May 4, 1993

Dear Fred –

Marble is now one of our favorite places; we assume it's one of yours, too. And we'd like you to have this book as a token of our thanks for your generosity.

Many thanks,
The Stowes and the Parkers

MARBLE
A Town Built on Dreams
— VOLUME I —
By Oscar McCollum Jr.

Creased Page

THE C.Y.M. CO. INITIALS of the Colorado-Yule Marble Company were carved into the marble bench behind the compressor house. This is located near the stone-quarry openings above the town of Marble.

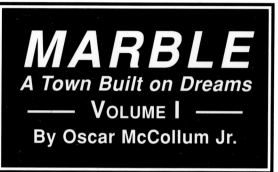

MARBLE
A Town Built on Dreams
─── VOLUME I ───
By Oscar McCollum Jr.

SUNDANCE

Books

MARBLE
A Town Built on Dreams

—— Volume I ——

By Oscar McCollum Jr.

SUNDANCE PUBLICATIONS *Limited*
250 BROADWAY, DENVER, COLORADO 80203

**Published by
Sundance Publications, Ltd.,
Denver Colorado**

**Graphical Presentation and Printing by
Sundance Publications, Ltd.,
Denver Colorado**

Production Manager — Dell A. McCoy

Photographic Director — Steven J. Meyers

Editors — Russ Collman & Theo J. Berlyn

ISBN 0-913582-55-7

ACKNOWLEDGMENTS

The publisher is grateful for the splendid co-operation offered in photographs for use in this book. The people living in Marble were especially helpful with their photographic collections. One primary source of never before published material came from Jack Clemenson. Who was most fortunate to have stayed with the town photographer for a while — Henry L. Johnson — a great many details came with that collection, stories of the town and mill operation. It was most fortunate that family of the late William McManus loaned their original photos to be used in this book. A good many Henry L. Johnson original prints were loaned by Esther Baumli Sanchez from a rare album produced by the Colorado Yule Marble Company. A large number of prints became available from family members that had lived and worked in Marble which were subsequently given to the Marble Historical Society. These and other contributors names appear with each photo reproduced among these pages. The publisher is extremely grateful for all of their help in this project.

—Dell A. McCoy, 1992

The page layout, choice of photos, and photo captions were designed by Dell A. McCoy.

OSCAR D. McCOLLUM JR.

THE AUTHOR organized the Marble Historical Society in 1977, and opened its museum in the old Marble High School building during the following year. He had been collecting information about the Marble area since 1941, when he was a student in a geology field camp in Crystal City. The beauty of the Marble area and the stimulus of the then operating marble quarry and mill started a life-long interest, which, with summer vacations in Marble every year, finally brought him back there to live after retirement. This field camp program of the Geology and Geography Department of the University of Kansas City — now part of the University of Missouri — was later interrupted by World War II. His studies were continued after the war with graduate work in geography at George Washington University.

A career, starting as a cartographer with the Army Engineers and the U.S. Geological Survey, soon evolved into one in the intelligence field. Employment for 25 years with the Central Intelligence Agency, including four years in the Far East, culminated in an award of the Agency's Certificate of Distinction, "...for outstanding performance of duty."

Moving to Marble in 1976, Oscar soon became involved in local civic-and-historical affairs. He served as a member of the Town of Marble's Board of Trustees for eight years and as mayor pro-tem. During this time, his efforts contributed to the acquisition by the town of the historic marble-mill site as a town park. The historical society prospered, and finally, the old high-school building was donated to the society by the Gunnison County school board. Oscar edited and published *Marble Chips,* the newsletter of the Marble Historical Society, for 15 years. This publication, containing historical vignettes, news of former residents and items of current interest, helped to bring together again many early residents of Marble. Two old-timers' reunions provided opportunities for nostalgic visits. In 1989 Oscar was awarded a Certificate of Commendation "For leadership in preserving and promoting Marble, Colorado, history," by the American Association of State and Local History.

The author and his wife, Lois Ann, now live in Glenwood Springs, Colorado, where he is the vice-president of that city's Frontier Historical Society.

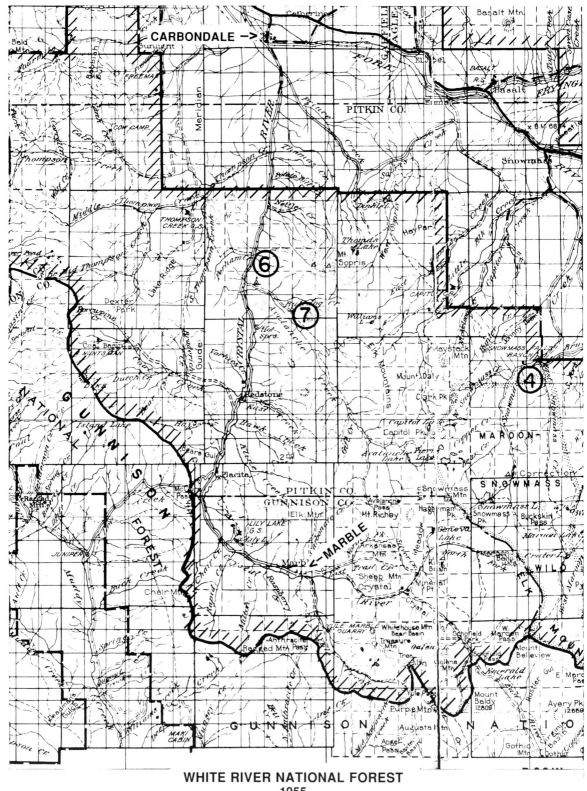

WHITE RIVER NATIONAL FOREST
— 1955 —
Carbondale to Marble, Colorado

TABLE OF CONTENTS

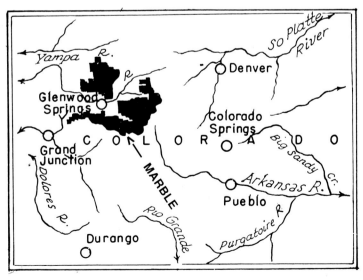

WHITE RIVER NATIONAL FOREST MAP
MARBLE, COLORADO

INTRODUCTION

AS A YOUNG MAN and new arrival to the Colorado Rockies in 1962, I spent much of my time in the beautiful Crystal River Valley. It was then a valley nearly unpeopled and very tranquil, dominated by high-and-rugged mountains, deep canyons, sparkling clear streams and stunning beauty. The valley was one I grew to love, and in 1970, Rex Myers and I authored the book *Marble, Colorado: City of Stone.*

During the past quarter of a century, Marble and the Crystal River Valley have changed. The town has seen the re-emergence of marble quarrying from nearby Whitehouse Mountain, more people have arrived, and the environment has become a matter of concern. In *Marble... A Town Built on Dreams,* Oscar McCollum in words and photographs brilliantly depicts the history of a unique and once-great mining town in Colorado.

Oscar McCollum first came to Marble as a geology student in 1941. The town never left his heart, and after many subsequent visits, he moved to Marble in 1976. For a decade he was the mayor of the community and did yeoman·duty in collecting and preserving Marble's rich heritage. This book takes us on an entertaining ride through Marble's history, told by the people who were part of its past.

The upper Crystal River Valley, dominated by the town of Marble, is a land rich in heritage. Its past has been highlighted by different ethnic peoples, enormous problems in transportation, a great mining industry and colorful figures like John C. Osgood, Sylvia Smith and Channing Meek. All have been influenced by the rugged Elk Mountains, violent weather and a magnificent-and-beautiful panorama.

Marble... A Town Built on Dreams covers this rich history and all Coloradans hope that this pristine-and-wonderful region continues unspoiled for another century or more.

— Duane Vandenbusche, Professor of History
Western State College, Gunnison, Colorado

PREFACE

WHEN DELL McCOY suggested that I compile a book about Marble, at first I thought another book on this area's history was not necessary, since the excellent account by Duane Vandenbusch and Rex Myers of the history of the upper Crystal River Valley, *Marble, Colorado: City of Stone,* has been available for many years. However, after more thought on the subject, it became obvious that much more could be told about the area's history.

The greatest source of information about the early history is found in the old newspapers published in Marble and Crystal City. While these accounts of the then current events — as seen by the local editors such as Evan Williams of the *Crystal River Current* and Frank Frost of *The Marble Booster,* are not always completely accurate or unbiased, at least they present a contemporary view of happenings. All these newspaper editors had various kinds and amounts of experience, and the style of writing in the years before World War I often seems quaint to us today.

Since it is interesting to read the old newspapers, it was decided to include in this compilation as many direct quotes from them as possible. As this could result in a rather disjointed account, I have provided some background and continuity to the subjects covered, with some personal comments that seemed appropriate.

All direct quotes are attributed to the source in footnotes, so serious readers can do further research in the originals. Most of these newspapers are available in microfilm at the Colorado Historical Society in Denver, as well as in some other libraries.

This publication also offers an excellent opportunity to publish many old photographs of the area, some of which have never appeared in a book. Many persons have been generous in allowing photographs from their collections to be included, and they have our sincere thanks.

— Oscar D. McCollum Jr.
Marble, Colorado, 1992

DELL A. McCOY PHOTO

LOOKING UPRIVER toward the Crystal Mill's water-power structure (looking toward the east), the North Fork headwaters of the Crystal River form at the left of this view, where Lead King Basin is located. Mineral Point is the name of the mountain beyond the mill, portrayed in this late fall scene. The Crystal River turns to the right, on the far side of the powerhouse, where the headwaters gather in Schofield Park, several miles upriver.

9

GEORGE YULE was the first promoter of the Yule marble deposits. He stumbled across the white rock during 1874 while prospecting along the creek that bears his name. Later, George Yule became the sher-

iff of Gunnison County.

LIZZIE A. McBURNEY married George Yule on January 15, 1896.

THE MARBLE TIMES issue of April 7, 1899, carried this photograph of a chain carved from one block of marble, by workers of the Marble City Quarry Company.

DREAMS OF RICHES

The upper Crystal River Valley, known as the Rock Creek Mining District, was first entered by prospectors with the dream of finding gold and silver. They discovered the area was full of rich mineral deposits consisting mostly of silver, lead, copper and iron. Many claims were staked out and patented in the county seat at Gunnison. A few of the mines proved to be large producers in the 1880's and 1890's, and the ore was hauled out on the backs of mules or on wagons to the railroads at Crested Butte or Carbondale. By the turn of the century many of the richest mines had played out but there were plenty of lesser veins of ore which attracted much attention. **The Marble Times & Crystal Silver Lance,** a weekly newspaper published in Marble, contained in every edition, reports on the activity at the mines. This mining business was the economic base for the area in 1900 and 1901.

The Marble Times & Crystal Silver Lance,
September 28, 1900.
J.C. Butler of Denver, accompanied by Mr. Lockridge of Chicago, came in the middle of last week to look over some mining properties.

A number of mining men are on Sheep mountain these days examining the mineral possibilities on the rugged slopes of that famous old mountain.

Last Friday, F.A. Fisher departed for his home at Aspen, having completed his work in Crystal basin, and the results of his summer's operations have proved highly satisfactory.

At the Bon Ton, on Crystal mountain, preparations for winter's work are proceeding favorably; the house will be completed this week. W.H. Hoagland expects to visit Colorado in a day or two.

W. Porter Nelson was over from Aspen during the week looking after his mining interests. We are not informed whether or not Porter found that "lost mine" the Aspen papers talked about.

Robert Harper, after an absence of two years, departs for his home on the 25th. The bonding and leasing of Mr. Harper's claims completes a valuable group that will be systematically developed in the near future.

• • • • •

Of course, in the part of the valley below Marble, coal was the most valuable mineral deposit.

The Marble Times & Crystal Silver Lance,
October 5, 1900.
Pete Doty has gone to Placita where he expects to secure employment in the mine for the winter.

• • • • •

Local men worked their own claims or found em-

ployment in the mines which had attracted outside investors.

The Marble Times & Crystal Silver Lance,
October 5, 1900.
T.A. Boughton has quit work on White House mountain and accepted a job at the Milwaukee.

Mr. Harding, a mining man from Denver, reached here last night and will spend a few days looking around the district.

Joe Barns came down from the hills Wednesday night and says they have four feet of fine ore in the Augusta and that other claims in that vicinity are looking exceedingly well.

• • • • •

Every community had an assay office and the quality of the ore from the various mines was closely watched by everyone.

The Marble Times & Crystal Silver Lance,
October 5, 1900.
Assayer Begar departed Tuesday for Florence, where he has secured a position in a cyanide mill at that place.

The Marble Times & Crystal Silver Lance,
October 5, 1900.
Dr. Keyes and another gentleman came in [to Redstone] from Colorado Springs Wednesday and yesterday went up into Crystal basin, accompanied by T. O'Bryan, to make an examination of the Buffalo Lode, with a view of extending the tunnel to a greater depth. This property is said to have a strong vein of mineral containing copper and lead, with gold-silver values.

J.C. Wise, having completed his assessment work,

Continued on Page 25

THE HEADWATERS of the Crystal River join those of the North Fork at this location beside the Crystal Mill's powerhouse, which was built in 1893. This is a summertime view, when the river water is fast-moving and dangerous to cross. North Pole Mountain can be seen above the powerhouse.

Crystal River Current

VOL. 1. No. 3.　　　　CRYSTAL, COLORADO, SATURDAY, OCTOBER 16, 1886.　　　　PRICE 10 CENTS

THE WEEK'S DOINGS.

Proceedings of the Passing Week—
A Few Interesting Lines From
S. A. 10—Local Notes.

Latest New York Quotations.

Bar Silver is worth .96⅜ cents bar oz.

Lead $4.35 per 100

Frank Fortsch is kept busy with his team hauling in supplies for the two coal companies.

Williams & Batt are packing up winter supplies to their mine on Sheep Mountain, and will have things all snug for a solid winter's work.

M. J. Gray, of Crested Butte, is having considerable trade from this section at present, and it keeps him rustling in goods by the car load over the D. & R. G.

For the use of man or woman. The most useful article ever invented. Price $1. Put up in a neat box with full directions. M. E. A. Co., P. O. Box, 1993, N. Y. City.

Monday and Tuesday nights we had our first real signs of winter. Considerable snow fell making very heavy roads for our freighters hauling in supplies over the divide.

Henry Anderson and W. W. Wood are hard at work opening up the Midland's marble ledge, and show some very solid pieces. They are also building a cabin on the property.

BORN—On Sunday morning, the 10th, inst., at McClure's ranch, down the river, to Mrs., wife of Mr. A. E. Johnson, a daughter, weight 11 pounds. Mother and child doing well, and the doctor thinks Andy will pull through.

On Monday last the most severe wind storms we ever had in these parts made things lively for teamsters. The roads were covered with fallen trees, and upon the South side of Sheep Mountain we have any amount of fire wood ready to haul in for winter use.

Proceedings of Mines and Marble.

Dick Lloyd and Will McLaughlin are doing contract work for Frank Parish up in Parish Basin.

Wm. F. Mason has been over on the Muddy getting hold of some anthracite coal on Ragged Mountain.

Baker Phillips is finishing up a 50 foot contract in Crystal Basin on property belonging to Mead, Wall & Hart.

A. W. Brownell has gone down to the Grand River Coal & Coke Co's. property, to take charge of the anthracite camp.

Fish & Harris are working assessments on their iron claims at the head of Avalanche Creek. They have a large body of fine iron.

John McKay has completed his assessment upon the Fargo. He has timbered up the incline in shape so it can be worked to advantage.

Capt. S. A. Barbour came over from Aspen on Wednesday last, to look after his marble interests, on White House Mountain. He experienced quite a time upon the range.

Uncle John McLaughlin completed his assessment work around Elko and will shortly go down the valley to open up the Alta. He has some of the best lead ores on Galena Mountain.

Lew Huffman and pard. have completed work on their mining property, upon Mineral Point, for this season, and started east on Tuesday morning. They have some very promising property up there.

A. F. Lawson, city attorney of Gunnison, is up from that city having the assessment work done on the Last Chance. He is part owner of the property and has one of the boss claims of Sheep Mountain.

The J. C. Osgood Co. have placed their diamond drill up at Barbour's Lake, on the hill side above camp, they are putting a hole down to see whether there is any workable coal seam close to the surface in that neighborhood.

Frank Royer came up from Gunnison with a party of men to work the Bonanza and Lead Chief properties on White House Mountain. Both claims show large bodies of lead ore, and are owned by A. Veil Capt Kingsbury and Mrs Jack.

Ed Skinner, one of Gothic's old timers, has beeen rewarded for his energy and pluck in standing by his mining property, on Copper Creek. He is now sacking and shiping some fine ore taken out of the Grey Copper mine. We are glad to see some of the boys strike it rich.

In and Out of town Personals.

Uncle John Howser has gone down the valley to rusticate a short time.

Wilber Wright was up from the coal camp on Tuesday last, shaking hands with the boys.

Henry Anderson was in camp Sunday looking for men to help him finish his contract work.

Mose Renoe came over the range last Sunday with a load of shingles for the J. C. Osgood Coal Co.

W. D. Parry and John McKay have gone down the river to see their old friends at Carbondale.

E. L. Jones has gone over to his ranch on the Muddy. He has a fine crop of potatoes and turnips over there.

Ira Cline was up from the Midland Coal Co's. camp on Sunday last, to see about having his mining claims worked.

Judge E. F. Colborn paid our camp a visit last Wednesday where he met many warm friends who will show their appreciation for him on Election Day.

Col. Bill English took a sudden trip over to Crested Butte last Wednesday. He commenced to think that he should see his best gal and look after the interests of the Boss.

G. D. Griffiths one of our old timers started for Denver on Wednesday. He was very fortunate this season in selling his marble claims, and is well provided for He will get one of his eyes operated upon in the East this winter. We hope to see him come back next spring with an eye as sharp as lightening.

Crested Butte Pointers.

A very agreeable surprise was given Mrs. M. F. Stiles at her new residence, on Thursday evening of last week. Card playing

urchin herder, Miss Bessie.

The Good Templars gave a very pleasant entertainment at the Odd Fellows' Hall on Thursday night of last week. It consisted of select readings, vocal solos, farces, ice cream, cake and fruit. As vocalists Mr. and Mrs. Miller have no peers as far as volume is concerned.

A very queer looking zoological specimen was captured and brought into town a few days ago. It is a very tender article and therefor it is looked after by female attendants. The manager of the As-pen museum evidently is very careless.

An observing young man was heard to remark, that, some of the ladies in town had got considerable ahead of their "bustle."

Misses Nina Jackson and Louie Hookey returned from Aspen on Monday. The young man smiles again.

Geo. Barnes, of Gunnison, returned to his "first love," on business, this week.

M. J. Gray had two car loads of goods arrive on Monday.

S. A. 10.

Don't You Think They Ask Tomuch.

A young lady in the east who speaks for herself, and a few others, desirous of securing western men for husbands, writes the following lines for the benefit of the batchelors of Crystal River:

The man who takes the red, red wine,
Can never glue his lips to mine.

The man who chews the navy plug,
Will in our parlor get no hug.

Who smokes or drinks or cuts the deck,
Shall never, never bite my neck.

Don't you monkey with the cards,
Or we can never more be pards.

The man who guzzles lager beer,
Can never, never chew my ear.

Drink nothing stronger than red pop,
Or in your lap I'll never flop.

If aught but water you e'er taste,
Just keep your arm off my waist.

If you drink wine or other slop,
You can never hear my corset pop.

The man who smokes the cigarette,
Can never, never take me out west.

If the young lady can comply to the following there is undoubtedly a good show for her to catch on to our editor. He is badly in need of a wife, and this is the kind he don't want:

The girl who loves the glittering jewls,
My lips to hers I'll never glue.

The girl who is known as a big-bug,
Shall my coat collar never hug.

She who wears the long ugly bangs,
Shall on my arm never hang.

She who wears her corset tight,
Will catch this chap, Ah-Ah! Not quite.

She who wears shop made curls,
Shall never, never be my best girl.

And if your bustle's like a shock,
In my lap you'll never flop.

One who wears a powdered face,
Won't get my arm around her waist.

If you flirt with every man.
I ne'er shall squeeze your little hand.

The girl who wears a low necked dress,
I never, never shall bring out west.

GOLD fields are scarce, but those who write to Stinson & Co., Portland, Maine, will receive free, full information about work which they can do, and live at home, that will pay them from $5 to $25 per day. Some have earned over $50 in a day. Either sex, young or old. Capital not required. You are started free. Those who start at once are absolutely sure of snug little fortunes.

13

CRYSTAL RIVER CURRENT

A. A. JOHNSON,

EDITOR AND PROPRIETOR.

STATE NEWS.

A revival is in progress at Brush.

General Sheridan has been visiting in Denver.

A Chautauqua club has been organized at Saguache.

There are 1031 pupils enrolled in the Leadville schools.

The bank clearings in Denver last week were $3,602,258.

A destructive forest fire has been raging in Grand county.

Seven buildings are in process of erection at Eort Morgan.

The tobacco crop of Virginia has been damaged by a heavy frost.

There are twenty-five carriers employed at the Denver postoffice.

A number of costly residences are being erected in Colorado Springs.

Horse thieves are making things lively down in San Miguel county.

The Greystone is the name of a new Democratic club organized in Denver.

The wages of smelter hands in Leadville range from $2.50 to $5 00 a day.

Ducks and geese are swarming in the Platte and other streams of the State.

A very extensive timber fire has been raging on the Dry Woody, near Aspen.

A second crop of strawberries has been raised at Grand Junction this year.

Sixty car loads of ore valued at $90,000 were shipped from Georgetown last month.

Aspen claims to have more sidewalks for its population than any town in the State.

The Argo Smelter exhibit $120,000 worth of silver bricks at the Denver Exposition.

The agricultural implement house of H. C. Babcock & Son, Denver, have made an assignment.

An exhibition of farm products will be made at Monte Vista on the 15th and 16th of this month.

The citizens of Durango and La Plata county are excited over the prospects of a number of new railroads.

An estimate just made fixes the number of range cattle in Montrose county at 32,000 and the sheep at 25,000.

There have been 105 entries of fruits, including more than 160 varieties, made for the Manufacturers' Exposition.

They are already quarreling in Denver over the question whether or not their exhibition shall be kept open on Sunday.

Some of the farmers in the great Platte valley are cutting their fourth crop of alfalfa this season. Verily alfalfa is king.

Colorow and his band of outlaws are reported to be on Douglass Creek, near the Utah line, and will probably remain there during the winter.

Rico has ordered a hose cart and organized a hose company. The company is composed of the business men and permanent residents of that place.

The Rio Grande will give half rates to Denver and return during the Manufacturers' exposition on such days as are designated for the various counties.

Many farmers throughout the State are cultivating the sunflower. As food for poultry the seed of that plant is unexcelled and the yield is enormous.

The Board of Trustees of Glenwood Springs have ordered their attorney to draft an ordinance to adopt the new town plat, which settles all disputes between the town trustees and the town site company.

The excellent display of grains and grasses which Prof. Cassidy of the State Agricultural College has had on exhibition at the different fairs in the northern part of the State, have been taken to the Denver Exposition.

An excellent mineral display was made at the Boulder fair; the rivalry between the precious metal department and the agricultural department was quite spirited, and it was difficult to determine which was the more attractive.

Nearly ten thousand dollars have been subscribed towards a permanent endowment fund for Colorado college, at Colorado Springs, since the beginning of the fall term. The amount was received from citizens of Denver, Colorado Springs and Manitou.

The total value of gold and silver received and purchased at the Denver mint during the month of September was $213,500.20. Of that amount $211,577.46 was gold and $1,922.74 silver. Idaho, New Mexico and Wyoming sent in bullion, as well as Colorado.

A petition is circulating for the purpose of obtaining signatures for a road from Glenwood to Meeker. The proposed road would make the journey 15 miles nearer and over a smoother country. It would be over what is known as the Old Ute trail, which is up Elk and down Flag creeks.

There is an immense demand in Eastern Colorado at the present time for feeders, and the cow centers are said to be thronged by buyers from Kansas and Nebraska. While the eastern beef market is paralyzed the demand for Colorado feeders is fairly stiff with prices satisfactory to the growers.

There were 32 male and 178 female teachers employed in Arapahoe county last year. The average monthly salary for male teachers in graded schools was $132, and for female teachers $76. For ungraded schools the average monthly salary for male teachers was $53, and for female teachers $50. The number of pupils enrolled in the schools was 9,839.

The population of Garfield county has nearly doubled within the past twelve months. The assessed valuation of the county was one-third greater this than the previous year, and a large number of cattle and horses have been driven in since May 1 last. Great activity has been displayed in securing coal land since work was begun on the Midland. Those holding such lands previously were promptly on hand to perform the requirements of the law, and the season has been one of unparalled activity.

The third annual convention of the Colorado Wool Growers' Association was held in Greeley on the 5th. Nearly every wool-growing county in the State was represented. President Wilder, in his address, estimated the wool clip of this year at 7,000,000 pounds. The Association represents an invested capital of more than $5,000,000 and a yearly revenue of over $2,500,000. Resolutions were adopted demanding the restoration of the tariff of 1867 on wool and woolen goods; requesting the Legislature to pass a law authorizing the payment of $2.50 for each wolf or coyote scalp; requesting that a member from this association be appointed a member of the State Veterinary Board; and asking that the tariff on wool from here to the Missouri river be reduced. The following officers were elected for the ensuing year: President, W. F. Wilder, of Colorado Springs; Vice-Presidents, William Milliken, of Las Animas county, H. Lanborn, of Arapahoe, C. E. Noble, of El Paso, N. E. Wheeler, of Weld, Charles Thurlow, of Bent, I. W. Bennett, of Larimer, Frank Willard, of Elbert, Henry Daigre, of Huerfano; Recording Secretary, C. L. Sullivan, of Greeley, Corresponding Secretary, F. B. Hill, of Colorado Springs, Treasurer, George H. West, of Greeley.

A FRIGHTFUL ACCIDENT.

The Boiler of a Mississippi River Steamer ... Causing Great Loss of Life.

ST. LOUIS, Missouri, October 6.—No cause is assigned as yet for the explosion last evening of the boiler of the river steamer La Mascotte, which caused such great loss of life. The boat is said to have been steaming along under 150 pounds of steam, her usual amount to carry, when the explosion suddenly occurred, blowing the fire in every direction. The utmost confusion prevailed. The pilot taking advantage of her heading, turned her towards the shore, but the flames caused him to abandon his post before the stage-plank could be lowered. After leaving his post the current turned the boat's bow out into the river again, and her stern swung close to the bank, which afforded a means of escape for several who were at that end of the boat, the pilot and one cabin boy getting ashore without any injuries or even wet feet. The stage plank was lowered and many were placed upon it, mostly women and children, who would have been saved had not the smoke-stack fallen squarely across it, and all who were not killed by it were drowned.

Captain Thompson, after doing all in his power to save the passengers and crew, jumped overboard and swam ashore, the boat having by this time drifted fully 200 yards out into the river. La Mascotte drifted over to the Illinois shore opposite Willard's Landing and sank, the only thing visible at present being her wheels.

J. S. Hanlon, the second pilot, says: "The Eagle was near us when the disaster occurred and she could have easily pushed us ashore without much trouble and danger, but I understand the Captain did not care to render any assistance. Adolphus Evelyns, the pilot of the Eagle, told me that the Captain ordered him not to go near the Mascotte, as he did not wish to endanger his boat. If he would have pushed us ashore not a single person would have been injured, except from scalds and burns."

The wreck of La Mascotte resulted from a collapse of one of the boiler flues. The explosion spent its force directly backward into the engine room, and only the crew and roustabouts suffered by scalding from the escaping steam. Eleven of the latter were so terribly burned that huge pieces of flesh peeled from their bodies. Six have died and the lives of the other five are despaired of. There are sixteen persons known to be drowned. D. S. Davidson is so badly burned around the face and throat that he will probably die. The register of passengers was lost and it is thought that some were drowned or killed whose bodies have not been recovered.

The total number on board as far as known are: Passengers, 16; cabin crew, 25; deck crew, 26. Passengers rescued, 8; drowned and recovered, 3; missing, 8; cabin crew rescued 19; dead and missing, 5; deck crew rescued uninjured; 10; rescued burned, 11; missing, 5. Albert Rice, one of the roustabouts living here, died this evening at the hospital, and two more are not expected to live until morning.

The crew on the Eagle as well as those who were rescued from La Mascotte censure the Captain of the Eagle for not making greater efforts to save the victims. Captain Thompson of La Mascotte and several of the rescued people state that the Captain of the Eagle refused, until he (Captain Thompson) and his crew threatened to take charge of his boat by force, to take the rescued and injured to this city, where assistance could be rendered them, but he said he would take them to Grand Tower, where little if any aid could be given them. After getting the injured aboard the Eagle he locked the staterooms on his boat and refused the use of covers for the wounded.

Three members of my family, says Mr. James A. Sample, Cash Room, office of the Treasurer, U. S., who were suffering from aggravating coughs, have been much benefitted by taking Red Star Cough Cure. None of the ill effects so noticeable in other cough remedies, have followed the use of this.

TELEGRAPHIC BREVITIES.

The town treasurer of Pittsfield, Mass., has embezzled $80,000.

President Cleveland and his wife will visit the Virginia State Fair at Richmond.

Thirty deaths have resulted from the explosion of the steamer La Mascotte, below St. Louis.

It is intimated that Federal officeholders who dabble in politics will be compelled to walk the plank.

The President has pardoned three Mormon Bishops who were convicted in Arizona of unlawful cohabitation.

Destructive prairie fires are reported from Northwest and Southwest Manitoba. The settlers have suffered greatly.

Hon. Austin F. Pike, United States Senator from New Hampshire, dropped dead while walking around his farm.

The steamer La Mascotte exploded her boilers near Cape Girardeau, Missouri, killing a large number of persons.

There are now 60,139,952 standard dollars in circulation. The issue of one-dollar certificates is expected to reduce his amount.

At a bull fight near the City of Mexico, on Sunday, six bulls and six horses were killed, and two picadores were severely gored.

A deputation of women from Ireland visited Mr. Gladstone and presented a petition with 50,000 signatures in favor of Home Rule.

The Trustees of the Peabody fund, in view of the earthquakes in South Carolina, have increased the allowance to that State to $10,000.

The Pope, through the Papal Nuncio at Madrid, has asked the Queen of Spain to pardon General Villacampa, who led the recent revolt.

The receiving teller of the Union Dime Savings Bank, of New York City, has left for parts unknown taking with him $20,000 of the bank's funds.

The freight brakemen on the Mahoming Division of the New York, Pennsylvania & Ohio Roads are on a strike for more wages. They refuse arbitration.

All the idle workmen in London have been summoned to follow the Lord Mayor's procession next month and make a silent demonstration of their needs.

The New York Court of Appeals has confirmed the sentence of ex-Alderman Jaehne who was convicted of bribery, and now other prosecutions are likely to follow.

In Silver Bow Canon, on the Montana Union Railroad, some miscreant fired 24,000 cords of wood, which was totally consumed. Loss, $100,000; insurance, $50,000.

Four men were blown to pieces and half a dozen others were injured by the explosion of thirty pounds of giant powder in the Caledonia mine at Deadwood, Dakota.

Mrs. Craig Alexander, whose husband was once a prominent business man of St. Louis, committed suicide by jumping from the roof of the dwelling of her son in-law.

A band of Salvationists at Wilkesbarre, Penn.. who persisted in Sunday parades regardless of the authorities, were arrested, and in default of payment of their fines were locked up.

A broken trestle on the Canadian Pacific road, 175 miles east of Winnipeg, resulted in a fatally scalded engineer and lesser injuries to seven passengers. The mail car and four coaches were burned.

There are rumors that the Texas cattlemen are seriously affected by the shrinkage in values and the cattle diseases throughout the country. It is thought that extensive failures may follow.

Earthquakes destroyed every village on the Island of Niapu, but the inhabitants escaped. The island is covered twenty feet deep with volcanic dust, and a new hill 200 feet high has been formed.

Fourteen of the parties implicated in the recent rebellion in Spain have been sentenced to death. Among the number are General Villacampa, three other officers, five sergeants, three corporals and two civilians.

While weighing out gunpowder, a merchant at Bringhurst, Indiana, dropped a lighted cigar into the keg. The building was wrecked by the explosion which followed, and three men can not survive the injuries received.

The employes of the Chicago packing houses, to the number of nearly 20,000, are on a strike because of the demand of the packing-house owners that hereafter they work ten hours a day instead of eight. Trouble is anticipated.

The Utah Commission in their annual report express the opinion that polygamous marriages are less numerous in Utah, and they say further that if the present laws are not equal to the emergency, further legislation must follow until the evil is blotted out.

Queen Christina has signed a decree commuting the sentences of the condemned insurgents. The Queen also signed a decree freeing the slaves in Cuba from the remainder of their terms of servitude. The whole Cabinet has decided to resign. It is believed that the Queen will ask Senor Sagasta to form a new ministry.

A curious phenomenon has occurred at Chimapla, in the State of Mexico. Within a few days past tremendous subterranean reports were heard, though at the time meteorlogical conditions were perfect. There was no unusual aspect in the sky nor the slighest rain. The people of the town were filled with alarm and an investigation was made by which it was discovered that a high hill in the vicinity had been completely divided into two parts by some powerful force.

At the Mormon General Conference at Coxville, Utah, an epistle was read from Presidents Taylor and Cannon, who sent it from their hiding place. It urges the Mormons to maintain their faith and bitterly assails the United States Court officers for their persistent prosecutions of the Saints, and says these prosecutions are the fulfillment of an old prophecy. It calls upon the Saints to cling to their principles and trust in God for their deliverance, which will surely come.

General Jackson presented his letter of recall to President Diaz on the 7th and left the same evening for the United States. In the railway depot he received from the American colony and other foreigners and Mexicans the greatest ovation that was ever given to any American in Mexico, with the single exception of General Grant. The American colony presented him with a handsome oil painting of the Valley of Mexico, which he accepted in a feeling speech, full of gratitude to his countrymen here.

A special from Washington says: "The President's back is up. He is indignant at the violations of the Civil Service order of July, which forbade federal officials from taking any active part in politics, and he proposes to make some striking examples, which will be a warning to minor officials. I think that those who will be selected for sacrifice at first will be Delany, United States District Attorney in Wisconsin; the Collector of Internal Revenue at Indianapolis, and the postmaster at New Orleans."

An attempt was made early Sunday morning to wreck the East-bound passenger train on the Missouri Pacific at Greenwood, thirty miles east of Kansas City. Rails, ties and other rubbish had been piled upon the track in a curve, and had the obstruction not been discovered by a farmer who flagged the train, a disastrous wreck could not have been prevented. There is no clue to the perpetrators, but as it was in the old train robbery district it is suspected that robbery was intended.

The American Board of Commissioners of Foreign Missions is in session in Des Moines. The report of the foreign secretary, Dr. R. N. Clark, of Boston, stated that but four missionaries out of 400 had died during the past year, while four veterans, with an average term of service of forty-six years, had retired. Then followed a general survey of each foreign country where missions are conducted by the boards. The report closed with the following summary: Number of missions 22, number of stations 85, whole number of laborers sent from this country 434, whole number of laborers connected with the missions 2,398, and the whole number of pupils in the mission schools 39,877. Following this report came that of the treasurer, Langdon S. Ward, of Boston. It gave as the cost of missions for the past year $620,640.50, cost of agencies $9,533.82, cost of administration $22,855.60—total expenditures $658,285.71, and total receipts from all sources for the year $659,667.20.

The large number of discharges made at the Government Printing Office, in order to reduce the service to the limits of the appropriation, creates the wildest excitement, especially among the female employes, whose distress, accompanied by tears and protestations, is most painful to witness. Public Printer Benedict, however, has discriminated, so far as possible, in favor of those having families to support.

An Appeal for Aid.

LINCOLN, Nebraska, October 2.—President Fitzgerald of the National League of America to-day sent to the officers and members of the League a long address in response to an appeal from Charles Stewart Parnell. After referring to the good results of the Chicago convention, to his desire in accepting the Presidency of the League to become an active assistant of Mr. Parnell, and to the benefit which the Irish cause has already received from the support of the League in America, the address says there now exists a most urgent demand on the Irish race throughout the world, and it continues:

On the twenty-second of September the Tory government of England decided by the rejection of Mr. Parnell's land bill, on the eviction and consequent starvation, or the banishment of thousands of men, women and children. Mr. Gladstone has truthfully said that every such eviction is equal to a sentence of death. Alas! Many single evictions have resulted in several deaths, but this was prior to the organization of the Irish National League, and I am greatly mistaken in the present temper of the Irish race and other friends of humanity if that barbarity will ever again be permitted on God's creatures anywhere.

"Until recently the sad story of Ireland was only known to her sons; now it is uppermost in the minds of all Christendom. The outspoken sympathy of the world is with her children in their struggle for home and liberty; hence Lord Salisbury and his Government will soon discover that they can never starve, exterminate or subdue by coercion the Irish people.

The fights on evictions for the non-payment of impossible rents have commenced. God's creatures are being rendered homeless, and they are turned out on the roadsides, but they shall not die the death that was planned for them by these heartless tyrants. Therefore I appeal to every man and woman with Irish blood coursing through their veins to aid in resisting this inhuman brutality. Let every branch of the League at once start an anti-Eviction fund, and send its contributions to the National Treasurer, Rev. Charles O'Reilly, at Detroit, Michigan. Branches should be started in every town and village in the country, in the workshops and on the railroads. Rich and poor alike should unite in this humane and patriotic work. Organization is necessary to resist organized tyranny."

As a horse and cattle lotion, Salvation Oil has proven itself an infallible remedy, it has received the hearty indorsements of many old and well-known horsemen.

OPENING OF THE MANUFACTURERS' EXPOSITION.

A Splendid Exhibit of Colorado's Industrial and Agricultural Advancement.

Residents of the Eastern States who have been taught to think of Colorado as a portion of the Great American Desert where nothing is raised except cactus and prairie-dogs, and where the inhabitants are all wild and woolly imitators of Will Bill and other heroes of yellow-covered literature, would have been astonished and incredulous if they could have stepped into the Mammoth Rink in Denver last Thursday evening and seen the beauty, variety, and extent of the agricultural, mechanical, mineral and art display and had been told that all those beautiful and useful things were either grown or manufactured in this State.

Denver has had more ambitious expositions; expositions on which more money has been spent and which have been more widely advertised, but none which actually showed to such good advantage the enormous resources of the Centennial State and the prodigious advances it has made as an agricultural and manufacturing community as the one now in progress. This may truly be called an exposition of the people, by the people and for the people. There is no suspicion of jobbery or real estate speculation connected with it, and its managers have the confidence of everyone.

The attendance on the opening night shows that Denver people are proud of it. The large building was crowded almost to suffocation by a well-dressed, fine-looking, pleasantly-surprised and highly good-natured mass of humanity, and even the most enthusiastic lover of this fair State could not but have had his pride and affection greatly increased by what he saw and heard.

The opening exercises were interesting and appropriate, and consisted of an address of welcome by General R. W. Woodbury, President of the Chamber of Commerce, an eloquent oration by the Hon. T. M. Patterson, and a short address by Governor Eaton. A magnificent orchestra and a well-drilled chorus of one hundred voices furnished delightful music.

Although it was intended to be principally an exhibit of manufactures, and although this department is wonderfully full and interesting, yet the admission of horticultural and agricultural products adds vastly to its interest and value. The display of apples, pears, crabs and grapes is a revelation to even old settlers, while the vegetables and grains surpass in size and quality even the boasted products of California. Perhaps the displays which attracted the most attention were the ones from the eastern part of Weld county grown without irrigation on sod ground, and a wonderful collection of fruits, grain, and vegetables brought by Mr. Pabor from Fruita, in Mesa county. The collection includes eleven varieties of pumpkins, three varieties of beets, the largest weighing 37 pounds; three varieties of potatoes and two of onions, a Chili squash, weight 88½ pounds; two varieties of field corn, the Colorado Dust and Golden Beauty; two of pop-corn and one of Evergreen sweet corn, a Brazilian or Flour corn and specimens of Kaffir corn, said to make excellent biscuit and bread; a Russian sun flower, measuring fourteen inches in diameter; Yelow Nansemond sweet potatoes and the Brazilian yam, sheaves of wheat, oats, rye and barley, with jars of the grain, stacks of broom corn, measuring ten feet; stalks of sorghum, including amber cane, black Imphee and the Leborian cane. Specimens of forest trees, showing a growth of two years—ailanthus, box elder and American elm. A branch of grapes—white Frontigroin—showing growth of one season. Also branches of the apricot, peach, hard-shelled almond, Russian mulberry and Russian olive. A specimen of cotton plant, two varieties of peanuts, the Spanish and the Virginian, castor oil beans, two jars of sorghum syrup, jars containing chufas, coffee pea, peanut, the hard-shelled almond.

The enthusiasm displayed on the opening night presages success, and success means the erection of an exposition building in the heart of the city where suitable accomodations can be given for such exhibits. It also means a new era of progress and prosperity for Colorado.

The Increase of Bald Heads'

To a person. who has a thoughtful turn of mind there can be no more fruitful theme for meditation than to go into our large halls, theatres, churches and others places of public resort, and, securing a seat in the gallery or in the rear part of the room, look at the heads of the audience for no other purpose than to ascertain by actual count how many show signs of baldness. Unless the experimenter has been in the habit of counting for this object he will be surprised to learn that in most of the Eastern cities fully 30 per cent, of the men over thirty years of age show unmistakable signs of baldness, while nearly 20 per cent. have spots on their heads that are not only bald but actually polished with the gloss that is supposed to belong to extreme old age alone. Bald-headed men are most plentiful in New York and Boston. After these come Philadelphia, Washington and the Western towns. Here are a few observations taken in Boston: Trinity Church—243 men; 71 actually bald, 45 indications of baldness. Kings Chapel—86 men; 38 actually bald, 14 indication of baldness. Hollis Street Theatre, orchestra at performance of the "Mikado"—63 men; 27 actually bald, 10 indication. Boston Theatre, Judic—126 men; 51 actually bald. 43 indications.

THE late failure of "Professor" Wiggins should teach him that American earthquakes are entirely too patriotic to verify the predictions of a Canadian weather prophet. Mr. Wiggins should confine his guesses to the British possessions.

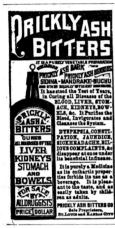

The Romance of True Love at Long Branch.

Correspondence New York World.

Four years ago there came with the blaze of summer society a beautiful young southern lady. Her form was fragile, her face was pale and spirituelle, almost angelic in expression, but upon her cheek was the hectic rose that bade soon to blossom for the grave. She was rich, well educated, and possessed of many friends. Courtiers? Yes, lots. She turned them all away kindly. Her principal charm was a sweet, mournful, lute-like voice, that touched the melancholy chords in the hearts of all her hearers. She rather shrank from using it, but it was called into use with overpowering effect at several quiet cottage parties. To sing was but to charm.

A little over a year before one of the most beautiful belles in all Southern Louisiana became betrothed with the gallant son of a still more gallant planter. They lived but for each other. They lived but to love. Changes came and made it essential that the planter's son must seek a livelihood for himself. He received a flattering offer to enter into business in Chicago. Partings are always sad, but when miles separate heart from heart that twine as closely to each other as the ivy and the oaken tendril, it is plunged into the very abyss of sadness. Well, they parted; mutual promises to write early and often, of course. For a while letters flew thick and fast; but not too fast for the lovers. Then came a silence, strange, unaccountable silence. The silence of a day lapsed into that of a week, a month, six months, yes, a year. And all the while away down there where the mocking bird sings and the southern breeze blow, there was a fond true heart that was breaking. Father and friends saw she was slowly fading. In alarm for their loved one they hurried away to this far-off resort.

One evening the young lady above alluded to attended a cottage party. She had sung twice to an admiring audience, when a brief anonymous note was thrust into her hand, with the request that she sing her favorite song. She trembled as she recognized a well known chirography. The piano resounded with a soft prelude. Then a sweet, dove-like voice floated out upon the air with the words "Must we, then, meet as strangers?" How the listeners were charmed with the pathos of the warbler. The poor girl struggled bravely through the first verse, and essayed a second. She turned ghastly pale and her form trembled convulsively as she finished the first line. Then, turning her eyes, she met those laden with reciprocal love, and, with a pitiful cry, she sank senseless to the floor. Loving hands raised her gently, and her form rested in manly arms. She soon regained consciousness, and—well, let's draw the veil. The affair, of course, created a great sensation among the guests, and one gentleman remarked that he never heard Balfe's gem sung with as great effect.

To-day I dandled a baby on my knee upon the sands near the West End. Beside me sat a lady upon whose cheek there bloomed no hectic rose. Can you guess who the lady was? Can you see through the whole story? There is a moral in this tale. It's all well enough for objecting parents to intercept some girls' letters, but circumstances alter cases. Also, love is a wonderful panacea at times for aching hearts and hectic cheeks.

"One of the Finest."

Chicago Herald.—"Captain Williams of the New York force, is one of the best known police officers in the United States," said a Manhattanite at the Palmer House the other night, "but I don't believe the story of how he got on the force has ever been told in print. It must have been twenty years ago or more when Williams was a strapping big youngster, crazy to be a patrolman. He was always around headquarters begging for a job. Finally one of the captains said he would give him a chance to see what kind of stuff he was made of, and immediately rigged him up with a uniform and club, gave him his instructions and sent him into the Bleeker and Wooster street district, with orders to keep the sidewalks cleared. Now, that was about the toughest corner in New York. The hoodlums used to run the streets there, and if a policeman failed to carry himself to their satisfaction, they proceeded to do him up. On this day the toughs were out in force, and right among them Williams walked.

"'Ye'll move on, now," he sang out, 'that's the order.'

"'Wat yer givin' us, Mr. Fresh?' was the defiant response, as the gang gathered to wipe the gutter with him as with so many of his predecessors.

"But Williams waited to hear no more. In a jiffy his club was out, and that terrible right arm of his at work. He is a powerful, agile man, and in all of his experiences he never handled a willow with such telling effect. In less than two minntes he had eight toughs stretched out on the sidewalk in front of him, and as fast as they attempted to get up he knocked them down again, and walked over their prostrate bodies whacking them right and left. He is a tiger when roused, and such a clubbing bout was never before seen in New York. Having pounded the eight toughs into subjection he stood them up in line and marched them to the station-house. As you may imagine, his temporary appointment was at once made permanent."

In every land and clime, the merits of St. Jacobs Oil as the only conqueror of pain, are being acknowledged by the press and people.

Mr. Frank Nicholson, of St. Louis, who recently visited Leadville, gives the following report of that district: "I regard Leadville as the best camp in the world. It produces annually more bullion than the whole republic of Mexico. It is not necessary to go to Mexico while such a camp exist, in this country. The Adams has struck several patches of ore, but has not yet reached the second contact. Neither has the Small Hopes, but in my opinion both will eventually. Small Hopes is the finest mine in the camp, the finest, in fact, I have ever seen. You strike ore at 100 feet from the surface, a vein about forty feet wide. The deep shaft, which is down about 500 feet, is not in ore, but the mine has enough ore on the first contact to last several years. Adams has enough to last two years, at least. Tiptop is a good piece of property. The ore is a sulphide and requires costly treatment, but there is a lot of it."

CATARRH, CATARRHAL DEAFNESS AND HAY FEVER.

Sufferers are not generally aware that these diseases are contagious, or that they are due to the presence of living parasites in the lining membrane of the nose and eustachian tubes. Microscopic research, however, has proved this to be a fact, and the result is that a simple remedy has been formulated whereby catarrh, catarrhal deafness, and hay fever are cured in from one to three simple applications made at home. pamphlet explaining this new treatment is sent free on receipt of stamp, by A. H. Dixon & Son, 315 King Street West, Toronto, Canada.—*Christian Standard.*

When the geysers began to spout down in South Carolina last week, the people thought that another political campaign had prematurely opened.

An Awful Doom

of any nature is usually avoided by those who have foresight. Those who read this who have foresight will lose no time in writing to Hallett & Co., Portland, Maine, to learn about work which they can do at a profit of from $5 to $25 and upwards per day and live at home, wherever they are located. Some have earned over $50 in a day. All is new. Capital not required. You are started free. Both sexes. All ages. Particulars free. A great reward awaits every worker.

A Lucky Student.

Boston (Mass.) Courier, Oct. 3.

Mr. Amaro Arango Bibeiro, who in the last drawing of the Louisiana State Lottery, held in New Orleans on the 14th inst., drew one-tenth of the capital prize of $150,000, is a senior in Tuft's College and resides at 17 Wellington street in this city. When visited by a *Courier* reporter last week Mr. Bibeiro was in a very happy frame of mind and expressed himself as being much pleased at his good fortune, as even to a man in well-to-do circumstances the unexpected receipt from the Adams Express Company of $15,000 was an event that did not happen every day. Mr. Bibeiro is a native of St. Peaulo, Brazil, about twenty-eight or thirty years of age, and first came to the United States in 1879. Some ten or eleven years ago he, together with his brother, inherited a small Brazilian coffee plantation, but this they soon disposed of and established themselves in their present business, that of railroad and commercial brokerage. His time in this country has been passed at Lehigh University, Penn., in New York city, and at Tuft's college, where he is at present making a specialty of civil engineering, and from which he will graduate in June. He has always had great faith in the possibilities and fairness of the Louisiana Lottery, and when in Lehigh, with a number of other students, was a constant purchaser of tickets, and was rewarded on one occasion while there, by receiving a prize of $750. About a year and a half ago he began investing two or three dollars a months in tickets again, as, he says, he thought he might as well invest his money in that way as in any other. A few months ago he drew five dollars and finally, on the 14th, a tenth of the capital prize. Mr. Bibeiro expresses himself as perfectly satisfied with his experience and says the windfall is just what he needs to put into his business.

Ever since the Michigan Central Railroad was built it has been a favorite with the traveling public, because its roadbed was smooth, its cars elegant, and its service admirable, but since the road built a new bridge across the Niagara river below the falls, and a station, called Falls View, right beside the horse-shoe falls, everybody wants to go that way. Many people cannot stop at Niagara Falls from one train to another, and they never could see enough of the Falls from the old bridge to amount to anything, but now, by the new "Falls Route" of the Michigan Central, they can stand on a high bluff for ten minutes, right above the seething, boiling cauldron, and see more of the falls in that time than they could to stop over for a day. From "Falls View" station the Michigan Central gives its passengers the most beautiful view to be seen on this earth. There may be more beautiful views on some other earth, but no railroad runs there yet.—*Geo. W. Peck in Peck's Sun.*

The United States has been charged with wanting the whole earth, but she is evidently becoming shaky on that subject.

That Bearing Down Pain

Is cured by CARTER'S IRON PILLS. At druggists'.

The sea serpent would make a good actor. He has got the "big head."

GET Lyon's Heel Stiffeners applied to your new boots and shoes before you run them over.

"BURNS AND SCALDS."—If you are so unfortunate as to injure yourself in this way, we can suggest a remedy that will soon relieve you of all pain and quickly heal the wound; it costs but twenty-five cents and is sold by all druggists. Ask for PERRY DAVIS' PAIN-KILLER.

Johnson says it is mighty hard to be a Christian when a man has a boy who will ring a chestnut bell on him at family prayers, when it is impossible to resent it.

Smoke "*Harvest King*," full Havana filled 5 ct. cigar. Hand-made, free smoker, delicious flavor. Sold by all dealers. Struby-Estabrook Co., Sole Ag'ts, Denver.

Bronchitis is cured by frequent small doses of Piso's Cure for Consumption.

The Frazer Axle Grease is better and cheaper than any other, at double the price.

We call the particular attention of the readers of this paper to the advertisement of the Pierce Well Excavator Co. of New York whom we know to be a perfectly reliable concern and the largest manufacturers of Well Drilling and Well Boring Machinery in the United States. They will send a beautifully illustrated catalogue, showing how artesian and oil wells are drilled, to those who will send them four cents in stamps to pay postage.

The authorities of Kansas confiscated and destroyed 3,600 bottles of beer at the National Fair in Lawrence, under the prohibition law.

Be merciful to dumb animals. Heal all open sores and cuts with Stewart's Healing Powder, 15 and 50 cents a box.

All the calcining furnaces of the various smelting works in Leadville are running at full capacity, and the amount of sulphide ore treated is very large.

What would our Forefathers have said if they had imagined that a cough could be cured for 25 cents—as by that reliable remedy—Dr. Bull's Cough Syrup

To be free from sick-headache, biliousness, constipation, etc., use Carter's Little Liver Pills. Strictly vegetable. They gently stimulate the liver and free the stomach from bile.

Not a Purgative; Carter's Little Liver Pills; their action is mild, pleasant and natural.

Miss Mamie Bratt, who has been attending Elliott's Business College at Burlington, has just returned home. She speaks in the highest terms of this excellent school.

General Booth, of the Salvation Army, will mount the big drum in the United States somewhere about November.

THE LOVE OF HOME

Is much increased by those refining influences which make the heart tender and the affections warm, and music is a leading factor. It fosters the affections of the children to all that is good and pure and noble. Many families may not be financially able to possess the benefits in music lines were it not that the KNIGHT-MCCLURE MUSIC CO., of Denver, Colo., are in shape to give easy terms on Pianos & Organs. To call or write them at 413 and 415 Lawrence St. is to be convinced that every industrious family may have a Piano or Organ of their own.

The only potentate who has occupied a throne for more than fifty consecutive years is Dom Pedro, Emperor of Brazil.

PATENTS obtained by Louis Bagger & Co., Attorneys, Washington, D. C. Est'd 1864. Advice free.

PRICKLY ASH BITTERS warm up and invigorate the stomach, improves and strengthens the digestive organs, opens the pores, promotes perspiration, and equalizes the circulation. As a corrector of a disordered system there is nothing to equal it.

In court. "You admit, then, that you forged these bills?" "Why, yes, your honor; you wouldn't have me go and steal good ones, would you?"

The Galatea draws more water than the Mayflower, but she doesn't draw it so fast.

If afflicted with Sore Eyes, use Dr. Isaac Thompson's Eye Water. Druggists sell it. 25c.

Chief Geronimo to Prince Alexander, of Bulgaria—"Uneasy lies the head that wears a crown."

Buckingham's Dye for the Whiskers produces in one application a permanent color.

We have used Ayer's Ague Cure, and have found it invaluable in malarial troubles.

If Gen. Miles had been vaccinated perhaps he wouldn't have caught Geronimo.

BARBED WIRE.

If you have barbed wire fences, keep Veterinary Carbolisalve in your stables. It cures without a scar and renews the hair its original color. 50 cents and $1.00, at Druggists or by mail. Cole & Co., Black River Falls, Wis.

When writing to advertisers say that you saw the advertisement in this paper.

Crystal River Current.

Published by the Current Publishing Co

A. A. Johnson,   Jos. A. Bray,
Editor.   Manager.

ENTERED AT THE POST-OFFICE AT CRYSTAL, COLORADO, FOR TRANSMISSION THROUGH THE MAILS AS SECOND-CLASS MATTER.

TERMS-PAYABLE-IN-ADVANCE:

One Year,.................$3 00
Six Months,..............1 75
Three Months,............1 00

SATURDAY, OCTOBER 16, 1886.

Crystal Post-Office Directory.

Mail arrives and departs every Tuesday, Thursday and Sunday.

Democratic State Ticket.

For Congress:
Myron W. Reed, of Arapahoe.
For Governor:
Alva Adams, of Pueblo.
For Lieutenant Governor:
H. B. Gillespie. of Pitkin.
For Secretary of State:
Here Mahoney, of Lake.
For Treasurer:
James F. Benedict, of Weld.
For Auditor:
Casimiro Barela, of Las Animas.
For Attorney General:
E. I. Stirman, of Ouray.
For Regents of State University:
Fred Lockwood,
O. A. McFarland, of Boulder.
Frank P Bertchy, of Sagauche.

Democratic Senatorial Ticket.

For Senator—Thirteenth District:
John Kinkade, of Gunnison.
For Representative:
Amos Hatchkiss, of Delta.

Democratic County Ticket.

For County Commissioner:
John F. Perkins, ot Pitkin.
For County Judge:
J. M. McDougal, of West Gunnison.
For County Commissioner:
Louis Grasmuck, of Gunnison.

THE Democratic ticket is a strong one, and Republicans will have to be up and doing.

GEO. C. ROHDE, the Prohibition candidate for county judge, is made of good timber, but will have to go in with the culls this time.

WE publish in to-day's issue of the CURRENT the Democratic ticket which is a strong one, and will carry weight with it the coming election.

UNCLE JOHN PARLIN will be our next commissioner. He is an old timer and knows the wants of the people, our Democrats and Republicans can count on him to work for the best interests of the county.

WE are glad to see our friend John Kinkaid receive the nomination, on the Democratic ticket, for State senator for the 13th district. He is a good man for the position, yet he may have a hard fight before him.

THE Aspen Democrat-Press will hereafter appear as an evening instead of a morning paper. This change will give the Dems. a chance to keep up with the Times, but we should think a morning paper is what the merchants want.

THE White Pine Cone must be trying to run the twin racket with James Rice and B. Clark Wheeler, their pictures are so much alike we cannot tell one from the other. Mr Rice, see that your picture is in it, it might take with the ladies, you know?

J. N. BENNETT at the mouth of the river, is running for county commissioner of Pitkin county. Citizens along the valley should give him their hearty support, as he can be of great benefit to us in having a road built up the river, and look after the general interests of his section which is one of the most important in the county.

THE Prohibitionests have nominated a State and county ticket, and the following are those running for county offices. Citizens who take water straight, what do you think of them? Geo. C. Rohde, of Crested Butte, for County Judge; D. A. McConnell, of Dovleville, County Commissioner; Capt. E. Bunn, of Gothic, for County Coroner.

THERE will be three times the vote cast in this precinct on Election Day than there was a year ago, yet the vote will not represent our population, as a number of citizens live to far away and cannot spare the time to come to the polls. We always claimed our State elections should be held earlier in the season, when people have better chances to leave their work, as every fine day counts at this season of the year.

PITKIN county is entitled to a representation upon the State ticket, but we are inclined to believe the wrong man was chosen to represent us in the senate, although he is a rustler in his own behalf, he does not fully represent the puclic, and cannot bring harmon into Republican ranks. Democrats and Republicans of Pitkin county would support a good man from that county irrespective of politics, but as matters now stand the Republican ticket will be scratched.

J. F McLEES, who at one time, while on the police force in Gunnison, shot and killed Col. Hayes, was hung on a gate beam in the stock yards at Montrose, on the night of the 7th, instant. He was always too ready with his threats and gun. A vigilance committee, determined upon stumping out men of his character, helped him over the range. It is to be hoped those who are in the habit of carrying guns, will take warning, as the practice is a bard one that should be put a stop to.

OUR roads are in horrible condition for travel, and more freight is coming in this way than to any point in the North end of the county, yet we cannot persuade our county commissioners to expend a dollar in repairs. Our citizens worked out their poll tax with a good will, but now it has became necessary to keep men constantly making repairs on the road. If our commissioners cannot expend any money towards encouraging capital into our county they should turn the road over to a toll company.

THE mail services between here and Crested Butte is something that should be regulated. At present mail arriving in Crested Butte for Gothic, Scofiel and Crystal, also for Aspen, is detained 24 hours to accomidate the Crested Butte & Aspen Stage Co., who are desirous of securing what few passengers arrive on the mail train for Aspen, but they do not await the sorting of the mail, only taking that which comes in the day before.

We inst upon having faster service as it is an imposition upon the public, we should have the mail that arrives in Crested Butte start out promptly, so that the mail carrier from Gothic could bring our mail the following day. The distance from Crested Butte to Crystal is only 19 miles, and yet it takes three days to hear from that point. Gentlemen change your time, we have to receive our mail faster.

THE iron claims around Snow Mass Mountain and the head of Avalanche Creek will be of great importance to this section and the mines around Aspen, as the finest kind of iron has been opened up. Within the last two months over a dozen locations have been made that show large bodies of magnetic and oxide ore very free from pyrite or other impurities, in fact we can say it is the finest body of iron in Colorado and contains as high as 70 per cent iron. Little importance was attached to the iron, although we knew it existed, until we became satisfied there would be a market, but developments the past

year insures us that such bodies of ore will become valuable. With the opening up of coal mines along the valley and the railroads to handle the ore and coal, whereby the two articles can be brought together and handled cheaply, we would not be surprised to see a blast furnace and smelter in operation at some point along our valley in the near future, for there is everything necessary for such an establishment. We always had a good impression of Crystal River's resources and believe the advancement our district has taken the past season will bear out our ideas of the wealth contained in the Elk Mountains.

Mining Application.

NO. 120, Ute Series.

Survey No. 4298.   District No. 3.
        U. S. Land Office,
Gunnison, Colo., Oct. 12, 1886.
Notice is hereby given that the Silver Ridge Mining Co. by T. A. Boughton, its attorney in fact, whose post-office is Scofield, Colo. have made application for a patent for 1500 linear feet on the Fourth of July Lode, bearing silver, the same being 750 feet N. Westerly and 750 feet S. Easterly from discovery shaft thereon, with surface ground 300 feet in width, situate in Rock Creek or Elk Mt. Mining District, Gunnison County, State of Colorado, and described in the plat and field notes on file in this office as follows, viz: Var. 14° 5' to 14° 20' E.
Begining at Cor. No. 1, whence U. S. L. M. Elk Mt. bears N. 7° 47' E. 635.4 feet, Thence N. 70° W. 1509 ft. to cor. No. 2, Thence S. 70° W, 300 ft. to cor. No. 3. Thence S. 20° E. 1500 ft. to cor. No. 4. Thence N. 70° E. 300 ft. to cor. No. 1, place of begining, containing 10.32 acres and forming a portion of the unsurveyed lands, said location being recorded in the records of Gunnison Co., Colo. Adjacent claim sur. No. 2546.
         John J. Thomas,
              Register.
First publication, October 16th, 1886.

Crystal River Current.

VOL. 1. No. 37. CRYSTAL, COLORADO, SATURDAY, JUNE 11, 1887. PRICE 10 CENTS.

LOCAL SPLINTERS.

Snow has all disappeared in Galena park.

Evan Williams was up from the lake this morning.

The road up the canon is being cleaned out and the bridge repaired.

Jim Livingston goes over to the Anthracite mine to work when it starts up.

The D. & R. G. will have to keep dirt flying if it reaches Aspen before the Midland.

It is probable that the Midland will not reach Aspen before the latter part of October.

Uncle John McLaughlin is on his way up the river to commence work on his property at Elko.

Will Parry is up from the Hot Springs, and reports prospectors as numerous up Avalanche creek.

Roses are in full bloom along this side of Sheep mountain. Who said this isn't an early spring?

Jim Usher had the misfortune to run a pick into his foot the other day which laid him up a few days.

There will be four railroad bridges across Roaring Fork and Crystal river in the vicinity of Carbondale.

John McKay has sold his house at Scofield to the Osgood Co. and they intended hauling it down to Prospect.

New oil companies are being formed to further develope that important industry along the Arkansas river.

Hon. A. M. Stevenson is hard at work these days securing right of way from Glenwood to Aspen for the D. & R. G.

Thirteen head of horses came over the range this morning and proceeded down to the Osgood Co's. camp at Prospect.

Andy Burnett and France Armstrong have gone up to Coal basin to work on the Midland company's coal land at that place.

Charlie Johnson went over the divide to the Anthracite mine on Wednesday last with a number of men who will work in the mine.

Dick and Will Lloyd have considerable surface water to contend with at present in their mine and have been laid up with rheumatics.

George Brown came over the divide this morning with Charlie Johnson, who has charge of the Osgood Co's. pack and saddle animals.

James Lovsey and son Charlie, of Crested Butte, came over the divide on horseback yesterday. They are going down to look over the lower country.

A fashion itemn says, 'The new pocket-books are long and slender." Yet, as we remember it, this is the way they have been worn for years and years.—[Ex,

Supt. J. W. Phillips, of the Grand River Coal Co., is erecting a comfortable cottage down at the Penny Hot Springs and expects to move into it as soon as completed.

Prospectors will be able to get around on the high peaks and basins inside of the next two weeks and we may expect to see a number in these parts this season.

For the use of man or woman. The most useful article ever invented. Price $1. Put up in a neat box with full directions. M. E. A. Co., P. O. Box 1993, N. Y. City.

Subscribe for the CURRENT and keep posted on the richest country in the State.

The Osgood Co. is completing the road from Melton's ranch down to Prospect on the north side of the river. This will be a great convenience to them and citizens along the valley.

"There are over three thousand medicines in the world," and of this number over five thousand are prescribed by friends for the man who is suffering from an attack of rheumatism.—[Ex.

In St. Louis the mining millionaire finds rest and solace in progressive euchre. In the West his flannel-shirted brother is not satisfied with anything milder than "producive poker."—[St. Louis Mining News.

Mr. Curtis, an eastern gentleman, accompanied Mr. Kebler on his trip from Glenwood to Crested Butte. He has fallen in love with our climate and mountain scenry and will locate at Glenwood Springs for the summer that he may bask in their buties.

John McKay arrived in camp the first of the week from Scotland where he has been on a visit for the last six months. While absent he met many of his old friends and had a gala time courting the Scotch lassies, but could not induce any to return with him.

Wm. Batt arrived in camp the first of the week wearing a broad smile. He got away with his bachelor friends in good shape while on his eastern visit. He left his bride in Gunnison a guest of Mrs. W. E. Jarvis, where she will remain until the roads are open over the divide.

The Odd Fellews, of Crested Butte gave a grand ball on Tuesday last. which was one of the most successful that ever took place in that burg. There were over sixty couple present- Will Lloyd, Tom Boughton, Frank Williams and ye editor were the ones representing this section.

Circumstances alters cases. Head of the house (to young man at front door)—"Havent I told you, sir, never to call here again?" Young man—"Yes, sir, but I haven't called to see Miss Clara this time. I have called for the gas bill." Head of the house (in milder tone)—"Please call again."—[Ex.

J. A. Kebler, general superintendent of the Whitebreast Coal Co., arrived in camp on Wednesday last from Glenwood Springs, and has gone to Crested Butte. He will start up the Anthracite mine at once which will give employment to qute a number of coal miners and help business generally.

Col. Peter Churchfield came up from his ranch on the Grand river last Sunday. He has been kept busy all winter surveying ditches etc., and has come up to look after the surveying of mining claims in these parts, Crested Butte and Irwin, and will reside in Crested Butte during the summer.

Careful experiments on the sense of smell in dogs have been made by George J. Romanes, who has communicated the results to the Linnæan Society of London. He finds that not only the feet, but the whole body of a man exhale a peculiar or individual odor, which a dog can recognize as that of his master amid a crowd of other persons; that the individual quality of this odor can be recognized at great distances in windward, or in calm weather at great distances in any direction; and that even powerful perfume may not overcome the odor. Yet a single sheet of brown paper, when stepped upon instead of the ground, and afterward removed was sufficient to prevent Mr. Romane's dog from following his trail.

MINING BREVITES.

"Doc" Bradbury has started up work on his mine at Elko.

Silver 95⅞ cents per ounce; lead steady at $4.65 per hundred pounds.

Myron Robbins and George Turner are prospecting on Avalanche creek these days.

J. O, Jordan has arrived in Gothic from Boston and predicts that our section will have a prosperous season.

George W. Farnham has arrived from Gunnison and started in working assessments on his Sheep mountain property.

W. E. Jarvis was in Gothic Wednesday last looking over one of his bonanzas that he intends opening up this season,

A. B. Fish is working the Bankers Daughter which is one of the claims on Sheep mountain that can produce considerable lead ore when we have a smelter down the valley.

Gran Griffin has a fine streak of ore in his property up Rustler gulch which assays up in the hundreds. He intends to open it up as soon as possible and make shipments to Gunnison.

Ashby & Eastop arrived from the lower country on Wednesday last and are located at their old camp on East river where they have a number of properties they intend developing.

Frank Williams brought some splendid looking iron ore into camp a few days ago which is certain to be of value to the smelters or blast furnaces that will no doubt be erected before long in this vicinity. The ore is solid and will carry about 70 per cent. in iron,

Mr. J. G. Hungerford came over from Crested Butte on Monday last and went up to the Milwaukee, on Sheep Mountain. He expects they will do considerable work on the property this season. It would justify opening up and we would like to see work started upon it.

Patterson and Judd are preparing to do considerable work on their mine, up Rustler gulch, which shows twelve inches of splendid lead ore that will stand shipment to Gunnison. The property is looked upon as one of the most promising around Gothic and when fully opened up should be a large producer.

It is not generally known that a nickel mine exists in this county, but Ed Cole and W. E. Dayton have got it and could supply Uncle Sam with the material for his small change. They have been at work on the lode during the winter and now go to Gothic, Elko and Galena mountain to work their properties there. Their nickel lode, the "Smooth Eph," three miles up Little Ohio creek, is said to be fourteen feet betwen walls of gneiss and trap rock. Specimens of the mineral in Dr. Jennings' cabinet look like the "pure quill,"as they are pronounced by experts to be.—Review-Press.

Mining Patents.

CROSS LODES—Where a patent issues for a lode which crosses a lode already patented, the surface ground in conflict is excepted fpom the second patent.—[Landowner.

ASSIGNMENT—There are no regulations or rules governing the assignment of patents issued by the General Land Office. Such patents are deeds, conveying to the grantees the title to certain land previously existing in the United States; and if these parties desire to transfer the title thus acquired, they must of cource conform to the laws of the "locus rei sitæ" [State or Territory] relating to the conveyance of realty.—[Mineral Lands.

LODE CLAIM IN TOWN SITES—EXCEPTING CLAUSE—Mining claims within town sites are patented with an excepting clause, as follows: "Excepting and excluding, however, from these presents, all town property rights up the surface, and there are hereby expressly excepted and excluded from the same all houses, buildings, structures, lots, blocks, streets, alleys, or other municipal improvments on the surface of the above described premises, not belonging to the grantee herein, and all rights necessary or proper to the occupation, possession and enjoyment of the same.—[Mineral lands.

Citizens of Aspen have formed a fish association for the protection of fish in Pitkin county, and offer a reward of fifty dollars to parties reporting or furnishing proof of anyone killing fish with giant powder. They are raising a subscription to place 150.000 eastern brook trout in the streams around Aspen.

Subscribe for and advertise in the CURRENT.

Something New.

Outsiders frequently wonder where the railroads obtain proper return for some of the ingenious but costly methods adopted in advertising their lines. One of the latest to attract our attention is a nicely bound 64-page book entitled, "What to Do," containing discriptions and the correct rules of a large number of games suitable for parlor or lawn, which has been issued by the Passenger Department of the St. Paul, Minneapolis & Manitoba railway, and will, we understand, be forwarded postpaid upon receipt of 8 cents by C. H. Warren, General Passenger Agent, at St. Paul. It is a book that would ornament almost any table and interest both old and young.

And He is His Own Grandfather.

A young man who is his own father, thus explains through the press; "I married a widow who had a grown up daughter. My father visited our house very often, fell in love with my daughter and married her. So my father became my step-son and my step-daughter my mother, because she married my father. Some time afterward my wife had a son. He is my father's brother-in-law and my uncle, for he is the brother of my step-mother. My fathers wife, namely my step-mother, had a son. He is my brother and at the same time my grand-child for he is the son of my daughter. My wife is my grandmother, because she is my mother's mother. I am my wife's husband and grand child at the same time; and as the husband of a person's grand mother is his grand father, I am my own grandfather.—[Pueblo Merry World.

Astonishing Success.

It is the duty of every person who have used Boschee's German Syrup to let its wonderful qualities be known to their friends in curing consumption, severe coughs, croup, asthma, pneumonia, and in fact all throat and lung diseases. No person can use it without immediate relief. Three doses will relieve any case, and we consider it the duty of all druggists to recommend it to the poor, dying consumptive, at least to try one bottle, as 80.000 dozen bottles were sold last year, and no one case where it failed was reported. Such a medicine as the German Syrup cannot be too widely known. Ask your druggist about it. Sample bottles to try, sold at 10 cents. Regular size 75 cents. Sold by all druggists and dealers, in the United States and Canada.

Elk Mountain Assay Office.

Assays of all descriptions promptly and carefully attended to when sent by mail. Address;

S. C. ROBINSON.
Pittsburg, Colo.

Only a letter.
Yellow and dim with age;
Wistfully gazing,
I hold the torn old page.

Only a token
From one who loved me well;
The faded writing
Scarce the fond words tell.

Only a letter,
Yet dearer far to me
Than all else beside,
Minding me, love, of thee.

Only a letter,
Yellow and old and torn;
On my heart it lies
Now I am old and worn.

Only a message,
Tender and true and sweet,
The writer long dead—
Never again we meet.

Only a letter,
Hid in an oaken chest;
Close, close to my heart,
When I am laid at rest.
—*Chambers' Journal.*

Baby's Golden Curl.

John Challoner was feeling utterly miserable. He was a brown-bearded, sturdy-looking man, with every outward appearance of health and prosperity; but as he sat there in the corner of the railway carriage, with his hands thrust deeply into the capacious pockets of his fur-lined coat, and with his traveling cap pulled low over his eyes, I doubt if there was so wretched a man in the whole of that London express.

There was a terrible storm on, for it was the Christmas eve of '78, and destined to be a memorable night in the annals of the weather almanacs; but as he sat there watching the snow being hurled in compact masses against the windows, John Challoner felt a certain grim satisfaction that nature should be in accordance with his own tempestuous thoughts. He was not very sure of their present whereabouts, but as far as he could judge, the train was already some hours late, and was progressing at a very slow rate indeed. Well, what did it matter, after all, whether or not he was home in time for the Christmas Day? The big dreary house, that a girl's young presence had seemed to flood with sunshine, would appear even bigar and drearier, now that that girl had left it forever. There would be Sarah, of course, the silent elder sister, who had watched over John's motherless boyhood, and who loved him with so jealous a devotion; but then—Sarah wasn't Madge, and it was Madge he wanted. Not that he would have admitted as much for a moment; that would have been too rediculous; when it was only last night, after a somewhat prolonged visit to the Scottish metropolis, that he had been talking to a lawyer in Edinburgh, and giving him instructions about the drawing up of the paper which was to separate the husband and wife. John was to go his way, and Madge was to go hers. And this was the end of those four years of married life which had opened so brightly, and only the first few months of that first tiny quarrel, when Challoner had forgotten the promise to take his gr l-wife to an especial dance, and had spent the evening amongst the books which had been the sole companions of his hitherto solitary life. Whose actual fault was it that things had come to this pass? In what had the trouble consisted, that there had been such jarring in the home that they had ultimately decided to live their lives apart?

The train went slower and slower, the freshly fallen snow lay in high banks on either side; but John Challoner's thoughts never wandered from the old sore subject. One by one he recalled the various landmarks of those four years. How bitterly Sarah had resented the advent of the young bride; how impossible he had found it to live a society life with Madge and yet get through the necessary literary work which meant his livelihood; how eagerly his young cousin, Charles Thorne, had volunteered to take her to dances and so on in his stead. Then he recalled that little daughter's birth, and the glad hopes that had sprung into life as he took his tiny Christmas rose in his stalwart arms and tried to trace the mother-look in the baby features. But the baby had only lived to see her second birthday, and with her death "the rift within the lute" had slowly widened, and the faint music which still had echoed in their daily lives was turned into jangling discord. Madge was fonder of young Thorne than of John himself," Sarah had averred; and the poor fellow had been forced to acquiesce, when barely had the dead child been laid to rest, before her mother had taken up the old whirl of dissipation, with Charl e Thorne in constant attendance.

There was nothing, I think, which John Challoner felt so b tterly as this same apparent hard heartedness. It is not often that men care for very young children, but this curly-headed little daughter had been simply worshiped by her father. The fact that he was a poet both by nature and profession may perhaps have helped him in his love and comprehension of what Theodore Watts so beautifully calls "the music of human speech—the beloved babble of children;" but certain it is that he had set high hopes upon this little one. The highest of all was that she would b nd his beautiful wife closer to him; but the baby had died and was under the snow, and the dead hopes were buried in the scrap of lawyer's parchment which another week would see signed and attested.

How bitterly cold it was to be sure! the hot water cans had been useless long ago; and the windows were coated with frozen snow; but yet he never regretted having taken the journey. Albeit they were English folk, Madge's home and belongings were in Edinburg, and Challoner had preferred leav ng the question of settlements with those who would be careful for Madge's interests, rather than less friendly hands. Of course there had been no actual obligation to go north in person, but Challoner, jealous for his wife's reputation, had dreaded the matter being discussed by unnecessary tongues. The separation was purely a personal affair, and was being settled by the family solicitors without any further appeal to the law.

There were only two other passengers in his compartment, and to arouse himself from his gloomy abstraction, he began listening to their conversation. They were both young, rather sporting-looking men, and one had evidently been describing to the other the personal appearance of some unknown lady.

"She is a thorough little beauty, I tell you, and I flatter myself I'm a good judge," was his enthusiastic conclusion. "Shouldn't mind traveling up to town with her myself."

"Why don't you, then?" came in answer.

The first speaker laughed. "I daren't, my boy. She has a gorgon of a maid with her, who is even more freez ng than this beastly weather. But you what, though; at the next station I'll try to get her some tea or something, and that'll pave the way to a chat."

Challoner frowned involuntarily. Such talk was peculiarly distasteful to him; and for the first time it struck him that for the future his Madge would be open to any and every chance insult which men such as his fellow-travelers might choose to put upon her. The very thought of it made his blood bo l. Madge was so pretty, so young, and in many ways so thoughtless, that even more than another, she might be made to feel her unprotected state; and whatever might happen he himself would be powerless to shield her. He became so absorbed in this new thought that he hardly noticed when the creeping train came to a stand-st ll; and it was only when a sudden blast of cold air made it apparent that his companions had thrown down the window and were leaning out that he roused himself to inquire the cause. He was putting his head out of the window to look about him, when the guard came along the footboard, feeling his way laboriously in the blind ng snow, and shouting at the top of his voice that all passengers were to descend.

Instantly all was in confusion. "Cries of Why?" "What's the matter?" "Are we in danger?" and "Guard! guard!" resounded on all s des. Immediately the younger of his companions unfastened the door and ejaculating, "Now for that pretty girl!" jumped out; while the other more slowly collected his wraps, and observed that he "supposed the snow had been too much for the engine."

This, indeed, proved to be the case; and after some pardonable grumbling, Challoner got out of the train and followed in the track of those who were picking their way towards a roadside station at some forty yards distance. As he did so, he caught the rough, persuasive tones of his late companion: "Really, now, you had better take my arm; we shall get on first-rate."

The door of a first-class carr age was swinging open, and standing before it —so directly in his path that Challoner almost fell over him—was the young gentleman who had vaunted his appreciation of feminine beauty. Naturally, Challoner's glance follow d his; and although he could not distinguish the lady's, he was becoming dimly conscious that the brown velvet coat was strangely familiar, when she spoke a few words in a tone which sent the blood coursing through his veins: "Thank you, I will not trouble you; my maid is with me."

Madge's voice! Challoner dropped his rugs, scrambled up on to the footboard, and held out his arms. "Come down at once!" he cried, authoritatively. "It may not be safe for you to stay there. Jump, and I'll catch you. May I troub e you to get out of the way, sir? This lady is my wife."

Madge flung herself instantly into the outstretched arms, and burst into hysterical sobbing. "O John, John! I have been so cold and so frightened. And the l ght in our carriage went out, and I thought something might happen to the train and hurt you."

"Why, Madge!"

Never before had Challoner seen his wife so thoroughly unhinged and frightened, and his heart gave a great leap as he noticed her last words: "Hurt me? Of course not. But how came you to be traveling to town? Why didn't you stay in Ed nburgh? Do you think you have taken cold?" He asked the questions all in one breath; but when she began expla ning that she wanted to spend Christmas in town with her aunt, he hastily cut her short.

"There is no time to talk; we must get on to the station. Parker (this to the maid), follow me closely, and try to walk in my footsteps. I shall carry your mistress; the snow is too deep for her."

While speaking he took the trembling g rl in his arms, and began slowly plodding along in the direction the guard had indicated. Of course it was only a chance meeting, and Challoner was too free from superstition to look on it as anything else; but even while he was reminding himself that it was a terrible pity they had met—that their tempers were wholly incompatible—and that it would be misery to live again through the last few months, he was still holding the girl very close and tenderly, and wishing in spite of himself that the distance could be doubled.

When they reached the little country station, they found it to be better provided with shelter than is usually the case; and though there was only one man in charge, he was a sensible, good-natured individual, who did his best for the poor travelers thus thrown upon his hands. Either the sight of Mage's white child-like face, or the pleasant stirring memories which he had summoned would make it worth his while, indeed him to open a little box of a room which appeared to be his special property and to motion to Challoner to enter.

"Your lady will be more comfortable there, sir, than in the big room along o' the third-class passengers and all," he suggested; and as the other husband nor wife could think of a sufficient excuse for protecting the company of their fellow-travelers, they were obliged to follow the man lead.

"I will not intrude upon your privacy," said Challoner stiffly, as soon as the station-keeper had left them alone. "You and Parker will be quite comfortable here, and you'll soon get warm by the fire."

Madge watched his broad form disappear through the doorway with a sinking heart. "He hates to be with me even for these few minutes," ran her thoughs; "and yet," with a piteous little quiver on her lips, "oh how delicious it was to be held in his arms. If he had held me like that oftener, we shouldn't be hating each other to-day! If he had but kissed me in the snow!"

The dismal train of thoughts was suddenly broken by the discovery that one of her trinkets were missing, and Mrs. Challoner was instantly on her knees. "Come and help me find it, Parker. she cried. I have lost my locket."

The excitement both of mistress and maid seemed considerably more than the occasion warranted; but only Madge herself and the faithful woman who had nursed her as a child knew of the serious trouble such a loss would entail.

"Could you have dropped it outside, ma'am?"

"Not possible. The chain couldn't catch on anything, when I had my cloak fastened. No; it must be on the floor. Do look for it, Parker."

And look for it they did, but without success; and when the long fruitless search was over, the expression on the girl's face was very woe-begone indeed.

"The mistress has lost her gold locket," whispered Parker when John Challoner came again to the door. "It's my belief, sir, that she dropped it on the floor of the carr age. Can't you send some body after it, sir?"

"What locket?"

"The gold one she always wears around her neck," exclaimed the maid, regardless of the urgent "Parker! You are not to trouble Mr. Challoner," which came from behind her. "She is fonder of it than any thing else, s r; it seems a pity it should be lost."

"Parker!" again broke in the pretty girlish voice, "I desire that you do not trouble Mr. Challoner."

The man's lips tw tched involuntary. It seemed to him that his young wife was only playing a dignity when she preferred addressing her remarks to him through the medium of a servant.

"Don't be foolish," he said peremptorily. "Of course I'll go after your locket. I only came back to tell you that I am afraid you will have to spend several hours here. The snow has broken down the telegraph w res, so the men can't send on a message to the next place for assistance. They must wait until this storm is over, and then get help from the village to dig out the train and clear the lines. But of course it will be the work of a good many hours."

"Thank you," said Madge meekly. "What s the time?"

"Nearly ten." He was turning away, when something in his wife's voice struck h m, and he re-entered the room. "You are still cold? Wear this," he said shortly, rapidly unbuttoning his fur-lined coat; and in spite of her remonstrances, he wrapped it round her, and then went hastily out into the bitter night-air.

Left alone, Madge leaned back in her corner and sat for a long time crying softly to herself. Being thoroughly unstrung by terror and fatigue, she was in just the impressionable mood wh ch made her husband's little act of kindness very precious in her eyes, and she nestled into the thick warm fur as though cheating herself into the belief that it was John himself who was holding her. She remembered a t me—it was during the happy weeks which followed the wedding day—when she and John seemed to be all in all to each other; but when they were finally settled in the staid London house, over which Miss Sarah's chilly influence hung like a pall; it had all been altered then. John had gone back to his beloved books, in apparent forgetfulness of the solitary l ttle wife in the big drawing-room up stairs; and if she proposed invading his precincts, it was only to be met with Miss Sarah's reproachful stare, and the words: "My brother never allows even me to disturb him." And then baby's birth, and—baby's death! In nervous terror of her own great grief, the poor young mother had flung herself into every kind of dissipation, for the dead child seemed hardly farther from her than the silent man who was buried in his books, and to face her sorrow alone was more than she could do. O dear! the life that henceforth would be lived apart, might have been so happy!—and the tears flowed on.

Meanwhile, Challoner had started for the railway carriage. The blinding snow, the flickering lantern, and the difficulty of picking his way, made the short journey a long one, but his busy wonderments made the time pass quickly. For the first time in his life, John Challoner was feeling curious. What made his wife so fond of that particular locket? What did it contain? He was still pondering on the mistery when he reached the carriage. Parker had been right; the little engraved locket lay upon the floor; but beside it lay something, at the sight of which the man's heart gave a great throb. A little curly head, a pair of sweet blue eyes, a soft uncertain voice trying to stammer the word "mama!" They all rose vividly before him as he stood there with the tiny ring of silky brown hair lying on his open palm. And it was Madge who had cherished the curl, which his own lips had seemed to press so much oftener than had hers! Madge, who had thought to keep the token that he had forgotten, and had regretted so vainly. Well, before they parted, he must ask her to halve her treasure wit him.

There were very tender memories stirring within him as he plodded his way slowly back to the station; when he at last reached the little room, his face was very gentle, albeit very grave. "Yes, I have it, Parker. Thank you," she said coldly. "I hope it was not a difficult matter to get the carriage?"

Challoner bit his lip. Do you think I minded the difficulty?" he retorted passionately. "Don't you know I'd have risked my life for the sake of rescuing this?" He laid the locket on the table; but as he spoke, he opened his clenched hand, and the soft curl glistened brightly in the firelight.

Madge started violently. "You opened it?"

"No; it had opened itself by falling on the floor." He leaned forward and looked at her curiously.

"And you cared to keep it, Madge?" "Did I—care?"

Only three words, but the tone went straight to the husband's heart. So she had cared after all, and yet—. "You went out again so soon," he said doubtfully.

"And could I help that?" The girl clasped her hands, and looked steadily at him with great sorrowful eyes. "You were always with your books and could I bear to live alone in these rooms where every cha r that her hands had touched, every picture that her eyes had seen, spoke to me of my lost darling? No; I would go to dances, theaters, anywhere where she had never been, and therefore could not haunt me."

"You might have come to me."

"To you?" The dreary little laugh which she echoed his words were not good to hear. "You had your work. You had never asked me to share it, and you had always left me alone."

Challoner's face had grown very white. "Madge," b said solemnly. "God is my witness that if I have wronged you, it was through a mistaken love, and not through carelessness. When we—marr ed (the loving stress he laid upon the word was not lost upon the girl, although her face was turned upon him), Sarah impressed upon me that if I pursued a plan I had already suggested to her, and asked you to ask as my secretary, I should be dealing unfairly in letting you expend your youth and sprits on me and my work, instead of on the amusements and society life which was natural to your age."

His very anxiety was making him speak in a stiff, unusual fashion; but the little clasped hands moved restlessly at his words. "I should have loved the work."

The murmur was too soft for the other to catch, and he went on slowly: "Right or wrong, I believed her. I said to myself: 'You are a poor man, and must work hard; but however great the strain may be, it must never touch your wife. If you can not take her out yourself, let your cousin do so in your stead. Let——'"

"Don't talk like that—don't talk like that !" Madge had risen to her feet, and the words came with an irrepressible sob. She waited a full m nute and then added: "It makes one wish that things had been different—almost."

When Challoner spoke again, it was after a long pause. "When d d you cut this curl?"

"On your birthday," said Madge with an effort to speak easily. "I brought her into your room, and she was dressed all in white——"

"I thought it was blue."

"No, John; all in white, with coral beads."

"Ah! yes, to be sure. I remember. The young rogue broke the string, and you were so proud of her strength that you would not have it mended;" and Challoner actually laughed at the remembrance of the scene.

"You took her in your arms," went on Madge bravely, "and kissed this very curl, and then you gave her back to me and said——"

She broke off suddenly; but though Challoner's face was flaming as hotly as her own, he went on stendily: "'I said, God bless my wife and child, and spare them to me for many, many years."

"But baby died in the autumn, and——"

In the intense stillness of the little room, John Challoner finished her sentence. "And you are leaving me," he said hoarsely. "Ah, Madge, for baby's sake, give me but that curl."

Her gloves were off and as she silently leaned forward to loosen the silk that held the pretty hair, their hands touched. She drew back for a moment, looking at him piteously, and the next, with a long sobbing cry, she fell forward into his out stretched arms.

* * * * *

It was a long trying night for many people at that little snow-bound station. And how sorely would the chance of the lines; but it was only when the first gray glimmer of light was stealing over the darkened skies, that they were able to pronounce progress possible. The passengers in the waiting-room had kept up a perpetual chorus of grumblings and abuse; but in the little room where the station-keeper had placed his two most favored guests, there was nothing but deep thankfulness for the enforced wait. During the long night hours, with only a tender memory to share their vigil, husband and wife had grown very close to each other. The long series of jars and misunderstandings which had grown up from their two several mistakes—from Challoner's erroneous belief that they could follow two distinct and separate courses and yet remain united; and from Madge's half-wounded, half-defiant pride, which forbade her to take the initiative in drawing nearer to each other—one and all they had been discussed—discussed gravely and penitently, as became two souls in whom fresh hopes were springing, and who, but for an apparently chance meeting, would have broken with each other forever. But when the sad reviewing of the r past failures was at an end, and with full hearts they dared to speak of a brighter and more trustful future, the tears that rose to their eyes were tears of happiness. "It shall be the talisman of our love," Challoner had said as he divided the tiny ring of hair; and the kiss that followed was fraught with all the solemnity of a renewal of marriage vows. It is needless to add that the services of the Edinburgh lawyer were not required.

As under the law only railway employees are entitled to passes, it is possible that the rush for positions in the service of the transportation companies will relieve the pressure upon politics.—*Chicago Herald.*

THE CATTLE LOSSES IN MONTANA.

Stockmen Very Much Discouraged by the Experience of Last Winter—The Rustling System Must Go.

The present winter marks, without a doubt, an epoch in cattle-raising in the northwest, writes a Fort Assiniboin, Montana, correspondent of *The New York World.* Despite the stories of the Arctic rigors of other winters, "'way back in the '60s," told by an occasional old timer, it is doubtful if this country has seen for twenty-five years any season more severe. Nowhere have its effects been more seriously felt than in Montana. The territorial papers are full of the tale of disaster to the ranges, but in the dispatches to the press much of the truth is naturally suppressed.

The losses of cattle up to March average throughout the territory probably not less than 30 per cent., and although the situation gives signs of improvement, yet hundreds of thousands more must succumb ere the snow entirely dissapears. For over two months the stock has been almost entirely without food and exposed to intense cold, and when the spring thaw does come, numbers of the worst sufferers will be too weak, and, as stockmen say, "too discouraged," to recover.

The thermometer has recorded as low as 57 degrees below zero in northern Montana, and for many weeks it has remained steadily at extremely low figures. For the first ten days in February the average was 20 below. This extreme temperature combined with lack of grass and hard crusted snow two feet deep, has exhausted even the hardiest animals on the range. Many thousands of foreign cattle, too, were driven into the territory last summer, and among these, unacclimated and wearied with driving, the havoc has been fearful. At no time was stock ever less prepared for such a winter than during the present autumn. The range, already half bare in many sections from over stocking had been shriveled by a drought, the likes of which was never known before. Grass was scorched as if by fire and springs and creeks never dry before in the recollection of the oldest settlers presented to the thirsty animals up to the time of the first snow-fall nothing but beds of sun-baked mud. Large numbers of cattle, through some agreement between their owners and the agents, were driven upon the large Indian reserves of the north where feed had not been entirely consumed, but where thousands of them have since met death upon the open, unsheltered prairie.

Stockmen who have recently ridden the ranges are very reticent, but occasionally a whispered report is heard from a reliable source, revealing a frightful state of affairs. At some points hundreds of cattle have been found dead in a single coulee, and one man, recently in from a trip up the Missouri, claims to have counted several thousand carcasses in five days of travel. Cattlemen of sound and conservative opinions assert their belief that the average loss will be fully 65 per cent. for the whole territory under the most hopeful issue of affairs. Sheep-raisers are suffering to almost the same extent as the cattlemen, despite the extra shelter and feeding that their bands get. Now, all of this disaster, unprecedented as it is, has long since been expected and foretold. Frank Wilkeson's letters foreshadowed the situation in the press during the past year, and in some cases cattle-owners themselves, seemingly struck by a presentiment of the future, made liberal offers last fall to purchasers or insurers of their herds. One of the largest of these owners near Helena offered $200,000 for such insurance without finding any takers.

By the blind confidence hitherto displayed in what is called out here the "rustling" system of wintering cattle, the greater portion of the whole wealth of the vast territory of Montana has been staked each year, as it were, on the single turn of a die. Such a winter as the present may happen any year; but "sixes" have been thrown nearly twenty times in succession, and the stake has each year been doubled with the gambler's unfailing confidence, in his ability to turn the lucky number forever. Now, on the first trick of the die, he loses his entire pile, minus perhaps what he has spent on cigars and drinks during the game. His losses involve thousands of friends who have backed his luck. Among these the banks are the principal sufferers. In the town of Helena alone, it is said, loans upon cattle security inflict most serious loss. In the territory itself, the money depression, extending as it does, to nearly all branches of trade and employment, will be felt for years to come, and, of course, many capitalists in the east are severely injured. The result of all this is inevitable and will soon appear. Stock-rising on the "rustling" plan must cease and stock-farming take its place. The days of the cattle kings are virtually over— here, as elsewhere. Many of the territorial papers are already urging a change in the system of raising, both on the ground of pecuniary policy, and—what is really singular and indicative of revolution in western ideas—of humanity to the stock itself. Their arguments will receive especial respect at the present moment, for a few well-known raisers have for a year or to past practiced the feeding system, and the contrast between their experience and the general ruin of the rest during this season points a moral that all must read.

Another transcontinental line will push its way across north Montana during the coming summer, and in very few years the vast ranges and their wealthy kings, the round-up and the cowboy, all of the romatic features of "cattle raising in the far west," will have become but traditions, and in their stead will reign the prosaic but humane, thrifty and successful methods of the eastern cattle farmer.

Closer than a Brother.

Stubbins—"Who was that sandy-haired fellow you spoke to just now?"

Grabber—"That? Oh, that's my bosom friend."

"Your bosom friend?"

"Yes, he makes my shirts."—*Cleveland Sun.*

War is A Bad Thing.

"People talk about war with Mexico and war with England, and the newspapers print plesant incidents and glorious achievements of the noble soldiers who figured in the late War, which is all well and as it should be, but," said old man Plunket, looking over his spectacles, "thar's none of 'em what knows what war is lessen, they's been thar.

"I tell you, stranger," said the old man, "you may read and you may look at pictures of battles, and you may go to all these 'campments and see them have their sham fights, but you won't know a bit more about what real war is than a man who would suppose your Gate City Guard could thrash old England. War is a bad thing, mister, war's a bad thing sure!"

"Do you see that house up the road?" asked the old man, pointing with his finger. "Well, stranger, right by that window thar by the chimney is a vacant chair. Not more'n a week ago the dear old woman who sot in that chair, right by that window, with her eyes looking right down this big road ever since Lee's surrender, was buried over yonder at the church, and that's not a man nor woman in this settlement but what has shed a tear over the grave whar she lies."

The old man wiped his spectacles with his red bandana, and with his head bent and his eyes cast down shook his head and uttered, "War's a bad thing, stranger; war's a bad thing."

"That old lady," continued the old man, "had four as fine boys as ever shouldered the musket for the confederacy—and that's saying a right smart. They all went to Virginia, and one by one they were killed till there was only one left. Tom, he was the oldest, and I never shall forget when the news come that he was killed at Seven Pines. Squire Adams he lived cross over on the other road yonder, and the mail for the settlement went to his house during the War, and the neighbors would get their letters from thar. We'd done heard thar'd been a big fight at Richmond, so I was settin' right here in this piazer smoking after supper and I hered Jim, one of Squire Adams niggers, start from the Squire's house down the path that led across the fields to yon house, hollowing and blowing his quills, and I told my old 'oman thar was a letter for our neighbors. Jim, he went on down the path, and directly he crossed over the branch yonder, and the sound from his quills came up the branch, and I could hear the doleful tune he was blowing as well as if I'd been in 200 yards of him. I followed the sound of his quills till he struck the path through yon pine thicket, and then he quit blowing his quills and sung:

> "Down in the cornfield,
> Hear dat mournful sound,
> All the darkies am er weeping,
> For massa's in the cold, cold ground.

"I told my old 'oman I was afered that nigger had bad news for our neighbors, and so it was, for no sooner than he'd got to the house I hered screams and hollerin, and me and the old 'oman put out over thar, and what I seed then makes me know war's a bad thing, mister, war's a bad thing."

"Then," said the old man "thar was more fighten and the army went into Maryland and our neighbors they'd sorter calmed themselves in their anxiety for the other three sons, and the army come outen Maryland and then pretty soon we hered of a big fight at Fredericksburg, and a few nights arter I was sittin right here in this piaza alone, and I hered Jim start from the Squire's agin, and as he went down across the field yonder he was singin'

> "I cannot work until tomorrow,
> Bcase the tear drops flow;
> But I'll try to drive away my sorrow,
> Pickin on de old banjo.

"And then he'd blow his quills and then sing another verse till he'd got over yonder to our neighbors, and then I listned to hear any weeping, if he carried bad news, but thar was no fuss this time, but I went over thar, me and the 'old 'oman,' and when we got close to the house we seed the spinnin' wheels nor the loom warn't running, and we knowed something was wrong, and sure enough the letter brought the news that two of the boys—the two middle ones, Bob and John—had been killed in the battle, and there was only one left—William, the youngest; and that poor family was too sad to weep; they couldn't cry; they were huddled down in the middle of the room on the floor, leaning one upon the other, and not a word spake they. I tell you, stranger, war's a bad, bad thing."

* * * * * * * *

"Well," resumed the old man, "the War went on, and at last news came that Lee had surrendered and that all the soldiers would soon be at home. My neighbors over thar sorter brightened up then, cheered with the hope of soon having William with them. The railroads 'twixt here and Virginia was all tore up, so the boys all had to walk home and get home the best the could. They paired off in little squad and started, every man for himself and pretty soon this one, and then another, according to their ability to make the trip, came in, and several brought the news that William was on the road and would be here at any moment, and that dear old mother, who we buried last week, took her seat by that yonder window every morning, and thar she set watching down this road for William, her baby boy, who has never come yet, and never will come. She set by that window over twenty years, waiting and watching, with a ball of thread in her lap and a half-finished sock in her hand that she held to all this time, never saying a word, but looking down the road so anxious, O, so anxious. Last week about 3 o'clock one day she raised her arms and with a cry of joy; 'My boys! O, my boys!' she fell over on the arm of the chair, dead. War's bad, stranger, very bad."—**Atlanta Constitution.**

GIVING AND TAKING A LIGHT.

The Manner of Spanish, German, English, and American Smokers.

There is a certain variety in the manner of giving and taking a light for a cigar that is interesting to all smokers. The Italians and French successfully copy the Spanish style, which is the the most graceful and elegant of all, the only possible objection to it being that they sometimes carry politeness beyond a reasonable range. But, after all, it is simple and friendly enough. The Spaniard bows and asks his neighbor for a light. The latter, returning the bow, immediately presents him with his cigar, holding out the lighted end at a slight angle between the thumb and second finger. The other takes the cigar and after procuring the needed fire from it, reverses it skillfully and returns it, the entire operation being accompanied by another graceful bow and each raises his hat as he turns to go away. The Spaniard always smokes through his nose. He considers it extravagant to waste any good smoke through his mouth, and inveterate smokers in all countries agree with him.

The German is more polite in asking for a light than he is in giving it. Even with the best intentions in the latter case his efforts have all the appearance of reluctance. Sometimes, when a cigar is smoked down nearly far enough, he throws it away immediately after granting the request for fire. This among the Italians is considered rude and boorish in the extreme, and is sometimes regarded as positively insulting.

The average Englishman before he gives a light, and finally acts as if he had achieved a mighty feat in condescension, Instead of lifting his hat his hand is more likely to go into his pocket, and he is apt to give a parting puff with an air of indignation as he stalks away. Possibly this comes from the fact that he never asks for a light himself, and is always well armed with matches.

The American of late, seems to be somewhat averse to letting anyone take a light from his cigar. He takes it for granted that it must be much better than his neighbor's and not wishing to contaminate it, he answers an appeal for the fire with a match. Sometimes he politely lights the match, and in some cases he presents it with an air good enough for any Spaniard. But this somewhat new custom may possibly be of Irish parentage. The Irish peasant generally strikes a match for his fireless friend or fellow traveler, and even in a gale of wind he will hold a lighted match in the hollow of his hands and humorously issue orders for the capture of the precious flame.

The giving or taking of a light, for a cigar is a small affair, but little things often reveal a great deal of the character, disposition, and breeding of men. It should alway be offered cheerfully and taken politely. In this country it need not be done with the extreme politeness and elegance which may be said to be the exclusive property of the Latins, and which is probably beyond the reach of colder and more sober races; but it should be accompanied by that good-fellowship which is governed by common sense, the foundation of all politeness.—*New York Sun.*

Advice To Young Men.

And as for the men we respect, let them give up a part of the time they spend in money-making to put on the polish that may seem a superfluity, but which women love, nevertheless, as they love all superfluities. A few trifling airs and graces, a suavity of speech, a neatly turned compliment, a profound bow—these are bagatelles, it is true, but in their way they work wonders and open a highway to the hearts of the simpler and weaker sex that has before been closed by gates of adamant. They are easily picked up in youth, but the old tongue trips awkardly over honeyed words and phrases, and the stiff old back at 40 odd can never achieve a bow which is much better than none at all. Even the men of Juabourg St. Germain—every city has its Faubough St. Germain—think better of one possessing these social embellishments, and there is not in the world a talisman of such potent magic as the nameless and irresistable spell of a charming manner. It ought to be innate, of course, but it can be in a great measure acquired.

The plodders upon whom Dame fortune is turning a dawning smile may pause awhile on the way. The smile and the good luck are bound to come, the brighter and better for the delay, and the young man who looks forward to one day being a man of millions may just as well fit himself early for the proud position he means to occupy.

What He Wanted to Say.

The conductor had his eye on the man for five minutes before he went in to collect his fare, and he was therefore somewhat prepared to hear him answer to the call of "fare" with:

"Really, but I beg your pardon, but——"

"Fare, sir!"

"Yes, certainly, but as I told you, I have——"

"Oh, I can change a twenty."

"Yes, I know you can, but I wanted to tell you that——"

"I must have your fare, sir."

"Yes, I know you must, but owing to the luxurious manner in which this car is fitted up I'm willing to pay double fare. Here is a dime, sir, and please turn it all over to the company."—*Detroit Free Press.*

A Frank Avowal.

Chicago Man—Yes, sir, I have brought suit against him for $500 for defamation of character.

"Isn't that very little?"

"Not as characters run in Chicago?"—*New York Sun.*

Copyright Their Fairy Tales.

People who tell big yarns ought tobe compelled to take out a special license.—*Pittsburg Chronicle.*

Denver W. N. U., Vol. V., No. 18

Crystal River Current.

Published by the Current Publishing Co

A. A. JOHNSON, Editor.   Jos. A. BRAY, Manager.

ENTERED AT THE POST-OFFICE AT CRYSTAL COLORADO, FOR TRANSMISSION THROUGH THE MAILS AS SECOND-CLASS MATTER.

TERMS—PAYABLE-IN-ADVANCE:

One Year,.................$3 00
Six Months,...............1 75
Three Months,.............1 00

Crystal Post-office Directory.

Mail arrives and departs every Tuesday Thursday and Saturday.

SATURDAY, JUNE ,11 1887.

EDITORAL ETCHINGS.

ANOTHER earthquake has visited the continent; this time in the Province of Quebec which shook up the mountains, but no lives are reported as being lost.

THE snow is disappearing at a rapid rate these days and we believe that a number of the mines in Crystal basin can be worked after the eighteenth of the month.

PACK animals can get over the divide at any hour of the day. Very little snow remains in the timber on the old road, and wagons will be going over by the middle of the month.

MAIL going to and coming from Aspen, Glenwood, Satank and Carbondale should go over Maroon Pass as it would save considerable time. A good idea would be to address it via. Maroon pass.

BUSINESS relations between the United States and Canada appear to be assuming a more satisfactory shape than formerly and if reciprocity is fully carried out it cannot help but benefit the two nations.

THE outlook for an active season in mining operations keep improving and should some plans that are now under way be carried out this district would be immensely benefited and come to the front in good shape before the next snow fall.

HON WILLIAM W. WHEELER, Vice President during Ex-President Hayes administration, died at his home in Malone, N. Y., on the 4th instant. For years he had been failing, and brain affection was the immediate cause of his death. He had a quiet burial.

ARRANGEMENTS have been made with the Denver mining Review whereby we can offer the CURRENT and Review to new subscribers for the reduced price of $4.00 per annum. This offer will give mining men the advantage of securing news from all sections of the state, also secure the latest news from this section. Mining is now attracting public attention therefore send in your subscription at once.

THERE is nothing small about the Security Mining company after all. 5,000 tons of ore was knocked down with seven shots the other day when an inspection was being made of the mine by a party of gentlemen from the east, who are interested in the property. For the sake of the mining industry of the state we hope the above is a fact; yet it seems too large a dose for the ordinary Colorado miner to swallow.

MAIL CONTRACTOR W. F. BLISS arrived in Gothic on Wednesday to make arrangements for carrying mail from Gothic to Crystal and Prospect under the new contract which will come into effect the first of July. Uncle Sam made a good contract in letting the route to Mr. Orr who will be out of pocket about $1.000 a year on the job. This should be a lesson to mail contractors to find out what mountain routes are before putting in bids. Ed Barthel will carry the mail for the contractor during the next quarter.

PUBLIC attention is being turned toward the mining industry and in eastern mining centres there is more activity in mining stocks. The surplus capital of the east could not find any more profitable industry in which to invest and to-day Colorado stands at the head of the list as a mineral producer, which is almost certain to attract more investors in this direction than to any other

point. The railroad building that is now going on throughout the state is advertising the country, and capitalists must see the advantages that will be gained by cheap transportation of ore from our mining centres.

GUNNISON and Pitkin counties should take immediate steps towards getting up a creditable collection of all kinds of mineral, coal and marble for the exhibition to be held at Denver. There will undoubtedly be many visitors from the east, and if a good display was made we believe it would be of great benefit to us. The mine owners should take an interest in the matter and see what can be done. This district could make a good display of silver, lead, and Iron ores, coal slate and marble, and we would like to see our miners get out samples and show up the resources of this section.

THE large carbonate belt between here and the head of Avalanche creek should attract the attention of prospectors this season along the mountain sides there is an outcrop of vein matter that is from 200 to 600 feet in width that shows a lead and iron carbonate in spar. Several locations are upon it, but there is still a splendid opportunity for the prospector along the belt, and we believe if shafts were sunk on it there would be large bodies of ore discovered. Some large pieces of heavy lead float that undoubtedly come from the vein have been found, yet there has not been enough work done to prove the value in the belt.

WE understand the county commissioners will make an effort to complete the Paradise gulch road this season. It is to be hoped they can see their way clear to do so,for it would certainly be of great advantage to the miners of this section. The distance to the railroad would be shorter some six miles. Mine owners around Galena, Crystal and Treasury mountains should then be able to send ore to Gunnison at a cost of not over $10. per ton from the mine to the smelter. The early season offers a splendid opportunity for considerable work to be done in the mines and there should be some shipments made before fall if parties would commence work at once.

WE are in receipt of a letter from Andy T. Anderson who is now in Juneau, Alaska, which is a lengthy for publication. His pen picture would make that land of promise equal to the climes of Southern California and her resources as boundless as those of Colorado. We have no doubt but what the country has resources that will pay the government on the investment and numbers of citizens will make their fortunes in the gold mines of that country. Yet we believe fully as good investments can be made in this state. However, those who are anxious to learn something about the country can call into this office and we will gladly give them the opportunity of reading the letter themselves.

THE companies interested in the mines of this section should take advantage of the present time and commence to open up their properties so they would be in a position to commence making shipments. Considerable work is required to be done to open up the mines before any amount of ore can be taken out, or returns made upon the investments, and the sooner claims are put upon a paying basis the better for all concerned. The Gunnison market is open for the purchase of all classes of ore, and if there was a sufficient amount of inducement for a smelter to be erected down the valley it would not be long before we could have a home market. A sufficient amount of work has been done in the camp to demonstrate the fact that we have mines that will pay to work; but so long as those most interested hold back we may expect to see a number of our mines laying idle.

ROYAL BAKING POWDER

Absolutely Pure.

This powder never varies. A marvel of purity strength and wholesomeness. More economical than the ordinary kinds, and cannot be sold in competition with the multitude of low test, short weight alum or phosphate powders. Sold only in cans. ROYAL BAKING POWDER Co., 106 Wall St., N. Y.

DURING THE FALL of 1975, the old log powerhouse for the mill at Crystal was still reasonably sound. The adjacent stamp mill ruins now litter the bank beside the Crystal River (at the right). This location is approximately five miles beyond Marble, reached by what is generally considered a road for four-wheel-drive vehicles.

THE CRYSTAL MILL'S powerhouse was built in 1893, where this wooden dam was constructed to raise the water level, so it would drop down the wooden shaft (at the right), which by turning a horizontal wooden water wheel powered an air compressor inside the mill. This dam washed out during the high runoff the next spring, but it was rebuilt. After the second dam washed out, water reached the shaft by means of a long wooden flume. The roof tops of Crystal City appear beyond the dam.

LOOKING DOWN on the settlement of Crystal City (toward the west), the Crystal River became a raging torrent of water during spring runoff — in the rocky gorge beyond. A long wooden flume crosses the photograph (beyond the town) to feed water into the mill shaft.

THE EAST WALL of the Crystal mill's powerhouse shows the water flume, positioned against the building, running beneath the shaft housing, where the water dropped onto the horizontal wooden water wheel. This photograph was taken in 1937, and it shows the adjacent stamp mill, which was worked by an air compressor that got its power from the water wheel. Riffle tables inside the mill recovered precious metals from the ore.

IN THE VIEW BELOW, you are looking in the direction of Crystal, while the stamp mill was still standing — beside the old powerhouse. It fell down during the mid-1940's, after snow and rain had taken its toll on the old wooden structure.

THIS SPECTACULAR VIEW was taken from Sheep Mountain, overlooking the town of Crystal. The Crystal River is in this scene, flowing past the little settlement, where it makes a turn to the right, toward Marble. Schofield Park is cradled below the distant mountain range. The town of Gunnison is beyond. If you follow the trail out of Crystal (at the left), it will lead you to Lead King Basin and the Snowmass Wilderness.

CRYSTAL CITY was a booming mining camp in 1890. It is located beside the Crystal River, seen at the right, flowing from the headwaters in Schofield Park. The North Fork of the Crystal River is to the left. Originally, the Crystal River was named Rock Creek, until the name was changed in 1886.

left for Aspen Tuesday, where he will remain during the winter with his family.

Saturday, Gus Brockway departed for Carbondale, having completed his work on Galena mountain. He has a nice showing in the Philadelphia lode.

A.R. Burnett is getting in timbers at the Lead King mine, and contemplates working that valuable property this winter.

H.H. Williams has moved into the rooms [in Crystal] heretofore occupied by Geo. C. Eaton's family, next to the store.

B.W. Cass and another man are working on the North Pole group, in Crystal basin.

• • • • •

Local newspapers were always trying to boost the economy by urging development of local resources.

The Marble Times & Crystal Silver Lance,
October 12, 1900.

The large amount of zinc ore found throughout this district affords a great opportunity for the establishment of a plant for the treatment of this class of ore, but such a plant should be located as centrally as possible. There are two or three properties in the district that disclose large bodies of this character of ore running a high percentage.

Now that the marble beds are being opened up we hope some responsible parties will soon take ahold of the excellent slate deposit adjacent to this town [Marble] and open the same up in a systematic manner. There is money in an enterprise of this nature, as the western demand for this class of stone is constantly increasing and would be more so if the long haul from the east for such material could be done away with, thereby reducing the cost of the same. Undoubtedly some enterprising company could reap a nice thing out of our slate beds if taken ahold of at this time.

. . . . .

These slate beds were opened later but soon closed down, either because of a poor market or because the quality of the slate was not adequate.

Continued on Page 32

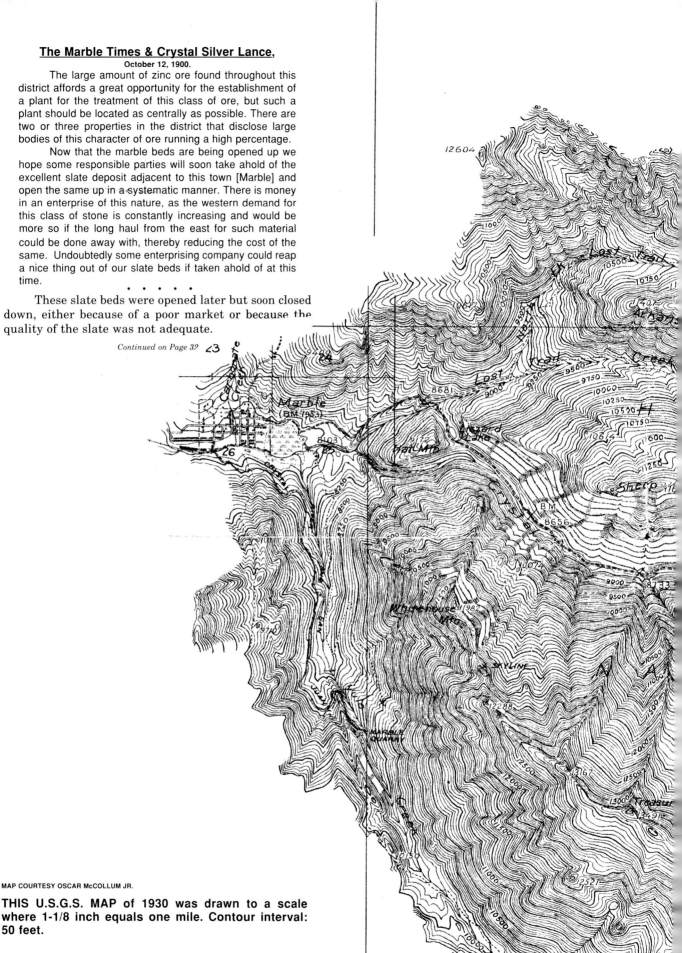

THIS U.S.G.S. MAP of 1930 was drawn to a scale where 1-1/8 inch equals one mile. Contour interval: 50 feet.

Glenn S Smith Division Engineer
Topography by C.A.Ecklund, S.T.Penick and R.O.Davis
Control by U.S. Geological Survey

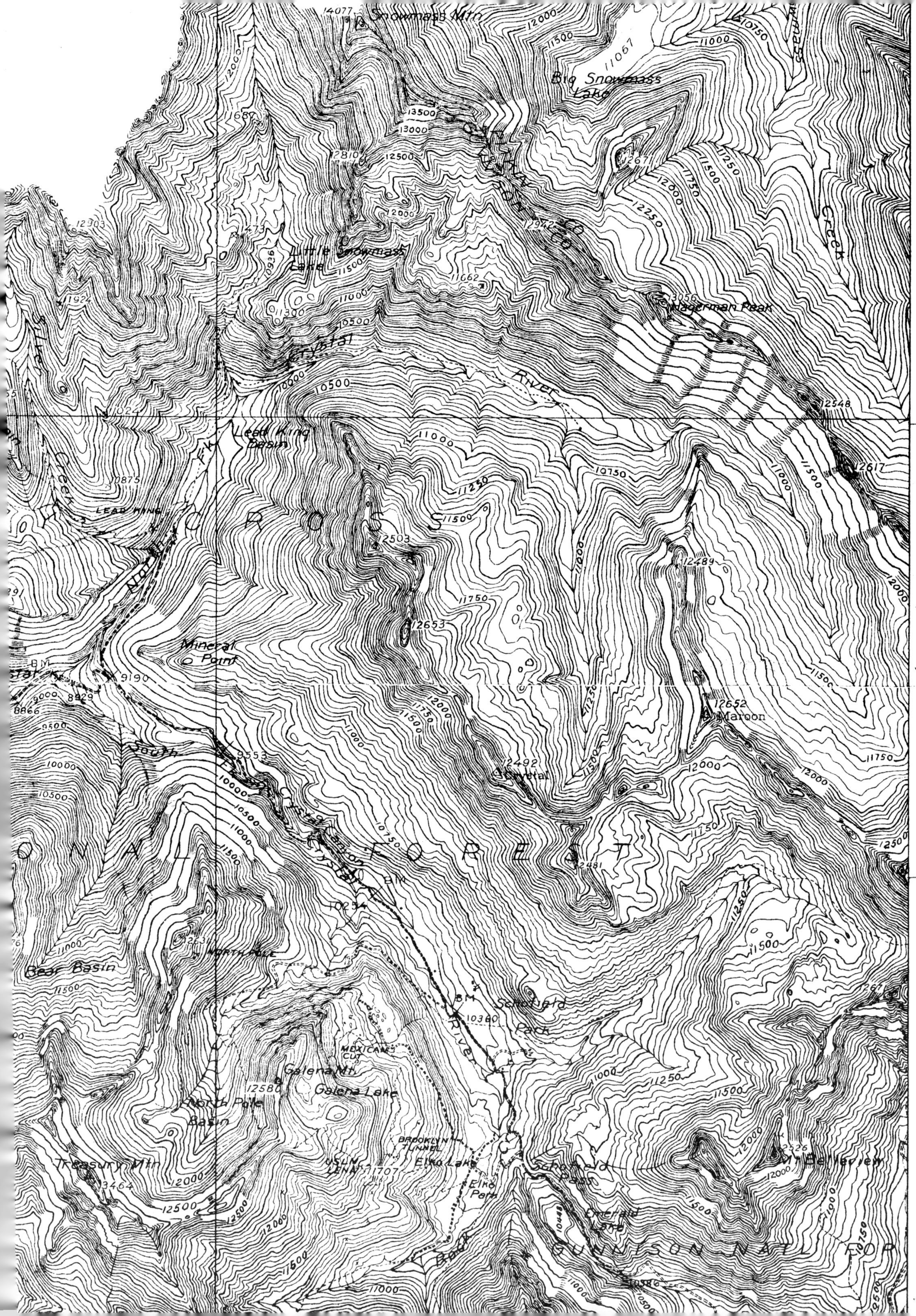
Snowmass Mtn
14077
Big Snowmass Lake
11067
Little Snowmass Lake
Hagerman Peak
13056
Crystal
River
Lead King Basin
LEAD KING
Mineral Point
9190
8929
8866
South
9553
Crystal Canyon
Crystal
12503
12653
12489
12652
Maroon
12492
Crystal
12481
Creek
Bear Basin
NORTH POLE
Schofield Park
10360
River
MEXICAN'S CUT
Galena Mtn
12580
Galena Lake
North Pole Basin
BROOKLYN TUNNEL
Elko Lake
Elko Park
Treasury Mtn
13464
Schofield Pass
Emerald Lake
Mt Bellview
12526
Rock
GUNNISON NAT'L FOR
12548
12617

(Aspen)

Crystal River Current.

VOL. 1. No. 48. CRYSTAL, COLORADO, SATURDAY, SEPTEMBER 3, 1887. PRICE 10 CENTS.

LOCAL SPLINTERS.

Tom Motheral came up from Prospect on Wednesday.

Buck Calvert took in the county seat the first of the week.

Our rainy season is playing thunder with work in the high basins.

Black currants are quite plentiful on the mountain sides this season.

The boys are all so busy at present that they cannot find time to attend the dances which are being given along the river.

Jim Jennings came up from his ranch with his pack train on Thursday, and went over to Crested butte after a load of provisions.

H. D. Penny came up from the Hot Springs yesterday, and was a caller at this office. He reports everything as flourishing down that way.

Joe Anderson, one of the old timers around Gothic came up the river the first of the week and has gone to work upon the Norman lode in Galena park.

Just received, from Philadelphia a splendid line of Wanamaker & Brown's fall and winter samples. call around at the store and examine them if you want a new suit.

Charlie Johnson went over to Anthracite the first of the week to meet Mr. Kebler. of the Osgood Co. who is upon a vacation, and intends camping out for a couple of weeks.

A female evangelist in Indiana is telling the girls that not five men in a hundred are good enough for them to marry. The girls go right along marrying,however, and every blessed one of 'em thinks she gets one of those five white sheep.—[Ex.

Helen M. Coke writes that "Kisses on her brow are the richest diadem a woman's soul aspires to." And yet the fellow who kisses a young lady on her brow while her rosy lips are making motions like a patent clohtes wringer is not the man for the position.—[Siftings.

C. H. Frohne,one of the boys who has stood by the camp for the past six years, started for his home in Detroit, Michigan, last Sunday. He will visit his parents whom he has not seen for the past seven years. Carl is one of the rustlers who believes perserverance is the road to success.

Mrs. Andy Johnson and Mrs Paul Blount paid us a pleasant visit last Saturday and took in the scenery around Crystal. This was their first visit up this way. Messrs Booton and Foster accompanied them. All were delighted with their trip and returned to Prospect the same evening.

Business First; Pleasure Afterward.

Matrimony is not allowed to interfere with business in Colorado. Recently a young man was going to be married and while out after the license he got interested in a poker game and was there long after the guests had arrived at the bride's house. The minister who was to perform the ceremony grew tired waiting, went to hunt the bridegroom and he also took a hand in the game, and the bride, to while away time between acts, opened a game of faro to amuse the guests, and when the lover hove in sight she had all the money in the party and a mortgage on the town site. This is an enterprise that is not met with in the slow going east. Some girls would have wept and bemoaned their sad fate and the big brother would have gone hunting for the lover with bad words and a shot gun loaded for bear. But this young damsel of the rugged hills took a different view of the matter and combined business with pleasure.—[Dakota Bell.

A Trip Down Yule Creek.

We clip the following from the Elk Mountain Pilot which is of interest to the miners of Yule creek and these parts:

"Your correspondent left Crested Butte on Wednesday the 24th, and after a very hard trip over a very bad trail,succeded in reaching the scene of the new mining excitement on Yule creek. At the point where the trail crosses the divide near the head waters of Slate river the formation changes from shale and slate on the southern slope to lime,quartzite and diorite on the northern side. It is in the lime and quartzite formation where the new strike is located as well as a number of other mines, such as the Justice and Knight property, the Pacific lode and several others.

We did not have time to see or visit a number of very good looking locations near the head of Yule creek, but continued our trip down to where the Hanlon Bros. are camped. The distance from the head of the creek to their mine is five miles. The new strike is a contact vein between marble and quartzite, marble being the hanging wall and quartzite the foot wall. The vein is about three feet in thickness and the ore an iron carbonate, carrying gold, silver and lead. The average value being, as I am told, about $200, principally gold. From the amount of development on the property it is hard to determine at present what it will amount to. One thing may be safely assumed, Mr. Hanlon has an excellent prospect in an excellent mineral formation.

Close to Hanlon Bros'. camp I found that genial old timer, Joe Barnes, and his partner Bennett, also Phil Pratt, the man who made the first location on Aspen mountain. I think Mr. Pratt's presence a good indication of the value of this new mineral field, and from the character of the formation and the mineral found therein I predict a valuable mineral section.

From Mr. Hanlon's camp I proceeded down Yule creek to where it empties into Crystal River, and on our way saw one of the prettiest sights the eye of human being ever rested upon. Marble walls hundreds of feet thick enclosing a stream of Crystal water. Marble as white as snow in blocks several feet square laying alongside of the trail. Lower Crystal river, or in fact all of that section that is tributary to it, is in a state of useless inactivity. This state of affairs is not owing to a lack of mineral, or that the ore is not of a sufficent grade, but is owing to the fact that most all the best mines are patented, and the owners, who live in the east and let their property remain idle, while the few poor men who have unbounded faith in the country, and I believe their faith is well founded, keep doing as much as their limited means will allow, while those who have means to develop their property await the results of the hard labor of others. This is a good subject for our law makers to take hold of, and as soon as some measure is enacted taxing the owners of patented mines this state of affairs will cease.

Crystal river and the mining country adjacent to it ought to produce 500 tons of ore per day and give employment to 1,000 miners, and the time is not far distant when such will be the case.

It is the same old story of mine experience. Some poor devil of a prospector will come along, strike it big in one of the numerous gulches around Crystal river, and there will be a boom. Capital will become interested in the country,prospects that are now idle will become producing mines, wagon roads that are now deserted will hum with busy traffic, and the few that now stick by their claims will receive the reward of their years of toil and preserverance." * *

MINING BREVITES.

J. O. Jordan is shipping a car load of ore from the Jenny Lynd at Gothic.

James Nelson has completed the work for Doc Shores and Charlie Gray in Chicago basin.

John Lawson has completed the assessment on the Last Chance, on Sheep mountain, and returned to Gunnison.

John McKay, George Farnham and George Barney have been busy putting up a cabin at the Fargo mine, on Sheep mountain. Farnham and Barney will work the property all winter. This is one of the most promising properties on the mountain, and we may expect to see the boys open up something big before spring. It shows a large body of lead ore which runs high in silver.

The Norman is showing up a fine body of galena and copper ore, which has improved considerable since work has been started up. The property is located alongside of the Gothic road in Galena park which makes it quite accessable, and we believe it would become a pay mine with a little more development. G. R. Read, one of the owners is hard at work running a drift upon the vein, and is highly pleased with the outlook. Major Fitch has become interested in the property, and they propose to see what they have got.

The Silver Chief, which is owned by Denver parties, is being worked by Williams & Batt. The property is located about three miles from Crystal, in Chicago basin, and shows up one of the best defined veins in granite that there is to be found in these parts. There is a body of mineral wider than the drift which is being run upon the vein, and we should judge there is fully three feet of pay ore in the drift, composed of copper and galena, and is one of the best showings we have seen. When proper facilities are at hand whereby work can be done to advantage and a good trail built from the wagon road we may expect to hear good reports from the property. The ore assays upwards of 100 ounces silver and a fair average in gold per ton.

Gothic Grabs.

Editor CURRENT:—

No doubt you have been awaiting a few items from this section, but as all the excitement is over on Yule creek we have a right to be excused for not writing sooner.

Things are moving along nicely here; although the country is large enough to support several mines in place of one. The Sylvanite is producing a larger and better grade of ore than ever before. Wire, native, brittle and ruby silver all blended together is enough to cause the eyes to stick out of any old timers head, let alone a tender-foot. The recent strike made in the lower working shows a breast of from five to six feet of high grade ore, consisting mainly of native and ruby silver; while in the upper workings they have wire, native and ruby. But the biggest item is that they have struck good ore where it was supposed there was none. Some fifty jacks are now engaged in packing from the mine to Gothic, where it is transferred to wagons and taken to Crested Butte.

A sad accident occurred here today; Burt Cowell, while attempting to ride one of his burrows, was thrown of and his collar bone broken. But Dr. Everett says not badly.

Sorrell and Robberts have been sorting over their ore on the Jenny Lind. They expect to make a shipment next week.

Bennett and Hammond were in the city to-day from their property on Rustler. They report their ore as improving, but not widening as fast as expected but are confident that they will get it in good quantities soon. They are two of the boys everyone would be delighted to see strike it.

Holloway and Griffin are still thumping away on the Venus in Rustler; but do not think that they have struck it yet as Grant has not reported lately.

A. Breed and Mart Yetter have "folded their tents and gone." Breed to Illinois and Mart to California. Cause, altitude too high for one and climate too much for the other.

Archie McLeod is driving in on the Jim Blaine, while J. J. Lockhart is looking for someone to do the work on the Buck and other properties, but, owing to the Indian outbreak, men are scarce.

Judd is doing assessment work over at Elko where he has some good lead property. Bob Eaton also put in an appearence and has gone to Elko to look after his claims.

Johnson & Steinmeyer are making preparations to work a location in Bunn basin. They, of course, expect to ship ore "poko tempo."

Charlie Howe, these days, dons a duster and acts as groom for his stable.

Thos. Crawford still supplies the boys with the necessaries at reasonable rates, also with smoking and "chawing" tobacco.

A. B. Davis still slayeth the fat steer for the consumers of Gothic, which delights the boys, as their mouths are watering for fresh meat after living on bacon and ham during part of the week Uncle Bob dishes out the stimulant for an appetite and Archie sells meat to satisfy it. Quite a combination, is it not?

Quite a bit of snow fell a night or two since, and the boys naturally ask themselves what they have done with their summer's wages.

—M—

WANTED:—A young printer, or boy, who is capable of doing the mechanical work on this paper,such as type setting, press work, on hand press; making up forms, etc., etc. No job work. For further particulars, terms, etc. address this office. Apply at once.

Why Women Don't Snore.

"Fergy, dear," said Mrs. Montgomery, the other morning, as Mr. Montgomery came down to breakfast looking as cross as two roads; "why do men snore?"

"Give it up," he replyed shortly, with a suspicious look.

"You snore dear," she continued, "what do you do it for?"

"I don't snore at all." replied Mr. Montgomery, emphatically. "Its that dad-gasted fool in the next house."

"Women never snore," remaked Mrs. Montgomery reflectively, as she dropped a pinch of salt in her husband's coffee. "I wonder why?"

"Can't," replied Mr. Montgomery

"Why?"

"Well,you can't snore unless your mouth is open. A woman works her jaw so confoundedly hard during the day that when night comes it is so tired that she has to close it up and give it a chance to recuperate.—[Exchange.

In Brief, and to the Point.

Dyspepsia is dreadful. Disordered liver is misery. Indigestion is a foe to good nature.

The human digestive apparatus is one of the most complicated and wonderful things in existence. It is easily put out of order.

Greasy food, tough food, sloppy food, bad cookery, mental worry, late hours, irregular habits, and many other things which ought not to be, have made the American people a nation of dyspeptics.

But Green's August Flower has done a wonderful work in reforming this sad business and making the American people so healthy that they can enjoy their meals and be happy.

Remember:—No happiness without health. But Green's August Flower brings health and happiness to the dyspeptic. Ask your druggist for a bottle. Seventy-five cents

FOR LEASE:—The Eureka mine, on Treasury mountain, will be leased upon reasonable terms to parties meaning business. Apply to; A. A. JOHNSON, Crystal Colo.

WHITE SLAVERY IN PENNSYLVANIA

Miners Who Are Threatened as If They Were Dogs—"Pluck Me" Stores and Cut-throat Leases.

A correspondent of *The New York Herald* telegraphs from Wilkesbarre, Pa., as follows: Not one word sent out concerning the condition of the striking miners at the Hazelbrook colliery of S. Wentz & Co., their grievances and their oppression, has been overdrawn.

To-day your correspondent spent some hours among the miserable hovels in which are herded the men who work for the company. In no other way can an idea be gained of the condition to which these unfortunates have been reduced by years of systematic oppression.

The colliery is situated in the heart of the wilderness, some two miles from the line of the Hazelton division of the Lehigh Valley railroad. About four hundred yards from the colliery, scattered amid rock and tree stumps stand a collection of shanties, some twenty-five in number, each containing two rooms and a little extension, which answers the purpose of a kitchen. The houses are built of rough hemlock boards and are elevated some four feet above the ground. In the floors and walls are gaping cracks between the boards through which you could thrust your head.

In these huts, with wind, rain and snow driving through the crevices, the miners and their families have to exist the year around.

They have no option—for two miles in every direction there are no other houses. The company, though it does not own the land, controls it under a lease. They will not sublease one foot of it, and, even had the poor miner the means, he is given no chance of making for himself a better home.

But the company has taken effective means to prevent him ever getting the means to live better where he is or move to better places. The iniquitous company-store system, the evils of which were so glaring that the legislature of Pennsylvania forbade it under heavy penalty, is in vogue here in its worst and most oppressive form. The company have established a store at which they claim to sell everything needed, and have issued their fiat that the men must trade nowhere else.

They have also effectually taken it out of the power of the men to go elsewhere if they wished. Completely controlling the land, they have forbidden any other merchant or dealer to come on the ground, and if the men purchase goods elsewhere they cannot have them delivered. There is no public roads through the land, and several merchants in Freeland and other neighboring towns who sought to sell their goods to the miners have been warned, under penalty of arrest for trespass, not to venture on the company's land.

The company thus enjoys a perfect monopoly of the trade, and can extort what they please. They charge fully 20 per cent. more than the regular rate for all goods sold, and—in direct violation of the law of the state—deduct the bills from the miners' pay.

Besides the deductions for store supplies the miners' rent, his powder, oil, coal, use of team to haul the coal, his board, if he is a single man, and even the charges for the priest and doctor (who are paid monthly by the company to look after the spiritual and physical welfare of the men), are deducted from the miners' pay. No matter how much a man may earn in a month the deductions invariably amount to as much or more than his wages, and it is an actual fact that out of fourteen men spoken to by your correspondent not one had received a cent of money for nine months for wages earned, except one, who a few days ago received $2.80.

Thus deprived of everything but the bare necessities of life, never allowed to obtain possession of a few dollars to enable them to better their condition, what are the men to do? They can do nothing but submit to the shameful system of oppression.

Six months ago the men commenced to join the Knights of Labor. The foreman exerted all the pressure possible on men known to be Knights and succeeded in getting many to withdraw. The engineer, Frank Steele, refused to leave the order and shortly afterward was discharged, ostensibly for negligence. The men believed he had been victimized and demanded his reinstatement. This was refused and a strike followed.

Then the company proceeded to show their power. Miserable as are the huts in which the men live they can only gain the right to occupy them by signing leases which place them beyond the pale of legal protection. In there iron-clad documents, copies of which are now on file in the court-house in this city, the men waive all the rights and protection to which they are entitled under the law. They agree that the moment they cease to work for the company they must leave the house; they agree that the company may at any time, on ten days' notice, evict them and their families, and each has to sign an "amicable suit in ejectment," by which they formally admit that they are illegally occupying the premises. On one of the documents a writ can be issued without a trial and the tenant and his goods thrown out at the company's pleasure.

Acting on these leases the company eight days after the strike served notice on nineteen families to get out, and on Saturday last brought the deputy sheriff and a force of Coal and Iron police to enforce the notices. Six families were driven from their miserable homes and all they possessed in the world thrown out after them. Not one of these was possessed of a single dollar to help him in his need, and his neighbors were as poor.

One woman, Mrs. Dunlavey, who had never left her house for two years on account of sickness, was ordered out. She refused to go, when the company's hirelings threw out every stick of furniture, drove out her family, and left her alone in the empty house. For three days the household goods lay as they were thrown; out and several of the evicted families passed both day and night in the open air, and had it not been for the assistance of the charitable would have been without food. They had nothing wherewith to move their goods, nor could they take them, and could not even bring a wagon on the ground without the consent of the company, which they knew full well was refused.

Other evictions were announced for Monday next, but in the face of the indignant popular voice it is not thought probable that they will be attempted.

J. S. Wentz & Co. are now attempting to operate the mine with Hungarian labor. About fifty of these people have been brought on the ground. They were given houses to live in, armed with revolvers, and put to work in the mine. When the men struck they left a large quantity of coal ready cut in the mine, and the time of the Hungarians who are now taking out this coal is being charged to the strikers.

The strikers, it is said, have ample legal remedy, which is to be at once resorted to. Under the law the company can be made to disgorge the amounts stopped out of wages, and can also be subjected to penalties for violation of the statute.

CRAZED BY BAD TEMPER.

What Befell a Beautiful Mexican Bride.

One of the prettiest girls of Zacatecas, belonging to one of the best families in the state, has just been admitted to the insane asylum in that city, a hopeless maniac. The story of the trouble which wrecked her for a season is one of the saddest that has ever been written. Born the daughter of wealthy parents, an only child, she was indulged in everything, and in concequence her naturally sweet disposition was thoroughly spoiled, and whenever an attempt was made to cross her wishes she had the most frightful outbursts of temper, which always ended in all around her yielding and allowing her to carry her point. On the 4th of March of the present year she was married to a wealthy hacendado whose extensive place is located near Zacatecas. The wedding was a grand affair, and the young couple started life together with the brightest prospects. Soon after marriage, however, there arose slight disputes between husband and wife, which ended, as has been the case all through the girl's life, in her favor, the husband, naturally a highspirited man, yielding invariably before her awful fits of violence. This, finally, however, became unbearable to the young married man and he determined to break his wife's frightful temper and assert his manhood, trusting that they would live more happily together in the end. So upon the next occasion when there arose a difference of opinion on some trifling matter he remained firm and utterly refused to yield his point. His wife stormed and flew into a perfect rage of passion, but he remained unmoved, and finally, when the exhibition of temper was assuming a phase where the young woman commenced breaking the breakfast dishes—they were at their morning meal when the trouble arose—in the impotency of her wrath, he clutched her tightly by the arm, and in a rough tone insisted that she should quiet down. She gave him one awful look, then with a wild shriek she tore herself from his grip and moving away a few steps fell to the ground foaming at the mouth. Medical aid was at once summoned, but for hours she lay unconscious, occasionally struggling violently, and then relapsing into quietness again. After a while she opened her eyes, took a long look around upon the people gathered about her bed, and with a bloodcurdling shriek sprang from the bed, and before any one could prevent her was out of the house and racing madly over the fields. All present gave chase, and after a long, exhausting run the mad woman was overtaken by her husband, and held fast until assistance arrived. The best medical aid procurable was obtained for her, but her reason remained in darkness and, the physicians predict there is positively no hope for her recovery.—*Two Republics.*

Dry-Goods Packing-Boxes.

Space is so valuable to New York merchants, and particularly those engaged in the dry-goods trade, that they prefer purchasing the packing-boxes in which they send off their goods to making them upon their own premises.

To manufacture a sufficient number for their daily need would require considerable room, and the rent for such accommodations would more than offset the amount saved. Therefore they purchase them from men who make the sale of such boxes a specialty. Their places of business are to be seen in all quarters. Generally they choose some piece of property which through litigation or other causes has not been built upon, where the rent is trivial and the lease of short date, and buy up all the old boxes they can lay hold of. These they patch up and sell at a considerable advance. There are others in the business, however, who are in the true sense of the word, manufacturers. Some of them conduct a safe and profitable business upon a small scale, while others launch thousands of dollars in the enterprise. These latter are mostly men residing in Michigan, who buy lumber by the wholesale. They have saw mills of their own, in which they manufacture the parts of a box complete, according to careful measurement. The different portions are numbered and sent to eastern shippers, who have only to nail them together according to directions to have a perfect packing-box. Such boxes can be produced at remarkably low prices, and the dealers in this city cannot successfully compete with their western rivals. In fact, the business has grown to such proportions in Michigan that several firms have invested thousands in forest lands in order to procure timber at the lowest possible cost."—*New York Mail and Express.*

A FUNERAL IN A TENEMENT

The Unostentatious Service Over the Death of a Baby.

A little girl in a red-checkered apron stood on tip-toe to tie two pieces of white ribbon to the front door-knob of the big tenement where she lived. It was in Rose street just around the corner.

The ribbon was limp and old, and hung in a lifeless way against the worn panels of the door. She stepped back to note the effect and another girl about the same age came out from a door in the lower hallway and joined her. The two little ones were the only signs of life about the great building that looked black and forbidding with its range of grated fire-escapes giving it the air of a barred prison. The second comer stared at the first girl with bold eyes for a moment and said, pointing to the fluttering ribbons:

"What did you do that for?"

"Baby is dead."

"Do you live in this house?"

"Yes; on the fourth floor."

"Huh," with a sniff of contempt. "We live on the first floor and we've got a baby carriage." Then in a more conciliatory way: "May I come up and see it?"

"I guess so," and the two children, hand in hand, went up the dark steps to the little room fronting on the street, where the mother and the woman of the next room were preparing the child for burial.

It was a bloodless little thing, the piece of clay the women fondled in that lingering way they have with those they love. The mother seemed jealous of the attention her friend showed the child. She wanted to attend to the last rites herself. She could not bear to have other hands to touch the little thing. No other hands but hers should smooth the pillow for its last sleep. There was no wild outburst of weeping on her part, and beyond a certain querulousness, no demonstration of affection. The mother did not even cry. She was too used to suffering for that. She talked reminiscently of the bundle of white on the bed. She told how she never expected to raise it; that it had always been thin and sickly; that it was the best child in spite of all that the world had ever seen; that she knew it could never stand the warm weather and a thousand little details that only a mother could remember and repeat. And every now and then she would begin again and go over its peculiarities, finding some new charm to tell of.

The other woman was sympathetic and receptive, petting the mother and calling her "Dearie" and "My darlin'" and flitting about the room putting things to rights with an air of proprietorship that would have been hotly resented at any other time. The two neighbors living so close together had been great enemies and had fought royally over the petty privileges of the fourth floor hallway. But all that was forgotten and laid aside now.

Pretty soon a young man with a week's growth of beard and a furred silk hat came in softly without knocking at the door. He said he was the undertaker. Nobody knew how he had found out about the death. He had a book with pictures of coffins in it. He stepped on tiptoe across the room and asked in a subdued voice whether to-morrow morning would suit for the funeral. Then he said for $14 one could get a beautiful casket. He always called his coffins caskets. The neighbor took him aside and conferred with him, finally getting the $14 casket for $11. Then he went away, after leaving a receipt for the $5 cash that had been paid on installment.

The mother took the cold form of her child in her arms and rocked it as she had done so often in life. It had a long, white gown, with a bit of lace down the front. She took a wisp of pink ribbon and fastened it at the baby's throat. The neighbors protested that she must not do that; it would never do. But the mother peristed and the bit of bright color remained.

The husband came home from work at the usual hour and did not grumble at the cold supper that was spread for him. He kissed his wife in a way that he had not done since they were married. They were a loving couple, full of the truest affection for each other, but the affection did not often find outward expression. He sat with his wife for half an hour and then feeling himself in the way went down and joined the group on the stoop. She did not care to leave the room.

He was working on a particularly urgent job and went off with his tools as usual the next morning. He kissed the mother of the little one again before he left. The woman across the hall came in early and put things to rights. Then she disappeared for a little space and returned, dressed in a newer gown of black. She brought a bunch of ox-eyed daisies with her and put them in the baby's hands. The little girl who had tied the white ribbon that served as crape to the front door-knob, came up wonderingly and felt of the flowers. Then she took one for herself. The neighbor and the undertaker arranged the casket, the woman quietly slipped the bit of pink ribbon from the shroud. But the quick eyes of the mother saw it and would not have the child deprived of the bit of color. It had always loved the bright string she pleaded. So the pink knot rested there.

A young minister came—he was hardly more than a boy—and read a chapter from the Bible and said a few words of consolation in German. There were ten or twelve persons in the room. He prayed for the bit of clay in the coffin. Then the undertaker's man took the coffin in his arms and carried it down to the hack that stood waiting at the door. The mother cried softly to herself during the services, and her little girl stood by her side and stared at the minister. There was no hearse, and only one carriage. The man put the coffin in the front seat of the hack, the mother and her little girl and the neighbor who had been so kind to her got in with it, one of the group waiting on the sidewalk slammed the door, and the carriage took its way over to Long Island to Cypress Hills Cemetery. Nothing was said at the grave by any one. They took the little box and put it in a great grave with half a hundred boxes of the same kind of precious dust that had been already laid away to rest.

In the afternoon the three mourners came home. The mother went up to her room and the little girl again stood on tip-toe at the door to untie the fluttering white. She took the ribbons up stairs, folded them carefully and put them back in the box where they had been at first. They were the ribbons that her mother had worn the day she was married.—*New York World.*

Mind Cure.

One of the most unreasonable and best patronized humbugs of the day is what is known as Christian science, or mind cure. It pretends to cure human diseases after the apostolic fashion, which it claims was not miraculous, but simply the successful exertion of mind upon matter.

Its teachers, or practitionists, argue that in olden times devout Christians were able to cure disease by the exercise of faith and will power, and that there is no good reason why such people may not do the same thing now. Their plan of operation is to impress upon the mind of the patient his ability to receive such a cure, and the power of the operator to bestow it, and then induce him to act upon his faith. For instance, a lady is afflicted with heart disease. The physician and the patient unite in a determination that the disease shall depart, they concentrate the full power of their minds in an intense effort to believe that the disease can and will be—nay, is driven out, and as a result the lady is no longer afflicted. The absurdity of the method, however, is readily demonstrated by applying it to strong cases. For instance, if a man should have his hand mashed to a jelly, or his foot lacerated, or his skull fractured, there is no sensible person will imagine these injuries could be instantly healed by will power or any other human agency.

There are some cases where people are afflicted with imaginary complaints, caused by a diseased state of the mind, and such ailments, it is not unreasonable to suppose, may be removed by merely mental process. Existing simply in the imagination, it is only necessary to convince the sufferer that they are gone and he is cured. But where there is an actual, unmistakable physical affliction, a concentration of all the will power and faith in the universe could not perform a cure without the application of material, tangible remedies and treatment. As a cheerful disposition is conducive to a healthy state of the body, it no doubt aids a cure of the patient to be hopeful and contented; but such aid is comparatively feeble, and could not effect a cure of itself.

The case which recently occurred at Tokepa, wherein a woman was permitted to die through the ministrations of one of these scientific quacks is to the point. She was afflicted in the lower limbs with some disease, and was depending on a so-called Christian science doctor, who was in attendance, to cure her. No remedies were used but mental ones, and the disease was allowed to progress to such a point that mortification set in and death resulted.

However nice a theory may be built upon a consideration of the powers of Christian faith, the days of miracles are past, and no amount of human ingenuity or science can resurrect them. That fact cannot be shaken. All pretended faith, or will, or word cures of positive bodily ills are humbugs, and those who practice upon the credulity of the people to rob them of their money by such means are impostors and swindlers. There is no such thing as mind cure or Christian science.—*Emporia Republican.*

A Wonderful Typesetter.

Minneapolis printers have in their midst what they regard as a phenomenal typesetter. The gentleman's name is Miln, and he hails from Sioux City. He is known as the "Missouri River Rusher," but his experience until very recently was confined wholly to country newspapers. He was employed for a time on *The Sioux City Journal*, and subsequently went to Chicago. His first work on metropolitan papers was in Chicago. He is now employed on a Minneapolis paper. He was put on a case a week ago Friday night and worked seven successive nights, putting up a "string" of 101,000 ems. The work was on "straight matter," Miln having had very little "phat" and no bonuses during the week. He can set 2,000 ems per hour with comparitive ease. Minneapolis printers are thinking of putting Miln against any printer in the country for a week's typesetting match.—*St. Paul Pioneer Press.*

A Very Sacred Oath.

They have no Bible in the French courts to swear on, and the crucifix which was used for that purpose has been removed. But now and then a witness needs to swear by something, as in a judicial examination at Marseilles lately of a man accused of murder. A cab-driver was asked if he could swear to certain testimony he had given. He raised his hand in a tragic manner toward Heaven, and exclaimed, in stentorian tone: "I swear it, Monsieur le Juge, by the ashes of my poor sister who died of the cholera!" He had something sacred, if not a Bible or crucifix.—*Independent.*

Overheard at the Kennel.

"Don't disturb me," remarked the faithful dog, pausing in his self appointed task of polishing a bone of the thirteenth century. "I am all in a snarl this morning." And the cat who was rather a nicerly thing and kept her purrs to herself instantly got her back up and remarking that she felt a little ruffled herself, went away to the dairy, saying she thought a churn at the cream pans would tone her up. Only poor ignorant dumb brutes, who know no better, would talk in this idiotic strain.—*Burdette.*

PITH AND POINT.

Hoop-springs eternal in the human bustle.—*Cleveland Sun.*

Will somebody please sit on the thermometer and hold the mercury down?—*Albany Argus.*

The Anti-Poverty Society is closely allied to the Help Yourself Association.—*Philadelphia Inquirer.*

Woman has a tender heart, but very often she prefers to hire some one else to tend her baby.—*Somerville Journal.*

The captain of the Moscow (Russia) Bicycling Club is named Kominoff, but of course he has got over that now.—*New Haven News.*

Man is not apt to fall down and worship the golden calf unless he has some hope of being the golden calf's owner.—*New Orleans Picayune.*

Miss Catharine Heathorne, known as "the maid of Kent," has just celebrated her 103d birthday. The maid of Kent seems to be made of iron.—*Boston Transcript.*

Solomon's advice to the sluggard to go to the ant and consider her ways, is seldom taken. The sluggard prefers to go to the uncle as long as there is anything to hang up.—*Springfield Union.*

When a New York man buys brass bricks for $20,000 each, upon the theory that they are gold, we object to putting him on the wires as "an old Californian."—*San Francisco Alta.*

The man who is too busy to be a gentleman during his active business life, generally finds it impossible to be one when he retires from trade.—*Arkansaw Traveler.*

Science says that man is 90 per cent. water. This can hardly mean Kentuckians and Milwaukeans. There is too much beer consumed in Milwaukee and too much whisky in Kentucky to leave any show for water.—*Peck's Sun.*

At the begining of every dramatic season, the newspapers say that the minstrel show is dead. Yes, the minstrel show is dead, but the people never grow tired of sitting up with the corpse.—*Arkansaw Traveler.*

A large number of bottle-fillers have struck in Chicago. It is not stated that they will try to boycott their employers by inducing the bottle-emptiers to let up for a season.—*Detroit Free Press.*

The painter who fell from a ladder went down with colors flying.—*Texas Siftings.*

Somebody claims to have discovered a substance which is "300 times as sweet as sugar." The "substance" is supposed to be about sixteen years old, and wears a bustle.—*Norristown Herald.*

The new glass works in Birmingham are probally called into life by the extra demand for bottles in prohibition towns.—*Louisville Courier-Journal.*

Pending a settlement of the hod-carriers' strike, access into the best families will be conducted on a less extensive scale.—*Philadelphia Times.*

Writing a letter is, to many people, an irksome task, but it isn't half so irksome as it is to hear a lawyer reading your letter aloud five years afterward in open court.—*Journal of Education.*

A St. Paul paper persists in offering its readers "Stray Sunbeams." Nobody has any use for stray sunbeams these days. Some stray chunks of ice would be more acceptable just now.—*Minneapolis Journal.*

There is a man in Copiah County, Miss., who is known to have killed twenty-seven men. Here is a chance for some philanthropic journalist to receive subscriptions with which to purchase him a medal.—*Chicago Mail.*

Scarecrows are much needed in the Sandwich Islands, and Harlem people are considering the propriety of offering to send a consignment of street corner, skating rink mashers without brains.—*New York Morning Journal.*

Gentleman in drug store—"That is a very spruce young man, who just went out." Druggist—"Yes, he chews more gum than any two girls in town—*Burlington Free Press.*

A writer, named Kane, professes to have discovered that Washington Irving, and not John Howard Payne, wrote "Home, Sweet Home." This gentleman wishes to raise Kane with our literary traditions.—*San Francisco Alta.*

"What causes all this drunkeness?" asks a prohibition journal. It is safe to wager that whisky and other intoxicating beverages cause the most of it. A prohibition editor should have known that much.—*Norristown Herald.*

He was a Street-Car Conductor.

"That man over there has had more women running after him than anybody I know of," said a San Franciscan to an eastern visitor, as he pointed out a stylish dressed young man on Kearney street.

"Is he an actor?" asked the stranger.

"No."

"Man with a divorce scandal hanging around him?"

"No."

"May be he is an acquitted murderer, or possibly a British bank clerk?"

"No."

"Well, if he is none of these, I'm hanged if I know why the women should have chased him?"

"He was once a street-car conductor."—*San Francisco Post.*

At the Panorama.

Little Girl—Is that you, papa, on the brick-colored horse that is up on its hind legs?

Parent—Yes, my child, that is usually pointed out as me.

"And did you cut that other man's head off and ride right straight over him into the fort?"

"Yes, my dear, I presume I did."

"But mamma didn't say anything about it when I asked her what you did in the war."

"Why, what did she say?" (looking around at the spectators proudly).

"Oh she said that all you did that anybody ever heard of was to fool around and get kicked by an army mule, and that now you haven't sense enough to get a pension."—*Dakota Bell.*

Speech Derangement.

There are several forms of speech-derangement, caused by a paralysis of a portion of the brain—the speech centres. They are known by the general term aphasia, which means simply speechlessness. The Medical Record has an interesting paper on the subject, to which we would refer those who care to study the scientific explanation of the matter. We give some of the prominent facts:

There are three forms of aphasia: (1) the sensory, in which the printed words are clear enough to the eye, but convey no impression to the brain (2) the motor, in which the patient can read, and understand the printed words, but cannot utter them, uttering instead unintelligible sounds; (3) the sensory and the motor variously mixed.

The following case illustrates the first form. A cultivated woman, being taken with a severe pain above the left temple, was surprised next morning to find herself unable to read a word, although she plainly saw the letters and words, and every object in her room. The largest letters, the heading of the daily papers, were as unrecognizable as the smallest. In about two weeks she began to recover, and could read again with tolerable facility in about three months. This was a case of word-blindness.

A somewhat similar case of word-deafness is reported. A well-educated gentleman, who fully understood what he read, was nevertheless able to utter only gibberish. Thus the sentence, "The Odessa line is again working properly," he read, "The assoil lens a puff niff miss corres povety."

The second, or motor aphasia, is the more common form. In this the person may fully understand all that is said to him, and yet be unable to speak or write the word he wishes to; and even if he seeks to express his meaning by gestures, he makes the wrong movements.

In the mixed forms, the patient, in some cases, cannot speak the words, and yet can write them; in others, he can write, and yet is unable to read his own writing. The power of speech is, in general, however, left unimpaired.

Allied to aphasia is so-called paraphasia. In this disorder, the patient, thinking to use a particular word, uses one not having the slightest resemblance to it. Sometimes he loses a whole class of words, most commonly nouns, and is forced to supply their place by a description, as "what one cuts with," for "scissors," or for "window," "what one sees through."—*Companion.*

A Swing Instead of a Gravestone.

Not long since a little girl in this city not over 10 years old was very ill. One day she insisted on seeing her father at once. He was telephoned at his counting-room, and on reaching the house the little girl said: "Papa, I think I am going to die, and I want you to do something for me instead of building a monument over my grave. What would a monument cost?" The father tried to dissuade the child from speaking of death, but she persisted until finally he said a monument would cost any amount of money that might be desired to expend on it. "Well," said the child it would not cost less than $100, would it?" The father said he thought not, but begged the little one to change the conversation. "No," said she, "I want you to promise that if I die you will give the $100 to build another swing in the park for the little children instead of building a monument for me." This promise was given with tears. The child had been in the habit of walking in the park and had noticed the delight that many poor children have in swings, and the thought had come to her that might have suggested itself to many of our philanthropic citizens, long ago. It is a pleasure to say that the little girl recovered from her illness and that is the reason, perhaps, why her father's promise has not been kept.—*Albany Household.*

The Poor Man's Help.

No business that we know of offers to the poor man better inducement, such equal rights and division of labor as the culture of domestic fowls. There is no monopoly, and, what is better, never will be. It is nicely balanced, not given to fluctuation, permanent and staple, and of all home industries it is the one for the "sons of toil." There is pleasure in it aside from its pecuniary advantages; does not cost much to start it; it commands ready sale on a cash basis, and it is light and healthy. One has not to wait years for something to come in, for, when once fairly started and properly attended to, there will always be more or less revenue coming in.

Many a poor man in and around the suburbs of our cities and towns is day after day waiting for something to "turn up," and wasting the most precious part of his life in visionary ideas, who would, we are sure, be vastly benefited in pocket, in brain, and in self-respect, if he but turned a part of his time and attention to the breeding and raising of thoroughbred poultry for his own use, for the market or for sale to those who like himself contemplate keeping fowls for pleasure and profit.—*American Poultry Journal.*

A Wise Son.

It is related of a well-known merchant of a neighboring city that, after making his will and leaving a large property to a trustee for his son, he called the young man in and, after reading the will to him, asked if there was any improvement or alteration he could suggest.

"Well, father," said the young gentleman, lighting a cigarette, "I think as things go nowadays, it would be better far if you left the property to the other fellow and made me trustee."

The old gentleman made up his mind then and there that the young man was quite competent to take charge of his own inheritance, and scratched the trustee clause out.—*Texas Siftings.*

HOUSEHOLD HINTS.

POTATOES EN GALETTE.

Take a dozen large potatoes, and many more if new potatoes are used, after steaming or boiling them peel them hot into a large dish with a good quarter of a pound of fresh butter; salt, pepper and a glass of rich sweet milk, mash them until the butter be well mixed and melted and the whole is free from lumps. Thickly butter a baking dish; then put in the potatoes; smooth the top. Bake in the oven. When the top is a yellow-sh-brown and forms a crust, serve.

POTATOES EN SALADE.

Boil, peel and slice some potatoes, and season them with oil, vinegar, salt, pepper and fine herbs; in place of oil butter may be used; mix in, if you like, some gherkins cut into slices, anchovies and capers.

POTATOES WITH CREAM.

Boil, peel and slice the potatoes, put a good piece of butter in a stewpan, adding a spoonful of flour, salt, pepper, or a little grated nutmeg, some parsley and cives chopped finely, and mix the whole together; then add a glass of cream; set the sauce over the fire and stir it until it boils; then put in the sliced potatoes, boil up and serve very hot.

POTATOES A LA MAITRE D'HOTEL.

Boil the potatoes and peel them, cut them into slices, and then put them into a stewpan with fresh butter, parsley and cives chopped up, salt, pepper and a dash of vinegar; warm them up and serve; in place of butter oil may be used, if the pottoes are very small they need not be sliced in the receipts where slic'ng is directed.

BAKED MACARONI.

Throw about clean macaroni into boiling water; when it is soft and swollen take it off the fire and pour in a little cold water to prevent its boiling any more. Take out the macaroni and drain it quickly, mix with it a quarter of a pound of cheese to a pound of macaroni. You can mix the cheese half of each; always have good cheese; more cheese can be used if the cheese is mild. Season with pepper and salt, put it into a buttered dish, put in bits of butter among the macaroni. Put some grated cheese on top and brown in the oven.

POTATOES A LA POLONAISE.

Boil some potatoes, peal them; if large, slice them, if very small it is not necessary. Warm them up in a white caper sauce or with pickled gherkins, cut into dice as a substitute for capers.

BECHAMEL.

A simple bechamel is made by putting a lump of fresh butter into a saucepan, when it boils add a glass of sweet m·lk into which a spoonful of flour has been beaten, stir the sauce to keep it smooth, remove from the fire. It is then fit for warm·ng up anything in. It is best to let it bo·l slowly and strain it. A fine bechamel is seasoned with fine herbs, celery, essence of mushrooms, and is made of cream instead of m·lk. It is stra·ned.

GOOSEBERRY PUDDING.

Make a paste of flour and beef-suet chopped fine, five well-beaten eggs, half a nutmeg grated, a little ginger and spice and some salt; roll out the paste, put it into a cloth, fill it with gooseberries and sugar and let it boil three hours. This is an English recipe.

GOOSEBERRY TARTS.

Prepare a pie paste, as l·ght as convenient, cover the bottom of it with powdered sugar, then place alternately a layer of p·ckled and washed gooseberries and one of sugar. Bake it three-quarters of an hour.

AUNT JENNY'S ROLLS.

Take three p·nts of warm water in which some peeled Ir·sh potatoes have been boiled, stra·n your water, add a tablespoonful of butter or lard, one teacupful of warm yeast; thicken it with flour to make a dough. Let it stand to rise, then work into rolls. Let it stand to rise fifteen or twenty minutes then bake about three-quarters of an hour. You can make this into loaves, as it is a good bread recipe.

VEGETABLE OYSTER CAKE.

Select good, large-sized oyster plant roots, grate them and add m·lk and flour sufficient to make a stiff batter, about a g·ll of grated oyster plant, two eggs, one pint of milk, and flour to make a batter, and salt. Drop it by tablespoonfuls into hot lard. Fry till brown.

The Pacific View.

There is much benefit to be gained,
And·advantages great and untold,
From an intellect skilfully trained
And a memory ably controlled.

'Tis a very commendable plan,
That occasions no loss or regret,
To imbibe all the facts that you can,
But always know what to forget.

The power of much information
Is something on which you may bet;
But, when cramp·d in a tight situation,
Then forget what is best to forget.

When by lawyers much worried and goaded,
Be pleasant and affable both;
But remember not things that are loaded
When you shoot off you mouth under oath.

Keep your knowledge in perfect control,
And when danger ahead comes in sight,
Then uncover memory's scroll
And run the blue pencil aright.
— *New York World.*

Humor in Signs.

Isaac Came, a rich shoemaker in Manchester who left his property to public charities, opened his first shop opposite to the bu·lding where he had been a servant, and put a sign which read: "I. Came—from over the way." Somewhat like this was the sign of a tavernkeeper named Danger, near Cambridge, who, having been driven out of his house, built another opposite and inscribed it: "Danger—from over the way." The successor retorted by putting up a new inscription: "There is no Danger here now."—*Living Church.*

Are the Puritans Degenerating?

Boston still cries for coast defenses, but never a dollar should be voted for that purpose. Let a foreign foe bang down this glittering dome of Boston's State House whenever it will. On a door in that State House is the sign "Gent's Gallery." No wonder a Boston cloth·er advertises "pants for gents."—*Milwaukee Sentinel.*

Who Are Good Farmers?

The good farmer is he who conducts his business as does every good business man in other departments of labor, says *The Farm and Stockman.* Prosperity comes of intell·gent enterprise and industry w·th a thorough knowledge of the business in hand. It is not the education of schools and colleges that gives industry and enterprise, but, all else being equal, education assists largely. In fact, it is a most important integer to success in any calling, and quite as much so to the farmer as to any other business man.

A good farmer is· methodical. He does his work at the proper t·me and in proper season. He keeps himself posted on market prices and never refuses to sell when values show a proper profit for his labors. His circumstances may not permit him to hold a crop for some possible larger price in the future, yet he never sells at a loss to himself, except in such cases, for instance, when an untoward season may have reduced the yield and quality of the crop below the cost of the production. Yet here the good farmer will get all there is possible out of the crop. Why? He is a reading man. Reads the best journals devoted to his calling and thereby keeps himself fully posted in all that pertain to the present value, and also the future probab·l·ties, of the markets of the country. The good farmer never runs needlessly into debt, trusting to "luk" to get out. He knows that blind chance never gave any man prosperity; that honest prosperity comes only by labor and honest intelligent endeavor, and never allows himself to be seduced from his integrity because some other man, by ch·canery or fraud, has gotten money rightfully belonging to another. In brief, the good farmer is a good man, physically, morally and intellectual·y.

Work and Brains Prosper as Partners.

Building air castles, and that alone, will not bring success; neither will the most energetic manual labor succeed without it be attached to correct management, which means a careful study of our business. Our own observations teach us this. That the man who is known as a "chronic theorizer" seldom makes a success of the business he would fain··instruct others in, and on the other hand some of our best workers are closely pressed, living one day on the fruits of the prev·ous day's labor. However much he may make in summer, it goes; he apparently, not looking into the future and real·z·ng that winter requires more money to live while the reward of labor is less. We all acknowledge the importance of preparing for a ra·ny day, and he who fails to do this certainly fails to use forethought enough to see how nearly he may be in the near future. No, mental and physical labor cannot be seperated; like the Un·on, they are "one and inseparable," indissoluble, and the breeder who thinks he can sit in h·s office and dictate to his servants, and make a continual success of breeding, will find ere long that his happy thoughts are not realized. If he has established a reputation and a reputable business before he adopts this plan, he may be able to hold his reputation sometime, but sooner or later his business must wane or fail. My observation has taught me that the most successful breeders are those who are penetrative and thoughtful, and not afraid to carry a slop pail. Every successful breeder must, to say the least, personally superintend the work, unless he has a partner equally interested, who can give the matter his superv·s·on.— *W. W. Prigg, in Swine Breeders' Journal.*

Advice to a "Short."

As m·sery likes company we refer a certa·n prominent bear of New England—who is now trying hard to cover his shorts—to turn for consolation to the·21st Psalm, in which he will find that David apparently passed through an ordeal similar to his own, for he uttered this lamentation:

12. Many bulls have compassed me; strong bulls of Bashan have beset me round.

13. They gaped upon me with their mouths, as a ravening and roaring lion.

The way of the bear on a bull market is, like that of the transgressor, hard.— *The Investigator.*

A Milk Ghost.

The cream takes out of the milk about four parts of its solids, which are rated at 13 parts of 100. This leaves 87 parts water. On this basis some writers contend that a calf should never be fed skimmed milk, as there is not enough food in it. Well, if it is sour it is worse yet. Admit it all. When are the four parts of solid in the cream worth the most? As veal or butter? They are worth four times as much butter. All right! Do not starve the calf, but make up the four parts of solids with o·her food costing less than two cents a pound. This is business sense and science combined.— *Farm and Household.*

What Mrs. Brown Thought.

"Where have you been?" asks Mrs. Brown at the theatre of Mr. B., just out between the acts.

"Oh, just out to see a man," replied Brown.

"When did he die?"

"When did who die?"

"The man that you went to·see."

"What are you talking about?"

"Well, judging from your breath, it must have been a spirit you saw."— *New York Sun.*

Antidote for Snake Bites.

In a letter from a German physician who is a resident of Brazil, it is stated that permanganate of potash is as infallible an antidote for snake bites in that country as it is in India and that every farmer keeps some of it in his dwelling.— *Brooklyn Eagle.*

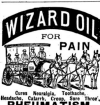

Crystal River Current.

Published by the Current Publishing Co

A. A. JOHNSON,　　　　Jos. A. Bray,
Editor.　　　　　　　　　Manager.

ENTERED AT THE POST-OFFICE AT CRYSTAL COLORADO, FOR TRANSMISSION THROUGH THE MAILS AS SECOND-CLASS MATTER.

TERMS-PAYABLE-IN-ADVANCE:

One Year,...................$3 00
Six Months,................1 75
Three Months,.............1 00

Crystal Post-Office Directory.

Mail arrives and departs every Tuesday Thursday and Saturday.

SATURDAY, JULY 23, 1887.

EDITORAL ETCHINGS.

We are of the opinion John Arkins, of the Denver News, had better draw in his horns a little bit on the convict labor question. Odds are against him.

THE Aspen Mining & Milling Co. contemplates employing 100 additional men on their properties within the next twenty days. So says the Aspen Times.

THE D. & R. G. railroad in adopting the broad-gauge system, has not forgotten Colorado editors, and still maintains its reputation as the Scenic Line of America.

WHEN a tramp comes along these days, from the lower country, he asks for whiskey, and says he has to keep up the fire to feel as warm as it is around Glenwood.

WE are in receipt of The Arbitrator a new weekly paper published in Denver, which is devoted to the interests of labor. It has a good field before it and we wish it success.

PEOPLE are suffering from intense heat in the eastern States. The thermometer registered 106 degrees in the shade at Lychburg, Va., and 102 in St. Louis on the 18th inst.

MORE anthracite coal land has been sold by the locators within the month. It would appear that when the banks are opened up there will be sufficient to supply all the people in America.

LAST Wednesday night the waterworks that run to Charlie Howe's stable, in Gothic, froze up. If people in the east would only visit the mountains they could avoid the present warm weather.

QUITE a prosperous town promises to spring up at the Penny Hot Springs. The mining interests of that section and Avalanche creek is bringing it to the front, while numerous citizens are desirous of erecting summer resorts around the springs as they prefer the location to that of Glenwood, on account of the excessive heat and dust at the latter place.

THE time is coming when the varried resources of this section will attract wide attention. The building of the B. & M. and Midland railroads to the marble ledge will open up the only industry of this kind in the west and give employment to large forces of men. The slate quarries that are being opend up will also benefit us; aside from our silver and coal mines.

PITKIN county is taking steps towards building a road up the river as far as the Penny Hot Springs and road viewers examined the route the first of the week. The county could not expend money to better advantage. We hope to see the road built before fall, and possibly the toll road company will build the road down the river to connect with the county road at the springs.

THE emigration we want from now on is men from the east with capital to develope our vast resources. The large amount of railroad building going on has brought in a sufficient number of the working class of people. We have plenty of inducements for capital to invest in the resources of the State, and can give better interest on investments than there is to be found in the east.

OWNERS of the slate quarries which have been opened up down the river, would do well to prepare samples of the article and send them to the coming exhibition in Denver. We believe the article will attract a large amount of public attention. The better class

---

of buildings that are being erected in the west are bringing slate roofing into greater demand, and considerable is being brought from the east, that can be furnished from these quarries at half the cost as soon as we have railroad facilities at hand to ship it to different towns in the state.

WE believe there will be some interest taken by the miners of this section in making a collection of silver and iron ores, marble and slate for the Exhibition at Denver. A good showing can be made from these parts if all take hold with a will. We will leave the coal companies furnish samples of coal if they wish, but that will make little difference, as it is now a pretty well known fact that this section has the finest and largest bodies of coal in the world, which will be sent out by the train load when the railroads get this side of the divide.

FROM what we have seen of the iron claims around this section we believe it to be valuable property. There is a large quantity of it, and the quality is good. Quite a number of claims have been opened up, and there seems to be but little doubt but what blast furnaces will be erected close at hand, that can turn the ore into pig iron for shipment. The iron will also be valuable for fluxing the silver ores of Aspen and this section, as smelters are certain to be erected close to the coal fields. It is the intention to send samples of the ore to the Denver exposition when outsiders can examine the article for themselves.

WE clip the following from the Alaska Free Press, of Juneau, which was published on the 25th of June, and congratulate Howard & Sons upon their lucky strike, and hope when they get a million or so they will "divy" up with their Colorado brethern:

"The Free Press has struck it rich, having this week located a 200-foot vein some 1500 feet from the beach, adjoining the famous Tredwell property, with equal advantages in the way of water. Only a few days out and here we are with a million. K. Valentine and Albert Wilson are our pards. The next issue of the Free Press will be printed on type of solid gold—possibly."

THE Denver Republican of the 18th instant, in an article upon the stone and marble interests of Colorado, urges the owners of the property to make exhibits of the same at the coming exposition in that city, and has the following to say regarding our marble:

"It is said that the marble of Rock creek is as good as the Carrara, in Italy. From the indifference which the owners manifest in regard to exhibiting specimens of it, this would, however, seem to be doubtful. We hope they will not be so modest in the future, and that they will let the world see some of their marble at the Denver Exposition."

When it comes to marble we certainly can produce as fine an article of white and colored marble as there is to be found in the world, and can show a ledge 100 to 150 feet in thickness covering several hundred acres. Although there has never been any of the marble placed on public exhibition in Denver, there are numerous samples of it in the hands of parties in the city.

A large tract of the ledge has been purchased by officers in the B. & M. and Midland Railroads, who have had it tested and know the quality, and contemplate running their roads to the ledge in the near future. There is, however, a large number of claims owned by private individuals who will possibly send specimens to the exhibition and make a showing. The apparent indifference in not exhibiting specimens of the marble is, that purchasers have been found without going to the expense of making public exhibitions of it. Nevertheless, we believe it a good thing to show the world what we have got, and have already urged the owners to send samples to the exhibition.

ROYAL BAKING POWDER

Absolutely Pure.

This powder never varies. A marvel of purity strength and wholesomeness. More economical than the ordinary kinds, and cannot be sold in competition with the multitude of low test, short weight alum or phosphate powders. Sold only in cans. ROYAL BAKING POWDER CO., 106 Wall St., N. Y.

Notice of Application for U. S. Patent.
No. 128 (1st Series,)

Survey No. 4411, Mineral District No. 3.

Notice is hereby given that in pursuance of the United States Mining laws, James J. Hagerman, whose post-office address is Colorado Springs, Colorado, has made application for patent for 1500 linear feet each on the "Blue Marble," "White Marble," "London" and "New Discovery" Lodes, situated in the Rock Creek Mining District, Gunnison County, State of Colorado, as described by the Official Plat, herewith posted, and by the field notes on file in the office of the Register of the Gunnison Land District at Gunnison, Colorado, as follows, viz:

Blue Marble Lode beginning at cor. No. 1, whence U. S. location monument "Sterling" bears N. 66 deg. 59' E. 222.3 feet; thence N. 16 deg. W. 300 feet to cor. No. 2; thence N. 70 deg. E. 1500 feet to cor. No 3; thence S. 16 deg. E. 300 feet to cor. No. 4; thence S. 74 deg. W. 1500 to cor. No. 1, the beginning.

White Marble Lode beginning at cor. No. 5, whence cor. No. 1 bears S. 73 deg. 39' W. 382.3 feet; thence S. 16 deg. E. 900 feet to cor. No. 6; thence S. 52 deg. 58' E. 600 feet to cor. No. 7; thence S. 55 deg. 56' W. 315.55 feet to cor No. 8; thence N. 52 deg. 08' W. 600 feet to cor. No. 9; thence N. 16 deg W. 900 feet to cor. No. 10; thence N. 55 deg. 56' E. 315.55 feet to cor No 5, the beginning.

London Lode beginning at cor. No. 11, identical with cor. No. 7; thence S. 25 deg. 12' E. 407.29 feet to cor. No. 12; thence S. 20 deg. 45' E. 1092.34 feet to cor. No. 13; thence S. 55 deg. 56' W. 348.29 feet to cor. No. 14; thence N. 20 deg. 45' W. 1151.66 feet to cor. No. 15; thence N. 25 deg. 12' W. 348.75 feet to cor. No. 16; thence N. 55 deg. 56' E. 303.61 feet to cor. No. 11, the beginning.

New Discovery Lode beginning at cor. No. 17, thence S. 16 deg. 29' E. 505.29 feet to cor. No. 18; thence S. 26 deg. E 996.06 feet to cor. No. 19; thence S. 55 deg. 56' W. 303 feet to cor. No. 20. thence N. 26 deg. W. 1063.94 feet to cor. No. 21; thence N. 16 deg. 29' W. 434.71 feet to cor. No. 22; thence N. 35 deg. 58' E. 19.27 feet to cor. No. 14. 314.96 feet to cor. No. 17, the beginning.

Containing together a net area of 41,372 acres and forming a portion of the unsurveyed lands of Township 12 South of Range 37 West 6 P. M., Gunnison County, Colorado.

The locations of unsenteed locations of these lode claims are recorded in the Office of the Recorder of Gunnison County, Colorado, as follows:

Location of Blue Marble claim on page 158 of book 65, Location of White Marble claim on page 159 of book 65, Amended location of London claim on page 297 of book 64, Amended location of New Discovery claim on page 296 of book 64.

Adjoining claimants are Henry Anderson, et al claimants of the "Scranton" claim, and Fredrick K. Copeland of the "Dolomite," "Emperor," "Empress," "Italian," and "Prince Arthur" claims.

This affiant further saith that the said claimant is not a resident of the Land District in which said claims are situate, but resides at Colorado Springs, Colorado, and that affiant is the duly authorized agent of said claimant and is conversant with the facts stated in this notice.

Any and all persons claiming adversely any portion of said lodes, mines, or surface ground, are required to file their adverse claims with the Register of the United States Land Office at Gunnison in the State of Colorado, during the sixty days' period of publication hereof, or they will be barred by virtue of the provisions of the Statute.

FRANK P. TANNER,
Register.

First publication May 28, '87. 7-30

Mining Application No. 135.

United States Land Office,
Glenwood Springs Colo., May 25th, '87.

Notice is hereby given that the Colorado Coal and Iron Company, J. E. Rockwell its agent and attorney infact, whose post-office addres is Aspen, Pitkin County, Colorado, has this day filed its application for a patent for one hundred and twelve acres and 515-1000 of an acre of Placer Land known and called the Castle Creek Placer, situate in Columbia Mining District, Pitkin county, Colorado, and known and designated by the field notes and official plat on file in this office as lot number 4430, in about township 12 S. R., 84 W. of the 6 P. M. The exterior boundries of said lot number 4430 being as follows: to-wit;

Beginning at Cor. No. 1, whence U. S. L. M. Columbia, bears N. 27° 35' 05'' E. 777.85 ft; thence s. 4° w. 244.69 ft. to cor. No. 2; thence s. 40° w. 209.96 ft to cor No' 3; thence s. 50° s. 1500 ft. to cor. No. 4; thence s. 40° s. 290.23 to cor. No. 5; thence s. 27° s. 1332.71 ft. to cor. No. 6; thence n. 63° s. 300 ft. to cor. No. 7; thence n. 27° w. 1292.56 ft. to cor. No. 8; thence n. 19° 54' s. 264.9 ft to cor. No. 9; thence n. 70° 06' w. 1151.04 ft. to cor No. 10; thence s. 18° 19' s. 996.72 ft. to cor. No. 11; thence n. 4° s. 210.94 ft. to cor No. 12; thence s. 27° 10' s. 725.76 ft. to cor No. 13; thence s. 81° 49' s. 891.4 ft. to cor. No. 14; thence s. 27° 10' w. 592.15 ft. to cor. No. 15; thence n. 77.69 ft to cor No 16; thence s. 46° 08' 30'' s. 1220.2 ft. to cor No. 17; thence s. 31° 53' s. 745.4 ft to cor. No. 18; thence s. 19° 15' s. 1869 ft to cor, No 19; thence s. 56° 11' w. 2131 ft to cor. No. 20; thence s. 43° 34' 48'' w. 1606.85 ft to cor. No. 21; thence n. 49° 51' s. 476 ft to cor. No. 22; thence s. 14° 50' s. 462.92 ft to cor. No. 23; thence s. 85° 57' E. 255.08 ft to cor. No. 1 the place of beginning.

S. J. DELAN,
Register.

First publication, June 11th, last Aug. 18, '87.

Notice of Forfeiture.

To Ronald Morrison, his assigns or legal representatives.

You are hereby notified that I have expended 100 dollars in labor and improvements upon the Gray Copper lode in the Elk Mountain, (or Rock Creek,) Mining District, County of Gunnison State of Colorado, as will appear by certificate on file in the recorders office of said county, in order to hold the said premises; under the provisions of Section 2324, revised statutes of the United States, being the amount required to hold the same for the years ending December 31, 1885 and 1886. And if within ninety days from this notice of service by publication, you fail or refuse to contribute your portion of said expenditure as co-owner your interest in said claim will become the property of the subscriber, under said section 2324.

Witness my hand this 15th day of April, A. D. 1887. F. C. JOHNSON.

First pub. April 16, last p. July 8, '87.

Notice of Forfeiture

To Charles Stearns, his assigns or legal representative:

You are hereby notified that I have expended one hundred dollars in labor and improvements upon the Lincoln lode, situated in the Elk Mountain Mining District, Gunnison County, Colorado, as will appear by certificate on file in the Recorders office of Gunnison county, in order to hold the said premises under the provisions of Section 2324, revised statutes of the United States, being the amount required to hold the same for the year ending December 31st, 1886. And if within ninety days from this notice of service by publication, you fail or refuse to contribute your portion of said expenditure as co-owner, together with the cost of this notice, your interest in said claims will become the property of the subscriber, under said section 2324.

Witness my hand this 5th day of July A. D. 1887 WILLIAM BOUCHER.

First pub July 9, last Oct 1, '87

Notice of Forfeiture.

To Robert MacGregor or his legal representatives:

You are hereby notified that I have expended, during the year A. D. 1886, one hundred dollars in labor and improvements upon the Last Chance lode mining claim, situated in the Elk Mountain Mining District, Gunnison, county State of Colorado, in order to hold the said premises under the provisions of Section 2324, of the United States Revised Statutes.

And if within ninety days from this notice by publication, you fail or refuse to contribute your proportion of said expenditure as co-owner, your interest in said claim will become the property of the subscriber, under section 2324 above mentioned. A. F. LAWSON.

First pub. April 23, last July 15, '87

C. J. S. HOOVER,
ATTORNEY AT LAW
Mining Patents Secured.
SCOFIELD, COLORADO.

JOHN KINKAID,
ATTORNEY-AT-LAW
GUNNISON, COLO.

EDWARD R. WARREN,
U. S. DEPUTY MINERAL SURVEYOR
—AND—
CIVIL ENGINEER,
OFFICE: NEXT TO DRUG STORE,
Elk Avenue, - CRESTED BUTTE, Colo.

JOHN McCOSKER.

Blacksmith & wagon maker
Blacksmith & wagon maker

Horseshoeing and Wagon Repairing upon Short Notice a Specialty.

SATISFACTION GUARANTEED

Jobs of all kinds promptly attended to.

CAN BE FOUND AT
MY OLD STAND OP-
POSITE ELK MT. STABLE
4th Street, CRESTED BUTTE, Colo.

JOHN ENGSTROM,
Shoemaker and Saddler
CRESTED BUTTE, COLO.

Boots and Shoes made to Order and Repaired on Short Notice.

A FULL LINE OF
SADDLES and HARNESS
ALWAYS ON HAND
Harness Repairing on Short Notice

FOR MAN AND BEAST!

Mexican Mustang Liniment

CURES

Sciatics,	Scratches,	Contracted
Lumbago,	Sprains,	Muscles,
Rheumatism.	Strains,	Eruptions,
Burns,	Stitches,	Hoof Ail,
Scalds,	Stiff Joints,	Screw
Stings,	Backache,	Worms,
Bites,	Galls,	Swinney,
Bruises,	Sores,	Saddle Galls,
Bunions,	Spavin	Piles.
Corns,	Cracks.	

THIS GOOD OLD STAND-BY

accomplishes for everybody exactly what is claimed for it. One of the reasons for the great popularity of the Mustang Liniment is found in its universal applicability. Everybody needs such a medicine.

The Lumberman needs it in case of accidents.
The Housewife needs it for general family use.
The Canaler needs it for his team and his men.
The Mechanic needs it always on his work bench.
The Miner needs it in case of emergency.
The Pioneer needs it—can't get along without it.
The Farmer needs it in his house, his stable, and his stock yard.
The Steamboat man or the Boatman needs it in liberal supply afloat and ashore.
The Horse-fancier needs it—it is his best friend and safest reliance.
The Stock-grower needs it—it will save him thousands of dollars and a world of trouble.
The Railroad man needs it and will need it so long as his life is a round of accidents and dangers.
The Backwoodsman needs it. There is nothing like it as an antidote for the dangers to life, limb and comfort which surround the pioneer.
The Merchant needs it about his store among his employees. Accidents will happen, and when these come the Mustang Liniment is wanted at once.
Keep a Bottle in the House. 'Tis the best of economy.
Keep a Bottle in the Factory. Its immediate use in case of accident saves pain and loss of wages.
Keep a Bottle Always in the Stable for use when wanted.

VICK'S FLORAL GUIDE

Is a work of nearly 200 pages, colored plates, 1000 illustrations, with descriptions of the best Flowers and Vegetables, prices of Seeds and Plants, and how to grow them. Printed in English and German. Price only 10 cents, which may be deducted from first order. Buy only VICK'S SEEDS. JAMES VICK, SEEDSMAN, Rochester, N. Y.

ONLY VICK'S SEEDS, AT HEADQUARTERS.

EVERY MINER IN THE DISTRICT
SHOULD SUBSCRIBE FOR THE

CRYSTAL RIVER CURRENT

IT IS THE ONLY PAPER PUBLISHED
IN THIS DISTRICT

The Current Will be Independent in Politics, and Devoted to the general interest of Crystal River. It will not only give all the Mining News of this District, but will keep posted on all important events transpiring in Gunnison and Pitkin Counties and also the State.

Subscription, - - - - $3.00 per Year

INVARIABLY IN ADVANCE.

Address

Crystal River Current,
CRYSTAL, COLO

A. A. JOHNSON,

DEALER IN GENERAL MERCHANDISE

MINERS' SUPPLIES,

Powder, Caps, Fuse, Steel.

TOBACCO AND CIGARS.

Choice Groceries,

BOOTS AND SHOES,

Duck Clothing, Gloves, Socks, Underware, Etc.

A Full and Complete Assortment of Goods and Miners' Supplies Always on Hand.

HAY AND GRAIN,

Supply Store for Coal Camps and Ranch Men

I make a Specialty of laying in Supplies to Miners wishing to work their Prospects during the winter.

A. A. JOHNSON,
CRYSTAL, COLO.

Branch Store at Prospect Camp.

TO THE BOYS
—OF—
Crystal River.

When You Want a Good Glass of Wine or Any Kind of Liquor, Mixed Drinks etc. etc.

Call on F. M. SHORT.
(BOB AGENT.)
Crested Butte, Colo.
A Full Line of Caigrs Always on Hand

MARRIAGE GUIDE

DR. HENDERSON,
605 & 608 WYANDOTTE ST., KANSAS CITY, MO.

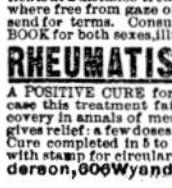

RHEUMATISM

WONDERFUL SUCCESS.

ECONOMY IS WEALTH.

Save the PATTERNS you wish to use during the year for nothing (a saving of from $3.00 to $4.00) by subscribing for

The Crystal River Current
—AND—
Demorest's Illustrated
Monthly Magazine

With Twelve Orders for Cut Paper Patterns of your own selection and of any size.

BOTH PUBLICATIONS, ONE YEAR,
—FOR—
$4.00 (FOUR DOLLARS).

DEMOREST'S THE BEST

Of all the Magazines.

CONTAINING STORIES, POEMS, AND OTHER LITERARY ATTRACTIONS, COMBINING ARTISTIC, SCIENTIFIC, AND HOUSEHOLD MATTERS.

Illustrated with Original Steel Engravings, Photogravures, Oil Pictures and fine Woodcuts, making it the Model Magazine of America.

Each Magazine contains a coupon order entitling the holder to the selection of any pattern illustrated in the fashion department in that number, and in any of the sizes manufactured, making patterns during the year of the value of over three dollars.

DEMOREST'S MONTHLY is justly entitled the World's Model Magazine. The Largest in Form, the Largest in Circulation, and the best TWO Dollar Family Magazine issued. 1887 will be the Twenty-third year of its publication. It is continually improved and so extensively as to place it at the head of Family Periodicals. It consists 72 pages, large quarto, 8x11¼ inches, elegantly printed and fully illustrated. Published by W. Jennings Demorest, New York.

AND BY SPECIAL AGREEMENT COMBINED with THE CURRENT at $4.00 Per Year.

THE CURRENT at $4.00 Per Year.

ONE OF THE LARGEST STRUCTURES in Crystal City was located on the main street. It is believed to be the building which had a foundation largely made of colored wine bottles, laid like cord wood. It was still there in 1942 — although the building was gone. Lead King Basin is behind this building, about two miles away. Boulders as large as this building roll down from the mountain, plowing a path through the "quakies" (aspen trees) and stop just short of houses.

The Marble Times & Crystal Silver Lance,
October 12, 1900.

The average prospector is the greatest optimist this world has ever known; it is utterly impossible to discourage him, says Mining Reporter.

With his pipe in his mouth, his trusty Winchester in the hollow of his arm, and his diminutive donkey walking by his side, he sets forth on his journey to find a mine. All he owns in the world is packed on the donkey's back, and consists, for the most part, of a sack of flour, a piece of "sowbelly," (bacon) a few potatoes, a little coffee, and (sometimes) a little dried fruit. These, together with a few cooking utensils and his tools, which are always of the best, make up all that he needs to make him happy.

The Black Queen mine on the steep south slope of Sheep Mountain halfway between Crystal and Lizard Lake, was one of the best mines in the area and in the 1890's produced about $100,000 worth of silver. So the following item in the The Marble Times & Crystal Silver Lance of October 19, 1900 resulted in quite a stir of interest.

The Marble Times & Crystal Silver Lance,
October 19, 1900.

Last Monday, at Denver, Messrs E.L. Ogden and Joe Scott of Aspen, closed a deal with the Crystal River Mining company whereby they secured a lease upon the Black Queen and Fargo lodes belonging to that company for a term of two and a half years, the lease expiring May 1, 1903.

Messrs. McVey and Moore were at Denver to represent the company in the transaction, but both returned to Missouri Monday evening.

By the terms of the lease, Ogden & Scott are required to commence operations immediately and to place a new hoister and other machinery at the mine and to do extensive development during the coming winter, which means the employment of a large number of men, resulting in putting new life into mining operations throughout this entire district.

The property is a valuable one and has produced in the past few years many thousands of dollars in ore, and at the present time there is a large body of high-grade ore exposed in the workings, besides a considerable body of mill ore.

Messrs. Ogden & Scott need no introduction from us as both are favorably known to many people here, and we welcome them to our midst hoping that their operations in this district will far exceed their expectations. The two gentlemen have been operating a valuable lead proposition at Elko for the past two years and we are glad to see them branching out, showing their faith in the mineral possibilities disclosed in this district.

TWO NEARLY IDENTICAL miner's shacks stand side-by-side in Crystal City. Notice the nearer of the two shacks had board nailed up the wall to keep melting snow from soaking through the walls into the structure. A pile of split wood and an ax stood near the front entrance, where family members posed for this picture.

Two weeks later the following notice appeared:

The Marble Times & Crystal Silver Lance,
November 2, 1900.

Supplies for the Black Queen mine are being hauled up, and timbers for the gallows frame for the new hoister are expected up this week. It takes time to make the contemplated improvements.

• • • •

When a prospector located what he thought was a worthwhile mineral lode he then filed a mining application with the U.S. Land Office in Gunnison for a patent. An example of a newspaper notice of such an application follows:

The Marble Times & Crystal Silver Lance,
September 21, 1900.

MINING APPLICATION NO. 251 UTE SERIES.

Mineral Survey No. 13862

U.S. Land Office, Gunnison Colo.

September 6, 1900

Notice is hereby given that Geo. C. Eaton, by T. O'Bryan, attorney in fact, whose postoffice is Crystal, Colo, has made application for a patent for 1500 linear feet on each of the Franklin and Eatonia lodes, bearing silver, with surface ground 300 feet in width, situate in Crystal River [or Elk Mountain] mining district, Gunnison county, state of Colorado, and described in the plat and field notes on file in this office, as follows, viz:

FRANKLIN LODE. Beginning at cor no. 1 whence USLM Elk Mountain bears s 82 10' e 1756.88 ft. thence n 55 02' w 1500 ft. to cor no. 2, thence s 38 54' w 300 ft. to cor no. 3, thence s 55 02' e 1500 ft. to cor no. 4, thence n 31 58' e 300 ft. to cor no. 1, the place of beginning.

EATONIA LODE. Beginning at cor no. 1 whence USLM Elk Mountain bears s 82 10' e 1756.88 ft, thence n 55 02' w 1500 ft. to cor no.2, thence n 34 58' e to cor no. 3, thence s 52 02' e 1500 ft. to cor no. 4, thence s 34 58' w 300 ft. to cor no. 1, the place of beginning.

Containing 17.849 acres, expressly excepting and excluding all conflict with surveys nos 7891, Cossewago lode; 2727, Garfield lode; 2728 Hancock lode; 2546 Lucas lode; and forming a portion of the unsubdivided twp 12 s r 87 w of the 6th principal meridian. Said location being recorded in Book 114, pages 309-10, of the records of Gunnison county, Colorado.

Adjoining claims those above specified, if any others, unknown. C.F. Hamlin, Registrer.

First pub Sept. 14—last Nov. 16, 1900.

• • • • •

A. A. JOHNSON'S STORE in Crystal City was on the main street. You are looking toward the west, and this location appears to have been a popular gathering place for outsiders coming into town to prospect in the nearby hills.

The newspaper printed the following guide for prospectors:

The Marble Times & Crystal Silver Lance,
October 26, 1900.

HOW TO FIND A POCKET.

First—Remember that the gold in the surrounding surface is the only guide of a pocket.

Second—Never dig a hole on a quartz ledge with the expectation of finding a pocket unless it will prospect at the start.

Third—When tracing for a pocket, if the gold is smooth, leave it at once, for it's ten to one you will never find it.

Fourth—If your trace runs to a deep bed of clay, don't lose much time in looking for the pocket.

Fifth—Beware of serpentine traces. Most all will prospect and not pocket.

Sixth—Remember fifteen or twenty colors of gold as fine as flour to the pan, and an occasional coarse color as big as a pinhead, is a better trace to a pocket than a single piece of gold worth $1, even if it is rough.

Seventh—The best place to look for pockets is in a coarse gold district. The pockets are larger and as easily found.

Eighth—Recollect that nine out of ten pocket ledges do not crop out near the pocket.

Tracing—Commence by panning the top of the ground. It will prospect better there than deeper, unless you are near the pocket or on flat ground. Then go deeper, even to the bedrock. If on descending ground, face up hill, panning from right to left as far out as you can get gold, and where you get the best prospect, move up the hill from that point, panning from right to left as before, and move up on the best prospect. Keep this up until you get above the prospects; then go back where you got the last best prospect, dig a small hole half way to the bedrock and take a pan. Then take one on the bedrock, and if the last prospect's best, rest assured you are near the pocket. From there trench up, and if you don't find the ledge and prospects give out, trench across, and you will be certain to find the ledge; if you do not find the pocket, trench both ways along the ledge, panning every inch, and you will be certain to find it, unless it has been distributed over the ground you have traced by the rocks decaying and rain washes. Where a pocket throws out a trace, you will find it at the top of the bedrock, if there is any left.

When you have taken out one pocket, note the formation around it; follow that and you will be likely to find another or a dozen. It is not advisable to sink straight down very deep unless it will prospect or the formation runs that way, which can be determined by black rock, caused by the stringers of iron and quartz running towards the ledge; where they strike the ledge, pockets are liable to occur.

Pocket chimneys—like those on the mother lode or any gold-bearing region—do not run straight down, but angle on the ledge. Pocket shoots are often not more than one foot wide, and even less. By the time your shaft is down eight or ten feet, you will have cut through your shot and lost it on the end of your shaft. The same system described to find pockets holds good in locating chimneys on milling lodes, if they contain free gold, or even gold bearing sulphurets.— Mining and Scientific Press .

More on the Black Queen mine: This mine, located up on the steep slope of the mountain, follows the slope of the rock layers down into the mountain at approximately a 30-degree slope. Ore taken out was lowered down the face of the mountain in a bucket moving down the mountain on a cable to the wagon road at the bottom. There, it was dumped into a tipple over the road, and later loaded into wagons. The stone wall which supported the tipple can still be seen alongside the present road.

The Marble Times & Crystal Silver Lance,
November 23, 1900.
The steel cable for [the Black Queen] was packed up on seven jacks last week. It weighed almost 1000 pounds, and its packing was accomplished without difficulty. It is between 800 and 900 feet in length and its quality is the best made.

• • • • •

At the end of the year, a summary of the year's activity included this opinion on the Black Queen.

The Marble Times & Crystal Silver Lance,
January 4, 1901.
Possibly, from a mining standpoint, the leasing of the Black Queen mine was the most important deal consummated in the district during 1900, and this valuable property is now being put in shape to more cheaply take out the ore bodies disclosed in the workings. Practically a new plant of machinery is to be installed, the incline is to be enlarged, a tipple built, and many other improvements are contemplated. A force of men is now employed getting things in such shape that when spring opens shipments will be commenced.

• • • • •

In 1898, the Hoffman brothers built a smelter across the Crystal River from Marble to process the ores from the area. During much of its life the smelter was not too successful; the owners claiming that the manager did not operate it right, and the latter insisting that the equipment was not suitable for the ores of the district. The smelter finally closed in 1911. But in the summer of 1901, it was operating.

The Marble Times & Crystal Silver Lance,
August 30, 1900.
Ore shipments from the Scott-Ogden lease [Black Queen mine] continue to the Marble smelter. The fourth carload having just been completed. There are 16 men employed and the force will be increased as opportunity offers.

The Crystal River Current,
October 28, 1904.
Assaying the samples from the Black Queen mine was completed a few days since [October 1904]. It is understood the values were entirely satisfactory.

The Crystal River Current,
July 7, 1905.
Mr. DeWolf, assayer for the Black Queen, is busy fixing up the furnace at the mill for future business [July 1905].

• • • • •

Sometime later the Black Queen closed because of lower prices for silver. The Missouri owner did not give up on it though and when conditions appeared favorable hoped it would resume production. The Marble Booster newspaper in November, 1915, reported this was about to happen.

HENRY L. JOHNSON PHOTO – JACK D. CLEMENSON COLLECTION

GOLD!... GOLD!... in the Colorado high country was on everyone's mind during the 1880's and 1890's. This Marble-area mine had penetrated the mountain to a considerable distance. Due to unstable rock, a large amount of lumber was used to shore-up the tunnel. Air was pumped through the pipe located above the miners' heads.

The Marble Booster,
November 2, 1915.
Harry S. Bryan of Denver, a mining engineer, spent a couple of days here since the last Booster looking over the Black Queen mine, four miles from Marble, on the road to Crystal, with a view of establishing a 100-ton concentrating mill there under contract with the company of capitalists who have leased the mine from A. McVey of Chillicothe, Mo., the owner. The lease was perfected through the promotion of W.J.H. Miller, well known in this mining district.

Mr. Bryan could not make a very extensive examination of the Black Queen mine itself, the lower levels being full of water that has gathered from disuse of the mine, but he was delighted with the location of the mill, saying that it is ideally situated for the purpose. And, as far as the mine is concerned, he is perfectly familiar with its possibilities and ores, anyway, having posted himself through assays of the ore and reports on the property.

• • • • •

By July, 1916, it appeared that Miller was not carrying out his obligations under the lease contract. According to a sworn statement by Bryan these obligations were as follows:

The Marble Booster,
August 6, 1916.

That said lease and contract provided that said W.J.H. Miller should rehabilitate the mill situated on the property, and should vigorously prosecute the work of mining, which included the unwatering of the mine, the rebuilding of the aerial tramway, and shaft house, and all the things necessary to producing ore. ...and would deliver into the mill from the mine the amount of 100 tons of ore per day, for which delivery said Miller was to receive $2 per ton as payment for mining. • • • • •

Bryan claimed that Miller had not lived up to his contract and, therefore, on July 21, 1916 the contract was cancelled. Thus, another dream of the investors to make some money through mining evaporated.

Another mine which produced rich ore over a number of years was the Sheep Mountain Tunnel. Its development resulted in construction of the Sheep Mountain Tunnel Mill, often referred to as the Crystal Mill, destined to become one of the most photographed sites in Colorado. **The Silver Lance,** published in Crystal in April 1893, trumpeted the news of its birth, as follows:

The Silver Lance,
April 20, 1893.
DID YOU HEAR THE
GLORIOUS NEWS
CRYSTAL'S BOOM ASSURED
The Sheep Mountain Tunnel
In the Swim
Another Producer Here

It is with the greatest of pleasure that we chronicle the fact this week that perseverance, pluck and industry is once more about to reap its proverbial reward—success. Messrs. Phillips and Eaton, the promoters of the Sheep Mountain Tunnel & Mining Company, have rustled with a vein for the past two years to push their tunnel into the heart of Sheep Mt. known to contain rich ore chutes in many places. Over 1,000 feet of exploration work has been done under great difficulties, but the work was kept moving, and the prophecies of these gentlemen are developing into actual realities; their undoubting faith is being justified, and new faith and new hope is being forced into every mind with reference to the value of Crystal's mineral riches.

In our examination today we found in the breast of the west drift on the Black Queen contact, about two feet of solid, though impure, baryta spar, well stained and mineralized in spots. This spar was encountered about ten days ago and has continued to widen out up to the present writing. We consider it a sure indication of the near presence of a rich and extensive ore body, and risk our reputation as a prophet on the fulfillment of our prophecy in this respect.

The air drills are not yet in operation, but the work will go on just the same until they are; meantime we are all cussing the weather, which continues to be simply wretched. The stockholders in this company can now congratulate themselves upon getting in on ground floor prices as the company will now undoubtedly hold the remaining stock at higher prices. • • • • •

The first enthusiasm was tempered somewhat by the reality of the area's isolation and lack of good transportation facilities, but the owners continued with their work on the mine, as reported in **The Marble City Times & Clarence Chronicle,** beginning in September, 1893.

HENRY L. JOHNSON PHOTO – JACK D. CLEMENSON COLLECTION

BILL BRINKMEYER was proudly holding "rich ore," where this tunnel of an unidentified mine entered the mountain. Bill became a local hero during a mine accident, when he held back collapsing timbers to save other miners. The incident strained his heart, forcing him to quit mining and become a constable.

The Marble City Times & Clarence Chronicle,
September 29, 1893.
Parties who have lately been in the Sheep mountain tunnel say that they have a large body of ore but that it is low grade in character, yet it would pay to ship if a railroad was close at hand.

The Marble City Times & Clarence Chronicle,
October 6, 1893.
Since we were up to Crystal the Sheep Mountain Tunnel company have done needed outside improvements and we understand that they are figuring on putting in a concentrating plant to treat the ore they have in the tunnel. Plans are now being prepared for the plant. Good for the Tunnel company.

THIS BOARDING HOUSE was situated above Marble, but it is unidentified on the back of this old photograph. Bill Brinkmeyer, standing at the left, was probably summoned for this photograph by someone ringing the dinner-bell triangle, which was hanging above the man's head at the right.

The Marble City Times & Clarence Chronicle,
October 27, 1893.

Work on the Sheep Mountain Tunnel's buildings and shops is being pushed vigorously and everything will be in splendid shape for the winter's campaign. Treasurer Eaton informed us that it was expected the drills would be started about the 1st of November and no let up again until daylight

shows at the other end of the tunnel.

• • • • •

With the completion of the power mill to provide compressed air, the tunnel into the heart of Sheep Mountain could be pushed more rapidly, as revealed in these occasional items in the newspaper. This activity was in spite of the national silver panic of 1893.

MARBLE HISTORICAL SOCIETY COLLECTION

THE ABOVE EXAMPLE of news is reprinted from *The Crystal River Current* of July 28, 1905.

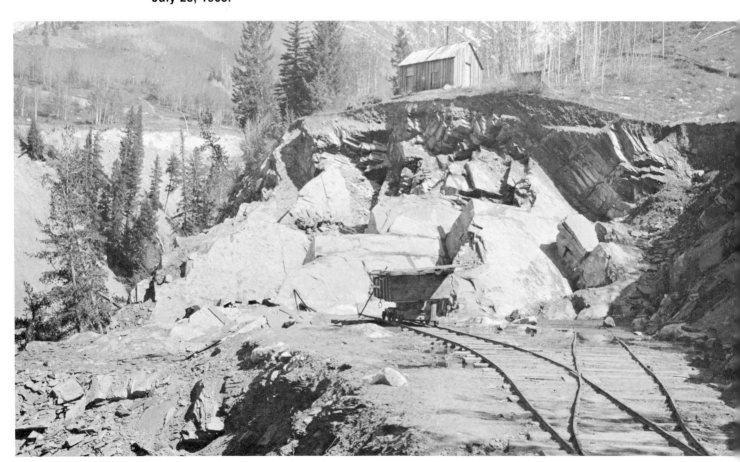

HENRY L. JOHNSON PHOTO – JACK D. CLEMENSON COLLECTION

THE MINING COMPANY in this scene financed the prospect opening ca. 1909. The mine was up Yule Creek, west of Yule Falls. It was a venture in quest of slate. Colonel Channing Meek dropped this search in favor of putting his efforts into the marble business.

The Marble City Times & Clarence Chronicle,
December 8, 1893.

The Sheep Mountain Tunnel company started up the air drills last Friday [December 1, 1893] and are running one shift at present, but will put on another, if possible, within the next ten days. We understand that the company is seriously contemplating shipping a car or two of ore if proper freight rates can be secured from Crystal down to the [Penny] Hot Springs. It is expected that some arrangement can be made with the Crystal River Railway company to place cars on the track at the Hot Springs for the use of the Tunnel company. By sorting the ore close it can be made to pay, even at the present low price of silver. Such a movement, if carried out, will not only benefit the Tunnel company but every property-owner in this district.

The Marble City Times & Clarence Chronicle,
December 22, 1893.

President Phillips showed us some good ore yesterday from the Sheep mountain tunnel, which is of the same character as that taken out of the famous Black Queen. Eight men are now employed in the tunnel and work is progressing satisfactory, while the outlook for a rich ore body is steadily improving.

The Marble City Times & Clarence Chronicle,
January 5, 1894.

The annual report of the Sheep Mountain Tunnel and Mining company has been published and mailed to all stockholders. It shows the work so far accomplished and all moneys received and expended. Since the company was organized they have sold stock to the amount of $71,005.83, and had a balance of $3567.78 in the bank on Nov. 20, 1893. The total work done under ground equals 1571 feet, aside of all outside improvements. The report is indeed very encouraging to the stockholders in this great enterprise.

The Marble City Times & Clarence Chronicle,
February 2, 1894.

The breast of the Sheep Mountain tunnel is being steadily pushed ahead through ore of increasing value. B.S. Phillips has been employed during the week in tightening up the [wooden] dam [at the powerhouse] so as to save some of the water now going to waste.

The Marble City Times & Clarence Chronicle,
March 9, 1894.

The Sheep mountain tunnel people have started an upraise [March 1894] to prove the extent of the ore body. They claim to have excellent ore but for some reason or other are keeping it kind of quiet.

The Marble City Times & Clarence Chronicle,
March 30, 1894.

Some stoping is being done in the Sheep mountain tunnel. It is understood they have a fair sized vein of high grade ore.

The Marble City Times & Clarence Chronicle,
April 13, 1894.

High-grade ore is still being taken out of the Sheep mountain tunnel. The ore body is improving with every shot.

The Marble City Times & Clarence Chronicle,
April 27, 1894.

Everything is running smoothly at the Sheep Mountain Tunnel. The breast of the tunnel is in ore of a fair value and in the up-raise streaks of high grade ore have been encountered, but so far no solid ore body has been disclosed. All the vein matter assays fairly well and now and then streaks of ore are encountered which run into the hundreds.

The Marble City Times & Clarence Chronicle,
May 25, 1894.

Tuesday [22 May 1894], about 4 p.m., flames were discovered issuing from the house at the mouth of the Sheep Mountain tunnel and in a few moments the entire structure was enveloped in a streak of fire. Soon all of our citizens, with several persons from Marble, who opportunely happened to be here, were on the ground with buckets. The fire was so hot water availed but little, and ropes were called into play, when the burning logs were soon brought to the ground and the mouth of the tunnel was cleared. The men worked as men never worked before for the reason that there were five men inside the tunnel while the flames were raging, but fortunately the air pipe remained unbroken and a full supply of air was pumped into the tunnel, and so well did this do that the smoke did not extend but a little back of the air shaft. The loss is not very great. The cause of the fire is explained by the candle in the box used for thawing powder, setting it on fire.

The Marble City Times & Clarence Chronicle,
July 13, 1894.

During the week [of 13 July 1894] the Sheep mountain tunnel has added some men to its working force and everything is moving along smoothly.

The Marble City Times,
July 27, 1894.

Mr. Fischel of Aspen, is at the Sheep Mountain tunnel making and putting in place 300 feet of air piping, and moving the air-sucker ahead that distance.

The Marble City Times,
August 24, 1894.

Frank Traynor is running the air drills at the Sheep mountain tunnel. It is presumed there will be less breakage of machinery. The tunnel is now in ore.

The Marble City Times,
September 14, 1894.

W.L. Davis, manager of the New York World, was a pleasant visitor in camp Saturday and Sunday [September 1894]. He was looking after his heavy mining interests on Sheep mountain incidentally, but more particularly investigating the merits of the Sheep Mountain Tunnel as a financial enterprise. After a thorough examination of the property he expressed himself as satisfied that it possesses great merit as a financial investment, and no doubt but what his company would become interested in the enterprise.

• • • • •

Such on and off development activities continued for many years at most of the active mines in the district. Some made expenses, and even some profit, but many were essentially losers. At the time Charles Bryan of the Black Queen was explaining the failure of that mine the Sheep Mountain Tunnel & Manufacturing Company property was taken over by Gunnison County for failure to pay taxes and sold at tax auction in July, 1916. At this same time **The Marble Booster** in its banner proclaimed:

The Marble Booster,
August 26, 1916

"Brighter Days for Marble Are in Sight. The End of Our Troubles is Nearing. So, CHEER UP."

• • • • •

This was an example of the continual optimism exhibited in all the mining camps and held by all the prospectors and mine developers. Mining was always a risky business, but they confidently expected their dreams to be fulfilled.

THIS IS TYPICAL of the road conditions near Crystal City and Marble before the days of pavement. Teams and wagons would often become bogged down in low spots, where water and mud had collected. Usually, another team of horses was required to pull them out.

IT IS BELIEVED that the mining scene below was in the vicinity of Crystal City, although there is no physical evidence available to prove exactly where it was. The mine portal was beyond the team and wagon, where the hillside was shored-up with rock.

THE CRYSTAL RIVER drops through a narrow, twisting canyon at this location, where it was impossible to build a trail. On the distant horizon, Chair Mountain appears beyond the town of Marble (due west). Lizard Lake is up the road (to the right), not visible in this view. The Colorado-Yule Marble Company dam for the collection of water to feed the power plant was down this gorge.

MAJESTIC MOUNT SOPRIS reaches an altitude of 12,823 feet above sea level. This scenic peak towers over Carbondale in this photograph, taken in 1906. The Crystal River Railroad (which later became the Crystal River & San Juan) made its connection here with the Denver & Rio Grande Railroad. Carbondale had a population of 500 at this time, with both railroads using the depot in the foreground of the wye (center). The Crystal River Railroad headed upriver (to the south, at the right) to reach Redstone and Marble, past the base of Mount Sopris.

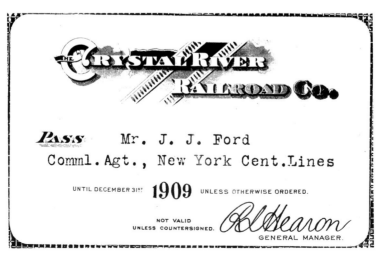

HOW THEY CAME AND WENT

When the Crystal River Valley was first settled by miners and prospectors about 1880 they came over Schofield Pass from Crested Butte. At that time the Crystal River was called Rock Creek and there was no road down the valley to Carbondale. Everyone walked or rode on horseback, or on the ubiquitous donkey. It was necessary to haul the hand-sorted ore laboriously extracted from the hard rock over the pass on the backs of mules to the railroad. Trains of 150 jacks would make the round trip of 30 miles in two or three days. Each jack carried 150 pounds of ore in sacks tied to their backs. It took expert mule skinners to handle so many animals on the narrow and steep trails. Of course, this trail was open only during the summer for about five months. After a few years a wagon road was built over the pass to enable the huge freight wagons to haul silver, lead and copper ore to the railroad at Crested Butte. It was then carried to the nearest smelter for refining.

In 1900 several newspaper reports indicate the enormous difficulties this mining industry had to surmount and the inherent dangers of operating in a wilderness. By 1893 a wagon road had been built down the valley to Carbondale and this made a much easier trip than going over the pass.

The Marble Times & Crystal Silver Lance,
August 24, 1900.
Phil Moore has commenced packing a carload of ore from the Undine mine to Placita, from whence it will go to outside smelters.

The Marble Times & Crystal Silver Lance,
September 7, 1900.
Henry Kirk was over at Bogan's camp the latter part of last week looking after some packing and he may move his jacks over there, as Frank Bogan has 300 or 400 tons of ore to move.

The Marble Times & Crystal Silver Lance,
September 7, 1900.
While rounding-up jacks on the hill side Wednesday morning, Charlie Nevin's horse fell in jumping a log and Charlie was quite severely hurt in the back during the fall. It was a lucky escape for him, however, and we hope he will speedily recover. • • • • •

The Marble Times & Crystal Silver Lance,
September 7, 1900.
John Larsen is sacking ore preparatory to its shipment to the Marble smelter.

The Marble Times & Crystal Silver Lance,
June 29, 1900.
The Carbonate mine is outputting a large tonnage of ore these days and the pack trains are kept busy transporting it to the Hoffman Smelter at Marble.
• • • • •

The Marble Times & Crystal Silver Lance,
September 7, 1900.
Three teams left here [Marble] Wednesday morning for Crested Butte to procure coke for the smelter as the coke from below here does not seem to give satisfaction. • • • • •

Travelers often caught rides on the wagons to avoid a long walk or riding horseback.

The Marble Times & Crystal Silver Lance,
August 24, 1900.
Dan Miner's team brought over Mrs. W.S. Smith and Miss Maud Foster from Crested Butte Wednesday. • • • • •

Much effort was expended in building trails and wagon roads in these rugged mountains, as many of the mines were in almost inaccessible locations.

The Marble Times & Crystal Silver Lance,
August 24, 1900.
Pete Mattivi is building a trail to the Hoffman tunnel site, on the northwest slope of Crystal mountain [above Crystal].

CRYSTAL RIVER & SAN JUAN RAILWAY
— Marble to Carbondale —
MAP DRAWN BY JIM KEY

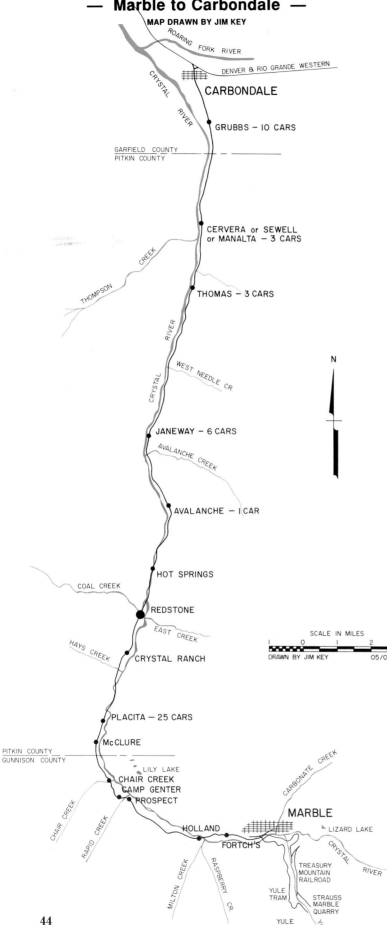

ROARING FORK RIVER

DENVER & RIO GRANDE WESTERN

CARBONDALE

CRYSTAL RIVER

GRUBBS – 10 CARS

GARFIELD COUNTY
PITKIN COUNTY

CERVERA or SEWELL
or MANALTA – 3 CARS

THOMPSON CREEK

THOMAS – 3 CARS

CRYSTAL RIVER

WEST NEEDLE CR

N

JANEWAY – 6 CARS

AVALANCHE CREEK

AVALANCHE – I CAR

HOT SPRINGS

COAL CREEK

REDSTONE

EAST CREEK

HAYS CREEK

CRYSTAL RANCH

SCALE IN MILES

1   0   1   2   3

DRAWN BY JIM KEY   05/06/92

PLACITA – 25 CARS

McCLURE

PITKIN COUNTY
GUNNISON COUNTY

LILY LAKE

CHAIR CREEK
CAMP GENTER
PROSPECT

CHAIR CREEK

RAPID CREEK

HOLLAND

FORTCH'S

MILTON CREEK

RASPBERRY CR

CARBONATE CREEK

MARBLE

LIZARD LAKE

CRYSTAL RIVER

TREASURY
MOUNTAIN
RAILROAD

YULE
TRAM

STRAUSS
MARBLE
QUARRY

YULE
MARBLE
QUARRY

YULE CR

The Marble Times & Crystal Silver Lance,
November 16, 1900.

The construction of nearly two miles of a wagon road up Yule creek to the marble claims of the Colorado Fuel company, and the shipment of the immense blocks already quarried to the eastern cities, means more to the town of Marble than most of our people realize. The road of itself, if nothing more, will materially benefit claim owners along Yule creek who desire to ship their products to the markets. The successful working of the quarry and the sawing of the stone for the market, means an increased number of workmen in this vicinity and the distribution of large sums of money among the people. Such industries will also be the means to stimulate and bring other industries into our midst, thereby benefitting all and make this a prosperous and lively locality. Enterprises of this or any other nature should receive the hearty support of all citizens alike.

. . . . .

After the wagon roads were built stagecoach lines were established to provide more convenient travel, though it is doubtful if this form of travel was much more comfortable.

The Marble Times & Crystal Silver Lance,
November 16, 1900.

Kirk & Shaw, since they took charge of the stage line, seem to be doing a good business. Almost every night they have a number of passengers and a lot of freight.

The Marble Times & Crystal Silver Lance,
August 10, 1900.

Crystal. B.W. Cass was an in-coming passenger on Friday's stage from Aspen to look after his mining interests here.

The Marble Times & Crystal Silver Lance,
August 10, 1900.

J.H. Hoffman took a spin down to Glenwood Springs on Monday's stage to attend to some business matters in connection with the various Hoffman companies.

. . . . .

This "spin" down the valley involved a trip of 42 miles from Marble over a track that was virtually impassable much of the year. Maintaining these "roads" was a never-ending task.

The Marble Times & Crystal Silver Lance,
November 16, 1900.

Roadoverseer Parry put in a new bridge at the top of Daniel's hill this week. It was needed badly. Nearly all the bridges in the district should be fixed up and replanked.

. . . . .

Building these roads was a dangerous business, usually involving much blasting with dynamite. One serious accident was reported in March 1901.

CARBONDALE, COLORADO, is located where the Crystal River has its confluence with the Roaring Fork of the Colorado River, and it was a natural place for a town to form. It served travelers as a stop-over for their treks up the Crystal River Valley. It was 1906 before the railroad laid track into Marble, making the trip upriver pleasurable. The Carbondale station grounds appear in this scene (at the left), with the Crystal River Railroad's wye off to the right, where the mainline left town toward the south. The business section of Carbondale appears beyond the railroad station.

The Marble Times & Crystal Silver Lance,
March 8, 1901.

About 9 o'clock last Friday morning a serious accident occurred on the new Marble road through the premature igniting of about 75 pounds of giant powder while being thawed out ready for use; the result of the explosion caused the death of one man and severly bruised many more, but taking everything into consideration the men escaped very luckily. It seems that the contractors had erected a shack for the purpose of thawing out powder and placed a small stove in it; the day before the accident the man in charge was transferred to the cook house and Foreman Frank Smith was delegated to look after the powder house, and while in there the explosion took place causing his instant death, but how it happened no one will ever know. Smith's hand was severed from his body and was found about 75 feet away, his leg was broken in two or more places, head, back and arms were terribly bruised; in fact, the poor fellow never knew what happened to him. Mr. Smith's remains were brought down to town that afternoon and Saturday he was given a Christian burial.

Before the interment Justice Fuller and six jurors held an inquest over the remains, the jury finding deceased came to his death through no fault of the contractors, but was caused by the explosion of giant powder, the cause of which was unknown to the jury.

. . . . . .

Two months later another, workman was killed while working on road construction. In those days, the hazards of employment had to be accepted by the workers, as it was considered an act of God when accidents occurred, but it appears there were not adequate safety precautions.

CRYSTAL RIVER & SAN JUAN locomotive No. 2 had arrived at the Carbondale, Colorado, station on July 4, 1940, with combination baggage-coach No. 9. One of the trainmen rested against the telegrapher's bay window, where the "order board" (semaphore signal) displayed red for "stop." The passenger train was standing on the Denver & Rio Grande Western's main track to Aspen — on the Aspen Branch. Passengers could wait in the relative comfort of the Carbondale depot, while interchanging from one railroad to the other. In times that train connections were delayed, passengers could find a room at one of the hotels in Carbondale, a short walk into town. The attractive little depot was painted buff and brown.

The Marble Times & Crystal Silver Lance,
May 17, 1901

Last Saturday, Angelo I. Giacomo, an Italian workman, was instantly killed while at work on the quarry wagon road. It seems that he was working on a very steep portion of the rock work, opposite the quarry, and while thus engaged his foot slipped and letting go of the rope he was hurled to the bottom of the canon, a distance of about 150 feet, causing his instant death.

While the death of the poor fellow is to be greatly deplored, no blame can be placed upon any one for such an accident. He was buried Sunday afternoon. We understand the deceased leaves a widow and four children in Italy to mourn his loss.

The Marble Times & Crystal Silver Lance,
July 12, 1901.

12 July 1901. The wagon road to the Osgood marble quarry has at last been finished. Messrs. Flaharity & Farrell, the contractors, had a hard proposition but kept at it until it was completed, and although way behind at one time we are pleased to learn they came out a little ahead on the job. The road itself is a fine one and cost the company somewhere about $12,000.

• • • • •

Local residents were constantly after the county and state officials to build new roads or improve old ones. The Marble Booster of 22 March 1913 reported on the latest efforts.

LEASED LOCOMOTIVE No. 701 of the Colorado & Wyoming Railroad was photographed at Carbondale while serving on the Crystal River Railroad in 1911. She was used extensively by the Colorado & Wyoming Railroad as a passenger locomotive. The Crystal River Railroad hauled coal and coke tonnage, along with passengers, out of Carbondale, Redstone and Placita, with connections for Coalbasin and Marble.

The Marble Booster,
March 22, 1913.

New Road Proposed to be Built From Marble to Redstone. At a meeting of the Marble Chamber of Commerce Wednesday night, with a large attendance, President Thode submitted a proposition to build a new wagon and automobile road from Redstone to Marble, thus connecting our town with the outside world and giving tourists and rigs a chance to come up here. Mr. Thode explained that the present "road" is a farce—little better than a trail, in fact, and that for a large part of the year it is entirely impassable. Marble being thus cut off from the outside except by train. Should the train service be interrupted there would be no way of getting food supplies in here except by horseback. . . . . .

While everyone wanted the road improved, the proposed methods of paying for it were in dispute.

The Marble Booster,
March 29, 1913.

Where The Booster Stands. With none but the kindliest feeling for the plan proposed to build a new road from Redstone to Marble, and giving due credit to the public spirited men who proposed it and are now working on the scheme, the Booster herewith declares itself unalterably opposed to taking any money now or hereafter out of the town treasury to devote to this purpose.

Walter Hood is in receipt of a letter from John C. Osgood in which the Redstone magnate says he will join heartily with Marble people in building a new road between the two points. He says the old road is out of the question—that the cost of repairs would be excessive and continuous, and that as soon as the snow goes he will take steps to survey a new route and estimate the cost of building same.

RAILROADS

It was early recognized by the pioneers of the Crystal River Valley that full development of the mineral and business potential of the area depended on good transportation facilities, and in those days, this meant railroads. The local area boosters, notably the small weekly newspaper editors, from the earliest times pushed the idea of railroads. It was difficult to build rail lines in these narrow mountain valleys but this did not deter the railroad men. **The Silver Lance of 20 April 1893** reported that two rail lines were being pushed up the Crystal River and there was hardly room enough for both.

Continued on Page 56

PASSENGERS ENJOYED the comfort of this combination baggage-coach-caboose when traveling to Redstone, Placita or Marble on the Crystal River & San Juan Railroad. This car was No. 02 and had been purchased from the Crystal River Railroad. It still carried the CRYSTAL RIVER name on the letterboard over the windows. The CRR was taken over by the CR&SJ on September 15, 1910, according to a conductor's book on the Crystal River & San Juan Railroad. In this photograph a baby carriage was being loaded aboard the car while it was in Carbondale. The car's diamond arch-bar caboose trucks had leaf springs, which cushioned the load of this car.

ANOTHER LEASED Colorado & Wyoming locomotive was on the Crystal River Railroad track behind the Carbondale depot in this photograph, taken sometime prior to 1909. A spool of wire cable was on the flatcar behind the engine. It was being transported up the line, possibly for use at the Colorado-Yule Marble Company quarry as replacement cable for the aerial tramway used to load electric tramway cars.

THE ENGINEER of the Crystal River & San Juan's engine No. 1 was waiting for the departure time in Carbondale on October 25, 1941, and would head this mixed passenger-and-freight train to Marble. When purchased from the D&RG, No. 1 had larger driving wheels than when the engine was originally delivered to the D&RG.

DENVER & RIO GRANDE locomotive No. 532, photographed in 1899, was purchased from the D&RG by the Crystal River & San Juan in 1915. With 55-inch drivers, this 4–6–0 was suited for fast passenger-train movements. Along the Crystal River, she was used on a tri-weekly mixed train between Carbondale and Marble.

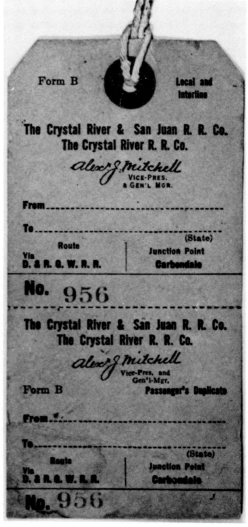

50

LOCOMOTIVE NO. 2 of the Crystal River & San Juan had pulled to a stop at the Carbondale depot on July 4, 1940, with combination baggage-coach No. 9 coupled on behind. The homemade universal piston-valve chamber gives this locomotive an unusual look — with her 51-inch drivers well-suited for mixed-train service.

TWO RAILROADS, the Crystal River & San Juan Railroad and the Crystal River Railroad, shared this baggage claim tag (printed on Page 50) between Carbondale and Marble. The two rail lines connected at Redstone.

THE ENGINEER'S SIDE of the Crystal River & San Juan engine No. 2 makes a good study as she was switching a livestock train in Carbondale on July 4, 1940.

THE CARBONDALE DEPOT was photographed one final time in 1958, before it was moved off the site — saved by the American Legion post in Carbondale. The freight end of the depot had a raised dock for wagon or truck delivery or pick-up. The depot outhouse stood beneath the tree (in the lower view), beyond the telegrapher's bay window, beside the D&RGW mainline to Aspen. In the view below, Crystal River & San Juan trackage was still in place along the town side of the depot.

MID-CONTINENT COKE & COAL loaded hundreds of trainloads of coal out of this facility in Carbondale. In the scene above, two Denver & Rio Grande Western diesel engines were moving a coal train through the east end of the yard in Carbondale. The year was 1971.

SPOTTED ON THE EAST LEG of the wye in Carbondale, Crystal River & San Juan combine No. 9 was photographed on July 4, 1940, while waiting to be picked up for a return trip to Redstone and Marble.

HAULED INTO CARBONDALE on the Crystal River & San Juan scrap train in 1942, this former Crystal River Railroad boxcar, No. 101, was purchased by a local resident for use as a shed. Buildings in downtown Carbondale are behind this boxcar body. No. 101 originally operated between Redstone and Coal Basin on the narrow-gauge branch of the Crystal River line. After 1908, the boxcar was used on the CR&SJ until 1942, on the standard-gauge Marble-to-Carbondale line (out-fitted with standard-gauge trucks).

CRYSTAL RIVER & SAN JUAN locomotive No. 1 had been plowing snowdrifts along the right-of-way from Marble, before she reached Carbondale. A Denver & Rio Grande Western milepost has the mileage from Denver at this point in the station grounds in Carbondale. A D&RGW section house and bunkhouse stood to the right of the depot.

HENRY L. JOHNSON PHOTO – JACK D. CLEMENSON COLLECTION

A LARGE "V" SNOWPLOW had been attached to the head end of an unidentified locomotive in this winter view, taken near Carbondale. In some cases, lives depended on the track being cleared, due to the poor conditions of automobile roads during the early 1900's.

A LIVESTOCK TRAIN was photographed on July 4, 1940, as it arrived in Carbondale about noon, with 12 cars. Engine 2 had been fitted with a spark arrestor for the hot, dry summer months. Summer grazing had become popular up along the Crystal River, and cattlemen and sheepmen utilized the pens at the west end of Marble for shipments by rail to Carbondale, where livestock continued on the D&RGW.

MORRISON A. SMITH PHOTO – JOHN W. MAXWELL COLLECTION

THE SETTLEMENT of Janeway was a small hamlet along the Crystal River line, near the point where Avalanche Creek empties into the Crystal River. However, it boasted of a post office during its early years. In this photograph, taken during 1978, one of the original log cabins still stood beside the main street. You are looking toward the southeast at the old townsite.

The Crystal River railway and the Elk Mountain railroad have some little difficulties still hanging in the balance. On Monday the first-named company appeared before Judge Rucker sitting at Glenwood and asked for an injunction restraining the other from interfering with the progress of their construction work. The granting of this injunction was resisted, but the court issued a temporary restraining order for five days.

These railroads have already met with many vicissi-tudes and embarassments, but it is believed there is room for both to operate in the rich country they are seeking to penetrate and tap, and that the best interest of the public will be served by the final completion of both lines of road.

Both railroads are pulling up the valley as rapidly as their circumstances will permit, and it looks to us as though the Crystal River company was playing hog a little more than is necessary, but that is the nature of the C.F.&I. brute.

• • • • •

A NORTHBOUND FREIGHT TRAIN, with combine No. 9 tacked on, was photographed as it passed the road crossing at Whitbeck on September 6, 1941. Large blocks of marble were en route to an unknown destination. The Crystal River is on the right (west) side of the train. This is the same train as the one on the following page.

Though the locals appreciated the business generated by the coal mining activities of the Colorado Fuel & Iron Company, organized by John C. Osgood, there were many complaints that the company was domineering and insensitive to the needs of individuals. Though this apparent company attitude was common in the business environment of those days, it also was ironic in that Osgood was a leader and experimenter in fostering the personal welfare of his employees. To that end, he designed and built the town of Redstone as a social experiment to demonstrate that coal miners did not have to be dirty and uncultured. By 1900 the new town was attracting attention as a place to enjoy the finer things of life.

The Marble Times & Crystal Silver Lance,
August 10, 1900.
Redstone. As your correspondent was piling lumber

in the yards the other evening a substantial gentleman, whose appearance looked the highest step of prosperity, approached him and inquired the time of the train's departure. It's liable to leave any time—just as soon as its switching is finished; those other three engines are doing all they can, was the answer. I inquired, he rejoined: because I wanted to sup over there—pointing to Hotel Legget—there's no better meals served anywhere.

• • • • •

The railroads were important employers and had a high profile in the community. Editors watched closely for every scrap of news which indicated their aims for the development and success of the area were being realized.

The Marble Times & Crystal Silver Lance,
August 10, 1900.
The C.R.R.R. [Crystal River Rail Road] advanced wages of common workmen from $1.75 to $2. per day. This affects about 300 workmen in the Redstone district.

ON A NORTHBOUND TRAIN near Whitbeck, Crystal River & San Juan locomotive No. 2 was hauling a Rock Island gondola and a long Pennsylvania mill gondola — both loaded with blocks of marble, which had been centered over the trucks for proper load distribution. The CR&SJ's combination baggage-coach No. 9 brought-up the end of the train. Blocks of waste marble had been dumped off along the grade of the railroad as "rip-rap," as protection against high water during spring runoff. This scene was photographed on September 6, 1941.

AN UNKNOWN PHOTOGRAPHER was sent out to make a pictoral record of structures along the Crystal River Railroad's right-of-way during September of 1911. It is quite possible that this water-flume collection box, with a spout for filling engine tenders, was located at Avalanche Creek, along the standard-gauge mainline to Redstone.

The Marble Times & Crystal Silver Lance,
August 10, 1900.

Three narrow gauge flat cars, capacity 50,000 lbs. each, reached here this week, heralding the approach of many more. 150 coal cars for the High Line are under way.

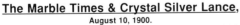

The High Line was the familiar term for the narrow-gauge railroad which ran from Redstone up Coal Creek 12 miles to the outcrops of the superior coking coal beds high up in an alpine basin (Coal Basin). Coal was hauled down to Redstone and converted into coke in the large bank of ovens across the river from the town. Then it was loaded into standard-gauge cars for the trip to the C.F.&I. mill at Pueblo.

The Marble Times & Crystal Silver Lance,
August 10, 1900.

We had quite a ride on the workmen's automobile early Sunday morning to the vicinity of Carbondale. Roadmaster Wallgren guided the machine and Foreman Galloway acted as "look out." We rode back on the top of a lumber pile and it was much smoother riding than on cushioned seats on many of our pretentious railways. Veteran railroaders remarked they had never seen such a good piece of mountain track.

PHOTOGRAPHED IN THE WINTER of 1942, rails were being pulled up near Mile-post 12, beside the Crystal River. Redstone is approximately three miles from this location.

The Marble Times & Crystal Silver Lance,
June 29, 1900.

A new narrow gauge engine, No. 101, the mate of 102, has arrived [at Redstone] and will be prancing around the yards in a day or two.

The Marble Times & Crystal Silver Lance,
October 12, 1900.

The first box car for the High Line has arrived and is now doing duty; it is of the "Palace" variety in its completeness.

• • • • •

This was in October 1900, at the time the Coal Basin mines were getting into production. Each delivery of rolling stock was greeted with enthusiasm as this translated into jobs.

The Marble Times & Crystal Silver Lance,
November 2, 1900.

Master Mechanic Gibb has returned from an extended eastern tour. He made a contract with the Cooke Locomotive Works of Patterson, N.J., for one of the latest and most improved snow plows. This is for use on the High Line and Mr. G. is satisfied will do the work for which it is designed most effectively. Mr. G. should know, if anybody; his wide range of experience upon many of the great railroad thoroughfares of the country, including the Union Pacific, with its extensive snow sheds, admirably qualify him for a competent judge.

• • • • •

Snowplows were extremely important to keep a line open during the severe winters. Great amounts of snow fall in Coal Basin and keeping the track clear for the trains was a monumental task.

The Marble Times & Crystal Silver Lance,
October 12, 1900.

The new locomotive, which replaces No. 1, arrived on Monday, accompanied by the General Master Mechanic of the Baldwin Locomotive Works for the western Division, Mr. W.J. Sweigard. A trial trip was made on Tuesday under Master Mechanic Gibb's supervision, and that gentleman pronounced her a success in all respects. She works with the smoothness and precision of an old timer. The weight of this engine is 90 tons, exclusive of the tank, which when full makes 48 tons additional. The boiler is 76 inches in diameter; the cylinder 22 x 28 and a 52-inch wheeler. This superb creation of the locomotive mechinist's art is every inch what it looks to be—a thing of strength and beauty, and Mr. James Cunningham is its living commander, although it looks to the beholder as if it was instinct with life itself.

From all indications, the Fuel Co. seems determined to bring this valley to the front if it is possible to do so, and our residents should encourage all efforts to this end, instead of the opposition that seems to crop out on every occasion. We need a railroad, we need the opening up of our marble and slate beds and our vast mineral outcroppings and the only way to accomplish this is by lending a helping hand to any individual or corporation that may undertake such an enormous task, and not throwing stones to block their way at every opportunity that offers itself.

• • • • •

At least the editor was objective enough to see what was good for the area, and counseled intelligent self-interest. Arrival of the railroad provided an opportunity for new adventures and exciting times and the editor tried to keep this before the public.

HENRY L. JOHNSON PHOTO – MARBLE HISTORICAL SOCIETY COLLECTION

BELOW PENNY HOT SPRINGS, the canyon narrows along the Crystal River. It was at this location that the Elk Mountain Raiway constructed a grade on the west side of the Crystal River, along what is now Highway 133.

CRYSTAL RIVER & SAN JUAN RAILROAD COMPANY						
21	23		STATIONS		22	24
1:35	5:55	lv.	REDSTONE	ar.	5:50	1:30
1:42	6:02	"	CRYSTAL RANCH	"	5:44	1:22
1:54	6:14	"	PLACITA	"	5:34	1:10
1:59	6:19	"	McCLURES	"	5:30	1:06
2:09	6:29	"	CHAIR CREEK	"	5:20	12:53
2:14	6:34	"	PROSPECT	"	5:16	12:48
2:23	6:43	"	HOLLANDS	"	5:10	12:39
2:26	6:46	"	FORTCH'S	"	5:05	12:36
2:30	6:50	ar.	MARBLE	"	5:00	12:30

JULY 1909   RR RED BOOK

The Marble Times & Crystal Silver Lance,
October 19, 1900.

While at Redstone this week we had the pleasure of taking the first ride on the High Line to Coal Basin and it was a grand trip. The road is narrow gauge and built in the most substantial manner and traversing one of the most picturesque canons in the state, affording the tourist much pleasure in viewing the grand scenery as the road winds up the canon. In the twelve miles of road there are over twenty bridges, and the way the locomotive crawls slowly from ridge to ridge is phenomenal. It is a grand piece of engineering, and the Marshall Pass road is not in it compared with this High Line. • • • • •

61

ORIGINALLY GRADED as the Crystal River Railroad in 1898, the Crystal River & San Juan leased running rights over this section of track during the years after the abandonment of the CRR by parent Colorado Fuel & Iron Corporation in March of 1938. This picture was taken near Milepost 12, where a siding had been constructed on the higher level in order to open a rock quarry at this location. The dirt road (Colorado Highway 133), alongside the Crystal River, was previously graded by the Elk Mountain Railway, which never laid any track. Penny Hot Springs is about a quarter mile from here, behind the photographer.

CR&SJ LOCOMOTIVE No. 1 was making her last trip down the Crystal River Valley, with the Morse Brothers Machinery Company dismantling train. The train was near Penny Hot Springs during the winter of 1942, as rail was winched up onto the flatcars. The hoist shed behind the boxcar contained a potbelly stove for the wreckers to warm their hands.

JOHN T. HERMAN COLLECTION

SUNDANCE COLLECTION

MUD AND ROCK SLIDES from heavy downpours were almost a yearly experience on the Crystal River & San Juan Railroad. This photograph appears to have been taken in the vicinity below (north of) Redstone, not far above Penny Hot Springs. Notice the track brace that had been installed between the rails to keep the track gauged correctly, at 4 feet, 8-1/2 inches.

SUNDANCE PUBLICATIONS COLLECTION

THIS "GS" (GENERAL SERVICE) GONDOLA of the Denver & Rio Grande and the Crystal River Railroad's Way Car 02 — outfitted for passengers, baggage and the conductor's office — had been cut off from the locomotive and was left sitting near Penny Hot Springs. The locomotive may have been detached in order to run for water, as sometimes happened when the tender tank had not been filled or had sprung a leak. Notice the person sitting in the baggage doorway of the way car (caboose / combine). This photograph was taken during 1908.

Even at this early date of 1900, it was recognized that one of Colorado's greatest assets was its scenery, and tourism was being actively pushed. These small Western weeklies had many subscribers in the East, including many who had invested in the various mineral ventures. These were the persons potentially interested in traveling to the West to see the scenery and the investment opportunities.

The Marble Times & Crystal Silver Lance,
November 2, 1900.
Two trains, instead of one, have run both ways most of the past week. Freight business is rapidly increasing.

Casually, we noticed on one freight 10 cars of cattle and 3 of sheep and on another 11 cars cattle, all from Placita.

The Marble Times & Crystal Silver Lance,
November 2, 1900.
A handsome "Way-car," fresh from the works reached the Branch a few days ago. It looks now as if the High Line would have its equipment of rolling stock before the main line.

The Marble Times & Crystal Silver Lance,
November 23, 1900.
Fourteen brand new dumping coal cars are in the yards awaiting the driving of the silver spike at Coal Basin.

• • • • •

Continued on Page 71

RICHARD A. RONZIO COLLECTION

THIS PHOTOGRAPH probably portrays the arrival of the first train into Redstone.
The first Crystal River Railway's standard-gauge locomotive was No. 1, a 2–8–0
built by Baldwin Locomotive Works in 1893. By October of 1900, a second No. 1
replaced the first engine. The second No. 1 was a larger engine, purchased to

haul longer, heavier trains. The Redstone depot foundation was being constructed
(at the right). During the interim, an old boxcar body was being used as a depot.
Coke ovens were under construction behind the train.

JOHN C. OSGOOD was in Redstone during 1903, when this photograph was taken. This was during the period when he was forced out of the Colorado Fuel & Iron Corporation as president of this major steel-maker. Mr. Osgood then applied more attention to completing his plans for developing the Redstone and Coalbasin company towns, along with his personal property at Cleveholm in Redstone, as well as at his ranch up along the Crystal River, in the direction of Marble.

THOMAS McCREA GIBB was J. C. Osgood's right-hand-man, and he had been placed in charge of managing and promoting Redstone, Coalbasin and the Crystal River Railroad — both the standard- and narrow-gauge portions of the line. (Note: Early maps show "Coal Basin" as two words; however, the Colorado Fuel & Iron Company used one word for this place name.)

CLEVEHOLM WAS DESIGNED and built for John C. Osgood and his wife, Irene, in 1901. It was here, in this dream castle, that Mr. Osgood entertained his friends from around the world — to impress them with the beautiful setting of Redstone and his ranch. Today (in 1992), this beautiful mansion is owned by Ken Johnson and is available for tours.

THE CLEVEHOLM DINING ROOM was decorated with a fireplace of red onyx, and the walls and drapes were made of red velvet. Before- or after-dinner drinks could be served at the table in the foreground. Notice the oriental rug and the extensive collection of silver, encased behind glass.

THE BIG HORN LODGE was built specifically for men to gather there before and after big-game hunting in the hills surrounding Redstone and Coalbasin. Wild game abounded in this rugged, mountainous, forested area during the early 1900's — including grizzly bears, black bears, big-horn sheep, Rocky Mountain elk and mule deer, not to mention smaller species of animals. The Big Horn Lodge was located west of the CF&I coke ovens in Redstone.

THE REDSTONE INN was constructed by the CF&I for bachelor workmen in 1901. Meals were shared in the large dining hall. Large stone fireplaces were featured, and hunting trophies adorned the walls, which were constructed with the finest woodwork of the day.

A COVERED TERRACE, with a globe-shaped "Inn" sign (lit at night), was located in front of the entrance to the Redstone Inn, which looked very much like a Bavarian or Swiss style building. The impressive Redstone Inn sits downriver from the Cleveholm mansion, at the edge of the colorful little town of Redstone.

THE COLORADO SUPPLY COMPANY'S store at Redstone was the largest commercial building in town. It was built in 1900; however, it disappeared from the scene many years ago. The main street through Redstone makes a curve over this property today. The building that is currently used as the Redstone Country Store (as of 1992) appears at the rear of the Colorado Supply Company store, a subsidiary of the Colorado Fuel & Iron Company. Notice the Crystal River Railroad spur, which ended behind the wall, alongside the store.

THE RED CLIFFS of Redstone — giving the town its name — are in this view (below, at the left), behind the Colorado Supply Company store. This picture was shot in 1902. Notice the barn and icehouse (to the left).

THE COLORADO SUPPLY COMPANY'S store interior held an excellent assortment of household items and groceries, which were personally gathered by the clerk (behind the counter) for customers to examine. Stools were next to the soda fountain. Notice the balcony where other goods were displayed.

DELL A. McCOY PHOTO

DURING 1958, the Redstone Country Store still retained its original exterior. The building was originally used as a barn, according to the 1903 property map of J. C. Osgood. The Elk Mountain Railway graded a right-of-way in front of this barn.

THE FIRST SCHOOLHOUSE in Redstone held classes in this building, constructed beside the Crystal River Railroad spur, near the icehouse. It was later used as a church, before the present structure was built.

JOHN B. SCHUTTE PHOTO

THE REDSTONE ICEHOUSE appears in this photograph, with a glimpse of the barn (at the left). Ice cut from ponds during the winter was stored inside the building, and it was used in "ice boxes" in the days before there were electric refrigerators. A team of horses and a wagon fitted with runners were on "River Road," known as Redstone Boulevard today (1992).

RICHARD A. RONZIO COLLECTION

THE REDSTONE CLUB building was located up the hill, beside East Creek. The clubhouse had a billiard and pool room, library and reading room, as well as a shower and bar — all on the main floor. A large auditorium, with a stage, occupied the second floor, where the band was posing. Their instruments were the best that money could buy, and they were all furnished by J. C. Osgood. Unfortunately, this once-fine building is now gone.

People are human, and men will act like boys:

The Marble Times & Crystal Silver Lance,
November 23, 1900.

A certain old gentleman presuming on the good understanding had with the Superintendent and Roadmaster, appropriated the latter's tricycle in order to interview an important witness in his election case. Everything ran smoothly until he picked up Mr. Horace Yewell, below the bridge. Mr. Y. was bound for home and had a lantern, and that lantern proved the undoing of both gentlemen. Getting below Janeway, Mr. Yewell, who became the engineer, gave his powerful muscles full play. Between mile posts 7 and 8 the party crashed into a car of steel rails; the tricycle raised at least 10 feet in the air, tumbled Mr. Y. in the ditch and powerfully embraced the O.G. in its ruins. It took the latter 5 minutes to extricate himself, his partner in the meantime unresponsive to his anxious enquiries. It developed that Mr. Yewell's respiratory organs had been brought to a stand still, but he finally recovered and proceeded to recover a shower of gold pieces sprinkled profusely over the road bed. The party appropriating the wheel returned to Redstone to make his peace with his superiors. He succeeded with the Roadmaster, but being leary of the Superintendent, kept dodging until Mr. Cornell overhauled him, when he paid his first reconing. As the wheel is a mass of smithereens, a hole being punched in the main iron wheel; the financial reconing, like the sword of Damocles, still hangs over him and threatens to absorb his "night school" earnings for the entire winter.

• • • • •

Continued on Page 75

"CAMP & PLANT" – THE CF&I COMPANY MAGAZINE

THE T. M. GIBB RESIDENCE in Redstone was located across from the Colorado Supply Company store. This was one of the largest houses in town (as illustrated in the view above, to the left). Medium-size homes are pictured (directly above), along with small, modest-size places, farther downriver (to the left), across from the Crystal River Railroad — which spanned the river on a through Howe-truss bridge (behind the houses in the view). The photograph below (at the left) was taken as the photographer was looking toward the north, along River Road (at about the center of town). Mount Sopris is in this view. The Redstone Fire Department (directly below) used a small hand-pumper, stationed at this firehouse, which was located high on the hillside, near East Creek.

THE REDSTONE PUBLIC SCHOOL was photographed sometime in 1903 at the main entrance, which faced east. A local quarry provided the rock for around the entrance (as shown above), and the main structure was of wooden-frame construction. These children had the advantage of obtaining an excellent education, not always found in Colorado's mining camps. Attention was given to the design of this structure, providing it with a friendly look — tucked-in among the trees of the forest, on the hillside overlooking the town.

By the end of 1900, the Crystal River Railroad had been completed to Placita and trains were running daily. The following time table shows that it took 2-1/2 hours to travel the line.

KENNETH JEYS COLLECTION

THIS PHOTOGRAPH (above, left) has been enlarged and printed across four pages (below and on the next two pages). The setting was in Redstone, beside the Crystal River. Coal Creek empties into the Crystal River at this point (at the lower left). The Colorado Fuel & Iron Company (CF&I) houses in Redstone had been built by J. C. Osgood. They can be seen across this view, from left to right. Notice the Pratt through-truss bridge on this page, which carried the Crystal River Railroad's mainline from Carbondale over the Crystal River. The boxcars had been spotted along the east bank of the river, to the rear of company houses. The public barn was on the west bank (at the far right). Coal Creek joins the Crystal River at the center of this view.

The Marble Times & Crystal Silver Lance,
December 7, 1900.
THE CRYSTAL RIVER R. R. Co.
Employees Time Table No. 8.

	South		North	
Miles	No. 1 Daily	Stations		No. 2 Daily
0	a.m. 10:05		Carbondale	p.m. 3:15
1.7	10:12	1.7	Grubbs	3:09
4.6	10:37	2.9	Cervera	2:57
10.5	11:01	5.9	Janeway	2:33
12.8	11:16	2.3	Hat Springs	2:24
16.6	11:31	3.8	Redstone	2:09
20.1	12:30	3.5	Placita	1:30
	p.m.			p.m.

John T. Kebler,   J.C. Cornell,
Gen'l Supt.   Supt.

The Marble Times & Crystal Silver Lance,
December 21, 1900.

Yesterday, the 20th day of December, 1900, was one of Redstone's red letter days. At ten o'clock a.m. a train load of coal arrived, under the immediate supervision of Master Mechanic and Acting Supt. Gibb, from the High Line. This is the first shipment of coal from Coal Basin, Denver newspapers to the contrary. It consisted of five of the new coal dumping cars, capacity 50,000 lbs. each, a total of 125 tons, and immediately passed through Redstone's new and immense tipple on its way to the coke ovens.

Continued on Page 84

BOXCARS ARE IN VIEW (below) up to the icehouse across these two pages. This was on a Crystal River Railroad spur on the town side of the river. The Colorado Supply Company store and Redstone Inn appear beyond the cars. More boxcars had been spotted along the CRR siding for loaded cars, which included a track scale for weighing cars (near the center), along the west bank. A number of cars appear at the right, along the beehive coke ovens, where carloads were ready to be moved over the scale and on into the holding yard (at the left). The wash house and carpenter shop were to the left of the Redstone depot. The coke ovens and the depot are at the far right, where a locomotive (out of the picture) was emitting coal smoke into the air. Nearly 100 boxcars and gondolas are present in this photograph, believed to have been taken in 1904. At this time, the Crystal River Railroad owned the railroad yard in Redstone, along with the line from Carbondale to Placita — as well as the narrow-gauge line between Redstone and Coalbasin. The Crystal River & San Juan Railroad interchanged their cars with the CRR at Redstone beginning in 1905, rather than at Placita, and they were hauled down the valley to Carbondale — where the Denver & Rio Grande (in turn) interchanged with the Crystal River line.

A FREIGHT TRAIN of merchandise had arrived in Redstone one day in 1902. The Crystal River Railroad's waycar (caboose) No. 1 — later the CR&SJ's No. 02 — was spotted beside the depot, where dual-gauge track was present to allow passengers from narrow-gauge trains to use the Redstone depot. Interchange of less-than-carload (l.c.l.) freight and mail was also facilitated by the use of dual-gauge track.

PHOTOGRAPHED DURING 1901, the Redstone coke ovens were in full production, all 200 of them. Two narrow-gauge Ingoldsby-patent dump cars had discharged their loads of Coalbasin coal on the trestle beside the coal-washer and screening plant.

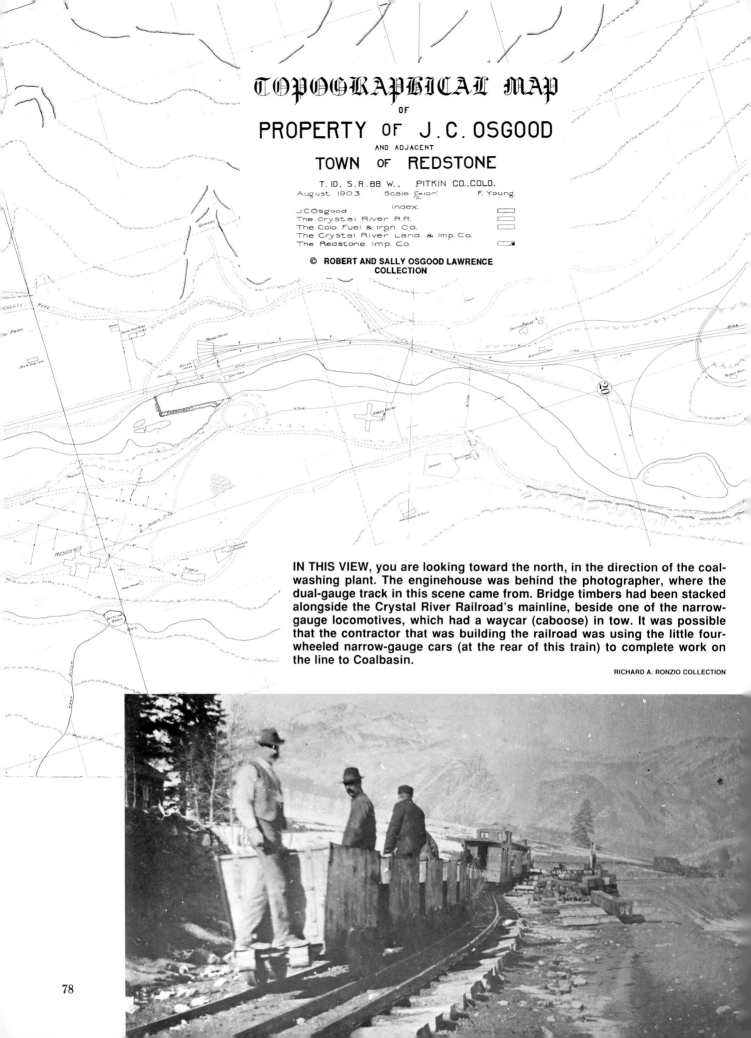

TOPOGRAPHICAL MAP
OF
PROPERTY OF J. C. OSGOOD
AND ADJACENT
TOWN OF REDSTONE

T. 10, S. R. 88 W., PITKIN CO., COLO.
August 1903   Scale 1"=100'   F. Young.

Index.

J.C.Osgood
The Crystal River R.R.
The Colo. Fuel & Iron Co.
The Crystal River Land & Imp. Co.
The Redstone Imp. Co.

IN THIS VIEW, you are looking toward the north, in the direction of the coal-washing plant. The enginehouse was behind the photographer, where the dual-gauge track in this scene came from. Bridge timbers had been stacked alongside the Crystal River Railroad's mainline, beside one of the narrow-gauge locomotives, which had a waycar (caboose) in tow. It was possible that the contractor that was building the railroad was using the little four-wheeled narrow-gauge cars (at the rear of this train) to complete work on the line to Coalbasin.

RICHARD A. RONZIO COLLECTION

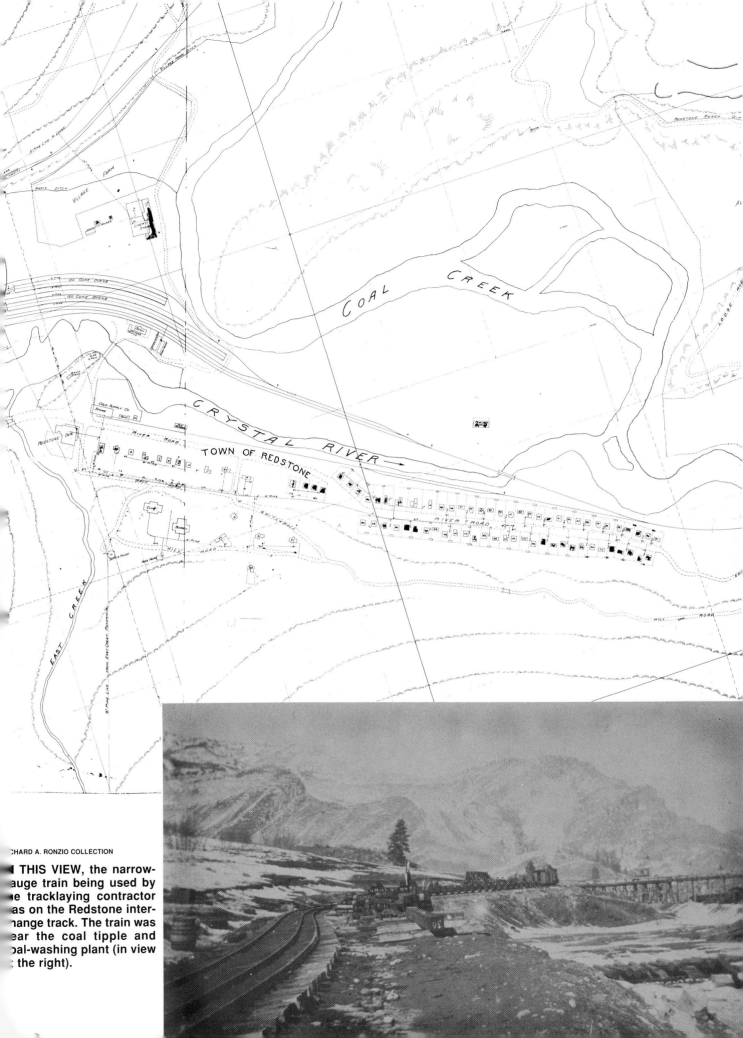

COAL CREEK

CRYSTAL RIVER

COAL CREEK

EAST CREEK

180 COKE OVENS

180 COKE OVENS

VILLAGE FARM

WASTE DITCH

COLD SUPPLY CO STORE

REDSTONE INN

RIVER ROAD

TOWN OF REDSTONE

CLUB

SCHOOL

SWITCHBACK

HILL ROAD

RIVER ROAD

HILL ROAD

REDSTONE RANCH DITCH

IN THIS VIEW, the narrow-gauge train being used by the tracklaying contractor was on the Redstone interchange track. The train was near the coal tipple and coal-washing plant (in view at the right).

THE PHOTOGRAPHER who shot this view was standing on the top platform of the coal-washing plant in Redstone as he aimed his camera toward the south, in the direction of Chair Mountain. Empty narrow-gauge Ingoldsby dump cars had been stored on the track leading to the coal-washing plant. The dual-gauge wye track was at the left, and the Coalbasin interchange track crossed-over to the right (hidden by weeds). A blacksmith shop was near the center of the scene.

THE REDSTONE YARD was photographed during September of 1911, at Milepost 17. At the far left was the blacksmith shop, and beyond it was the coal-washing plant, beside the dual-gauge siding, where two timber trestles crossed-over the mainline in a loop of track. Stored narrow-gauge Ingoldsby dump cars occupied the spur tracks. The mainline between Carbondale and Marble was next to the county road (at the right).

THIS WATER STANDPIPE for locomotive tenders received its water supply from Coal Creek, although it stood beside the Crystal River Railroad's mainline in Redstone. Notice the Redstone Inn, which is located across the Crystal River (at the left).

THE CRYSTAL RIVER RAILROAD'S enginehouse in Redstone was built in the style of a roundhouse, but it was minus a turntable. Engines were turned on a wye, instead. The enginehouse contained three stalls and could house narrow-gauge locomotives (at the left), as well as standard-gauge engines. The far-left stall could interchange narrow- and standard-gauge trucks under the rotary snowplow. The Gamekeeper's Lodge and barn were located to the right, as this photograph of 1901 shows.

NARROW-GAUGE LOCOMOTIVE No. 103 arrived on the Crystal River Railroad on April 18, 1903. This heavier outside-frame 2–8–0 steam engine allowed the railroad to increase their uphill trains to 10 empties, whereas Nos. 101 and 102 could pull only seven cars each. Link-and-pin couplers were used on the narrow-gauge Coalbasin line until its end in 1909. Note: The Colorado Fuel & Iron Company's magazine, "Camp and Plant," printed the name "Coalbasin" as one word, rather than "Coal Basin," as found on USGS maps and printed elsewhere. The publisher has decided to use the company magazine's rendering of this name.

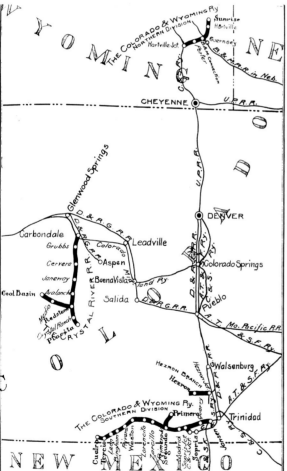

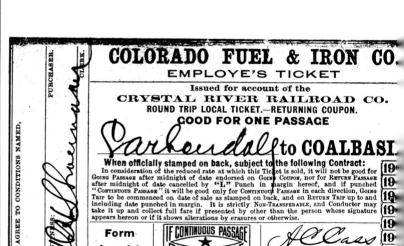

Crystal River Railroad "High Line"

BY DELL A. McCOY

Coalbasin
TURNTABLE
MEDIO
BEAVER PONDS
COW CAMP
COAL CREEK
Redston

THE CRYSTAL RIVER narrow-gauge 2–8–0, No. 102, was brand new in this picture, just out of the Baldwin Locomotive Works when she posed for this view in 1899. The slope-back tender was preferred for switching cars in freight yards, to provide better visibility back along the tender.

THE INGOLDSBY-PATENT dump cars were photographed after completion, with the drop-bottom doors in the open position, hinged from the center. The car was made primarily of wood, with steel support members. In the lower view, car No. 246 had been placed on a standard-gauge flatcar for shipment. Notice the operating end, showing hand levers, locks, air-dumping device, "U"-trussrod saddle and the door-raising gear, with safety disengagement. The first lot of 40 cars was shipped on October 30, 1900, while the second lot of 10 cars was shipped on November 15, 1902.

The Marble Times & Crystal Silver Lance,
January 4, 1901.

During the past year the Crystal River Railroad has done an immense business for a railroad in a new country, and its in-coming and out-going business shows material increase over 1899. The main line was not extended any during the year, but the road bed and equipment shows marked improvement, until today it is one of the smoothest running and best equipped mountain road in Colorado.

The Coal Basin branch, or the High Line as it is called, was completed last month [December 1900]. This is narrow gauge and runs a distance of 12 miles from Redstone to the coal banks in the basin, and the road is equipped with the latest improved patent dump cars. Traversing as it does one of the most rugged canons in the state the scenic features of this road are not surpassed by any in the West as to its grandeur. The construction of this piece of road is one of the greatest engineering feats of the nineteenth century, and is the pride of the officers of the Colorado Fuel company. In the 12 miles there are 22 bridges used in crossing and re-crossing this grand canon, and the loops, twists and curves are wonderful to behold while the iron horse is crawling slowly on its way up into the basin.

The Marble Times & Crystal Silver Lance,
February 8, 1901.

8 February 1901. The coal train on Sunday, from Coal basin, consisted of 11 cars containing 275 tons. Supt. Griffith is speedily increasing the output.

• • • • •

From the time the railroad reached Placita, the residents of Marble were constantly pushing to have it extended the last seven miles to Marble. Since the C.F.&I. was primarily interested in coal, there was not the economic incentive to extend this line. By February 1901 rumors were building.

The Marble Times & Crystal Silver Lance,
February 22, 1901.

Reports are current that at the present time the prospects are bright for the completion of the Crystal River Railroad into Marble the coming summer. For the past ten years, especially when the snow is deepest, the same rumors have floated around, and have not materialized so far; however, it is unquestionably true that just now all things look brighter for railroad extension up this valley than at any period in the history of the district, and we sincerely hope the first year of the twentieth century will fulfill all of our expectations in this regard.

• • • • •

J.C. Osgood during this time period was doing development work on the marble beds along Yule Creek and thus the anticipation was always present. His activities with the marble continued after 1900 even though he was fully occupied with getting the Coal Basin mines producing. So, when the following notice appeared in July 1905 excitement began to build.

Continued on Page 107

CRYSTAL RIVER narrow-gauge locomotive No. 103 was heading upgrade to Coalbasin with seven empty Ingoldsby automatic-dump cars. One of the railroad's sidedoor waycars was on the tail-end of the train, photographed at Milepost 2, . The head-end brakeman rode the cowcatcher to watch for rocks or trees that might have fallen onto the track.

BRIDGE NO. 3 on the Crystal River Railroad was just above Milepost 3. It was the second crossing of Coal Creek above Redstone, on the Coalbasin Branch. This span was a through wooden Howe-truss bridge, with wrought-iron tension rods running vertically. Notice the mortarless stone piers in these two photographs taken during September of 1911.

AT MILEPOST NO. 4 the Coal Creek Valley opened up where the narrow-gauge Coalbasin Branch made an extremely tight "S" curve and crossed three bridges. This freight train, with a load of bridge ties and steel bridge girders, was heading upgrade, with a locomotive cut into the middle of the train.

THE LONGEST BRIDGE on the Coalbasin Branch was located at Milepost 4.6, just below Cow Camp. This span was known as Bridge E-4. This bridge was constructed as a deck Howe-truss, which rested on cut-stone piers. Vertical tension rods can be easily seen along the span. Timber-bridge bents were used as approaches. In this view you are looking toward the north. Notice the erosion beneath the approaches.

CRYSTAL RIVER RAILROAD waycar No. 02 brought-up the rear of this freight train, which was hauling a load of bridge ties and steel-support members — presumably for the last crossing of Coal Creek, at the coal-tipple car loader in Coalbasin. This view was taken in the vicinity of Milepost 5, where a bridge crossed Coal Creek, above Cow Camp.

IT IS BELIEVED that this water tank was located at Medio, not far below Milepost 8, where a passing track was provided. With the continuous 4.0-percent grade out of Redstone, the smaller water reservoirs in the tenders of Nos. 101 and 102 were soon depleted, as a result of the climb from Redstone. A glimpse of the hillside above Coalbasin can be seen below the spout. A few cabins were located here for caretakers.

ROTARY SNOWPLOW AB2 of the Crystal River Railroad was being moved downgrade from Coalbasin by Nos. 101 and 102, in order to open-up the line after a heavy snowfall. The train is in the vicinity of Milepost 10.

HEADING FOR THE HEIGHTS of Coalbasin in 1903, narrow-gauge locomotive No. 103 was nearing the last horseshoe loop, midway between Mileposts 10 and 11. The ridge of hills surrounding Coalbasin are behind this train of empty cars.

ROUNDING THE LAST horseshoe loop, midway between Mileposts 10 and 11, this snow-fighting train was moving downgrade, with rotary snowplow No. AB2 on the head-end. The last three balloon-loop curves measured 265 feet in diameter — very sharp, even for narrow-gauge locomotives and cars.

CRYSTAL RIVER RAILROAD engine No. 102 had the lettering "Columbine Route" on the cab panel. She was posed with a downgrade train of coal, midway between Mileposts 10 and 11. The train crew, including the engineer, fireman and two brakemen, posed for the occasion. The hilltop behind the train is in back of Coalbasin. On the right-hand page, the photographer had moved down to the lower level for a view of the passing train of Ingoldsby dump cars. This train will eventually swing into view on this level.

IN THIS OVERALL VIEW of Coalbasin, taken in 1901, final finishing work was underway on the shed covering the funicular tramway line that lead to the coal-mine opening above the camp (to the right). This trestle was 1,400 feet in length. The old original part of this coal camp at Coalbasin stood just beyond the tramway line. Slag waste had been dumped beneath the two trestles (at the center). The end-of-track on the narrow-gauge branch was at the covered turntable (at the upper left). A string of five empty Ingoldsby dump cars sat in front of the ice-house, located beyond the mainline. The Coalbasin depot stood beyond the tramway trestle (near the center). The Colorado Supply Company store, No. 26, stood beyond seven carloads of coal, spotted on the siding (near the center). Newer homes constructed in Coalbasin appear in this scene (in the foreground). The Coalbasin Club was standing beside the mainline (at the far left).

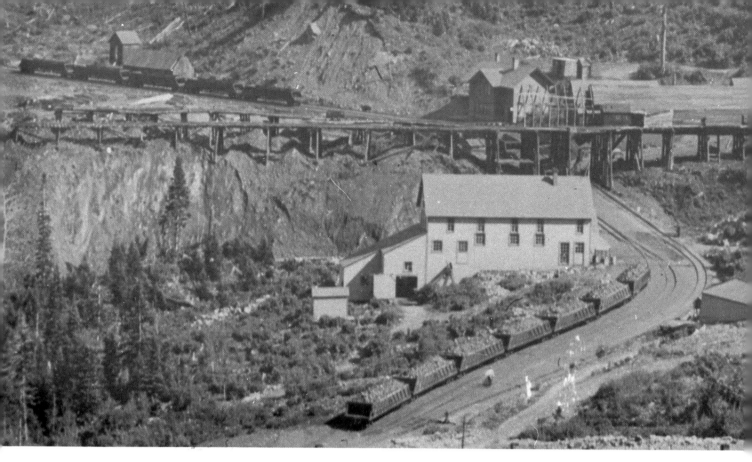

THE PRINT ABOVE is an enlarged section of the previous page and shows the icehouse and Coalbasin depot, beyond the funicular tramway that led to the coal mine. The Colorado Supply Company store, No. 26, can be seen beyond the string of loaded Ingoldsby dump cars, which had been spotted on the siding.

THIS COALBASIN PHOTOGRAPH was taken in 1904, and it shows additional homes that were built along a tributary creek, which fed into Coal Creek (shown in the foreground). Notice the Crystal River Railroad bridge. The covered turntable is visible (at the upper left), with a glimpse of the rotary snowplow nearby. The Coalbasin depot and funicular tramway to the coalmine opening (portal) appear in the distant background of this view.

A YOUNG OFFSPRING of one of the coal-mine burros was being admired at Coalbasin by visitors. At the left, the Colorado Supply Company store could be seen in this view of 1900. The mine had just commenced operations, as indicated by the small slag pile beyond the coal tipple (at the left). Ingoldsby-patent dump cars were allowed to drift downgrade by hand, to be spotted beneath the coal chutes for loading. They were then worked by hand onto the holding yard for a locomotive to pick them up.

ENGINE NO. 102 was spotted on the last bridge that crossed Coal Creek in Coalbasin. She was on the main-line track, pausing beneath the coal tipple. One of the two side-door waycars had been tacked-on behind the engine tender. The train probably had delivered seven empty cars in the holding yard below the turntable, and the crew was waiting for a few more loads before starting downgrade to Redstone. Notice the Ingoldsby dump car beneath the coal chutes.

THE COALBASIN SCHOOLHOUSE had 11 children in attendance when this photograph was produced during March of 1902. Dr. W. E. Ashby, resident surgeon, paid a visit while the teacher, Miss Josephine Macbeth, stood in the doorway.

IN AN ATTEMPT to have sober workers in Coalbasin, J. C. Osgood established the Coalbasin Club, shown in these two photographs. The club was located next to the track, with a short spur running in back for coal-fired stoves in the camp and for use at the club. The Coalbasin Club had a card-and-game room, with a separate reading room. Although bottled liquor was served here, a "no-treating" rule was enforced, in order to keep the men on their jobs. This also reduced the chances of accidents happening. Women and children could not enter the club except by permission of the board of directors.

RUSS COLLMAN PHOTO

THIS PLEASANT LOCATION is on the Coalbasin "High Line," near Milepost 6. Aspen trees abound in this area, which had been logged out. This is one of the most beautiful hikes in Colorado, along the old narrow-gauge grade, with very few obstacles en route.

ROTARY SNOWPLOW NO. AB2 had been placed on the special spur laid for it at the end of the Coalbasin Branch. The turntable was inside this covered building, constructed to protect it from the heavy snowfalls at this altitude, which was nearly 10,000 feet above sea level. This tail track allowed upgrade trains to switch their empties in the holding yard, behind the photographer.

MARJORIE AND ERNEST GERBAZ COLLECTION

97

THE CRYSTAL RIVER rotary snowplow appeared to have been moved onto the yard track used to hold empty coal cars, a short distance from the covered turntable. A plume of smoke gives evidence that one of the locomotives was at the end-of-track. In this view, where you are looking toward the east, preparations were underway to open-up the yard tracks, as well as the mainline on down to Redstone.

WORKING DOWNGRADE from the covered turntable, the Crystal River rotary snowplow was being put to work to open the mainline past the holding yard for empty coal cars. An engine and waycar were in the yard, at the rear of this string of Ingoldsby dump cars.

THIS IS ONE of the first views taken of Coalbasin, near the end-of-track. The photographer was looking toward the west. The depot in Coalbasin had not yet been built, which would later be at the left of the mainline that had been recently plowed open. A second siding, covered by snow, lay between the mainline and the snow-fighting train (at the right). This yard was laid with eight-foot crossties, which touched each other end-to-end, giving no clearance for brakemen on the sides of cars.

THE INGOLDSBY-PATENT dump cars were given a severe cold-weather test in Coalbasin during the winter of 1900. The crew had coupled rotary snowplow No. AB2 on the front of this snow-fighting train, with Engines 101 and 102, Waycars 01 and 02 and Flanger B1 following. The waycars were used as the conductor's office and for sheltering the train crew. The flanger was coupled onto the rear to clear snow, in case the train must back up. The train is on the mainline in Coalbasin, having passed under the coal tipple.

DELL A. McCOY PHOTO

SNOW-CAPPED MOUNT SOPRIS is in view, to the north of this location along the sparkling Crystal River. It is summer, and the water is crystal-clear. You are looking toward Redstone, downriver, in this scene photographed near the site of J. C. Osgood's ranch.

A ROCK RETAINING WALL had been constructed alongside the Crystal River Railroad's standard-gauge mainline, at J. C. Osgood's ranch above Redstone. This provided protection for his private car, the "Sunrise," which had a siding located here.

DELL A. McCOY PHOTO

THIS WAS THE SECOND standard-gauge 2–8–0 locomotive owned by the Crystal River Railroad — the second No. 1. This engine had 50-inch driving wheels and a large boiler. The fancy "Columbine Route" herald was painted on the cab side, below the engineer's window. Notice the rather small tender, which was considered large enough for the short run up and down the Crystal River Valley. Combination coach No. 1 was coupled-on behind, to bring passengers, less-than-carload (l.c.l.) freight and mail into Redstone. The train had stopped beside the wash house and carpenters' shop.

THE FIREMAN'S SIDE of the Crystal River Railroad's locomotive No. 1 was nearly identical to the far side. Notice the three-pocket link-and-pin coupler setup on the pilot beam, which provided for coupling with narrow-gauge equipment in Redstone. This husky 2–8–0 was originally Colorado & Wyoming No. 7 and was christened the "Bull-of-the-Woods" because of the unusual-sounding whistle that had been fitted on the engine. Reportedly, the whistle came off of a Mississippi River steamboat, and it had a moan like a bull about to break down an oak gate!

CRYSTAL RIVER & SAN JUAN locomotive No. 1 performed the sad duty of pulling the salvage train, which removed the rail between Marble and Carbondale in 1942. Freshly-fallen snow lay on blocks of marble used as rip-rap along the railroad grade — photographed here near Hays Creek Falls. The former Crystal River narrow-gauge boxcar, No. 101, was on standard-gauge trucks for the use of the CR&SJ.

THE STATION BUILDING of the Crystal River Railroad at Redstone was 16.6 miles from Carbondale, as shown on the station sign above the train-order semaphore signal. The telegraph operator inside the bay-window section of the depot operated the signal "board" to either the red or green position for train engineers. This train-order board is displaying red. The wooden-frame depot very closely resembles the Denver & Rio Grande structure at Carbondale. Passengers could enter the waiting room through the trackside door. This depot served the Crystal River's narrow-gauge Coal Basin Branch, as well as the standard-gauge main-line. Notice the third rail for narrow-gauge traffic on the mainline track in front of the depot. This picture was taken during September of 1911.

LEASED LOCOMOTIVE No. 701 of the Colorado & Wyoming Railroad, a 4–6–0, was photographed ca. 1912, near Hays Creek Falls. The engine was hauling a train-load of marble on flatcars. It was unusual to find that the engineer had cut the locomotive into the middle of this train of cars for the trip to Carbondale. Perhaps the marble was waste rock to be used for rip-rap along the river bank.

NEAR HAYS CREEK FALLS, men hired by Morse Brothers Machinery Company were busy pulling spikes, in preparation for removing rail up onto the flatcars with a winch, housed on the forward flatcar. The rather rough-and-rocky automobile road is visible (at the left). Notice the former narrow-gauge boxcar No. 101, tacked on behind CR&SJ engine No. 1.

LOOKING TOWARD THE SOUTH, up the Crystal River, Chair Mountain stands tall at the end of the valley — causing the river to turn from the east — to eventually empty into the Roaring Fork of the Colorado River at Carbondale. This location is a short distance upriver from Redstone.

IMPOSING CHAIR MOUNTAIN forms the rugged skyline in this view, where the photographer was looking up the Crystal River. The original wagon road to Marble and Crystal City was above the track of the Crystal River & San Juan. A wooden Howe-truss bridge carried the track over the river, which you can see in about the center of this view. This photograph was obtained from a point a short distance above Redstone, near Hays Creek Falls.

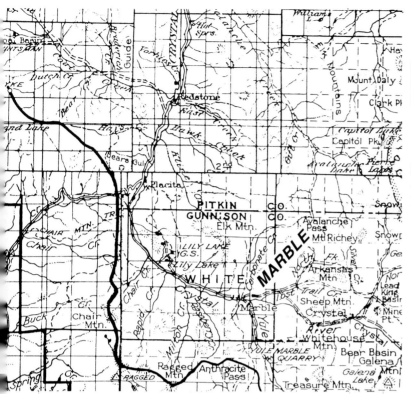

CRYSTAL RIVER & SAN JUAN RAILROAD

TIME TABLE
— 1922 —

Train No. 21			S T A T I O N S	Train No. 22		
LV	7:45	a.m.	CARBONDALE	AR	7:00	p.m
AR	8:55	"	REDSTONE	"	5:45	"
"	9:05	"	Crystal Ranch	"	5:39	"
"	9:15	"	Placita	"	5:31	"
"	9:20	"	McClures	"	5:25	"
"	9:30	"	Chair Creek	"	5:18	"
"	9:35	"	Prospect	"	5:14	"
"	9:45	"	Holland	"	5:09	"
"	9:53	"	Fortschs	"	5:04	"
"	10:00	"	MARBLE	LV	5:00	"

Crystal River Current,
July 7, 1905.

Surveyors McClung and Miller have been in camp all week estimating the cost of finishing the railroad from Placita up here for the Colorado Yule Creek Marble Co. and all of our citizens pray it will be completed.

Crystal River Current,
July 28, 1905.

Yule Creek Railway. On the 19th [July 1905] articles of incorporation were filed with the secretary of state by the Yule Creek Railway company and the capital stock is placed at $200,000. The promoters of this new road are G.W. Bowen, S.I. Heyn, Pope Clark, Alfred E. Davis and Rolla E. Black of Denver, and J.B. Bowen and W.R. Jewell of Redstone. The road is to run through Garfield, Pitkin and Gunnison counties. It will begin at Bryant in Garfield county on the line of the Colorado Midland and follow the Crystal river to its confluence with Yule creek. It will then follow this creek to its source.

• • • • •

This line was never built between Carbondale and Marble. The portion from Marble up Yule Creek was constructed to the Strauss marble quarries on the east side of Yule Creek. **The Marble City Times of 29 April 1910** reported this start.

Next week Clough & Cloug will begin completing the Crystal River Marble company's broad [standard] gauge railroad, known as the Treasury Mountain road. They are expected Monday with all necessary aparates for beginning work.

• • • • •

A year later the line was completed and operating though it is not clear how long and how much it ran. **The Booster** reported that:

The Marble Booster,
June 17, 1911.

John J. Jarrell has taken his old place as conductor on the Treasury Mountain railway. Joe Hall is again at the engine throttle.

• • • • •

When Col. Channing F. Meek purchased the marble beds on the west side of Yule Creek in 1905 he organized the Crystal River & San Juan Railroad to extend the line of the Crystal River Railroad the last seven miles into Marble. He then operated the two lines as one, as the C.R.& S.J. The rails, laid by imported Japanese laborers, finally reached Marble on 23 November 1906 and the town went wild with enthusiasm. Now there was nothing standing in the way of realizing their dream of a constantly expanding marble industry and lots of jobs.

The long-awaited solution to the transportation needs of the upper valley had finally arrived, and the Marble residents enjoyed the convenient train travel to Carbondale and beyond. But after a few years, they began to take the railroad for granted and assumed the trains ran for their convenience. Though the Coal Basin mines had closed J.C. Osgood still spent some time in Redstone and had some influence. He considered he had some personal prerogatives and did not hesitate to ask for special consideration. This did not set well with the editor of **The Marble Booster** and other Marbleites, as the following headlines of 11 January 1913 indicate:

"My! The Power This Man Has." "Anything Mr. John C. Osgood wants, he has to Have." "While 1500 Souls Wait." "Marble People are Deprived of Mail, Express, Freight and Passengers while C.R. & S.J. Does an Errand for Mr. Osgood."

Sane, sober and conservative people no doubt wonder sometimes what condition of mind so inflames a man that he will stick a gun in one pocket and a dagger in the other and go forth to slay a fancied enemy who belongs to what he is pleased to term the plutocratic class. Every so often something like this happens. Through a series of experiences, Marble people have come to a partial realization of how a man not entirely right in his upper story might

APPROACHING PLACITA, Colorado Highway 133 is in view (at the right), on what was formerly the grade of the Crystal River & San Juan Railroad. Chair Mountain is partially hidden behind the foreground hills in this autumn view, taken during September, about 10 years ago.

AFTER ABANDONMENT PROCEEDINGS had been granted by the Interstate Commerce Commission in September of 1941, CR&SJ trains continued to carry loads of marble down the valley to Carbondale before winter set in. On November 11, 1941, CR&SJ locomotive No. 1, two gondolas with loads of marble, a wooden boxcar and the combine (No. 9) climbed the short grade out of Placita. Waste blocks of marble re-enforced the grade against high water in the nearby river. The Placita coal bunker is visible at the curve in the mainline.

get up the indignation to bump off a bloated aristocrat. We wonder what creates anarchy; Marble people know something of the reasons, though, since the removal of a certain person [Sylvia Smith] last March, there are no anarchists in the town.

Last Wednesday the superintendent of the C.R. & S.J. railway here had orders from Denver to hold the Marble train at Carbondale for the private car of Mr. John C. Osgood. The train was held. When Mr. Osgood's car arrived late in the afternoon further orders were given to hook the engine of the Marble train to it, run up to Redstone with it and get Mrs. Osgood and return with her to Carbondale. The orders were obeyed.

The Marble train arrived here, after this errand-boy performance, at about 7:15 at night, instead of 10 o'clock in the morning, when it was due. The United States mail was delayed in distribution until after 8:15 o'clock at night.

A town of 1,500 people waited on the pleasure of one aristocrat—Mr. John C. Osgood. The train crews worked longer hours than the law permits, the postoffice people stayed over time, the transfer men had to dig into the merchandise car in the night and get out the perishable freight and deliver it to avoid freezing, while other freight and express was not delivered until the following day; passengers for Marble were held up in Carbondale all day, with extra expense for meals, and a great deal of extra trouble was made all around. And all because Mr. John C. Osgood had to have his private car sent up to Redstone to take Mrs. Osgood out on silken cushions.

Why [sic] the devil is this man Osgood, anyway? Is he some titled potentate, or is it a case of ME and god? This isn't the first time Marble has had to suffer for this man's convenience. Last summer a trainload of excursionists bound to Carbondale with a brass band to attend a big

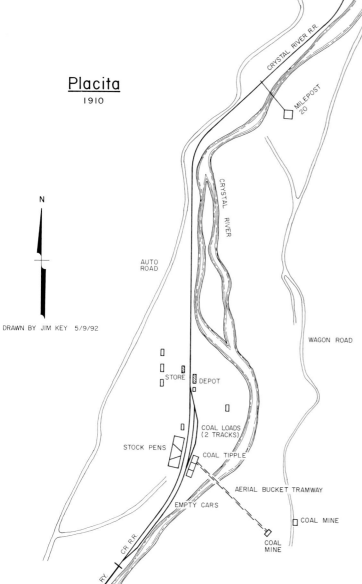

Placita
1910

N

DRAWN BY JIM KEY 5/9/92

CRYSTAL RIVER R.R.

MILEPOST 20

CRYSTAL RIVER

AUTO ROAD

WAGON ROAD

STORE

DEPOT

COAL LOADS (2 TRACKS)

STOCK PENS

COAL TIPPLE

AERIAL BUCKET TRAMWAY

EMPTY CARS

COAL MINE

COAL MINE

CR&SJ RY.

CR R.R.

THE ABANDONED DEPOT of the Crystal River Railroad at Placita was photographed during September, 1911. The mainline ran past this side of the structure, where the train-order board (signal) support rod hung off the wall. The Crystal River is in the background. This was the end of the line for the Crystal River Railroad, which leased running rights to the Crystal River & San Juan Railroad from Placita to Redstone, where the CR&SJ interchanged rolling stock and returned to Marble. Paint samples from this depot indicate that it had been painted freight-car red.

banquet were held at Redstone on account of that same private car until they missed the banquet. Even the nigger cook on the car was careful to see that he didn't get any marble dust in his clothes as he occasionally stuck his kinky head out. What do you think of it, fellow worms?

• • • • •

This was a rather unusual diatribe on the part of Frank Frost, the editor, as he usually was able to be more objective and keep a cool head. But Osgood was not directly concerned with Marble at this time and his patience wore thin. Col. Meek had died as a result of a trolley runaway, and the marble company was having financial difficulties, which threatened jobs and the security of the economy in Marble.

Changes in the Denver & Rio Grande schedule from Glenwood Springs to Denver resulted in suspension of the "stub" train to Carbondale since the eastbound train left Glenwood at 4:10 a.m. This forced Marble travelers to take the Midland, which left Carbondale about the same time the Marble train arrived, and the depots were a mile and a half apart. This problem got the attention of the local authorities and on 12 April 1913:

THE SMALL SETTLEMENT of Placita was photographed during the 1920's, where miners' families occupied the dwellings. In 1924 two coal mines produced anthracite coal here. The Placita depot, complete with a station sign on the north wall, is visible near the center of this picture. Notice the coal-mine portal — with a wooden platform — against the hillside, across the Crystal River. Aerial-tramway cable reached across the the river to the coal tipple (at the far right), where a bucket was hanging from the cable. Coal was still being trucked out of here until sometime in the 1950's. Howard Holgate related that the mine on the opposite side of the valley blew up twice from methane gas, and it was abandoned. However, in the mine shown in this view, he was personally digging coal, and it was so free of gas that he could use open-flame lamps. Curiously, the coal from this mine melted as it burned, and old-timers said it was excellent blacksmithing coal.

1918

1917   No. A 85

THE CRYSTAL RIVER RAILROAD CO.

PASS Mr. J. J. Ford

ACCOUNT Com'l Agent, N Y C Lines

BETWEEN All Stations

UNTIL DECEMBER 31ST   1917 { UNLESS OTHERWISE ORDERED AND SUBJECT TO CONDITIONS ON BACK

VALID WHEN COUNTERSIGNED BY L. B. HAIL
COUNTERSIGNED BY

VICE PRESIDENT AND GEN'L MANAGER

The Marble Booster
April 12, 1913.

R.J. Woodward, local general manager of the C.R. & S.J., has been trying to run the trains on his road so that connection could be made with the Midland and to that end he made arrangements with the transfer line at Carbondale to be in waiting at the street crossing near the Dinkel store as the Marble train came into Carbondale. The train is stopped at the crossing and passengers and express transferred with the minimum loss of time.

Mr. Woodward says further that an offer has been made to the Col. C.F. Meek estate for the automobile the Colonel owned and that if it is accepted car trucks will be placed on the machine and it will be converted into a passenger carrying conveyance, making a trip each afternoon, for passengers only, to Carbondale, leaving here at 1 o'clock p.m. and returning at 6 o'clock.

• • • • •

Weather conditions were often severe in the valley and the trains were harassed by mud slides and heavy snows. The incident reported in February 1916 was not unusual.

Continued on Page 117

A CLOSER VIEW of the Placita coal-mine operation shows greater detail of the coal tipple, which had two chutes. The coal bucket was tripped (or "tippled") so the coal would be unloaded into the storage bin. Metal aprons were lowered at the front edge of the chutes so that coal could tumble out into railroad gondolas on the siding. A track gang's push car had been pushed off the track to the edge of the grade. A wooden foot bridge (badly in need of repair) crossed the Crystal River to provide access to the mine on the hillside above the river.

CRYSTAL RIVER & SAN JUAN locomotive No. 1 was taking a load of anthracite coal in its tender at Placita when this photograph was taken. This was during the last years of the railroad's operation.

IN THE VIEW BELOW, you can see that there were two coal tipples at Placita during the last years of the mine's operation. The tipple at the right presumably was constructed by Howard Holgate because the old tipple was too small. Holgate trucked coal to customers in the area. A conveyor belt was in the angled part of the new structure (at the right) so that coal could be loaded into the bunker from the shed.

ALTHOUGH THE COAL MINE at Placita and the railroad had been abandoned by 1958, when these views were photographed, the original tipple was still standing, along with the later addition. The weathered logs (at the right) were part of the old livestock pens. Chair Mountain is in view (at the right).

THE PLACITA COAL TIPPLE was photographed from another vantage point revealing the south side for model builders. It appears that a conveyor-belt setup carried coal into the open bunker for coal storage. The Placita mine provided anthracite (hard) coal, with which the railroad also used for its engine tenders.

TAKEN FROM THE EAST BANK of the Crystal River, Placita had this appearance during the 1920's. At the far left, the coal tipple had a railroad gondola beneath its chute, being loaded on the siding. Livestock pens were located to the right of the tracks. At the center of the view you can see the old Crystal River Railroad's depot, with a lean-to attached to the east wall. The station sign had been mounted on the north wall of this little wooden depot.

BY THE TIME the Morse Brothers Machinery Company was on the scene at Placita, a second coal tipple had been constructed — several years before 1942 — south of the existing tipple. A smokejack for a potbelly stove appears on the roof of boxcar No. 101, spotted on the mainline, with a string of flatcars loaded with rail. Stock pens are at the right, and snow-covered Chair Mountain rises above the valley .

DELL A. McCOY PHOTO

SPRING HAD ARRIVED in the Crystal River Valley when this color view was taken at Placita. Only a few original buildings remained in what was formerly a coal-mining camp. Originally, this place was owned and operated by the Colorado Fuel & Iron Company, under the supervision of J. C. Osgood.

The Marble Booster
February 5, 1916.

Digging out R.R. Train left here last Friday at 10 a.m. and didn't get to Carbondale until 3:20 Monday morning. When the Crystal River & San Juan train left here last Friday morning, enroute to Carbondale on the daily trip, it was in the teeth of a storm that had been raging all night, snowing hard, and there was some doubt as to whether the train would get through. Had the management of the road known just what the train was going up against it is doubtful if they would have sent it out at all.

Leaving here, the train carried a crew of twenty-five snow shovelers and before they got to the lower end of the Marble yards these workmen were called into service. Late that afternoon the train had reached the bridge over the creek at Prospect, a scant four miles from Marble. Through the cut this side of Prospect, alongside the Gibb ranch, the snow had drifted in to a depth of seven and eight feet. The engine ran out of water at Prospect and the crew tied up the train there and walked back to town. Aside from two time-keepers at the mill, there were no passengers on the train.

Continued on Page 120

117

WORKMEN HIRED by the Morse Brothers Machinery Company prepared to dismantle a rail frog at the turnout (switch) for the Placita coal tipple, which is in view beyond the dismantling crew. It is interesting to notice the variations of grade at Placita, with its ups and downs. The siding had been slightly elevated at this end so that railroad gondolas could be rolled by gravity to the coal chutes and beyond.

Crystal River & San Juan Railroad

TRI-WEEKLY

TUESDAY
THURSDAY
SATURDAY

TRAIN SHEET

Time Table No.   Marble, Colo., APRIL 16   1940

EASTBOUND						WESTBOUND		
			2	TRAIN	I			
				ENGINE	I			
				CONDUCTOR SMITH				
				BRAKEMAN SMITH				
			Distance	ENGINEER CHIDESTER	Distance			
				FIREMAN WALTHER				
				TIME ORDERED FOR 8:00 A				
Dep	Dep	Dep 7:15 A	0	MARBLE TOW	27.5	Ar 2:00 P	Ar	Ar
				7.4				
		7:46 A	7.4	PLACITA	20.1	1:35 P		
				3.5				
		8:10 A	10.9	REDSTONE YW	16.6	12:50 P		
				6.1				
		8:35 A	17	JANEWAY	10.5	12:15 P		
				5.9				
		8:55 A	22.9	SEWELL	4.6	11:50 A		
				2.9				
		9:05 A	25.8	GRUBBS	1.7	11:40 A		
				1.7				
Ar	Ar	Ar 9:15 A	27.5	CARBONDALE Y	0	Dep 11:30 A	Dep	Dep

DELL A. McCOY PHOTOS

THIS GROUP of photographs was taken at the pithead of the Placita coal mine in 1958. The mine was above the mining camp, and three sides of the structure appear in this view, perched on the hillside above the Crystal River. Two of the mine's tramway coal-dump cars were outside the portal.

LOOKING SOUTH from the edge of Placita, Chair Mountain begins to recede behind the foreground rock formation, where the highway climbs over McClure Pass. This is the location where the Crystal River bends to the right, as it cascades down through the hills from Marble and Crystal City. This Indian-summer scene is typical of the colorful display the aspen trees present every autumn in the Crystal River Valley.

Saturday morning the crew and shovelers walked down to Prospect, melted snow to give water for the engine, and started again, reaching the Placita cut, adjacent to the stockyards, at 7 o'clock that night. After supper at the Placita mine the train got under way again and late that night reached the Williams ranch at a point nine miles this side of Carbondale, where the engine ran off the track on a crossing which was covered with ice beneath deep snow. An hour's work put it on the rails again and a fresh start was made, only to run off again on another crossing half a mile further on the Johnson ranch. This time the engine ran completely off, taking the front trucks of the caboose with it.

This last derailment tied the train up tight and the crews and shovelers abandoned it and set out on a foraging trip for something to eat. It was then 10:30 at night but the people at the ranch house were awakened and supplied food and hot coffee. All hands, after taking food, then went back to the caboose, built up a hot fire and spent the remainder of the night there. The first thing Sunday morning they tapped a wire and telegraphed to George B. Taylor at Marble the condition of affairs. Mr. Taylor wired for the wrecking car of the Denver & Rio Grande railroad at Glenwood which arrived at the scene of the derailment at 11:20 Sunday morning and set to work to get the train back on the track again. Working steadily, it was 1:30 o'clock Monday morning when the train was ready to proceed again and at 3:20 Monday morning the Marble train reached Carbondale, having been on the way since 10 o'clock the previous Friday morning, covering the thirty miles.

The crew and shovelers rested there until 11:45 that

ELMORE FREDERICK COLLECTION

DURING THE WINTER of 1908, heavy snow blocked the CR&SJ track into Marble, and the Crystal River Railroad's rotary snowplow came to the rescue. The rotary plow was probably assisted with one or more Denver & Rio Grande locomotives. The Crystal River snowplow, No. AB2, was later purchased by the D&RG and was renumbered "OO" ("double-oh"), where it was used on narrow-gauge lines — normally stationed in Gunnison. In use on the Crystal River, this plow was interchanged by switching narrow-gauge trucks to standard-gauge trucks, according to the need. This photograph was discovered inside the carriage house owned by Elmore Frederick during 1972, after Sundance Publications began to remodel the place for the company's second business location.

McCLURE FLATS on occasion would drift deep with snow, and on this particular day in 1916, CR&SJ engine No. 1 stopped to be photographed, with the snow level up near the top of the locomotive boiler.

COLLECTION OF THE LATE WILLIAM McMANUS

CR&SJ LOCOMOTIVE No. 2 was photographed with a southbound mixed train on September 6, 1941. The short train consisted of three freight cars and a passenger car. As always, the combination baggage-coach, No. 9, was coupled onto the rear of the train for the conductor and occasional passengers. Cookman Chidester opened the throttle for the climb up the 3.0-percent grade to Camp Genter — with the Yule Colorado Marble Company side-dump car cut into the train, as well as two livestock cars owned by the D&RGW. At the far right, across the Crystal River, the coal-mine opening located above Placita can be seen on the hillside. Mount Sopris is in the distance (at the left).

same morning, when they set out on the return trip to Marble, allowing no passengers except a few men. Several women, waiting at Carbondale to come up here, were not permitted to go on this train, it being feared that trouble might be met with in getting through. This fear proved unfounded, however, as the train came home in good time, without any trouble except occasional shoveling away of a drift.

Tuesday morning, when the train was ready to start to make another trip to Carbondale, it was discovered that the engine was frozen tight to the tracks in the local yards and three hours of work was necessary to release it. The train did not get out until 12 o'clock and it was after 9:30 when it got back here Tuesday night.

ALONG THE RIVER BOTTOMS south of Placita, snow usually piled up to a great depth during a typical winter. This condition would close down the railroad for days — and sometimes for weeks — at a time if conditions worsened. The Crystal River & San Juan Railroad could normally depend on the Crystal River Railroad's rotary snowplow for assistance once that line had been opened.

COMMUNICATIONS

Getting messages from one place to another was a major problem in the early days. It usually necessitated someone traveling on foot or horseback to the nearest town or other inhabited location. In case of illness or accident, this could involve a critical time period. After 1900, when the railroad was operating from Placita to Carbondale communications were aided by a telegraph line.

The Marble & Crystal River Lance,
August 1, 1900.
The telegraph line between Placita and Carbondale is now being put up and it will prove of great convenience to the company as well as those living in this district.

• • • • •

The Crystal River Current, published in Crystal, commented in several issues in February, 1905, on the convenience of having telephones in the area. The line between Marble and Crystal was installed in the fall of 1904.

The Marble & Crystal River Lance,
February 24, 1905.
We are glad the new telephone line to Marble is working good again. It will save Mrs. Hodges a great deal of worry to hear that her husband gets through safely while the slides are running every day. [Allen Hodges carried the mail to Redstone from Crystal, on skis in the winter.]

HENRY L. JOHNSON PHOTO – JACK D. CLEMENSON COLLECTION

THE SNOW-DISPOSAL CHUTE on the Crystal River rotary snowplow could be moved to one side or the other to aim the snow either to the left or right of the track — as the rotary blades chewed through the snowpack. In this scene the snowplow operator — unthinkingly — had aimed the chute toward the cleared mainline, filling-in snow, which had to be removed again.

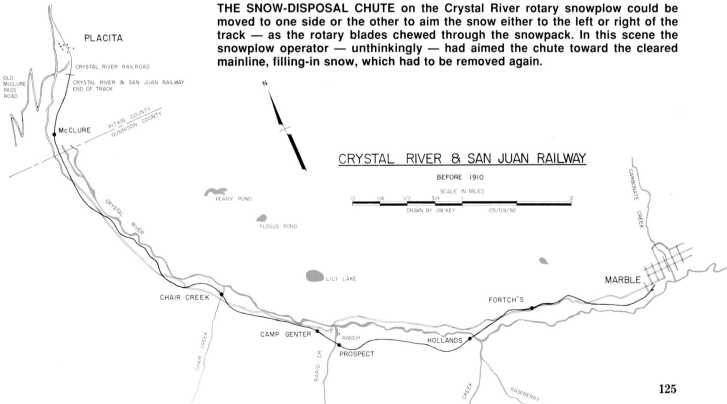

PLACITA

CRYSTAL RIVER RAILROAD

CRYSTAL RIVER & SAN JUAN RAILWAY
END OF TRACK

OLD McCLURE PASS ROAD

PITKIN COUNTY
GUNNISON COUNTY

McCLURE

N

CRYSTAL RIVER

PERRY POND

FLOGUS POND

CRYSTAL RIVER & SAN JUAN RAILWAY

BEFORE 1910

SCALE IN MILES

0   1/4   1/2   3/4   1   2

DRAWN BY JIM KEY   05/09/92

LILY LAKE

CARBONATE CREEK

MARBLE

CHAIR CREEK

CHAIR CREEK

FORTCH'S

CAMP GENTER

RANCH

PROSPECT

RAPID CR

HOLLANDS

MILTON CREEK

RASPBERRY CREEK

Make Plans right now to Spend your Vacation this summer in Marble

THE ABOVE picture shows a scene along the Crystal River, a fine trout stream that flows right through the town of Marble. Can't you feel your pulse gain a beat as you think of the big Rainbow in the pool beneath that rocky ledge ready to snap your fly?

There are good stores in Marble with everything you might need to take along on a fishing trip.

MARBLE BOOSTER AD – 1912

Crystal River & San Juan R. R.
TIME CARD
No. 2 leaves Marble daily ex. Sunday...5:00 a m
Arrives Carbondale.......................7:00 a m
CONNECTING WITH
Colorado Midland No. 3 for west........7:22 a m
     "   "   No. 6 for east........7:45 p m
D. & R. G. No. 228 for east and west via
    Glenwood Springs....................7:30 a m
C. R. & S. J. No. 1 returning leaves Car-
    bondale...............................7:45 a m
Arrives Marble........................10:30 a m

The Marble & Crystal River Lance,
February 10, 1905.
Received a telephone message from Al Hodges and Louie Idzenton Sunday morning that they were starting from Marble on snowshoes to bring the mail into Crystal. Tom Ramsey started early on this side to meet them. We would rather not have any mail for 60 days than see one of our boys covered up, so don't take any chances, boys.

The Marble & Crystal River Lance,
February 10, 1905.
Sunday morning Paul Tischhauser and Godried Roggl were detained 40 minutes climbing over the big snow slide between Crystal and the Lead King on their way to work. After arriving at the mine they phoned down to Mr. Peters not to attempt the trip without men and shovels. Now is the time when the phone line comes in good play.

Continued on Page 131

126

OLD CR&SJ ENGINE No. 2 was heading upgrade in this classic scene and was near Marble when Richard H. Kindig took this photograph on September 6, 1941. This grade crossing was guarded by a neatly-lettered sign, with "Stop, Look and Listen" on the upright post. A siding is in view at this location, at Camp Genter.

DELL A. McCOY PHOTO

WINTER ALONG THE CRYSTAL RIVER often appears to look very much like the proverbial "white Christmas" for many months of the year, being at a rather high altitude, above 7,000 feet. This photograph was taken approximately a mile below Camp Genter. Marble is a few miles distant, around the bend (to the left).

IT IS DIFFICULT to photograph the Crystal River along this stretch of the valley because of sunlight coming into the lens of the camera. Autumn — often referred to as Indian summer — is definitely the best time of the year to visit the Crystal River Valley. A good public campground is at McClure Flats, providing campers with a scenic place to stay overnight.

KNOWN AS CAMP GENTER to people living in the Crystal River Valley, this anthracite coal camp was operated by E. W. Genter of Salt Lake City. By 1927, the company began to produce coal at this location, about two miles below Marble, adjacent to the CR&SJ. The camp soon acquired a post office known as "Genter." Workmen were finishing the trackside coal tipple below the mine portal, which was situated up the hillside. Mine cars of slack (waste material) can be seen on the upper level. In the following photograph, the community of "Genter" was ready for business during the 1920's. The old road to Marble appears in the foreground.

The Marble & Crystal River Lance,
February 24, 1905.

Louie Idzenton went to Marble Monday morning with
the intention of fixing up the telephone line. Fix it up good,
Louie, so we can talk to the Marble people.

The Marble & Crystal River Lance,
July 7, 1905.

At the last meeting of the Crystal River Telephone
Co. it was decided to take the Black Queen in and allow
them to attach their wires at the most convenient place
o the mine and mill.

Solving the problems of transportation and com-
munication enabled the upper Crystal River Valley to
be developed into an active community, with an economy
based on marble production, coal mining and hard-rock
mining of the valuable "carbonate rock" minerals, such
as silver, lead, zinc, copper and iron pyrite. Even when
the local smelters were able to concentrate the ores by
their then primitive reduction processes, shipping the
minerals out to mills in Pueblo or Salt Lake City required a major expenditure of money and effort. This
made hard-rock mining an economically fragile enterprise, based as it was on intensive hand labor. The
silver panic of 1893 virtually closed down many Western mining towns. When Col. Meek developed the marble
industry in the valley, he relied on Eastern investors
for the extensive funds required up front to start a new
industry.

RAPID CREEK went on a rampage after heavy rains had soaked the mountains in 1908. CR&SJ locomotive No. 6, a small 2–6–0, was stopped short on her way to Marble with the daily mixed train, consisting of only the combination caboose-baggage-coach No. 02. During this time period, freight and passengers were interchanged at Redstone, where the Crystal River Railway picked them up for the trip on into Carbondale. There were numerous problems for Marble residents riding the train on the Crystal River line; however, the worst problems were caused by CF&I magnate J. C. Osgood every time he traveled on the line aboard his private car, the "Sunrise." When this took place, all other railroad traffic was halted.

THE FIREMAN'S SIDE of the Crystal River & San Juan Railway's locomotive No. 6 was photographed again at the Rapid Creek rock-and-mud slide, where debris covered the mainline. No. 6 was built in 1906, a small standard-gauge 2–6–0 Mogul, which was good for hauling short passenger trains, but had less tractive effort than needed for heavy freight trains, due to the size of the engine. This was the first engine the line owned and was second-hand.

THE HILLTOP in this view is the left-arm formation of Chair Mountain. Rapid Creek tumbles through the gully, past the old power plant (at the left). Camp Genter and the coal mine occupied space (at the right) next to where the Crystal River & San Juan Railway came up the valley from Redstone.

AUTUMN HAD ARRIVED at the Darien Ranch in this color view, shot a short distance below Marble — from the side of the road. Fresh snow can be seen at the higher elevation of Chair Mountain, visible across the gorge of Rapid Creek. Soon, snow will lie in a deep blanket over the landscape.

THE TOWN OF MARBLE is situated in the distance, beyond the first low hill in this color photograph. A part of snowcapped Whitehouse Mountain stands beyond the townsite (at the right). A Crystal River & San Juan Railroad bridge once crossed the Crystal River in this view (at the left).

THE DARIEN RANCH ran cattle for many years below the CR&SJ right-of-way, which ran along at the edge of this pasture land. Rapid Creek cascades down from the peak at the left, known as Chair Mountain.

THANOS A. JOHNSON PHOTO

DURING JANUARY of 1942, afternoon sunlight played across the snow-covered fields of the Darien Ranch, below Marble. Whitehouse Mountain is on the distant skyline (in the center) in this view, where you are looking toward the east and a bit to the south.

DELL A. McCOY PHOTO

AT THE WEST END of the Colorado-Yule Marble Company mill, blocks of low-quality marble were stacked alongside the grade of the Crystal River & San Juan Railroad. Whitehouse Mountain and Treasure Mountain are in the southwest in this autumn color view.

MORRISON A. SMITH PHOTO – JOHN W. MAXWELL COLLECTION

LEAVING MARBLE on October 25, 1941, the two Yule Colorado Marble Company air-dump cars had been loaded with waste marble, while two boxcars had been loaded with finished marble, outward bound for unknown destinations. Coach No. 9 brought up the rear of the train, with a coal fire burning in her potbelly stove to ward off the autumn chill in the air.

JACK D. CLEMENSON PHOTO

THIS SEPTEMBER, 1942, VIEW was taken from a departing coach on the CR&SJ, as a train left Marble. Notice the metal framework of the former shed that covered the Colorado-Yule Marble Company block yard, located at the mill west of town. Jack Clemenson took this picture from the rear platform of CR&SJ combine No. 9. At this time, John Petrocco and others were dismantling the frame of the block shed. At the same time, Jack Clemenson was working for Morse Brothers, taking out the tramway tracks to the quarry.

141

THIS QUAINT SPLIT-LOG DEPOT was the official CR&SJ station building and Western Union Telegraph office at Marble. The structure faced west, next to the main-line, and a bench provided patrons a resting spot if no agent was in at the time. The standard-gauge electric Colorado-Yule tramway line ran behind the building on its way into the mill yard. Notice the hand-carved marble depot sign, mounted on this modest depot. The sign now finds a home at the Marble General Store. Although the sign was broken while being moved, it provides a living monument of marble, displaying the craftsmanship that formerly was available in Marble.

THE CR&SJ STATION SIGN (below) was photographed when the sign was mounted on "Ken's Pop Stand" in Marble. The elevation for Marble was 7,950 feet above sea level at the depot.

Chapter 3

THE TOWN OF MARBLE

After the Ute Indians had been moved out of western Colorado in 1881, following the Meeker massacre, the area was opened to prospecting and settlement. Most of these early explorers and settlers in the upper Crystal River Valley came over Schofield Pass from the Gunnison Country. Two of these men were William F. Mason and John C. Mobley, and the latter also brought his wife and two children, Nellie and Chet. These men founded the town of Clarence, west of Beaver Lake, and began to sell lots to other prospectors. About this time William Walter Woods and William D. Parry also had a dream of establishing a town as a base for the prospectors, and platted the town of Marble, just to the west of Clarence.[1]

The Federal Census taken June 28, 1880, showed 50 "Inhabitants Camped on Rock Creek," later named the Crystal River. Of these, 14 of the men were married, and 11 of their wives and children were included in the count.[2] Most were listed as prospectors or miners and the majority of them were camped in Crystal City and the town of Schofield.

By early 1900, there were 150 persons living in the town of Marble and E.E.L. Reyland applied for establishment of a post office there.[3] About the same time, the leaders of the town of Clarence also filed for one. Several years before, Dr. Robert Hays Kline of Philadelphia had bought a one-half interest in Woods' Marble townsite, and he happened to be a friend of the Postmaster General. So, it is not surprising that Marble got the post office. The leaders of Clarence decided it would be unproductive to fight for dominance with the other town, and joined their forces with Marble, forming one town on July 4, 1892.[4] On August 24, 1892 the first newspaper was issued in the town of Marble, The Marble City Times.[5]

The town of Marble continued to grow because of the mining activity and even the silver panic of 1893 did not affect this town as much as it did Crystal City. The activities of John C. Osgood in developing his marble holdings on Yule Creek contributed to the economic

stability. The establishment of the Hoffman Smelter in 1898, across the Crystal River from the town added its twenty jobs and indicated that there was still active mining in the area. The 1900 census showed there were 110 persons in Marble Village, and in spite of the silver panic of 1893, there were still 101 persons counted in Crystal City. So, hard times in the mining industry could not kill the dream of prospectors and miners that they would achieve wealth.[6]

By the time of the 1910 census, only four persons were counted in Crystal, while Marble had grown to 806 people because of the opening of the marble quarry and mill.[7]

There had been much talk of incorporating the town of Marble, and by early 1899, meetings were held to pursue this goal. On June 20, 1899 the town held an election to vote on incorporation, and the measure passed 33 to 4. After an election to name members of a board of trustees and a mayor, the county court issued the incorporation. The first officers of the town, elected on June 20, were: J.H. Hoffman mayor, and trustees: P.J. Tischhauser, Evan Williams, D.M. Brown, A.T. Bush, G.H. Rummel and H.A. Mitchell. Nine days later, the Board of Trustees met to organize the town government, and the minutes of the meeting record their actions.

The First Meeting of the Board of Trustees of the Town of Marble was called to order July 29, 1899 at 7:30

[1] Vandenbusche, Duane, & Rex Myers, "Marble, Colorado: City of Stone." Golden Bell Press. Denver, 1970. p.10.

[2] 1880 Federal Census, Gunnison County, Colorado, T9, Roll 90, p.155.

[3] Vandenbusche & Myers. p.16.

[4] Vandenbusche & Myers. p.19.

[5] The Marble Times & Crystal Silver Lance, August 24, 1900, p.4.

[6] 1900 Federal Census, Gunnison County, Colorado, T623, Roll 124, Enumeration District 140, Sheet 19, p.137, Precinct 22, 15 June 1900. T.T. Higby, enumerator. See the Appendix for the 1900 census listing for Marble.

[7] 1910 Federal Census, Gunnison County, Colorado, T624, Roll 120, Enumeration District 64, Sheets 1A to 7B, Precinct 24, 15 & 16 April 1910, Herbert H. Lynde, enumerator.

THE ABOVE PICTURE is from a daguerreotype of William (Bill) Woods, taken when he was in Deadwood, South Dakota. This was at the same time "Wild Bill" Hickock was murdered in Deadwood. William Woods eventually trekked down to Colorado, and with W. F. Mason, he founded Clarence in 1881. This was at the confluence of Carbonate and Rock creeks. Later, William Woods and William Parry plotted the town of Marble — just west of Clarence. The marble deposits in the area received a considerable amount of publicity during 1881 and 1882, and Bill Woods hoped to be able to sell plots of land to prospectors. Reportedly, Bill Woods had flaming-red hair and wore it in curls to scare off Indians who might want to "lift his scalp." Notice the date of 1873 on the daguerreotype.

p.m., Mayor Hoffman presiding at the Marble Times office.

After rollcall with all present except A.J. Mitchell, the following nominations were moved, seconded and carried.

Mayor Pro-tem—Evan Williams
For town Clerk—F.W. Reyland
For town Treas.—W.D. Parry
For Police Judge—Leonard Hoffman
For Street Commissioner—Judge [Joseph] Bardine
For Marshall—J.M. Downing
For City Atty—Judge Bardine

The Candidates were unaminously [sic] elected. The name of E.W. Fuller was suggested as a candidate for Police Judge but after discussion it was decided not to nominate him. The following committees were appointed by the Mayor.

Ordinance Committee—Evan Williams, A.J. Mitchell, P.J. Tischhauser

Finance Committee—A.T. Bush, G.H. Rummel, D.M. Brown

Printing Committee—A.J. Mitchell, P.J. Tischhauser, G.H. Rummel

Streets, Alleys & Bridges Committee—D.M. Brown, A.T. Bush, G.H. Rummel

License Committee—Evan Williams, A.T. Bush, A.J. Mitchell

A motion was made and carried to issue a six months license to Pietro Sottile to sell liquor. A motion was also carried to pay Mr. Sottile $100 for services rendered to the town.

After considering a motion to fix the Town Treasurer's bond at $1000 an amendment making it $500 was offered and carried.

Mr. Williams was allowed a bill against the Town for $55.30 for incorporation matter printed by him.

A bill also was allowed to the County Court for incorporation fees of $68.42.

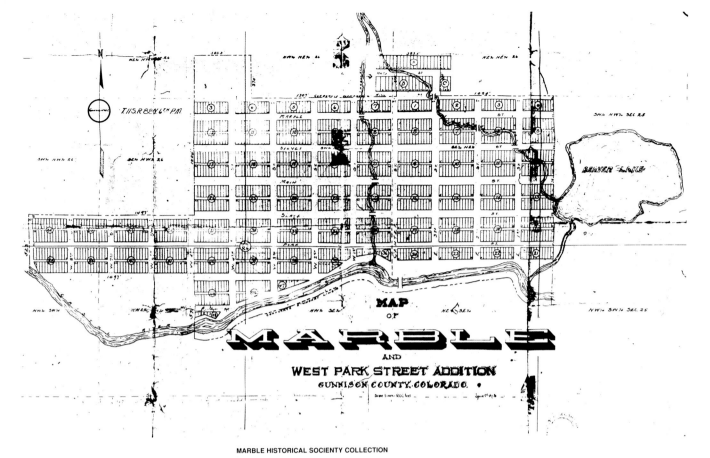

MARBLE HISTORICAL SOCIENTY COLLECTION

ONE OF THE EARLIEST KNOWN MAPS OF MARBLE

A motion was carried that Evan Williams be instructed to confer with the Town Atty. in regard to the books necessary for the Town officers. It was also agreed that an assessment of ten mils be levied upon the taxpayers and $200 was appropriated for work to be done on the streets.

By agreement Council meetings will be held every Saturday at 7:30 at the Times office until present business is straightened.

Adjournment until Sat. Aug. 5th.[8]

The minutes of following meetings were in similar vein and the board tried to take care of the most pressing community matters. But, since the officials were volunteers, they often did not perform their duties in advance of the trustees' meetings. This is a problem even today in small towns. The new Police Magistrate entered upon his duties with vigor, however, as indicated by this extract from the September minutes:

The Police Magistrate reported one arrest during the month of August which was a plain drunk. The offender's name was Ray Wright of Crystal. He was arrested by Deputy Marshall Bush and charged with being drunk and disorderly. The prisoner plead guilty and was fined $10 and costs.[9]

• • • • •

A.T. Bush died three months after election to the Board of Trustees and was replaced by William Fulton.

Officials had the same problem then as today in getting the voters to go to the polls.

The Marble Times & Crystal Silver Lance,
October 19, 1900.

The Board of Registration met here Tuesday [October, 1900] and 115 voters were placed on the poll books, but we do not expect there will be over 75 votes cast.

• • • • •

For several weeks before the November 1900 election the newspaper was devoted almost exclusively to election news, local and national. The opportunity to make it a festive occasion was not lost in the efforts to consider the serious issues concerning national, state and county offices.

The Marble Times & Crystal Silver Lance,
November 9, 1900.

Election night a very pleasant hop was given at the hotel and quite a number were in attendance from Crystal. All seemed to be enjoying themselves.

The election at Marble was carried on in a quiet and orderly manner, no excitement of any kind occurring. The vote shows that the people were almost unanimous for the fusion ticket. The following is the vote as cast:

For Presidential Electors the fusion candidates each received 70 votes, and 6 for the republicans...

At Redstone the vote approximated about 141 republicans to 25 fusion. • • • • •

In the new year, the politicians of Marble began to look forward to the town election in April.

The Marble Times & Crystal Silver Lance,
March 1, 1901.

NOTICE. The qualified electors of the town of Marble are hereby notified that a convention of the Citizens' Party of said town will be held at the Phillips hall on Saturday evening March 9th, at 7:30 p.m., for the purpose of placing

⁸ "Minute Book of the Town of Marble," July, 1899, to December, 1921, July 29, 1899; book is deposited at Colorado State Archives, Denver.

⁹ "Minute Book of the Town of Marble," July, 1899, to December, 1921, July 29, 1899; book is deposited at Colorado State Archives, Denver., September 2, 1899.

Continued on Page 148

WHEN PHOTOGRAPHED on June 18, 1908, Marble looked like this. The little town did not yet have electric lights; however, things were looking up because the Colorado-Yule Marble Company had secured the contract for the Cuyahoga County Court House for $500,000. Marble was being hauled down into town from the quarry at this time on heavy wagons with nine teams of horses. The population numbered approximately 700 residents, as hiring continued at the marble company. Not many businesses had set-up shop on Main Street as of this date, but the Marble City Hotel in view, at the corner of Main and East Third streets. Thode's Lumber Yard had begun construction of their shed near the Crystal River (at the lower center). The snow-capped peaks beyond Marble are above the area where Carbonate Creek had carved a deep gorge into the hillside (beyond town). Slate Cliff and Gallo Hill are at the left, where Gallo's coal mine was located, high on the cliffs. The coal was packed-out on burros. This photograph was taken from the road of the Colorado-Yule Marble Company, which led up to the quarry — on the hillside above the Hoffman Smelter.

THIS DRUGSTORE is believed to have been located near the southwest corner of East Main and Center streets when it was photographed prior to 1908. Kobey's Clothing Store later occupied the lot at the right. Whitehouse Mountain is in the view, at the left.

in nomination, a ticket, as follows, to-wit:

One candidate for mayor, to serve for one year; Three candidates for Trustees, to serve for two years; To be voted for at the annual election to be held on Tuesday, the 2nd day of April A.D. 1901.

EVAN WILLIAMS
Chairman Citizens' Committee

The Marble Times & Crystal Silver Lance,
March 15, 1901.

At the Citizens' convention, held last Saturday night, the following gentlemen were nominated by acclamation to fill the various town offices:

Mayor—J.H. Hoffman.

Trustees—D.M. Brown, P.J. Tischhauser and O.F. Tracy.

All are renominations, except Mr. Tracy, who was nominated in place of Mr. Mason.

The convention was a short one and the best of feeling prevailed.

• • • • •

The trustees continued to pass ordinances governing the operation of the town, and in March, 1901, appropriated funds for the coming year.

IT IS BELIEVED that this quaint little frame house was located on East Silver Street, between East Third and East Second streets. Notice the fence that had been placed around the property to keep animals out of the yard, so they could not eat the garden and flowers.

148

THIS COLOR PHOTOGRAPH provides an interesting comparison with others taken from nearly the same location. Trees have nearly hidden Marble's dwellings in the center of town — in this view taken during the summer of 1973. Marshland can be seen in the foreground, as the Crystal River crosses the scene from right to left. The former Treasury Mountain Railroad grade is visible (at the lower left).

149

A SHOEMAKER had set up his shop at the corner of Main and Center streets when this picture was taken during 1908.

The Marble Times & Crystal Silver Lance,

March 15, 1901.

Ordinance No. 13. Appropriation Ordinance for the fiscal year commencing April 1, 1901.

Be it ordained by the Board of Trustees of the Town of Marble:

Section 1. That the following sums shall be and are hereby appropriated to meet any or all expenses of the Town of Marble for the ensuing fiscal year, commencing the first day of April A.D. 1901.

Sec. 2. There shall be appropriated for the Street, Bridges and Alley fund the sum of Five Hundred Dollars ($500), out of any money in the town treasury, or that may come into said treasury during the year A.D. 1901.

Sec. 3. There shall be appropriated for the General Fund the sum of One Thousand Dollars ($1000) out of any money in the town treasury, or that may come into the treasury during the year A.D. 1901, not otherwise appropriated.

Passed by the Board of Trustees of the Town of Marble this sixth day of March A.D. 1901.

J.H. HOFFMAN, Mayor.

Attest: JOSEPH BARDINE,
Town Clerk.

• • • • •

Political parties were active in the town at this time.

The Marble Times & Crystal Silver Lance,

March 22, 1901.

On the night of the 14th, the Peoples' Labor party held their convention and placed in nomination the following ticket:

Mayor—J.M. Evans.

Trustees—J.F. Clayton, W.F. Mason, W.G. Miller.

We understand Mr. Clayton has declined the nomination tendered.

• • • • •

There was no doubt how editor Evan Williams of the local newspaper thought the election would come out.

The Marble Times & Crystal Silver Lance,

March 22, 1901.

If all the voters turn out on election day, the result of the town election will be about as follows: J.H. Hoffman, 47; J.M. Evans, 14.

The Marble Times & Crystal Silver Lance,

March 22, 1901.

FINANCIAL STATEMENT OF THE TOWN OF MARBLE.

Commencing July 29, 1899, the time of incorporation, up to the year ending March 18, 1901.

Receipts:

Total amounts from saloon licenses............	$1150.00
" " " Police Court................	20.00
" " " Dog Tax.....................	20.00
Total amount of receipts.........	$1190.00

Expenditures:

Paid for incorporating.................................	$ 575.73
" " Improvement of streets..................	486.90
" " Election and ballot box...................	86.64
" " General expenses.........................	119.83
" " Interest on warrants......................	23.72
Total expenses.......................	$1301.81

SUMMARY STATEMENT

Total amount Warrants issued......	$1269.12	
" " interest on warrants...	32.72	
Total indebtedness..	$1301.84	
Total receipts..........	1190.00	
		$111.84
Outstanding Warrants unpaid........	$125.63	
Cash on hand................................	13.79	
Net indebtedness.....................		$111.84

L.S. Rorher
Town Treasurer .

The Marble Times & Crystal Silver Lance,

April 5, 1901.

The dance election night was very largely attended and everyone seemed to be having an enjoyable time. The children danced the Oxford very prettily and gave the audience a selection or two of comic music, much to the merriment of all.

Continued on Page 155

RICHARD A. RONZIO COLLECTION

BUILT BEFORE 1908, the Marble City Hotel stood at the corner of East Main and East Third streets — with the front facing the south. It may be assumed that a restaurant was located on the main floor, with rooms on the second floor, up the flight of stairs. A kerosene lamp post stood at the corner. Plans were made to replace this structure with a marble building, but the idea fell through. This building lasted until after the 1941 flood, when it disappeared from the scene.

RICHARD A. RONZIO COLLECTION

LOOKING WEST on Main Street in Marble, prior to 1908, the Marble City Hotel still had a kerosene lamp post on the boardwalk. The Marble Laundry had moved into the new building next door, which featured a wooden canopy over the sidewalk.

ELECTRICITY WAS NOW AVAILABLE to Marble residents and merchants, and a street light hung at the intersection of East Main and East Third streets. Street and sidewalk improvements were taking place on the block where the Marble City Hotel stood in 1912. The sidewalk had been lowered about two feet, requiring steps up to the entrance of the hotel. The outside staircase had been removed from the east wall, and the Marble City Hotel sign was moved up to the roof for better viewing. Two doors farther west, on the block beyond the Marble Laundry, stood the two-story Dix Rooming House. P. R. Larson offered general merchandise in the log store beyond.

MERVIN C. AUDE COLLECTION

PHOTOGRAPHED FROM NEAR the top of McClure Pass, the town of Marble is situated toward the left of this autumn scene, below Whitehouse Mountain's unmistakable formation. Above it (to the right) is Treasure Mountain, rising to 13,484 feet above sea level. At the right, discernable behind the McClure Pass hillside is Chair Mountain. Chair Mountain Ranch occupies land adjacent to the Crystal River (at the center).

BEFORE DECEMBER 3, 1908, when the town of Marble voted to go "dry," Faussone's Saloon stood on East Main Street — on the south side of the block, next to the place where a channel would be dug for Carbonate Creek, to the left of the support pole against the building. The Imperial Beer sign announced the presence of the saloon. The men at the left were leaning against the weighing mechanism for a platform scale. Liquor was known to have had a serious effect on the workers at the mill and quarry. The date of this photograph is unknown, but the presence of the lawman at the entrance suggests that the establishment may have been closed. Prohibition caused the "good old boys" to lose their social drinking places.

"ROCKY MOUNTAIN SPRING WATER" was in full production around the town of Marble, in spite of Prohibition. In most cases, alcoholics spent much of their paychecks on "booze," rather than to put food in their children's mouths, and — unfortunately — alcohol can change a person's personality to such a degree that many drinkers became wife-beaters. In certain cases, drinkers died from "homemade brew," or they could become blind, due to the lethal type of alcohol produced. However, it was a big thing in those days to be "popular with the gang," just as it is with today's youth "getting high" on drugs. Drinking and driving did not have the same effect at that time; the drunk was placed on his wagon seat, and his horse knew the way home.

Election passed off very quietly here and not much surprise was manifested at the result of the vote. The number of ballots cast was 63, but one was spoiled, so far as the mayor was concerned, but the balance of the ticket was all right. Figuring on 60 voters we stated two weeks ago the vote on mayor would be 47 to 14, and we were not very far off, even if 63 votes were tallied. The following is the vote:

Mayor—	J.M. Evans	17
	J.H. Hoffman	45
Trustees—	D.M. Brown	29
	W.F. Mason	30
	W.G. Miller	29
	P.J. Tischhauser	37
	O.F. Tracy	46

• • • • •

Within a short time the activities of the marshal in keeping the peace required a more secure place to hold prisoners, most of whom were arrested for drinking and fighting.

The Marble Times & Crystal Silver Lance,
May 10, 1901.

The Town Board has let a contract for the erection of a jail building and had previously ordered two steel cells from a St. Louis firm. We understand the Hoffman bros. donated a lot on State street to put the building on for the present.

• • • • •

Efforts were made to improve town streets.

The Marble Times & Crystal Silver Lance,
June 28, 1901.

A force is at work opening and grading Centre street from its southern intersection with Main street to the town limits. It was needed to be done very badly as heavy laden teams traverse it to and from the smelter.

• • • • •

THE MARBLE TRADING store was located on the southeast corner of East Main and East Third streets. This was one of the more spacious structures in the town. The building had two small signs in front, reading "General Store" and "Butterick Patterns."

AN UNIDENTIFIED FAMILY was making the rounds in Marble (possibly about 1915, according to the lady's wearing apparel). This style of wagon could provide a shocking experience during sudden thundershowers, with no provision for a cover on the rig.

155

THANOS A. JOHNSON PHOTO

PAUL MARBLE WOODS, the son of the principal founder of Marble, William Woods, and an International Harvester dump truck are in this view. The road was raked, hoed and shoveled by hand. The enclosure on the side held tools and a four-gallon glass jug — heavily padded with burlap potato sacks — contained the workers' drinking water. This was taken ca. 1947.

RESIDENTS OF MARBLE were on horseback on Main Street, on a summer morning in 1914. Wooden-frame business buildings lined the block between Center Street (located in the distance) and East Third Street, where the photographer stood. The distant ridge of mountains (to the west) includes Chair Mountain.

COLLECTION OF THE LATE WILLIAM McMANUS

PAUL MARBLE WOODS, son of Marble's principal founder, is shown here at his log cabin by Lily Lake. This building was originally built next to the William Parry house in Marble. Mrs. Woods preferred the old house next to Carbonate Creek. After his parents died, Paul moved this cabin, log by log, and rebuilt it at Lily Lake. It had hot-and-cold running water and complete facilities, plus a water-powered washing machine. The photographer would snowshoe up to the cabin from Marble with his wash in his rucksack to do his laundry up there — at least twice a winter!

Life in town went on as usual.

The Marble Times & Crystal Silver Lance,

June 28, 1901.

We have anxiously scanned the town for items but saw nothing of interest. No fights, a few innocuous drunks, the dogs too busy with the festive wood tick to fight, a couple of rising young tots strangling a decrepit kitten, and all the little ones in town riding and falling off from, and being stepped on by burros, constituted the whole grist of excitement.

• • • • •

By 1905, interest in the town government was lagging.

The Crystal River Current,

March 31, 1905.

The registration board was in session last Tuesday and placed the names of some thirty voters on the books, but we don't expect to see half that number of votes cast.

The town election will be held next Tuesday. But little interest is being taken in the affair. Only the "Knockers" are dishing out a lot of tommyrot about town matters. They had a chance to show their ability two years ago, when three of these enterprising (?) people were in town and members of the board; but they did nothing at all. They kick about taxes and want the Wood part of town taxed as ranch land. We have levied no town tax but once— in 1889... If Mr. Wood wants to dissolve the incorporation why don't he go at it in a legal manner?... The voters here are tired of this "knocking" business and have expressed so at the polls many times.

• • • • •

The Board of Trustees passed an ordinance in 1901 requiring the registration of all dogs and payment of a dog tax, one dollar for males and two dollars for females. Within a few years, a pound was needed.

The Marble Booster,

June 24, 1911.

The new city pound has been properly dedicated, though the exercises were accompanied by no great applause. Instead, there were growls and yelps of anger and dismay from those owners of livestock who in the past have been wont to use the public domain as a feeding and exercise ground for their animals.

• • • • •

By 1911 Marble had grown to about 1000 persons[10], but there was still a lack of civic interest and only the People's Party entered candidates in the April election.

The Marble Booster,

April 8, 1911.

Only one ticket was in the field—that of the Peoples party. This ticket was composed entirely of business men of Marble and the voters were well satisfied with it. Not a single name was written in on any ballot cast. In all, 97 voters went to the polls but five ballots were cast out as defective. In these the voters tried to vote a straight party ticket but overlooked the fact that there was neither a Democratic nor a Republican ticket on the ballot.

• • • • •

[10] Colorado State Business Directory, 1911.

157

THE MARBLE CITY BAND was out in front of Carey's Ice Cream Parlour on a hot July day. The store had good shade from the awning, against the southern exposure on East Main Street, where the building sat. This location was between East Third and East Second streets. The awning also announced stationery for sale.

THIS HAPPY GROUP was on the front sidewalk of Carey's Ice Cream Parlour in Marble. From left to right were: Ike Robey, a lucky dog, June and Maude McManus, and Lena and Frank Gertig. Angelus marshmallows came in assorted flavors, according to a window sign. An Elite Bakery delivery rig was next door.

This turnout was less then ten percent of the town residents, if the number given in the Colorado State Business Directory is accepted. Several reasons could account for this lack of interest. The 1910 census shows that of the 806 then residents of Marble, 330 of them were born in some foreign country, and 115 could not speak English.[11] Many had been recruited in Italy and other European countries for work in Marble, and it is probable that most of these persons were not United States citizens. These foreigners were pretty much looked down upon, isolated from the original inhabitants, had their own stores and generally lived in company houses on West Park Street in "Dago town." Also, the marble company and the business men did not try to integrate them into the community, as they believed most would be here only a short while. They were seen by the biased and unthinking persons as a necessary but generally unwanted group. A few local citizens tried to improve their situation and "Professor" Aristotile R. Ambrosini offered evening trade school and English classes. For a while, Italian language articles were printed in The Marble Booster.

In May 1911 the town passed an ordinance to build wooden sidewalks along Main Street and certain other streets, and "The Town Rejoices. Marble Takes Her Place As A Progressive Town."[12]

The marble business was a going concern by 1909, and employed many Italians and East Europeans to cut and process the marble. In this year, the company officials decided that the problem of alcohol was interfering with the workers' efficiency. Therefore, the company caused the town government to pass several ordinances prohibiting the possession and consumption of liquor in the town. The foreign workers were in the habit of consuming alcohol daily and did not take to the new laws. Soon, a thriving illegal bootlegging business existed. One of the most active practitioners of this activity was Mrs. Curley, who was arrested for bootlegging.

At the prodding of the officials of the marble company, the bootleggers finally were targeted.

The Marble Booster,
May 27, 1911.

The Lid is On Again in Marble. Bootleggers Arrested and Heavily Fined. Marble has been housecleaning this week. It was just a question of time until something would happen to the bootleggers. They were getting entirely too "raw" in their work. It had reached the point where a number of persons were operating what practically amounted to open saloons. The foreign element, especially, grew very bold in their sales of beer, whisky and wine and a thirsty "gent" never had far to seek to appease his longing. So the big blow-off was due, and it arrived.

Early this week a real sleuth blew in from Denver. With a fried egg hat turned down around his ears, his coat collar turned up and a pair of green whiskers in his pocket he slunk up the alleys and appeared in unexpected places at unexpected times. With a typewritten list of suspected bootleggers and a revenue collector's commission in his possession, he didn't care a tinkers darn for outraged innocense [sic].

[11] 1910 Federal Census, Gunnison County, Colorado, T624, Roll 120, Enumeration District 64, Precinct 24, Sheets 1A - 8A, 15 & 16 April 1910, Herbert H. Lynde, enumerator.

[12] The Marble Booster, May 27, 1911.

AS EVIDENCED by this photograph, taken in the late 1920's, the Elite Bakery (the building to the left, near the northeast corner of East Main and East Third streets) was in need of paint. Notice the brick chimney hung on the east wall of the bakery, supported by pillars. Outbuildings at the rear provided cover for coal and wood storage. A team and wagon were at the front entrance of Carey's Ice Cream Parlour.

159

THANOS A. JOHNSON PHOTO

A GATHERING of "old-timers" occurred at Thanos Johnson's home in Marble during late August of 1945. Left to right, they are: Ambrose Williams, Demetra Johnson (holding Demetrios), Thanos, Mrs. Vanderpost (wife of an early ranger in the valley), Uncle John Williams and Mr. Vanderpost, who authored books about the early towns in Colorado. He was unaware that "Penny Hot Springs" — located a short distance north of Redstone — was the townsite of "Clifton," where an ochre deposit was mined. (Ochre is an earthy clay, often reddish brown, used as a pigment in paint.) William (Bill) Parry and his wife lived in a cabin there. Bill's wife would be visited by Ute Indians, who bathed in the thermal springs — often when Bill was away from home. Bill would leave a loaded revolver on a table for her, but she confided in her diary that she did not know how to shoot it. Nearly all of the old cabins of Clifton (or Penny Hot Springs) are now gone.

"You've got to come through with the license fee," he told the suspects.

This was all very well from the government's get-the-money point of view, but nobody was being actually arrested for selling liquor. All the sleuth wanted to do was to make 'em pay up. Those illicit sellers whom he found in possession of a license, he did not molest.

But, all this time, our own guardian of the peace, Marshal Mahoney, was doing some "sleuthing" himself.

He didn't wear any green whiskers but his gum shoes didn't make any noise. Judge Budlong was notified that there would be some business for him Monday evening.

When Monday came the marshal and his assistant, Perry Sallgren, went forth into the highways and byways and collected various citizens and sundry packages of wet goods. The gross receipts—both persons and packages—were turned into court at 7 o'clock Monday night.

Mrs. J.J. Curley was the first victim offered to the majesty of the law. Also, Mrs. Curley was the most extensively prosecuted, there being no fewer than eleven counts against her. She entered pleas of not guilty to each count and protested vigorously that she never had sold liquor to anyone in Marble. Marshal Mahoney and Ben Holland were the city's witnesses. H.W. Clark, an Aspen attorney, appeared as special prosecutor.

Judge Budlong found Mrs. Curley guilty on each count as charged and assessed her fine at $200 and costs on the first count and $300 and costs on each of the other ten counts. This made the total of her fines mount to $3,300, counting the costs. She served notice of appeal and her bond was fixed at $6,400.

The following day Sylvia Gowatch was arraigned on five counts and fined $1,400, the costs running the total up to $1,442.50.

Having not so much loose silver about his person and being unable to find a bondsmen, Mr. Gowatch went to jail, where-at the Italian population since has been much frustrated and full of woe—and garlic.

The real exhibition of hysterical gesticulations did not come, however, until the Bianche tribe struck court. Mary Bianche threw a fit when the judge soaked her $100. After she came out of it she dug deep into her roll and produced $108.50 in cash, the sum total of the fine and costs.

Dominick Bianche, also, was a good cash customer. The officers had two counts against him and the fines and

TODAY'S BEAVER LAKE LODGE in Marble (now enlarged), owned and operated by Hank and Pat Kimbrell, stands on the northwest corner of East Silver and East Second streets. River stones were used as the foundation and for front-porch supports. One porch-support column of river stones (possibly repositioned) was used as a bench mark for surveyors at this location. "Bill" Brinkmeyer was still living here until sometime after World War II (one of Marble's old, great story-tellers). It was said that the first school classes in Marble were held in this building prior to 1907. For today's hungry visitors to Marble, this is the only restaurant in the village proper that provides patrons with fascinating views of some of Colorado's tiny hummingbirds, who make use of the feeders provided for them by the owners of this delightful place.

costs assessed amounted in the aggregate to $317. The tribe of Bianche rose and howled at this and Judge Budlong had to threaten them with jail before they subsided. Then the judge told Dominick he would remit $100 of the fine if he would pay the remainder. The Bianche's went into executive session in one corner of the courtroom and communed. A great walling of eyes, shrugging of shoulders and hubbub of voices told how serious the question was. But at the end, Dominick emerged with the coin to satisfy the court, and the town of Marble now has $217 of Bianche money that never will see Italy.
• • • • •

This apparent attitude of Frank Frost, editor of The Marble Booster, indicating prejudice and lack of respect for the different culture of the Italian workers, is shocking to us today. And it is even more remarkable when it is considered that Frost was actually one of the more liberal, enlightened and level-headed members of the community.

The Marble Booster,
July 22, 1911.
City officials of Marble have been watching this week with much interest the course of the law at Gunnison in relation to the case against Mrs. J.J. Curley.

Mrs. Curley, who is the proprietor of the Main hotel, was recently arrested on a charge of bootlegging and tried before Judge Budlong, police magistrate. She was convicted on eleven counts and fined a total of $3300.00. She gave notice of appeal at the conclusion of the trial and the judge fixed the amount of her appeal bond, which according to law had to be filed and accepted by the judge within ten days after judgment had been rendered.

Continued on Page 169

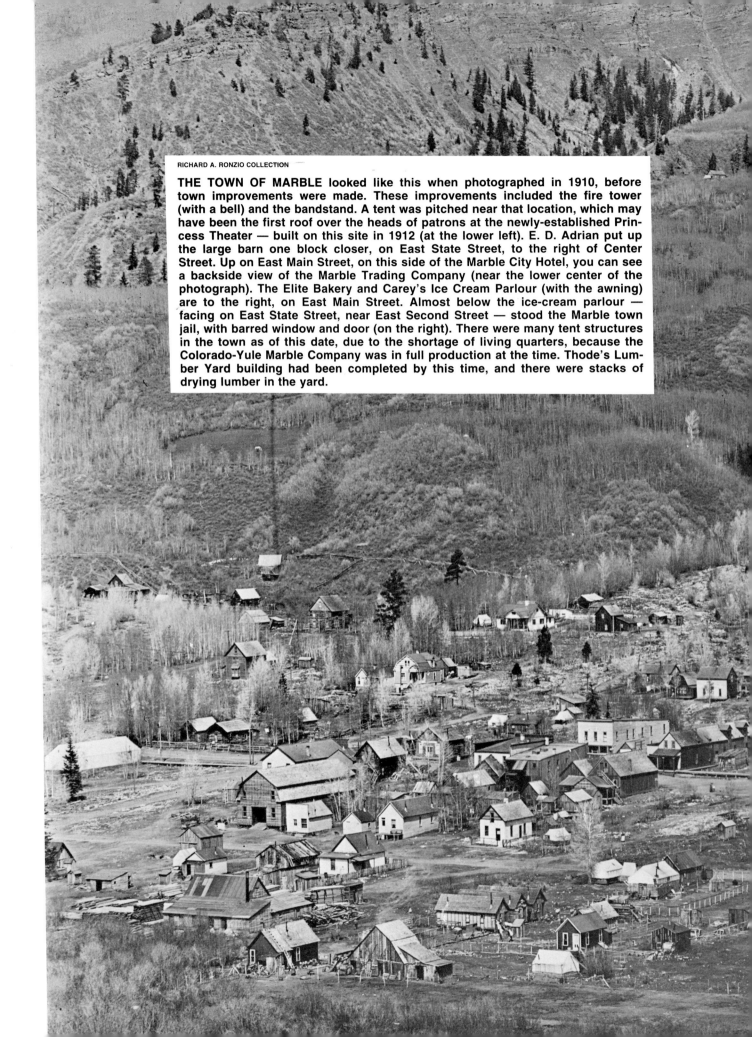

THE TOWN OF MARBLE looked like this when photographed in 1910, before town improvements were made. These improvements included the fire tower (with a bell) and the bandstand. A tent was pitched near that location, which may have been the first roof over the heads of patrons at the newly-established Princess Theater — built on this site in 1912 (at the lower left). E. D. Adrian put up the large barn one block closer, on East State Street, to the right of Center Street. Up on East Main Street, on this side of the Marble City Hotel, you can see a backside view of the Marble Trading Company (near the lower center of the photograph). The Elite Bakery and Carey's Ice Cream Parlour (with the awning) are to the right, on East Main Street. Almost below the ice-cream parlour — facing on East State Street, near East Second Street — stood the Marble town jail, with barred window and door (on the right). There were many tent structures in the town as of this date, due to the shortage of living quarters, because the Colorado-Yule Marble Company was in full production at the time. Thode's Lumber Yard building had been completed by this time, and there were stacks of drying lumber in the yard.

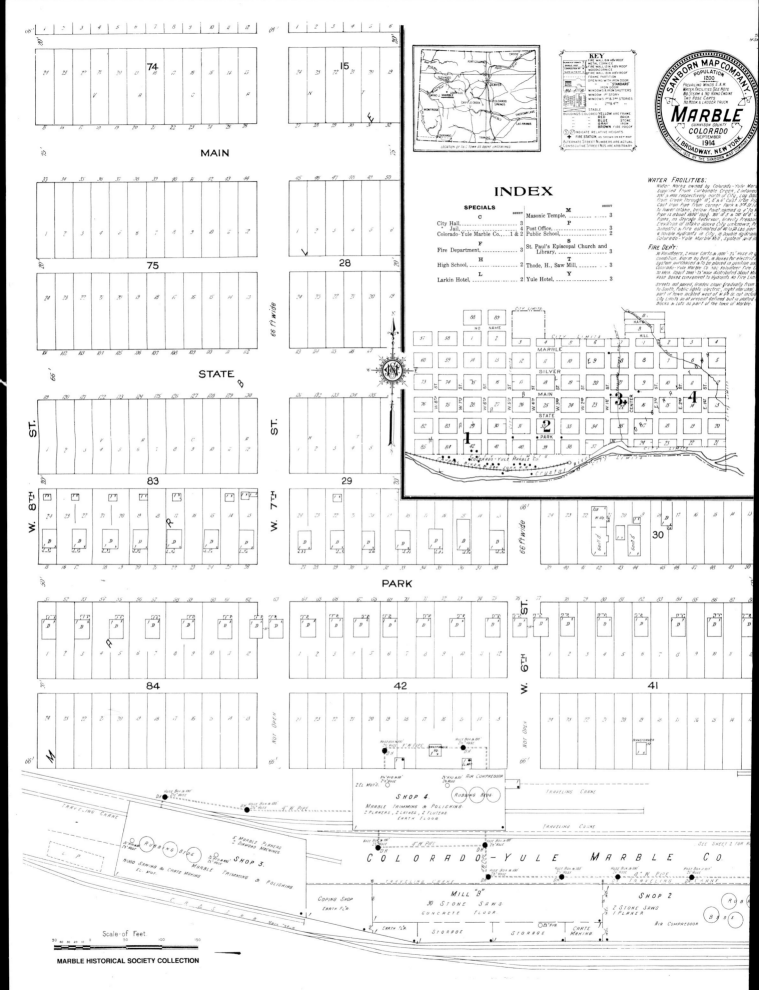

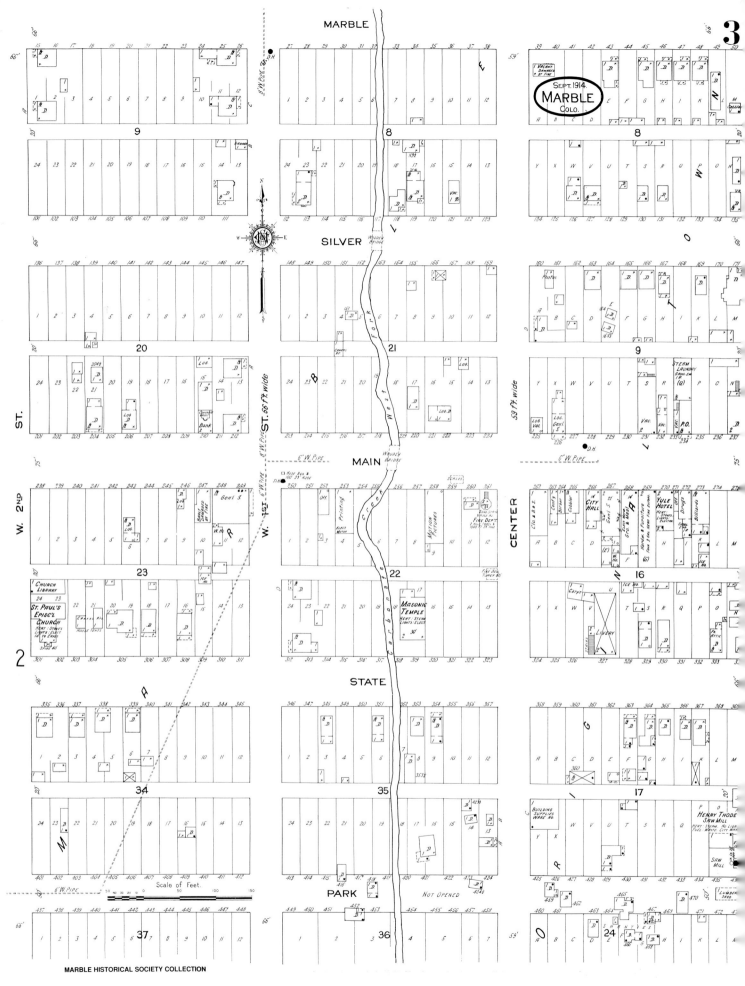

MARBLE

SEPT. 1914
MARBLE
COLO.

SILVER

MAIN

STATE

PARK

CENTER

ST.

W. 2ND

St.

MARBLE HISTORICAL SOCIETY COLLECTION

Sept. 1914. MARBLE COLO.

GEORGE L. BEAM PHOTO – D&RGW ARCHIVES

THE OFFICIAL PHOTOGRAPHER of the Denver & Rio Grande Railroad was in the Marble area on an assignment in 1910, when he photographed the busy community. He pointed his camera lens toward the northwest for this panoramic view. The tall white building toward the left was the Marble Masonic Lodge, No. 137, chartered on September 20 of 1910. Colonel Channing F. Meek's large house — with an excellent view from three sides — was located high above Marble, on the safety of the hillside above Carbonate Creek. Many tents were being lived in at this time, due to the lack of available homes. The townspeople were enjoying the growing prosperity of the Colorado-Yule Marble Company at this time.

Mrs. Curley did not file the appeal bond until June 28. The cases were tried May 23.[13] It was, therefore, more than a month afterward when she filed the bond.

The case was set for hearing in the county court at Gunnison last week and Mrs. Curley was there with her attorney, John Noonan of Glenwood. The attorney representing the city of Marble called the attention of Judge Hetherington to the failure of the defendant to file her appeal bond within the time specified by law. The court, therefore, had no option but to dismiss the case without hearing.

The action of the court makes it obligatory upon Mrs. Curley to pay the fine or appeal to the supreme court of the state, alleging error. It is likely she will take this latter course. If the supreme court affirms the judgment of the lower court, she must then either pay or go to jail.

---

[13] "Police Docket Town of Marble, Colorado," Gunnison County, August 1899 to August 1925.

The Marble Booster,
August 6, 1911.

The city is about to proceed to collect the enormous fines recently assessed in the police magistrate's court against Mrs. J.J. Curley. These fines, on eleven counts for bootlegging, amounted to $3,200. There have accrued about $100 in costs, also, which must be borne by Mrs. Curley. The council, at the meeting Wednesday night, instructed the clerk to communicate with the sheriff and levy an execution on the property owned by Mrs. Curley in Gunnison county.

• • • • •

Mrs. Curley apparently continued her bootlegging activities. In January, 1912, when the marshal was called to settle a fight at the Main Hotel he arrested J.J. Curley and a man called McHugh. The latter said Mrs. Curley was selling liquor.

Continued on Page 172

'20.

HENRY L. JOHNSON PHOTO – ESTHER BAUMLI SANCHEZ COLLECTION

WALKING UP EAST MAIN STREET in Marble, the photographer captured these wooden-frame buildings on his glass negative in 1909. Starting at the far right, the Kobey Clothing Store occupied the corner of East Main and Center streets. Next door was Dever Jewelers, and next to it is a former saloon building, with a stack of split wood out (to the left) next to the sidewalk. A platform scale was positioned at the edge of the street, with weighing controls housed inside the tall

vertical box (to the right). Notice the fire-alarm box on the pole beside the box in the street. The box was used to store fire hose. The arc light used for street lighting was fastened to a cable over the center of the street. A pulley and cord lowered the fixture within reach (at street level) for whomever maintained the lamp. Electric power reached Marble near the end of 1908.

WALKING FARTHER EAST on Main Street during 1909, Henry Johnson captured this interesting view. On the north side of East Main Street stood the two-story Dix Rooming House, an unidentified shop, a barber shop (with a red, white and blue "barber pole" painted onto the roof support), the Marble Laundry and the Marble City Hotel. The last two tall buildings are the Elite Bakery and Carey's Ice Cream Parlour (beyond East Third Street. A fire-alarm box (with a telephone inside) is fastened to the telephone pole (at right).

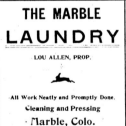

The Marble Booster,

January 20, 1912.

The Marshal, thereupon, called Fisher and raided the hotel. In Mrs. Curley's rooms were found two barrels of whisky in pint bottles and in the basement was found a barrel of bottled beer. The liquor was seized and Mrs. Curley was arrested.

• • • • •

She was tried on three counts and fined a total of $900 and costs. Since she was not able to pay the fine or supply bond she was put in the Marble jail.

The Marble Booster,

February 3, 1912.

Mr. and Mrs. J.J. Curley, who are confined in the city jail, the one having been fined for fighting and the other for bootlegging, have determined to serve out their time rather than pay their fines... If she stays in jail she will have to serve sixty days on each count, a total of six months. The fines will still stand against her at the end of that time. J.J. Curley will have to serve thirty-three days. The marshal took down to the jail last Saturday a stove, a supply of coal and a lot of dishes and cooking utensils, together with a quantity of flour, bacon, potatoes and other food supplies. Hereafter the Curleys will do their own housekeeping in the jail.

• • • • •

To prevent outside liquor salesmen from soliciting sales in Marble, the Board of Trustees passed on February 7, 1912 ordinance No. 30, "To prohibit the solicit-

AT THE RIGHT you can see the same wooden firehose box shown in the previous view, with the fire alarm on the pole. Beyond is a general store run by J. F. Parish. Next in line is the Mertens & Graham store, followed by the Main Hotel, the City Drug Store and the Aude Pool Hall. Across East Third Street is the Marble Trading Company store.

ing of orders for the sale or purchase of intoxicating, spirituous, malt, vinous or fermented liquors."[14]

None of these efforts succeeded in the long run as the demand for liquor was too great. But in early 1912 the "dry" boosters thought they had won.

The Marble Booster,
February 24, 1912.

For the first time since the saloons were voted out of Marble three years ago last November, this town is safely in the "dry" column. Not a drink nor a bottle can be had for love or money. Old "soaks" who have heretofore had no trouble obtaining liquor are saying to each other, "she's a tough country to live in," and they feel, like the immortal Casey, that "somewhere the sun is shining but there is no joy in Marble.

• • • • •

[14] The Marble Booster, February 10, 1912.

The town had grown to a respectable size and value by 1911.

The Marble Booster,
October 21, 1911.

The final account of the county assessor has not yet been made and will not be until December [1911], but the total assessed valuation of the town of Marble as it now stands is $92,480, according to information just received by The Booster from A.M. Thomas, the assessor.

In March 1913 Marble politics finally began to heat up. Eleven of the Democrats in the town held a "secret" caucus to nominate a slate for the coming April election. Nominated were: W.L. Girdner, cashier of the Marble City State Bank, for mayor; Charles Sistig, bar-

Continued on Page 188

WHILE ON EAST MAIN STREET in 1909, Henry Johnson turned his camera toward the south for this excellent "downtown" view. Left to right are the Aude Pool Hall, City Drug Store, a tiny tailor shop, Main Hotel (with what probably was a restaurant on the main floor), Henry Mertens' hardware store and a general store operated by J. F. Parish. Whitehouse Mountain looms over the scene (in the background, at the left).

175

GEORGE BROWN (left), Pete Lipson and Henry Mertens, the proprietor, are out in front of the Mertens & Graham hardware store. Rooms were offered for rent on the second floor of this building. The entrance to the overhead apartments was on the sidewalk, along East Main Street.

NOTICE THE UPPER WINDOW of the hardware store, which had been decorated for Christmas. Behind the outside window seat you can peer inside the lower store window to see an array of fancy dinnerware and home decorations. A thermometer was located at the entrance, so everyone could talk about the weather.

THIS IS THE EARLIEST KNOWN photograph that shows the Fire Bell Tower, which was located at the center of Marble in 1912. Marble Hose Cart No. 1 was housed in the base of the new Marble Bandstand, erected on the corner of Main and Center streets. Thode's Lumber Company had built a new office warehouse, shown this side of the Fire Bell Tower, painted white (with three small windows). A large quantity of cut timber was stacked in the lumber yard. This was the year that Colonel Channing Meek met his untimely death from a runaway train on the Yule tramway line.

AN UNKNOWN PHOTOGRAPHER took this unusual view of Marble as he looked toward the southwest one day in 1913. Mill Mountain, across the Crystal River from the Colorado-Yule Marble Company, had been nearly stripped of standing

trees because of snowslides that had occurred previously. On the next four pages, this photograph has been enlarged by 500 percent, so you can have a closer look at the town and identify buildings.

MARBLE BOOSTER AD – 1911

MAIN STREET IN MARBLE ran east and west, across this view. At the far left, on East Main Street, is the Marble Trading Company, on the corner of East Third Street. In the foreground are the backsides of Carey's Ice Cream Parlour and the Elite Bakery. The next block on East Main Street shows the rear of each property, including the Marble City Hotel, Marble Laundry and Dix Boarding House, as well as a general store next to Center Street, beside the shoe shop. The Kobey Clothing Store is across the street at this location. From the Marble Band Stand, on the southwest corner of Center Street, look toward the west and you will get a glimpse of an ice-cream store and the Fussone Theater. The Masonic Temple, with a dancehall on the second floor, is behind the theater. The Colorado-Yule Marble Company's electric-tramway line runs across the top edge of the scene.

IN THE LAST TWO FRAMES of this 1913 photograph you are looking toward the southwest. You can pick out West Main Street, where *The Marble Booster* newspaper was located (on the west bank of Carbonate Creek), with a small grocery store nextdoor. The Williams Brothers General Store and the Marble Post Office shared the same large building on the southwest corner of West Main and West First streets. The City Meat Market occupied the next building, and there is no identification for the third one. Higher up the hill, on West Main Street, is the old office building occupied by the Colorado-Yule Marble Company (before the firm moved their office into the mill). Two company-built cottages were up West First Street, across from the post office. William McManus invested his money in purchasing a row of houses, just being completed (lower center), facing East Marble Street — between West Center and West Third streets. Rooftops of the Colorado-Yule Marble Company's mill appear across the top edge of the view.

BLEU D. STROUD PHOTOS

THE DUFF HOME was one of the early dwellings built in Marble during 1903. The roof was canvas, with a smokejack passing through it. By 1905, the Duff home had taken on a new appearance, in the second photograph (below), where you are looking east. Notice the same tall pine tree that can be seen above. This property is located across the street from St. Paul's Episcopal Church on West State Street.

HENRY L. JOHNSON PHOTO – ESTHER BAUMLI SANCHEZ COLLECTION

WILLIAM McMANUS, one of the top men in management of the Colorado-Yule Marble Company, purchased this row of homes in 1913 with his savings. He was well aware of the need for comfortable family homes in Marble, which could be bought for a reasonable price.

A FEW YEARS had gone by when this photograph was taken of the McManus dwellings on East Marble Street. Changes include a new structure on the left corner of East Third Street, and the front porch on the fourth home was missing. The fifth home was missing, and an additional house was at the right.

HENRY L. JOHNSON PHOTO – JACK D. CLEMENSON COLLECTION

WINTER SNOW had made East State Street almost impassable in this view, ca. 1916. The cross street (at the left) is East Third Street. Residents often piled ashes onto the street in front of their homes when emptying their heating stoves — noticable in the black piles on the street (at the left). One resident was out shoveling, and a homeowner (at the right) was partially hidden behind a porch pillar. These houses were built with practically no insulation, making it necessary to keep a hot fire burning for many hours during frigid winter days.

ber, E.D Barton, blacksmith, and Ben Jorgenson, for trustees. The Booster stated that the caucus was the idea of Girdner, C.C. McWilliams and Tom Boughton. Frank Frost implied that Girdner was still a resident of Carbondale since he voted there last November. The editor questioned why this group felt it necessary to present a slate in opposition to the Peoples' Party. He said that of the current board of trustees, three were Democrats and three were Republicans. He asked if Girdner was against the marble company, since it was the greatest supporter of his bank.

Mr. Girdner's reply in the paper the next week did not really answer Frost's questions and made statements the editor claimed were false. It appeared that Girdner's approach was that of an unexperienced politician and Frost pretty well destroyed his arguments. The issues seemed to be the question of saloons in Marble, and more importantly, the personalities and principles of the candidates.

The election settled the controversy, apparently to everyone's satisfaction, as Girdner later told Frost that "he was glad it turned out the way it did, and he was sorry he ever went into the political arena."

The Marble Booster,
March 1 & 8, and April 5, 1913.

It's all over—the town election—and the Peoples' party ticket won out by a big majority. The people of Marble, given a chance to express themselves at the polls, did not hesitate to put their stamp of approval on the ticket that bore the indorsement of the Colorado-Yule company, just as The Booster predicted would be the case.

• • • • •

The town government managed to survive the ups and downs of the economy, caused by World War I and the Great Depression of the 1930's, but the onset of World War II was more than a one-industry economy could handle. In the fall of 1941, the quarry and mill closed, and the next year all the facilities of the marble company were dismantled and sold for scrap, which was badly needed for the war effort. All but 40 or 50 of the people moved out, and in 1945, the town failed to have an election to continue official functions. There seemed to be no need for a town then. The post office closed by 1943, and there were predictions that Marble would become a ghost town. However, higher prices for minerals stimulated an increase of mining in the area, and

this kept the remaining people busy. What had been left of the town after the August 8, 1941, flood of mud and rocks was further damaged by the even larger flood of July 31, 1945. The end of the war brought reduced demand for minerals, so most of the remaining people left. For several years, only Charles and Marjorie Orlosky and Theresa Herman remained in town. The Hammond Atlas published about that time listed Marble with a population of one, as the Orloskys had moved to the other side of Beaver Lake, leaving only Mrs. Herman in the town. In later years letters continued to be addressed to "The One Resident of Marble" by school children

around the country who were intrigued by a town of one person.[15]

This was a far cry from the formerly prosperous town of about two thousand persons. The dreams of the early prospectors and the developers of the superb marble deposit had finally died. Apparently, the officials in the Secretary of State's office in Denver did not notice the demise of the town. No action was taken to dis-incorporate it and former town officials held on to

town records they happened to have in their possession. Years later, Mrs. Herman told the author that she had been the last town clerk, and was still owed some salary when the town government died. She said she was holding some of the town records because she had not been paid. After her death, local rumor indicated these records were later destroyed.

REACTIVATION OF THE TOWN OF MARBLE

The government of the Town of Marble being dormant and inactive for twenty-seven years; conditions

[15] As late as 1988, letters so addressed were delivered by the Star Route carrier out of the Carbondale Post Office to the author in his capacity as president of the Marble Historical Society. Each letter was answered with information about the town's history and current situation, and in several cases, continuing correspondence resulted.

Continued on Page 192

THIS SMALL HOUSE is believed to have been built about 1910, on the north side of East Silver Street, which places it as the second house west of present-day Beaver Lake Lodge. Charlie Limerick's cabin in-between was moved by Brinkmeyer from Marble's Main Street to the present location. Adam Troha stood in his fenced yard, which had a sidewalk made of marble.

THIS LITTLE COTTAGE (on the following page) was located near East Hays and East Third streets, and it was occupied by the town's principal photographer, Henry L. Johnson. This house is on the highest-plotted street on the hill north of Marble. Jack Clemenson was fortunate in having stayed with the Johnson's during the fall of 1942. Currently (in 1992), Marshall Barnard occupies this home.

A DINING-ROOM TABLE, set for Christmas dinner, was photographed inside Henry L. Johnson's home before holiday festivities began. The Johnson's front door is at the left, with a Swiss cuckoo clock near the ceiling. A thermometer was mounted beside the living-room window, near Henry's desk.

PROBABLY A SELF-PORTRAIT, Henry L. Johnson was mining in South America when this photograph was snapped. He was known as "H. L." by some Marble residents and as "Old Shaky" by others.

HENRY JOHNSON
ART PHOTOGRAPHER
Portraits and Views

finally changed in the area enough to encourage local residents to resurrect the town government. These changed conditions were brought on by an increased population due primarily to greater interest by tourists. After World War II, this beautiful valley was discovered by some persons and re-visited by many former residents. One visitor from Arizona was Wade Loudermilk, and he fell in love with the pristine beauty, as so many others had before him. He purchased a house on the corner of East Second and Silver streets and converted it into the Beaver Lake Lodge. Several small, old houses were moved onto the property to use as cabins, and a new tourist industry was born.

Loudermilk and other developers learned that the public was interested in visiting the area, and old houses were renovated and new cabins and houses were built. This development was hampered by the great distance to the county seat at Gunnison, and it was felt the town could better control its destiny with a local government. The primary incentive to reactivate the town government was the birth of the Marble Ski Area, on the mountainside above town, in 1970. Several persons, led by Lloyd Blue, thought the ski area developers were trying to take over control of the area and were not adequately concerned with environmental preservation. Blue finally came to the conclusion that these develop-

ers were serious, and if their activities could not be prevented, the town should gain as much as possible from their actions. Thus, the idea developed to reactivate the town government and have a legal basis for some control over the ski area.

An attorney, J.E. DeVilbiss, was contacted for legal advice on the procedures necessary to have an active town government. Investigation produced the information that the town had never been legally de-activated, so that basically, all that was needed was for the town residents to hold an election to consider the question and elect a town board of trustees and mayor. This was done in March, 1973, with sixteen persons voting and approving the proposition. Lloyd Blue was elected mayor, and the five persons selected as trustees were: Sidney Baker, Kenneth Seidel, Karin Lindquist, Bill Deem and Stanley McKay.

On March 16, 1973, the representatives of the new town government took the oath of office administered by the state Lieutenant-Governor, John Vanderhoof. This event was appropriately celebrated with a party, and the new board held its first meeting. A Resolution was passed concerning the publication of ordinances and bylaws of the Town of Marble. A copy of all the ordinances of another small town had been procured and Marble Ordinance No. 1 was passed adopting all these

AT THE LEFT: The 1914 Fire Team of Hose Cart No. 1 was fully equipped with protective helmets and waterproof coats. The lower part of the Marble Band Stand was used for the storage of the firefighting equipment. The Woods' family home sat across East Main Street in this photograph. It was built of split logs and was one of Marble's oldest buildings.

OSCAR McCOLLUM JR. PHOTO

HOSE CART No. 1 of the Marble Fire Department is now on display inside the Marble Historical Society Museum, situated in the old school house on the hill. This cart originally was housed beneath the Marble Band Stand.

OSCAR McCOLLUM JR. PHOTO

JOHN T. HERMAN, former resident in Marble, tells that the Marble Fire Department's Hose Cart No. 2 was stored in a shed beneath the Marble Band Stand.

THE MARBLE Fire Department's Fire-extinguisher Cart (below, at the right) has been refurbished, and it is currently on display at the Marble Historical Society Museum.

OSCAR McCOLLUM JR. PHOTO

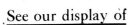

COLLECTION OF THE LATE WILLIAM McMANUS

THIS WAS THE SECOND business establishment set-up by Carey's Ice Cream Parlour, on Main Street. This place was located beside the Marble Band Stand, and it was built in 1912. The Fire Bell Tower is in the left background of this view. Potted plants are in the window, and a small sign read "Fresh Buttermilk." This building, which was owned and operated by Maggie Carey Brown, was gone from the scene after 1923.

PRIOR TO THE ARRIVAL of the railroad in Marble, the U.S. Mail and passengers traveled over the rough-and-rocky road into town in stagecoaches. Pictured at the Marble Post Office, located at West First and Main streets, U.S. flags were flying. The weary travelers were stretching their legs and backs in the warm Colorado sunshine at Marble's relatively high altitude of 7,950 feet above sea level.

RICHARD A. RONZIO COLLECTION

IT WAS THE YEAR 1910 on West Main Street, where Williams Brothers General Store and Post Office stood, beside the City Meat Market. Notice the new wooden boardwalks. This barn-type roof withstood deep snowfalls, as the building lasted until recent years. If the roof had been repaired, the place would still be standing.

THE WILLIAMS BROTHERS General Store and Post Office was still standing in 1979, although the building was abandoned many years before; however, it was torn down after the roof gave way. Unfortunately, roof shingles gave way, and this in turn rotted roof timbers, and they caved-in. On February 14, 1919, the Post Office Department ordered this post office to close, with no reason given. Five days later, the department ordered the Marble Post Office to be re-opened! Evidently, the Post Office Department had decided on their own — for no good reason at the time — that Marble had become a ghost town! This post office was still in operation in 1942. (For many years, men had swept snow off the roof during the winter to relieve the weight.)

ordinances by reference, as an interim measure. Sidney Baker was elected mayor pro-tem. The mayor produced a list of committee appointments, which were approved: I. Evalee Gifford, Municipal Judge; June K. Blue, Town Clerk and Treasurer; Judson E. DeVilbiss, Town Attorney. It was decided to post ordinances in three places in town, as provided by state statutes, in lieu of publishing them in a newspaper. The meeting was then adjourned, and the minutes were signed by Acting Clerk, Esther Fogle Neal.[16]

In the next few months, the town board considered many matters of vital interest to the town. These included: cooperation with the ski area and whether to include the town in the Marble Metropolitan District, possible sources of water, provisions for law enforcement, sewer system, zoning, Holy Cross Electric franchise, solid waste disposal, opening streets and possibly vacating some, and possibilities for a town park.

Dominant in most of these considerations was the effect the ski area would have on the town. Town citizens did not really trust the developers, and the trustees finally decided not to approve a proposed sewer line of the Marble Metro District to run through town, though by providing town taps it could have benefited the town. Ski area officials asked the town to speak on its behalf to the Forest Service for approval of use of forest land for ski runs.

[16] Board of Trustees Minutes, March 16, 1973.

Continued on Page 199

195

WEST MAIN STREET in Marble led a person up the hill to the two schoolhouses in session during 1910. The Williams Brothers' General Store and Post Office is to the left, on West First Street, with the City Meat Market next door. Beyond it stood a small building advertising chili (misspelled "chile"). Farther up the street was the original office of the Colorado-Yule Marble Company. At the far right is one of the general manager's cottages of the Colorado-Yule Marble Company, where a Mrs. Bantock advertised her milinery shop in *The Marble Booster* some

years later. The Marble City State Bank is visible west of this house, and a log structure is farther up the hill, while the porch of the Wilfred Clifton Parry house can be seen beyond the log structure. One of the children enjoyed this winter scene at the intersection, which had been equipped with an electric-arc street light. A fire-alarm box is fastened to the flagpole (at the left). As of 1942, there was a Conoco gasoline pump in front of this store. At that time, the only other place in the valley to buy gasoline was in Carbondale.

197

MARBLE HISTORICAL SOCIETY COLLECTION

THE MARBLE CITY STATE BANK moved into their new quarters in 1912 on West Main Street, across from the post office. An attached shed on the rear of the building probably held coal and wood, and stored other things as well.

FROM UP THE HILL on Main Street, the photographer was looking toward the east in this view. The downtown section of Marble appears in this photograph, which was produced in 1912. At the far left is the Marble City State Bank and a company-built house, at the intersection with West First Street. On the right side of this scene is the Williams' General Store and Post Office, with Mrs. M. Marcharenia's Grocery Store next to *The Marble Booster* newspaper, run by Frank P. Frost. The newspaper office was located on the bank of Carbonate Creek. The bridge over this creek is plainly in sight at this location. The Marble Entertainment Hall was just the other side of the bridge, while Kobey's shoe-and-clothing store is beyond, at the intersection of Center Street.

FRANK AND ROSE GERTIG COLLECTION

Land owners of the Woden-Eagle Millsite in the Mason Addition above town asked to be annexed, which later was done.

A lease was procured from the Gunnison County school district for use of the high school building as a town hall. A few years later, the town government moved to the former school house across the street so the Marble Historical Society could use the high school for its museum.

In 1974, the town filed on three cubic feet per second of absolute water and another three cfs of conditional water in Carbonate Creek, based on the appropriation of water in 1907 by the Marble City Water Company for the Colorado-Yule Marble Company. This water right had never been adjudicated by the Water Court, though used by the company and the town until 1942, as there did not seem to be any need to do this at that time. This new filing was approved by the court, and from that time on, the town has made a quadrennial filing each four years to prove beneficial use of the conditional water. This use was maintained in the first several years by running water from the approved point of diversion on the west side of Carbonate Creek, just above town, through the old water mains to the mill site. This amount of water diversion was adequate, and in 1979, the town leased one cubic foot of its conditional water to the newly established Marble Water Company.

HENRY L. JOHNSON PHOTO – JACK D. CLEMENSON COLLECTION

AT THE INTERSECTION of West Main and West First streets, the northwest corner was occupied by one of the Colorado-Yule Marble Company's cottages, constructed for the general managers. A second cottage (at the right) was being completed in 1912. The Marble City State Bank is at the left.

THIS COZY LITTLE HOUSE was on the north side of West Main Street, about nine lots west of the Marble City State Bank. The house is visible in the distant view of Marble, photographed in 1908. It was known as the Wilfred Clifton Parry house.

MARBLE HISTORICAL SOCIETY COLLECTION

On 14 September 1979 John Williams, great grandson of Horace Williams, who had established the Williams Brothers General Store about the turn of the century, made a presentation to the Town Board. His proposal was to organize a private, non-profit water company to lease water from the town and distribute it in new water mains. This seemed to be the best way for residents of West Marble to obtain water service, since the town was not able to provide it. Eight families agreed to each lend $7,000 to the new company, and a loan of $90,000 was obtained from the Farmers Home Administration to build a pump house, install a well and lay

OSCAR McCOLLUM JR. PHOTO

THIS PRESENT-DAY PHOTOGRAPH portrays the Wilfred Clifton Parry house, which was west of the Marble City State Bank building. An assay office was at the rear of this property. Lots with a house in Marble were taxed 25 cents each year by Gunnison County during the 1930's. Today (in 1992), one unimproved lot is taxed $400 per year.

about 5,000 feet of 6-inch and 8-inch water mains. It was agreed that any time the town could assume or pay off the company's debts, the water system would be turned over to the town at no additional cost. This seemed like a good arrangement to all concerned, and the initial system was built in the summer of 1980.

The Water Court, in 1981, approved a change in point of diversion to a well on West First Street, near the Crystal River, of 0.06 cfs of water for the Water Company to pump through its new water mains to serve parts of the town. This use of water made it possible to convert this amount of the conditional water to absolute, adding to the total amount of absolute water the town owned. In the next few years, the system of water lines was extended as there was demand.

In 1975, the town gave permission to Gunnison County for use of gravel in the bed of Carbonate Creek, along Center Street, if the county would dredge a chan-

nel for the creek in the process of removing the gravel. The county brought in a portable crusher and produced many tons of gravel in two large piles, suitable for roads. Part was given to the town for streets, and to sell to local residents. The lower part of the channel had filled up again within a few years.

The town applied for and received a $14,500 grant from the state Park Department in 1975, to develop a park along both sides of the Crystal River, fifty feet wide, where it passes through town. Several years later it was necessary to turn back the grant since the town could not provide the needed matching funds, and the town's rights to the property were in doubt.

The State Division of Local Government provided a $7,000 grant to fund a feasibility study for a sewer system for the town. When the study determined it would cost 1.5-million dollars to build an adequate system, nothing further was done.

Continued on Page 211

201

THIS WAS THE INTERIOR of *The Marble Booster* **news-paper, which was located on West Main Street, next to Carbonate Creek. We might imagine that Frank Frost was at the typewriter, with his wife next to him, while a pressman was operating one of the small hand-fed platen letterpresses (at the left). Paper stock was kept on the shelving (at the right).**

Anniversary Number of

VOLUME 5.   ::   NUMBER 1.

THE BOOSTER

2nd Section

FRANK P. FROST, EDITOR & PROP.

MARBLE, GUNNISON COUNTY, COLORADO
SATURDAY, MARCH 13, 1915

FRANK P. FROST, PROPRIETOR OF THE BOOSTER.

Some Inside Booster History

This issue marks the beginning of the fifth volume of The Marble Booster. Four years have I labored with this paper in Marble. The Booster has grown to be a darned good little newspaper and I'm glad of it.

Four years ago the first of this March I landed in Marble with about $200 in my pocket. I suppose it would be funny to say right here that I still have the pocket. But, to be accurate and cut out the comic stuff, I have made money in Marble. I have a plant that I wouldn't take $3,500 for and I have a few dollars besides, and I owe nobody anything.

It was Paul J. Tischhauser who started me on the road to Marble. I didn't know Paul at that time from a goat, but he heard of me through an advertisement I had inserted in a musical paper. I had left the Star at Kansas City, where I had been employed for a long term of years as a reporter, and had taken a flyer at country journalism, where my fancy was leading me, first at a small town in Kansas, where I thought I was going to have a chance to own an interest in the business. But the owner and I could never agree on terms. I was there for one year and it was while editing and managing this Kansas paper that I inserted the advertisement in the musical paper that caught the eye of Paul J. Tischhauser.

In our correspondence, Paul had mentioned that he thought a company could be formed here in Marble to buy the plant and good will of the late but not lamented Sylvia Smith. I had told him I was not overburdened with money and could not swing such a proposition by myself. Upon my writing him to see what he could do, he got together a bunch of loyal Marble men and put the proposition up to them.

The late Colonel C. F. Meek took a leading part in the preliminary plans which led to my coming to Marble and with him as leader in the financial arrangements, a sufficient number of business men took stock in the proposed company so that Paul was enabled to go to Miss Smith with a proposition to buy her out. She put a price on her outfit and it was accepted by Paul, representing the stock company. But when Paul went to make a payment and bind the bargain she refused to sign the papers. She had heard that the Colorado-Yule company was backing the proposition and she declined to leave Marble at the behest of the company which she so heartily despised.

So the deal fell through, but Paul wrote me at Kansas City to come on anyway, that a newspaper plant, good enough to start with, was in storage here and that I could get hold of it on terms that would enable me to start up a newspaper.

I well remember the day I landed in Marble. It was the 6th of March and I had on a thin pair of patent leather shoes in which I had to wade the slush, a foot deep, up to the sidewalks of Main street. I hadn't worn a pair of rubbers for years and had forgotten there was such a thing. Of course, I got a "beaut" of a cold the first thing.

It didn't take Paul Tischhauser long to put me in front of Colonel Meek and negotiations were at once opened for the sale of the plant of the defunct Marble Age, which the company had taken on a mortgage and had stored in one of the company buildings. The Colonel told me to go ahead and move the plant to the location I had determined upon for the paper's office, look it over, and then fix my own price for it; also fix my own terms of payment.

Fair enough proposition, wasn't it? And let me say right here that during the time I knew Colonel Meek I always found him just as fair on everything else we had in common.

I had rented a small building on a side street, next to a livery barn, for the office, and to this place I moved the outfit of the defunct Age. It took eleven days to straighten it out and get out the first issue of The Booster. I well remember that neither Colonel Meek nor Charles Austin Bates ever liked that name I gave the paper.

Mr. Tischhauser secured the first copy of the first issue of The Booster. I. M. Kobey ran him a close second. Both gentlemen came early to The Booster office on the eventful day and waited patiently until the press began turning out the papers. Mrs. A. B. Sharp was the first bona fide cash subscriber whose name was entered upon the subscription books.

For the first eighteen months of the life of The Booster the paper was printed with the old Washington handpress (man-killer, John Jarrell used to call it) that came with the Age outfit. In the summer of 1912 I began to think seriously of building a new home for The Booster on Main street. Again it was Colonel C. F. Meek who came to the rescue. The Colonel endorsed my note at the Marble City State bank for $1,000 and the building was soon under way. We moved into it on September 10, 1912. On the following October 26 we threw to one side the old Washington press and began the publication of The Booster in the form it comes to you today.

Colonel Meek died as the result of the injuries he sustained in the trolley accident before we had gotten into our new building. With his death the bottom at once dropped out of everything in Marble, as our citizens well remember. "Fate" Girdner, cashier of the bank here where I borrowed the money to put up The Booster building, has since told me that he never expected me to pay the note I owed the bank. He was, I think, agreeably surprised to find from the records of the bank that I paid off the note in full in just fifteen months after it was executed. This final payment was followed a couple of months later by the final payment on the note I owed the Colorado-Yule company for the old Age outfit with which I began business.

In this connection I am happy to state there remains nothing in the present Booster office to remind us of the old Age outfit except the Washington handpress which we now use to take proofs on. For this use it is good for many years to come. Every pound of the type has been sold as old material in Denver and the proceeds used as part payment on new type and material, with which The Booster is well supplied. The Age job press was smashed beyond redemption at the time we moved into our new building.

The Booster now enjoys a circulation of 1,000 copies each week. It is the aim of all who have any connection with its publication to make it as neat as we can and to give subscribers the worth of their money. There are just three of us in the harness—Mrs. Frost, who sets most of the straight matter for the paper; William von Mueller, foreman, who takes care of the mechanical end generally and is an exceedingly competent printer; and the writer of this article, who is the manipulator of the typewriter and general office ornament, also fishing editor.

The Booster today is conducted along exactly the same lines as it laid out for itself in the first issue. It is independent in politics and it aims to give local news in preference to trying to settle the affairs of the nation. It is loyal to the core and it will continue to do everything in its power for Marble and its industries.

VIEW OF THE TYPE-SETTING DEPARTMENT OF THE BOOSTER.

Both the mechanical and editorial force of The Booster is shown in the picture. Mrs. Frost sits on the stool by the front window; Mr. von Mueller, foreman, is composing one of his justly famous jobs, while the editor is stalling around at the imposing stone, so that he can get his phiz in the picture. In the room through the door at the right is really where the editor belongs, but you know how it is when a man with a photograph box comes along. The picture shows a front view of our former office stove, also, and you will observe that it isn't such a bum-looker from this angle as it appears from the back.

OSCAR McCOLLUM JR. PHOTO

THIS WOODEN-FRAME HOUSE has been extensively remodeled and stands at the corner of West First and West Silver streets, across from Horace William's house. It was built for Dr. Stevenson, ca. 1910. This dwelling is in sight, near the center, on the right side of the view on Page 185.

BLEU D. STROUD COLLECTION

DOCTOR H. H. SWIFT and family were enjoying their sunny front porch of their home on the north side of West State Street. This place was near the center of the block where the Episcopal Church stands today. Notice the doctor's "shingle" beside the front door, with visiting hours posted. This place was later used by Theresa V. Francis as a school.

COLONEL WILLIAM McMANUS was getting into Colonel Channing Meek's automobile, parked in front of the McManus residence. This was the second house down from the Episcopal Church in Marble. Colorado-Yule Marble Company homes are in view across the road, on West State Street. Dr. Swift's horse was grazing on the grass inside the front yard — a good way to mow the lawn! (William McManus was a nephew of Colonel Meek.)

COLLECTION OF THE LATE WILLIAM McMANUS

THE COLORADO-YULE MARBLE COMPANY built these supervisors' houses along West State Street, between West Second and West Third streets, a block up the hill from the Episcopal Church. These houses, constructed in 1909, had about six rooms. The lower view shows the same block during the grip of winter's snow. Altogether, the company constructed and owned 91 houses for employees. These houses rented for $6.00 and $7.00 per month.

HENRY L. JOHNSON PHOTOS – MARBLE HISTORICAL SOCIETY COLLECTION

VERY LITTLE TRAFFIC had moved through the foot-deep snow in this Christmas-card scene, illustrating company-owned cottages across the street from St. Paul's Episcopal Church in Marble. Heavy snowfalls are typical for this part of Colorado.

SEVERAL COMPANY COTTAGES were constructed along West State Street, on the same block as the Episcopal Church — with one lower down the street, still under construction. What was probably the roof of the Masonic Temple is barely in view beyond.

BLEU D. STROUD COLLECTION

207

THIS IS ANOTHER COMMON VIEW of Marble, believed to be taken in about 1914. On East Silver Street, toward the right, are the homes purchased by William McManus, and below this is an alley view of the backs of business buildings along East Main Street. Many new homes had been constructed by this date in the lower part of Marble. Thode's Lumber Yard was in the right foreground, with stacked lumber in view. The Masonic Temple appears as the tallest building in Marble (at the left), where additional homes had been constructed. At the upper left a larger company house is in view, with a barn-type roof.

THESE VERY EARLY-DAY slab houses in Marble were located fronting the Colorado-Yule Marble Company's mill property. This was at West Fourth Street, on lots owned by the company. The occupants probably had the interiors made-up into nice living quarters.

THIS STRUCTURE is one of the slab houses constructed shortly after the Colorado-Yule Marble Company mill was built in Marble. The house faced the oil-house building, and they were just to the left of the Drafting Room at West Third Street.

THE LARKIN HOTEL on the northwest corner of West Park and West Third streets fixes the position of these small Colorado-Yule Marble Company houses. They were equipped with electric lights, and outdoor running water was available from Carbonate Creek at the street hydrant. Fifty of these homes were built, and some were moved to Grand Junction during the 1940's, after the marble company was closed down. Others were sold on their lots for $2,500 each.

In the first three years after the reactivation of the town government, many items of concern to the town were taken up by the trustees. The mayor, Lloyd Blue, looked into many opportunities for the town to receive various benefits from state and federal programs. This included the following: A map of areas of the town subject to flooding was prepared and filed, which enabled property owners to obtain federal flood insurance. Government surplus items were obtained from the Four-Corners Agency, merely for paying the freight. This included two rubber tired dozers, two two-wheeled army trailers, ten metal storage cabinets, three metal office desks and four railroad flat cars to use as bridge decks. An army 2-1/2-ton truck was received on loan from the Civil Defense Agency and the State Forest Service provided a water tank for it, to be used as a fire truck. The State Centennial-Bicentennial Committee provided a grant to construct a new bridge over the Crystal River on the quarry road, using one of the railroad flat cars as the town's matching part of the grant, along with some public donations. The town received much advice and some engineering assistance from District 10 Regional Planning Commission. The State Department of Local Affairs also provided advice on town government problems.

Other activities of the town board included preparing a zoning map to attempt to put some controls on development, reconstruction of some of the old water ditches east of Carbonate Creek, some repair to the old bell tower and installation of a flag pole on East Main Street. The staff and students of the Outward Bound school, on the mountain side above town, were always helpful in providing volunteer labor for town projects.

In June, 1976, the town obtained a lease from the Small Business Administration on about 14 acres of the old mill site property, at a token rent of $100 per year, to use it as a town park. Later, on 7 February 1979, this important site was entered on the National Park Service's National Register of Historic Places.

Early in the summer of 1976, Lloyd Blue moved to Grand Junction, and on July 9th he resigned as the mayor of Marble. At this time, Kirk Blue resigned as trustee. Kenneth Seidel, one of the trustees, was appointed by the board to fill the position of mayor, and Mabel Lyke and Oscar McCollum were appointed to these vacancies on the board by the remaining trustees.

HENRY L. JOHNSON PHOTO – ESTHER BAUMLI SANCHEZ COLLECTION

ACCLAIMED AS MARBLE'S largest-and-best hotel, the Larkin Hotel was advertized as clean and comfortable, but was by no means stylish. Meals were well-cooked and wholesome. The daily rates at the hotel were between $1.50 and $2.00. A large veranda provided an excellent view of the mountains from the hotel. The hotel laundry was in the lean-to at the rear, on West Third Street. The Larkin Meat House is at the far right, behind the hotel.

HENRY L. JOHNSON PHOTO – ESTHER BAUMLI SANCHEZ COLLECTION

THIS REMODELED DWELLING is now on the site of the old Larkin Hotel, tucked away into the forest of deciduous trees — which was on the northwest corner of West Park and West Third streets.

About this time, Stanley and David McKay also resigned from the board, and Debra McKay resigned as Town Clerk, a position she had recently assumed from June Blue. David Beamis and Kenny Smith filled these vacant positions, and Lois Ann McCollum was appointed clerk. John LeMay and Dorothy Seidel made up the remainder of the board. The new officers were sworn in by Town Magistrate, Jack Orlosky. Thus, the first three years after the reactivation of the town government was ended, along with the board's domination by Lloyd Blue.

During this period many residents contributed much unpaid time to get the town functioning. It was common for the mayor and various trustees to travel at their own expense to Gunnison or Denver on town business, and several families made cash donations and interest-free loans of $100 to help the town with special needs. The town received a grant of $5,060, matched by $253 from the town, to purchase three police radios.

Continued on Page 217

THE MARCHESINI GROCERY STORE in Marble originally was located on West Park Street. This later became the residence of Mr. and Mrs. Reheuser. It was located on the block between West Fifth and West Sixth streets, facing the mill of the Colorado-Yule Marble Company.

MRS. REHEUSER, resident of the former Marchesini Grocery Store, was out back with her daughter, Leona, in front of the outhouse. They were busy feeding their chickens. Fresh eggs were an important part of their diet — and chicken and noodles was a sumptuous Sunday-dinner treat for the family.

HENRY L. JOHNSON PHOTO – COLLECTION OF THE LATE WILLIAM McMANUS

COLORADO-YULE MARBLE COMPANY houses had been built along both sides of West Park Street. They were just east of the mill. The photographer was looking toward the west. These houses rented for $4.00 per month, and they each had four rooms. They are shown here as they appeared in 1909. They had the luxury (for the day) of outdoor running water from a faucet, plus electric lighting. A fire-alarm phone box was mounted next to a water hydrant.

PHOTOGRAPHED SOMETIME later in Marble, the same company homes as shown above were in need of paint, probably postponed due to the financial condition of the company. Most residents would not take care of the exterior of their houses, considering that they belonged to the company. Larger houses farther west rented for $6.00 per month.

HENRY L. JOHNSON PHOTO – MARBLE HISTORICAL SOCIETYCOLLECTION

OSCAR McCOLLUM JR. PHOTO

DUNCAN McCOLLUM, the son of Oscar McCollum Jr., was at the Marble town jail, which sat on East State Street, midway between East Second and Third streets, near the alley. This jail housed numerous residents during Prohibition. This, in turn, brought in a considerable sum of money in fines, and the fines paid the wages for law enforcement.

LOOKING DOWN MAIN STREET from Center Street in Marble, some noticeable changes had taken place on the south side of the street in 1914. The Kobey shoe-and-clothing store (at the far right) had moved their sign to a higher position, fastened onto the false front. A confectionary shop was next door, shared with a barber shop. A barber pole was out beside the boardwalk. A cobbler occupied the early-day saloon, with a tall board fence alongside it. City Hall, next in line, had been built recently on a vacant lot. This building had a tall false front. A general store occupied the building made of marble, while the City Market & Grocery was east of it.

HENRY L. JOHNSON PHOTO – JACK D. CLEMENSON COLLECTION

This was considered necessary for emergency communications in the area as often the telephone service was unreliable. Snow plowing in parts of the town was a problem, as the county only maintained the main route through town. Clayton Kuhles suggested to the board that the town purchase a dozer for snow plowing and other uses. When this was approved, he located one in Gunnison for $9,650, which served the purpose for a number of years.

A major problem appeared for the town because of the manner in which the town was first incorporated in 1899, and its subsequent inactive status after World War II. In the 1960's, when the town had no active government, some property owners petitioned the Gunnison County Commissioners to vacate the streets and alleys. The commissioners took this action. After the reactivation of the town, several of the streets were reopened, after being effectively closed by the mud flows of 1941 and 1945. In 1978, Dr. Francis Burdick, who owned a house and lots on both sides of East Third Street at Hill Street, sued the town to quit title to his alleged ownership of portions of Third Street and the alley south of his property. The town attorney, Patrick Carrico, contended that the action of the county commissioners to vacate the streets was "null and void and has no weight nor legal significance," even though the town had no active government. At the trial in county court in December, 1979, the court agreed with Carrico, but ruled that Burdick had rights to the half of the street and alley bordering his property, since it was proved the former owners had fenced and used these portions for many years. This effectively reduced a portion of Third Street to a width of 33 feet, which seemed to be adequate under the circumstances.

The town election of April, 1980, stimulated much interest and many candidates for the trustee positions. A political rally was held and every candidate had a chance to express his opinions on matters of current interest. After the election the Board of Trustees met, and, "Beginning at 7:30 p.m. on 11 April 1980 the following newly elected officials took their oaths of office: David H. Beamis as Mayor; Danny H. Beamis, Martha Bontrager, Pete Bontrager, Oscar D. McCollum and Steven K. Wardrum as Trustees. Clayton A. Kuhles took his oath earlier in the week due to expected absence from this meeting." Kuhles expected to be absent because at that time he was incarcerated in the Garfield County Jail in Glenwood Springs. When it appeared he would not be released in time for the meeting, the Town Clerk, Lois Ann McCollum, accompanied by Martha

THE MARBLE BOOSTER

BY FRANK P. FROST   MARBLE, GUNNISON COUNTY, COLORADO, SATURDAY, AUGUST 26, 1916   VOLUME 6; NUMBER 25

FIRE TAKES HEAVY TOLL

Flames Start in City Drug Store and Destroy Five Business Houses, with Contents, Including Henry Mertens' Magnificent Store, U. S. Postoffice and Swigart Building.

FLAMES CHECKED BY GALLO 2-STORY MARBLE BUILDING

Dynamite Used to Blow up Swigart Building, Next to Gallo's, and Heroic Volunteer Firemen Fought the Fire to a Standstill at that Point---Losses Aggregate $35,000.

Fire which broke out at 1:15 o'clock Thursday morning in the rear of the City drug store, destroyed that building and contents, spread to the Athens pool hall, next on the East, and to the United States postoffice on the West, at the same time, and then to Henry Mertens' big two-story business house, reducing all of these buildings to ashes. The Swigart building, next to Mertens' store, was dynamited to help stop the flames at the Gallo marble building, and heroic work of the firemen kept the fire from entering the Gallo store, stopping the conflagration at this point.

What proved to be the worst fire in the history of Marble, and, in fact, the only big fire the town ever has had, was discovered by Tom Beck, who was asleep in a back room of the second story of the Mertens building. Mr. Beck heard the crackle of flames, smelling smoke at the same time, and he quickly located the fire out the window of his room, which directly overlooked the blaze, then under great headway.

Tom turned in the alarm at the fire bell and soon had practically the entire population of the town out. Three lines of hose were laid but it was quickly found that pressure was sufficient only for two, and neither of these as strong as was needed.

The fire by this time had crept into the main part of the drug store and communicated to the pool hall. It was then seen that it was to be a disastrous conflagration and citizens occupied themselves with trying to save what they could from the postoffice and the Mertens store. Nothing whatever was gotten from the drug store and only a part of one pool table from the Athens place.

The progress of the flames was very rapid, owing to the highly inflammable nature of the frame buildings, and it didn't seem but a few minutes until the postoffice building was all afire and it was seen that Henry Mertens' big store was doomed. Then it was that Mayor Stephenson gave orders to blow up the Swigart building, between Mertens' and Gallo's stone building. Frank Mueller laid thirty-five sticks of dynamite adjacent to the ice box in the Swigart building and then attached a fuse which N. W. Ward fired, after warning all persons to a safe distance from the building. The detonation of the explosion was terrific and the frame building collapsed like a house of cards, allowing the firemen to successfully stop the flames from creeping into the Gallo building through the windows at front and back.

The fire was stopped at this point although it was nearly two hours after the first alarm before it was certain that the blaze was confined. Some of the very hardest fire fighting of the night was done on the frame buildings lining the alley back of the Mertens' store, which, if they had got away from control, would, in turn have fired the big livery barn across the alley from Gallo's, and this would have touched off many other houses.

It was inspiring to see the manner in which the former members of the disbanded fire department buckled into the work of fighting this great fire. Among those on the front line were Ernest Mazza, Bill Aude, Ike Kobey, Joker Walsh, William von Mueller, Joe Gallo, Terry Mullen, Andy Carlson and J. A. Nall.

The losses aggregate $35,000, divided as follows:

Swigart building, loss $2,000, no insurance. Building owned by George Swigart of Carbondale; not occupied.

Henry Mertens, loss on building, $4,000, insured for $3,000; loss on stock $13,000, $4,000 insurance. Mr. Mertens allowed a considerable part of his insurance to lapse last week, being unable to carry it during present period of business stagnation in Marble.

Postoffice building, 2-story frame, formerly Curley hotel; owned by a bonding company in Denver, no record

(Continued on last page)

Bontrager and Martha Beamis, went down to the jail and gave the oath of office to him. Kuhles had been arrested when two Marble residents reported that he had stolen a dozer. This charge later proved to be false, but it succeeded in being an embarassment to Kuhles and the town. In this election, all but one registered voter appeared at the polls, and this 96 percent turnout was published nationally by the Associated Press.

Fire protection for the area was always a concern of the residents. Soon after the town government was reactivated, a committee of the Board of Trustees was set up to oversee this matter. Various persons served as fire chief and took care of the town's fire fighting equipment. Volunteers were organized, and from time to time, took training in how to fight fires and operate the equipment. In 1982 public donations and fund rais-

A MAJOR FIRE took place in downtown Marble on August 24, 1916. All of the wooden structures east of the general store (built of marble) were burned. A safety fence was erected to keep pedestrians off the sidewalk. The large livery barn across the alley escaped the blaze. It is in view (at the left), with an ice-house building in the foreground. Altogether, six building were lost to the fire.

ers provided money to construct a 2-bay firehouse at the entrance to the Mill Site Park. Application was made to the Carbondale and Rural Fire Protection District for inclusion of the Town of Marble in the district. This was approved in an election of the district, and the town granted the district a 99-year lease on the 100x100-foot lot containing the fire house. Also, the town turned over to the district all its fire fighting equipment, and as the district assigned appropriate fire trucks to Marble, more efficient service to the area resulted.

The reactivation of this once-dead town aroused some interest in the state. Several requests were re-ceived from other small communities for information on how this revival was accomplished. The problems of a very small community (in Marble's case, less than 50 residents) operating a local government are many. The few interested people meant that each had to wear "several hats." The greatest problems derived from the general lack of experience and knowledge on how a local government operates. The reconveners fostered the public's opinion that town board meetings were general town meetings, in the early New England sense. Whenever local citizens bothered to attend trustee meetings, they thought they should be able to speak at length on any subject, and this greatly prolonged the meetings. Efforts by the mayor or the trustees to run an efficient and business-like meeting were not taken kindly by the public and some of the trustees. It was difficult to get the trustees to carry out their assigned tasks on committees, so this resulted in lengthy discussions in the meetings among persons who did not really know the facts. What progress was made was by a slow and tortuous process. It is probable that towns of less than 150 residents should not try to have their own local government. This size population can barely generate enough tax funds to hire employees. Relying on volunteers entirely is not conducive to an efficient and well-run government.

AN UNKNOWN PHOTOGRAPHER took aim at Marble from across the Crystal River, shortly after the fire of August 24, 1916, which destroyed six business buildings. These buildings stood on the foreground lots, where the Marble City Hotel can be seen, on the far side of East Main Street. The general store, built of marble, appears at the left, and the Marble Trading Company's two-story building was at the right. A bit farther to the right and one block farther north — on East Silver Street — is a glimpse of the Beaver Lake Lodge, one of the few buildings standing today (1992). By this time, it seemed that Thode's Lumber Yard was out of business. Most of the small houses at the far-east end of Marble went unchanged through the years. In the past, a bridge had been in place over the Crystal River on Center Street, which led to the Hoffman Smelter. The Treasury Mountain Railroad's mainline and siding still existed at this time.

ELKS DAY IN MARBLE was on June 16 in 1923. American flags were waving, and there were speeches and ice cream, along with picnics. Notice the snow accumulation atop Whitehouse Mountain.

THE ELKS CONVENTION of 1923 had packed the town of Marble. The Marble City Pastime had hung their business sign over the sidewalk, on the front of the second story of a building made of marble. The building to the left of the Pastime housed the Walsh & Brooks Grocery Store. An American flag was hanging over the doorway of the City Hall. The Marble Trading Company, which was in the building down the street, ceased to advertise after 1918.

THIS MAY BE ONE of the last photographs taken of Marble before the disastrous fire of August 24, 1916. The Dix Boarding House, Shoehorn Lunch Room and Marble Laundry soon burned to the ground. They are visible in this photograph on Main Street; however, after the terrible fire, these buildings were leveled. This same photograph appears on the following four pages, enlarged for greater detail.

THE SHARPNESS of this photograph — enlarged by 300 percent from the original size — tells us that the photographer probably was Henry Johnson of Marble. In the first frame, taken ca. 1915, the Masonic Hall stood with a fire escape leading down from the dance floor. The Fire Bell Tower, a backside view of Carey's Ice Cream Parlour and the Marble Band Stand appear at the center of the town. The Adrian barn still stood at this time, with a rear view here of two buildings built of marble on East Main Street. Thode's Lumber Yard seems to be out of business. Main Street lots destroyed in the fire of August 24, 1916, are visible. Across the street are buildings that were destroyed by fire in 1923. Interesting details abound of the small dwellings, their yards, gardens, fields and sheds on this and the next three pages. These pages illustrate the town to the edge of East First Street.

THIS VIEW IS THOUGHT TO BE one that was taken on the Fourth of July in Marble during 1923. Only a short time had passed since the devastating fire of May 20, 1923, which had burned down the Shoehorn Lunch Room, Dix Boarding House and Marble Laundry. Charred remains of the fire still littered the lots in the foreground. Notice the latest building (at the far left), built of marble, thought to be occupied by the Walsh & Brooks Grocery Store. The Marble Band Stand can be seen above the crowd's heads (at the right), and the Princess Theater is in view farther west.

THE PHOTOGRAPH BELOW probably was taken at East Main and East Second streets, not far from Beaver Lake, at the east end of Marble. A sheepherder apparently had arrived in Marble, and his flock was wandering through the town after being turned loose from the livestock pens on the west end of town. These sheep were later herded up into the high country, north of Marble. Because of over-grazing, sheep were believed to have caused the disastrous mudslides during the years to come. If sheep were allowed to over-graze, heavy rains would wash much of the topsoil downhill through the town.

THIS PHOTOGRAPH probably was taken inside one of Marble's barber shops, not long after electricity had been installed. Notice the old wallpaper, hair clippers, shaving mugs and wicker baskets for trash. Hair-tonic bottles were in front of the mirror behind the barber.

THE ABOVE PHOTOGRAPH, taken in 1911, is a good example of the simple life-style afforded by persons living in and around Marble during the first half of the 20th century. A modest frame house, with a wooden sidewalk and bridge over a ditch, could be considered a "dream home" in the Rockies. The location of this dwelling is unknown.

THE WILLIAMS FAMILY CLAN was enjoying this gathering in the front yard, prior to the 1941 flood. "Uncle John" (at the far left) and Ambrose (at the far right) ran the last general store and post office, across from the Marble City Bank. This two-story house was located on West State Street, south of the Masonic Temple.

HORACE WILLIAM'S HOUSE was photographed during the winter of 1942. The Colorado-Yule Marble Company superintendents' houses still stood as originally built (beyond, at the left). Notice the beautiful snow sculpture on Gallo Hill, created by the warm sun melting snow, which formed into huge icicles. There had been a coal-mine operation near the peak of Gallo Hill in years past.

THE DAN BARNE'S RANCH was nestled up against the north hillside at Marble, near the east edge of town. These folks had the luxury of owning a wonderful Model "T" Ford sedan. (A second one can be made out near the trees, in the shade at the right, with its top down.) Notice the tent building (at the far right). A close study of this photograph reveals the Treasury Mountain Railroad grade, near the center of the view, and the Colorado-Yule Marble Company's electric-tramway line to the quarry is at the far right. Beaver Lake was not much more than marshland at this time. The marble company's powerhouse is visible (at the left center), beyond the Beaver Lake marsh.

THE GRAMMAR SCHOOL of 1909 stood on West Main Street, up the hill between Fourth and West Fifth streets. This was across the street from the Marble High School, which was built later. The building contained six rooms, and it was conducted by a principal and three teachers. It accomodated 100 pupils and was constructed for $4,500.00, a considerable sum of money at that time.

THE BIG DAY HAD ARRIVED for these students in Marble — the new grammar school had been completed in 1909, and the town's professional photographer had been called upon to perform the nearly-impossible task of gaining the children's undivided attention for long enough to obtain this group photograph.

TEACHING THE CHILDREN

First settlement in this district occurred in Crystal City about 1880, and soon after, families began to arrive. It is not known when the first school opened there, but in 1887 Mrs. J.C. Johnson was teaching school in Crystal. A school house was built north of the livery stable on the east side of town in May and June, 1891,[1] which still stands. From that time on, school was held in Crystal until at least 1905, and some of the teachers were as follows:

1887	Mrs. J.C. Johnson
1891	Miss Enwall
1894	Bertie Smelcer
1900-01	Hattie Evans
1901-02	Agnes Carlberg
1904-05	Miss Cross
?	Miss Edna Richards[2]

By 1893, the town of Marble had grown enough to need a school, and Hattie Evans was the teacher that year. In July a dance was held in Marble for the benefit of the school. First classes were taught in the house which now is part of Beaver Lake Lodge. Soon after, a little red school house was built on West Main Street, across the street from the present Museum, in the high school building. Some of the earliest teachers were:

1893-94	Hattie Evans
1900	Miss A.M. Malony
1901	Emily R. Johns
1901-02	Jennie Copeland
1906	Dolly Duncan Webb

A newspaper notice in 1900 reported:

The children held Thanksgiving exercises at the school house Wednesday afternoon. A number of visitors were present.[3]

This modest report was surpassed by one in the same paper concerning the Crystal school activities, taught by Miss Evans who had moved up to that school from Marble.

Miss Evans entertained her patrons with the following Thanksgiving program by the school children:
Recitation...When Thanksgiving Comes...Vera Finley
Recitation....John's Pumpkin ...... Albert Usher
Song.........The First Washington Day...School
Recitation....The Secret .... Helen Williams
Recitation....Thanksgiving Thoughts......School
Recitation....The Refuge of the Seeds....Albert Usher
Recitation....A Thanksgiving Ladder......Helen Williams, Eugene Rosetti, John Williams, Vera Finley, Rosa Rosetti.
"America"..............................School

The children acquitted themselves excellently, and reflected great credit upon the painstaking care and ability of the teacher.

Within a few years, the first school building in Marble was too small, so it was replaced about 1908 by a four-classroom building on the same site. This building finally was torn down in 1942.

The school population continued to grow to about 200 school age children, with the expansion of the quarry and mill production, and soon another school building was required. In 1910, the high school building was constructed, containing six classrooms and an office/library. This was a community effort, as the Colorado-Yule Marble Co. donated the marble for the foundation and lower floor, and the marble workers donated their time to cut and set the stone. The total cost to the district was about $7,000. This is the building now housing the museum.

After The Marble Booster newspaper began publishing in March, 1911, almost every issue contained an article concerning the school. Most of these were routine, listing students with perfect attendance and those

---

[1] Edgerton, Frank W. & Rose, "Journal of Events Jerome Park and Crystal," 1886 - 1895, p.116; deposited at Colorado State Historical Society, Denver.

[2] See the Appendex for a more complete list of teachers in the area, compiled from various sources.

[3] The Marble Times & Crystal Silver Lance, November 30, 1900.

OSCAR McCOLLUM JR. PHOTO

THE MARBLE HIGH SCHOOL was photographed during January of 1978, which is now the location of the Marble Historical Society. A fine selection of artifacts are now housed here for visitors to see during the summer months. Oscar McCollum Jr. and his wife, Lois Ann, worked diligently for several years to build-up the collection. One outcome of this interest in Marble's history stirred the fires that eventually resulted in the publication of this book. The society continues to strive to obtain additional artifacts and photographs to keep Marble's history alive.

on the honor roll. One of the first described a school entertainment program to raise money for school ground equipment.

The Marble Booster,

March 25, 1911.

The entertainment given in Yoeman hall last Saturday night for the benefit of the public school playground fund was one of the most successful held during the winter season. At the small admission fee charged—25 cents—a total of $38.56 was taken, which means that the hall was filled. The audience was appreciative, too, and every member of the excellent program was warmly applauded.

To attempt an individual mention of the performers would merely be to repeat over and over the word "meritorious." For each number was creditably rendered and the program was freely spoken of as one of the best ever arranged in Marble. The following was the program in detail:

Introductory remarks ....Prof. Walker
Clarinet solo...Canary Polka ....Frank P. Frost

Reading.........Shamus O'Brien ....Rev. Walton
Vocal solo......I'll Take You Home Again, Kathleen...June Carey
Reading.........A Pair of Boots ....Helen M. Tandy
Mixed quartet...Come Where the Lilies Bloom....

     Soprano—Mrs. L.P. Montgomery
     Alto—Mrs. Homer Harrington
     Tenor—Dr. F.B. Stephenson
     Basso—Charles Van Zandt

Reading.........How Rubenstein Played the Piano...Prof. Walker
Violin solo.....Sextet from Lucia............
Dr. Stephenson
Sketch..........The Widow's Mistake ....Mary L. Sharp, June Carey, J.T. Beasley
Instrumental trio....Berceuss......

     Violin—Dr. Stephenson
     Clarinet—Frank P. Frost
     Piano—Mrs. Stephenson

Clarinet solo.....Spring Song ....Frank P. Frost
Western sketch....Original..................
Messrs. Van Zandt, Stephenson, Cantello, Kobey, Sharp, and Saint

THE MARBLE HIGH SCHOOL was completed in 1910 and was constructed across the street from the grammar school — up the hill on Main Street. The bell tower and fire escape were added later. Notice the use of marble for the foundation and front-porch supports. The Colorado-Yule Marble Company mill site is down the hill from this location. During 1916, the school system had enrolled 120 boys and 100 girls.

The money realized is to be devoted to equipping the playground at the school and already a start has been made. Swings, a turning pole, another merry-go-round, see-saws, and a toboggan slide are among the devices planned for the entertainment and development of the little folks.

. . . . .

A further article described other school activities.

The Marble Booster,
March 25, 1911.

The pupils of the lower grades have shown much interest in planting different kinds of seeds during the past week.

August Fregosi deserves praise for excellent composition work.

Katherine Walton re-entered school this week.

The boys are showing their appreciation of the playground movement by helping to dig holes for swing posts.

The pupils of the sixth and seventh grades have made unusual efforts lately to do creditable class work. Members of the eighth grade often stay after school of their own accord to do unfinished work or to prepare work for the next day.

Ask John Tischhauser what he thinks of Cicero as an orator. John has the industry that wins.

The ninth grade pupils have had very good lessons in Ancient History during the week, although the lessons assigned were longer than usual.

In the next issue of the newspaper, an article on "News of the Schools" gives a further glimpse of what the school was like in 1911.

The Marble Booster,
April 1, 1911.

Miss Perdue's pupils have been quite regular in attendance.

Maggie Brown and Herman Hays have returned to school.

The work in Miss Tandy's room has been especially fine during the week.

Hurschel Adams, one of the earnest workers of the eighth grade, has been compelled to be absent from school on account of illness. It is hoped that he will soon be back at school.

The Principal listened with much pleasure on Thursday morning, to the analysis of examples by pupils of the fourth grade. Their statements showed that the class had been carefully trained.

Mrs. Montgomery's pupils have been cleaning their desks and are inbued with the spirit of cleanliness. They have been very active in making flower beds. They are preparing one bed for planting potatoes.

Attendance has been good in the Primary department. Tommy Stinson entered the first grade. The primary pupils enjoy making calendars for each month. For March they made a kite calendar. Miss Tandy reports an enrollment of twenty-five.

HELEN WILLIAMS was a grammar-school teacher in Marble and posed with this group of youngsters on the front steps of the school.

Mrs. Stephenson, Dr. Swift, Rev. Walton and Mr. Manning visted the schools during the week. Dr. Swift told the boys and girls how much they could help in cleaning and beautifying the school yards and the yards at home. Mr. Manning impressed the pupils of the grammar department and high school with the necessity of regular attendance at school and of making the most of their oportunities for advancement.

. . . . .

Apparently, not all persons were convinced of the importance of a good education. In a "School News" article in 1912, the principal felt it necessary to lecture the parents.

The Marble Booster,
January 6, 1912.
School is the pupil's business. The same attention is required here as elsewhere to command success. There is only one excuse for absence or tardyness—sickness. Parents who are satisfied with anything less than perfect attendance are handicapping their children with the characteristic habit of the man who cannot hold any position. The total absence for the year ending last May was 1472. We are doing much better this year but there is still room for great improvement.

. . . . .

Most residents of Marble considered Col. Channing F. Meek, the president of the marble company, a be-

nevolent master and friend of all community acitvities. This attitude also existed in the schools, and a large portrait of Col. Meek hung in the school entrance hall, gazing kindly down upon each student as he entered the door. This portrait was purchased by the students after his death. It is likely that the good colonel consciously cultivated this image.

The Marble Booster,
April 1, 1911.
In recognition of the closing of school for this school year, Col. C.F. Meek, president of the school board, sent each boy and girl in the schools a box of candy Wednesday afternoon, Mrs. W.D. Parry having charge of the presentation.

The Marble Booster,
June 8, 1912.
The graduating exercises held Thursday night of last week [June, 1912] in the Faussone theater, was attended by an audience that filled the theater and the program proved to be highly entertaining. The Address was given by the Rev. Father J.P. Carrigan of Glenwood Springs, who spoke on the subject of "Education." His address was a masterly effort, given in the style that has made Father Carrigan famous in Colorado.

Col. C.F. Meek, president of the school board, also

spoke to the class in presenting the diplomas, impressing upon the graduates the value of knowledge and what attributes are necessary for the best manhood and womanhood. In presenting the diplomas the Colonel had a word of advice and encouragement for each pupil. He also warmly congratulated the teachers upon their excellent work during the year.

The Marble Booster,
July 6, 1912.

Marble is to have a real public library of no mean pretensions. The school board this week [July, 1912] accepted a gift of 1,000 volumes from Prof. J.P. McCaskey of Lancaster, Penna. Prof. McCaskey is the editor of the Pennsylvania State School Journal and also a stockholder of the Colorado-Yule Marble company. He has visited Marble and has a deep interest in the town.

Included in the list of books given by Prof. McCaskey are 500 volumes of general library reading, including the Harvard Classics of President Elliot in fifty volumes, ten volumes of World's Wit and Humor, thirty volumes of Irish Stories and Literature, ten volumes of Thackeray, five volumes of Jules Verne, five volumes of the World's Great Events, five volumes of Short Story Classics, etc., etc. Then there are 300 volumes of reference books for teachers, educational series, professional and reference books, text books, books on music, etc.

The Marble school board at its meeting last Saturday night passed resolutions thanking Prof. McCaskey for his generous gift. It is the plan of the board to assemble the books given by Prof. McCaskey with those now at the church and place all of them in the principal's room and under the principal's charge at the school building. In the vacation season some one else will be secured by the board to have charge of the library. At all times the general public may draw books for reading from the library.

The two lots of books assembled will give Marble a collection of about 2,000 volumes which will make a mighty fine nucleus for a splendid library.

• • • • • •

In support of the schools an active and energetic Parent-Teacher Association met regularly.

The Marble Booster,
December 14, 1912.

The regular meeting of the Parent-Teacher association was held at the High school building December 6, 1912. A very entertaining program was rendered, consisting of the following numbers:

Selection..... High School Orchestra
Recitation.... Pansey Woodward
Solo............. Mrs. Mullin
Trio............. Mrs. Stanley, Mrs. Wade, Mrs. Robinson.

The executive committee appointed at the last meeting was dismissed and a new one appointed, consisting of Mrs. Sweet, Miss Parker and Mrs. Harvey. The minutes of the last meeting were read and approved and the meeting was opened for business.

Prof. Gray asked for an electric light for the high school orchestra for practice, which Mr. Thode promised to have put in place.

Mrs. Montgomery suggested that the association subscribe for some literature relating to the work and named the Child Welfare magazine as the best publication in that line. The magazine was liberally subscribed for.

The ten following questions of importance were suggested to be taken up by the association during the year for study and discussion.

1. What kind of food should children have? (What kind helps school work?)
2. How to keep children well. (Fresh air the basis.)
3. How to dress school children. (Simply and not fussily.)
4. Symptoms, treatment and prevention of contagious diseases.
5. What is obedience and when does training in it begin?
6. How to make dishonest and untruthful children.
7. How parents hinder the school work of their children.
8. Children's companions.
9. Do our children need play?
10. How to teach children to save and to spend. (Allowances, etc.)

These questions were adopted and on motion of Prof. Gray a committee of two was appointed to prepare especially on the questions; also, that the subject be open to discussion after being presented by the committee.

Mrs. Barnes put in a complaint on poor penmanship and Miss Phillips on unclean drinking cups and pails.

Prof. Gray explained the methods of teaching and writing in the grades quite satisfactorily, and Mr. Thode agreed, as a member of the school board, to see that the matter of sanitary drinking water receptacles be attended to.

The matter of Christmas entertainment for the children was taken up. A motion was made by Mrs. Goodwin that the parents assist the teachers in the Christmas entertainment. Motion carried. A committee of five was appointed to serve—Mrs. Goodwin, Mrs. Wade, Mrs. Sampson, Mrs. Woodward and Mrs. Mullin.

The question of a probable vacancy in the presidency of the school board was brought up by Mr. Thode for consideration.

The meeting adjourned to meet the second Friday in January.

Mrs. Harrington, Secretary

• • • •

The school year ending in June, 1913, was "A Very Successful One." Statistics show the following:

The Marble Booster,
June 7, 1913.

During the year just closed the whole number of pupils enrolled was 196. The number of days of teaching, including holidays, was 179. The average membership was 141 while the average daily attendance was 130. The average age of the pupils was 9-6/10 years. During the year 21 pupils had to be corrected by corporal punishment. In plain English these youngsters got a "licking." There were 134 visitors at the schools during the year and the average tardiness per pupil was 4.

• • • •

Subjects offered in the high school in 1915 were as follows: plain & solid geometry, English I, II, III & IV (composition & rhetoric, American & English literature), algebra I, advanced algebra, U.S. & ancient history, 3 years of science (physics & chemistry), Latin I & II, German I & II, domestic science and senior reviews (a good, stiff course in arithmetic, grammar, U.S. history & civics). Some subjects were offered in alternate years by the three high school teachers.

In May, 1915, at a well-attended public meeting in Marble, the citizens of the town decided to approve the school board's proposal to add several new courses to the curriculum. This would cost $2,500 more than the current budget, for an additional teacher and equipment. For some reason unknown in Marble, the

THANOS A. JOHNSON PHOTO

THERESA V. HERMAN was at her post in the old Masonic Temple, serving as a teacher in the classroom when photographed by one of the town's newest arrivals in 1942, Thanos Johnson. It was shortly after this that she moved the class into her home, which was much easier to heat for the two students.

county commissioners failed to increase the school mill levy to bring in the needed funds. What is worse, the Marble school board was not notified that the extra funds would not be available.

The Marble Booster,
January 22, 1916.

In June 1915, the school board made up the budget and certified it to the county superintendent of schools, who, in turn, certified it to the county commissioners at the regular November meeting of that body. She asked for and recommended to the commissioners that the tax levy for school District No. 4 be increased from 3.5 mills to 4.5 mills. The budget certified to the board was as follows: Secretary $80; domestic science $250; furniture $150; repairs $500; manual training $250; janitor salary $600; fuel and other incidentals $800; teachers' salaries $6130. Total, $7769.

Following, and in accordance with the expressed wishes of the patrons of the school district, the school board purchased the paraphernelia required for the added subjects and contracted to pay the additional salary for the teacher.

However, when the county commissioners met in November and made the tax levies, including the increase recommended for District No. 4 by the county superintendent, the commissioners contended that the increase wasn't necessary and made the levy the same as last year.

This arbitrary action on the part of the commissioners puts the district face to face with a deficit of $2500.

This means that the schools will very likely have to be closed down at least two months earlier than the regular closing time.

. . . . . .

The editor of The Marble Booster expressed the area citizens' righteous indignation.

The Marble Booster,
January 29, 1916.

The law which permits county commissioners to override the taxpayers of a school district and thwart their desires, even though, as is the case in District No. 4, the commissioners do not own a nickel's worth of property in the district, is a travesty and ought to be repealed. It is a fine commentary on law when the taxpayers of a school district vote unanimously to tax themselves a certain amount

THERESA HERMAN, an old-time resident of Marble, provided a school for the few remaining children in town in this house on State Street, near the east end of the block, almost at the corner of West First Street. This is the same block where St. Paul's Episcopal Church is located. This school lasted only a few years, from 1942 until 1950. Ralph Edwards, of radio-and-television fame for his "Truth or Consequences" show, encouraged school children across the nation in 1944 to collect paper for a drive to support the war effort during World War II. Theresa's students collected 5,120 pounds of paper, unfortunately including vital records from the marble quarry, mill and the CR&SJ railroad — all to fight the Japanese.

JOHN T. HERMAN COLLECTION

240

in order to have superior educational advantages and then three commissioners, sitting in solemn session over across a range of mountains, arbitrarily nullify the action without even so much as saying by your leave.

. . . . . .

The school board finally decided to keep the schools open until the end of the spring term, then hold a special election to raise the mill levy and issue bonds to cover the short fall. This experience heightened the feeling in Marble that this area, across difficult Schofield Pass from Gunnison, was a step-child of Gunnison County. Later, the chairman of the county commissioners duly responded to The Booster's charges and placed the blame on the county superintendent of schools. Bureaucratic ineptitude all around seems to have been the culprit.

When the marble quarry and mill closed in late 1917, because of World War I, the Marble grade school was barely able to stay open with one teacher. However, a lack of students caused the high school to close for some of the years after 1919. By 1922, the population began to build back enough to require two teachers, later increasing to six teachers in 1928. At the beginning of World War II, the population again dropped dramatically, though there were always a few students through 1950, which, after 1942, were taught by long-time resident, Mrs. Theresa V. Herman.

In the 1920's both school buildings were not required for the smaller student body, so the grade school building was not used for classes, which were all held in the high school building. The largest room in the grade school building was used for basketball practice, and other sports purposes. In 1927, there were about 35 students, and all were taught in the high school building. The top floor was for the high school, the main floor for elementary grades, and the primary grades met in the basement. The largest room was partitioned into two classrooms.

When it became impractical to hold classes for 3 or 4 pupils in the large school building, during World War II, the school board bought the residence east of Theresa Herman's home at West First and Park streets, and she taught her few students there. Later, this house was moved to the site of the old grade school building, which had been torn down in 1943. In 1980, this house was used as the town hall, and in 1985, the school district transferred its ownership to the town.

After 1950, Marble pupils were bused to school in Carbondale, so the school buildings were not needed. The high school building was boarded up in 1947, and the school board hired Charles and Marjorie Orlosky to paint the building and install the wood shutters over the windows. Later, the house was moved to the site across Main Street from the high school, and it was boarded up about 1950.

With the formation of the Marble Community Church in 1960, a building was needed for its services, and the Gunnison school board agreed to the request to use the high school building. The church group, with help from Outward Bound staff and students, opened the building, installed a stove in the large room, applied some paint to the walls and used the room for church services in summers. In 1973, the reactivated town government also started using this room for meetings.

The Marble Historical Society was organized in 1977, and in cooperation with the town government, started using the high school building for a museum. In a few years, the town moved its offices across the street, and the historical society took over the entire building. After protracted negotiations, the Gunnison school board gave the building to the historical society, which then made many repairs to the structure, but retained its school building character. Thus, its original intent for educational purposes was retained and the restored building is now included on the National Register of Historic Places.

PETER McCOLLUM PHOTO –
MARBLE HISTORICAL SOCIETY COLLECTION

THE PRESENT TOWN HALL in Marble operates in this house that is the former residence of Theresa Herman. Her home has since been moved onto the site of the old grammar school on Main Street.

MANY OF MARBLE'S original homes were still standing as of 1942, when this view was recorded. These company-built houses, across from St. Paul's Episcopal Church, were built with barn-type roofs, which withstood winter snowfalls better than flat roofs. Whitehouse Mountain is in view in this pleasant scene.

Chapter 5

RELIGION IN THE VALLEY

After silver prospectors discovered rich ore in Leadville in the 1870's, some of them immediately began moving over the passes into the Gunnison River Valley, founding towns as they went. These are the men who moved over Schofield Pass and down the valley of Rock Creek, as the Crystal River was called then. Settlers stopped at the sites of Schofield, Crystal and Marble, and towns soon began to grow in the early 1880's. Until families arrived, there was not much demand for churches, though itinerant preachers moved from camp to camp. In 1889, Crystal was blessed with two visiting preachers in one week, and they held their services in the Crystal Club.

Some of the miners developed large silver mines in Aspen, and that town grew rapidly. Spiritual needs began to be met after 1884, by the efforts of the Episcopal Missions of Western Colorado, and these supplemented the work of Congregationalists, Roman Catholics and others. In 1908, the Episcopal building known as St. Johns Chapel in Aspen, was declared surplus and moved to Marble. This building has an interesting history, affected by economic conditions of the time and the state of the Episcopal Missions.

To unravel the building's history, it is necessary to examine the entire Episcopal mission activity in Aspen in the 1880's, as there were two buildings of similar construction. The first Episcopal mission was established there in 1884, without its own building.[1] By 1886, the Christ Protestant Episcopal Church congregation was holding worship services in the Miners Union Hall on Hopkins Avenue.[2] In late December, 1886, a "neat little chapel" was completed by Christ Church at Second and Bleeker in west Aspen.[3] Pitkin County deeds show that on 12 May 1888, George Brown sold to Mary E. McMurray as trustee for the East Aspen Sunday School, for $200, Lot K, Block 33, on the northeast corner of Hyman Avenue and Cleveland Street, East Aspen, including "all improvements thereon," also known as "St. Johns Chapel."[4] It appears the structure later known as St. Johns Chapel, was built shortly before May, 1888, probably by or for the East Aspen Sunday School. On 1 February 1890, this property was sold to the Bishop & Chapter, Cathedral of St. John, for $1.00,[5] and renamed St. Johns Chapel. Therefore, this is the building moved to Marble and renamed St. Paul's Church.

Soon after prospectors and miners began to settle in the Marble area, after 1880, families began to arrive, and the presence of women and children increased interest in spiritual matters. By the summer of 1900, there were flourishing Sunday Schools for the children in both Marble and Crystal, though neither town had a church building.

On one Sunday afternoon in August of 1900, the Marble Sunday School paid a visit to the Crystal Sunday School. Teamster Oliver F. Thomas put hay in his wagon and gave the children a ride up the seven mile long canyon behind his team of fours. At 3 p.m. the Marble Superintendent, C. Ambrose Williams, joined the Crystal Superintendent, Leonard S. Rohrer, in calling the joint meeting to order. The program was typical of such events in that day, and was as follows:

1. Prelude ... Doxology
2. Prayer by L.S. Rohrer
3. Song - "Scattering Precious Seeds"
4. Recitation by Harry Ferris
5. Responsive Reading - 23rd Psalm
6. Recitation by Vera Finley - "Smiling Face"
7. Recitation by Herbert Hodges - "Do You Ever Think"
8. Song - "Never Alone"
9. Recitation by Marion Hodges - "Unselfishness"
10. Recitation by Eva Ward - "Little Children Love One Another"
11. Song by Zella Ferris - "Let the Sunshine In"
12. Recitation by Lela Ward - "Gift Bearer"
13. Recitation by Helen Williams - "The Master's Childhood"
14. Song by Primary Class - "There's Sunshine in My Soul"
15. Recitation by Zella Ferris - "A Humble Spirit"
16. Recitation by John Williams - "Brighter World"
17. Song - "Coronation"

Continued on Page 247

---

[1] *The Aspen Daily Times*, January 1, 1887.

[2] *The Aspen Daily Times*, November 8, 1886.

[3] *The Aspen Daily Times*, December 24, 1886.

[4] Pitkin County Deed Book 33, page 219 and Book 87, page 12.

[5] Pitkin County Deed Book 61, page 277.

HENRY L. JOHNSON PHOTO – ESTHER BAUMLI SANCHEZ COLLECTION

ST. PAUL'S EPISCOPAL CHURCH was also known as the Union Church, and it is located on the northeast corner of West State and West Second streets. It was moved from Aspen in 1908 on a railroad flatcar. Three denominations shared the little church, ministered by a resident Congregational pastor, an Episcopalian and a Catholic. A reading room on the rear of the sanctuary was supplied with numerous periodicals, and it held a good library of books, donated by friends. A large-sized Aeolian organ could be played manually, or it could be operated mechanically with perforated music rolls. There were two tent houses east of the church in this scene, and the Horace, John and Ambrose Williams house was next door.

DURING DECEMBER of 1912, scaffolding was placed at the front of St. Paul's Church for installation of a bell and tower. This bell weighed 500 pounds and was ready for the Christmas-season church services.

HENRY L. JOHNSON PHOTO – MARBLE HISTORICAL SOCIETY COLLECTION

BY THE TIME this color view was produced in 1985, new metal street signs were appearing in Marble, with the "State Street" sign attached to the tree in this scene. The new name for the church, "Marble Community Church," had been placed near the old wooden building. Jack D. Clemenson conducted a few Sunday services here in about 1960. Ambrose Williams would arrive at the church early on Sunday morning and stoke the wood-burning stove in the middle of the sanctuary, to take the chill off the place.

DEEP POWDER SNOW often piles up during winter storms at Marble's relatively high elevation, 7,950 feet above sea level. The Community Church (St. Paul's) had a Christmas look about it when photographed here during the 1930's.

PHOTOGRAPHED DURING 1988, the Marble Community Church (St. Paul's) still retained its original interior charm. Notice the pump organ, to the right of the pulpit.

18. Recitation by Bertie Usher - "A Willing Hand"
19. Recitation by Laura Hodges - "Yes, I'm Guilty"
20. Song - "Life's Railway to Heaven"
21. Remarks - L.S. Rohrer
22. Song - "Mother's Counsel"
23. Remarks - Judge Thomas O'Bryan
24. Song - "God Be With Us Till We Meet Again"[6]

By 1908, St. Johns Chapel was not needed in Aspen; as the silver panic of 1893 had caused a large reduction in Aspen's population. Also, the chapel at Second and Bleeker served the needs of the denomination. Since Marble was growing rapidly at this time and needed a church building, the Episcopal Diocese made it available for moving to Marble. In September, 1908, the Women's Guild of the Episcopal Church in Marble had 50 members and bought two lots at West 2nd and State streets from William W. Wood for $250.[7] The Episcopal Mission in Marble needed a building since the Sunday School had 55 members. That fall, the St. John's building in Aspen was dismantled and moved to Marble on a railroad car and rebuilt on its present location. Mrs. Anna Mae Brooks said that all the town turned out to see the material for the building arrive in Marble.[8] At this time, the two side rooms were added, and the church altar, rail and furniture was designed by the Venerable Archdeacon W.H. Doggett.[9] It was then renamed the St. Paul's Church. When constructed here, the building did not have a bell tower. In 1911, it was decided the church needed a bell to call the faithful to worship, so carpenter Roy Chambers built a tower, and Mrs. Mortimer Matthews of the Proctor family donated the bell.[10] It weighs 500 pounds and was cast in 1911 by the Moncely Bell Company of Troy, New York, and installed in the new tower in November of that year.

Marble was much in need of a church building by this time, as the marble quarries and the marble mill had been operating since 1906, and the town was growing rapidly. There were close to 1,000 residents by 1908, many of them immigrants from Europe, with large families. Large numbers of these expert stone workers were Roman Catholics and used to regular attendance at Mass. They, as well as the several Protestant congregations, needed a building in which to worship. The newly located St. Paul's Church provided this facility for all the religious groups. From this time on, several

---
[6] The Marble Times & Crystal Silver Lance, August 24, 1900.

[7] The Aspen Democrat, September 12, 1908.

[8] Personal interview by the author, 1983.

[9] The Marble Booster, September 23, 1911.

[10] Marble City Times, November 2, 1911.

IT IS BELIEVED that this group picture was taken during a meeting of Episcopal priests and choir members visiting Marble.

THE MARBLE FOUNDATION for the Columbus Catholic Church was photographed on its southern exposure in 1975. This illustrates the lasting beauty of marble, as well as the fact that it stands up against the severe weather conditions found in Marble.

COLONEL CHANNING MEEK donated marble for constructing the Columbus Catholic Church in 1912. However, the building program never got beyond the stone foundation, reportedly because of Colonel Meek's untimely death. This foundation still stands beside West Park Street, near West Second Street.

established congregations used the building for services. By 1909, the Rev. J.N. Trompon was leading a Union Congregational flock, with services in the "Mission House." Also in 1909, the Colorado-Yule Marble Company painted the church white, with green trim, the same as the school building. Episcopal services were conducted by priests from Glenwood Springs and Aspen, and in December, 1912, the Rev. Oliver Kingman became the resident Episcopal minister in Marble. Services for the many Roman Catholics were conducted weekly by priests who came over on the railroad from Aspen. This was a busy place on Sundays. The Congregational Union Church alone had services at 11 a.m. and 7:30 p.m., with Sunday School at 10 a.m.[11]

Though the Episcopalians did not have a resident minister in Marble until late the next year, they made a big event of the frequent occasions when the Episcopal Bishop came to town. In August, 1911, they held a gala reception for the Bishop, and Mrs. Benjamin Brewster. Several hundred persons attended the event at the Masonic Temple. The Marble Band played, with dancing until midnight, 75 couples dancing at one time in the beautifully decorated hall. There was so much food that after everyone was finished eating, there were 500 sandwiches left, plus 20 or 30 cakes and 10 or 15 gallons of ice cream. So, a party was given for the Marble children the next afternoon.[12]

Because there were many Roman Catholics in Marble, after several years of attending Mass in the St. Paul's Church, or elsewhere, they decided they needed their own church building. They appealed to Col. C.F. Meek, president of the Colorado-Yule Marble Co., for help in acquiring a building. In February, 1911, Col. Meek donated a couple of lots on West Park Street, between Second and Third for the church. He told the marble workers that if they would cut and lay the marble blocks on their own time he would donate the marble. They happily agreed, and the building was started.[13] The marble foundation was completed by September, 1912, and the cornerstone was laid by Father Corrigan. About this time, Col. Meek was killed when he jumped from a run-away trolley on the quarry road, and the marble company found it necessary to stop supplying the marble, since the company was in financial trouble. In the fall of 1912, a wooden building was hastily constructed on the marble foundation, but it collapsed the next winter from the heavy snow load. This church building was never completed.

The Roman Catholics continued to be served by priests who came from Glenwood Springs or Aspen and conducted services in the St. Paul's Church. Anna Mae Brooks stated that in the early 1930's, Father McSweeney came over from Aspen on the train every Sunday afternoon. Since he believed the people should not have their Sunday disturbed by having to go to church, their only day off from work, he usually conducted Mass early Monday morning before the day shift at the mill. He would stay with the Brooks family, or others, and usually John Brooks would drive him back to Aspen in his car.

Religion was important in those days, with some kind of activity or service almost every day. The Ladies' Aid Society met at the Mission House on Thursday, evening prayer services and choir practice on Friday, Women's Auxillary met every Thursday afternoon, Kindergarten at 2 p.m. Sunday; these were some of the regular events. Special religious activities were centered on Christmas and Easter with pageants by the children. In August, 1911, a worship service at the band stand, with sacred music by the Marble Band, was attended by 200 and repeated the next night.[14] The high school orchestra played at a Christmas party at Faussone's Theatre, and Santa was present with gifts for all. The church building was booked so fully that often religious lectures by visiting preachers had to be held in the high school building. The Ladies' Guild put on teas and bazaars from time to time.

When the Rev. Oliver Kingman arrived in 1913, he organized the Boys Club of St. Paul's Church. They had their own club house behind the church after 1914, and it contained a spacious club room, its walls covered with Indian trophies and antlers.

The Marble Booster,
June 26, 1915.

The large fireplace, built of pure white marble, is a gift of the president, J.F. Manning, of the Colorado-Yule Marble Co. Around it on winter evenings the boys gather to rehearse Indian and mining stories of bygone days of their regions, while the yule log from the mountainside sheds its cheer over the whole room. The boys have their club well organized and make their own rules and regulations under the supervision of the rector. Once a month there is a social function to break the monotony of the long winter season. In the summer, the boys go into camp in the mountains. We do not have to go far to find ourselves away from civilization. A few miles over some trail or mountain road brings one into wild regions. Late last summer the boys' club went into camp twenty miles across the mountains. We passed through a very wild canyon, over several avalanche-slides beneath which the river running its way through the mountains, forms a perfect arch-bridge over which we drove, and on which the boys had much sport throwing snow balls and playing tag while the men worked digging a road to drive the load in safety up over the snow.

．　．　．　．　．

The Marble Sunday School claimed to be one of the largest in western Colorado. For many years, John and Ambrose Williams were superintendents and at Easter presented each child with a small potted plant. This organization served as more than religious classes and had many social activities. In July, 1917, fifty children of the Sunday School had a picnic a few miles down the valley, and earlier the same year, Mrs. James Coryell's class had a party at the boys' clubhouse. The teachers of the various classes took part in leadership training classes, conducted by the several ministers.

St. Paul's Church continued to be a center of social and religious activities until the end of 1941, when the quarries and marble mill closed at the beginning of World War II. This resulted in the virtual death of the town, and it was not long until there were insufficient people in the area to support services. The building was neglected for a decade, except for general supervision

---

[11] The Marble Booster, June 17, 1911.

[12] The Marble Booster, August 12, 1911.

[13] The Marble Booster, June 1, 1912.

[14] The Marble Booster, August 12, 1911.

ST. PAUL'S SUNDAY SCHOOL claimed to be the largest in western Colorado for a time, a possibility in 1912, when the town of Marble had a population of some 2,000 hardy souls.

and maintenance provided by John and Ambrose Williams, who lived in the brown house east of the church in summers.

By 1950, the Marble area was beginning to stir to the growth of the tourist industry and summers found a growing number of people here. In 1952, the two teenage Loudermilk girls, Kareen and Raquel, began to conduct prayer meetings and hymn-singing services in the church building, and these attracted many of the summer residents and visitors. Whomever seemed to be the most qualified and willing was asked to lead the weekly services.

The regular summer residents, who liked to worship in the little church, had coalesced into a congregation by 1960, and adopted the name Marble Community Church. This group asked the Colorado Congregational Conference if it could provide a minister for the summer months. The Conference willingly complied and sent George Drake, then a young Seminary graduate and

college teacher at Grinnell College in Iowa, to serve the budding congregation. George and his new wife Sue were housed in the old residence, which formerly had sometimes served as the Marble Elementary School. George and Sue nurtured the fledgling flock for the summers of 1960 and 1961, with Sunday services, Wednesday night Campfires and Daily Vacation Bible School. Their efforts were so successful that the Weekly Sage newspaper in Glenwood Springs published a feature article on the church. This attracted the attention of the Rev. William O. Richards, the Episcopal minister in Glenwood Springs, and he asked George why his permission had not been asked for use of the church building. George replied that he thought permission had been granted. Soon Bishop Joseph S. Minnis determined that the Episcopalians needed to renew services in Marble, and asked the community congregation to vacate the building. They complied, but many Marble citizens were angered by the action of the Bishop.

IT WAS EASTER SUNDAY in 1923, at St. Paul's Episcopal Church in Marble, where a small crowd had gathered on the steps, in front of the church belfry. (John Williams was the second from the left.)

The congregation held one or two services outside under the trees and appealed to the Gunnison Watershed School Board for permission to hold services in the old boarded-up high school building, and was given immediate approval in August, 1961. Members of the congregation, with the help of Outward Bound students, proceeded to clean up the school building, paint the large meeting room, install a propane stove, put in temporary electric wiring and generally made the facility suitable for worship services. For twelve summers, the congregation continued to worship in the high school.

On September 28, 1962, the Marble Community Church joined the Western Association of the United Churches of Christ at its annual meeting in Grand Junction.[15] In 1963, the association provided a house trailer in Marble, and later, other housing, for the summer ministers to stay in, and the custom of inviting a succession of ministers to preach one or more Sundays

evolved. Most were UCC ministers who came to Marble for their vacations. In 1969, the Marble Church's Board of Directors decided to assume responsibility for recruiting the summer ministers and providing for their housing. From this time on, ministers from other denominations also were invited to serve. Since the congregation was made up of members from many denominations, it was truly a community church.

In the summer of 1963, the congregation decided it should build its own church. Howard and Bleu Stroud offered to donate a tract of land on Main Street, a half block west of the high school, and many individuals responded with gifts of money, some as a result of the national publicity on the eviction from the church building, via the Denver Post and Time magazine. Thanos Johnson constructed and donated an altar cross, Theodore Mularz of Aspen donated his architectural services, with a plan for a building, the Rev. Paul Roberts of Phoenix sent two stained glass medallions for the

---

[15] Minutes of the Board, Marble Community Church.

251

LOOKING TOWARD THE EAST on State Street in Marble, St. Paul's Episcopal Church also housed the Catholic Church congregation and a Congregational denomination. Notice the Colorado-Yule Marble Company houses along the south side of the Main Street. A bridge carried traffic over Carbonate Creek, farther

sanctuary, Mrs. Frank Reh gave a small pump organ, and the Aspen Institute donated the old benches from the Aspen Music Society tent.[16] Ground breaking services were held on August 18, 1963. At this time, the congregation was organized with an elected Board of Directors consisting of: Frank Reh, Ray Sommers, Fred Kallenberger, Clyde Kuhles and Howard Stroud; with Stroud as chairman, Reh as treasurer and Bleu Stroud as secretary. The Outward Bound students and staff helped clear the building site and cut 28 large spruce trees to use as beams. In April, 1965, the plans for building the new church building were published in a Glenwood Springs newspaper. But about this time, members of the congregation began to question the suitability of the building plans presented and the advisability of building, and no further progress was made on the intended structure.

The Episcopal Diocese, with donations of materi-

als and labor from others, renovated the St. Paul's church building in 1964, with a new foundation, sheet metal roof and paint. For a few years, the Rev. Fr. William R. Shannon came over from Aspen on Sunday afternoons in summers to conduct services for the few Episcopalians who happened to be in Marble.

In 1974, the congregation was able to obtain permission from the Colorado Episcopal Bishop to move back into the church building for services, in exchange for helping to maintain it.

Each summer, regular worship services were held and conducted by guest ministers, and occasionally extra services at Thanksgiving, Christmas or Easter were also possible. A more permanent status was achieved in the fall of 1980, when it was decided to continue services through the winter. This was made possible because of the fortunate availability of the Rev. Dr. Frederick E. Udlock, a Presbyterian, who had recently retired as

16. Minutes of the Board, Marble Community Church.

east in this view. Hat Mountain is in this scene, at the far east end of State Street, with Sheep Mountain in the background. The road to Crystal curves to the left, out of Marble and around Hat Mountain — past Lizard Lake — and it proceeds to the right, past Sheep Mountain.

a professor of religion at Hastings College at Hastings, Nebraska, and who was living six miles below Marble. Attendance and support during the winter of 1980-81, convinced the congregation that it was possible to maintain a full-time ministry in the upper Crystal River Valley, and it continued to grow and prosper.

In late 1982, the congregation of the Marble Community Church decided to withdraw from the UCC Association and reorganize as an independent congregation. The church also became incorporated under the laws of Colorado. This procedure was completed on January 16, 1983, when forty people were accepted into regular or associate membership of the newly reorganized Marble Community Church, with Dr. Udlock as pastor.[17]

For several years, the officers of the church had been negotiating with the Episcopal Diocese toward purchase of the building in Marble. This discussion finally came to fruition when the Rev. Fr. Cyril Coverly,

Director of Operations of the Diocese, came over from Denver to present the deed to the building and land at an impressive dedication service, conducted by the pastor, on July 7, 1985.

With ownership of the building secured, the congregation proceeded to upgrade the structure with insulation and paneling of the two side rooms, a new brown metal roof over the entire structure, new electrical wiring, strengthening of a sagging beam and a new stove and ceiling fans. Most of these improvements were possible through generous gifts of money and labor from members and friends.

The year 1988, marked the 100th anniversary of the construction of the venerable building, and it started its second century in good condition for its service to the community and to God. Further evidence of its importance to this community is its current inclusion on the National Register of Historic Places.

17 Minutes of the Board, Marble Community Church.

Chapter 6

THE GOOD OLD DAYS IN MARBLE

About one hundred years after the miners and other settlers began to move into the upper Crystal River Valley of western Colorado, it is worthwhile to look back and review what the living conditions were for those intrepid pioneers. Much has been written concerning the hard work required to settle and conquer a new country, with the hardships occasioned by lack of adequate transportation, isolation and a shortage of most of the amenities we all so quickly take for granted as being essential to a civilized existence. In most of the fast-growing communities many men and even families had to live in tents for some months until log or frame houses could be built. This was the situation in Crystal City as well as in Marble during the periods of rapid growth. But primitive conditions and difficult times did not mean these people worked all the time. To enable them to survive the hard times they occasionally took time off for relaxation and enjoyment of the very special conditions and beauty which surrounded them. How did these hard-working men, women and children entertain themselves when the occasion permitted?

One person who grew up in Marble in the early 1930's remembers it this way: "It seems so long ago when I was a little girl up there and played out every day no matter what the weather was. Winter fun was a big thing, and everyone had an old pair of skis, several sleds, innertubes, bob sleds and a few toboggans, and nearly everyone had some kind of ice skates. Many times we had to wait our turn to wear our brothers' or sisters' skates, and kept warm by the fire 'til our turn came around. No thought of how cold it was or how it was storming, we just made it part of our growing up and enjoyed it."[1] This attitude seemed to be current among most of the children during these early days. It was a great time and a great place for them to grow up, as there were plenty of things for them to do. In the summer, there was the fishing, hiking and exploring in the mountains, and hunting for the older boys, when their family chores were done. Winter brought its own special activities because of the snow and frozen lakes. Besides their special childish play, the youngsters took part in many of their elders' recreational activities.

Social activities were very important, especially to those miners' and ranchers' families living an isolated existence. The townspeople organized many clubs and associations to foster their desire to inter-relate with their fellows. The old newspapers are full of accounts of social events, such as dances or "hops," parties at Halloween, St. Patrick's Day, Christmas, New Years Day, or any weekend the mood struck them. The surprising thing about these "socials" was the great distance people would travel by horseback, wagon or on foot after working hard all week. In August, 1887, Mrs. Dan Penny of Crystal held "a pleasant hop," and about twenty-four showed up from as far away as Prospect, Coal Basin and Thompson Creek. This is even more remarkable when one remembers that the first wagon road down the Crystal River Valley was not built until five or six years later. Music for the dancing was provided by Mr. and Mrs. Wilson, vocal and instrumental music by Mrs. Andy Johnson and Miss Alice Penny, as well as the Crystal River Glee Club. Supper was provided, and they all danced until daylight. They then ate breakfast before starting for home.[2]

A Halloween party at the Holland Ranch in 1909 drew 19 guests, in spite of a bad storm. They were greeted with refreshments of popcorn, fresh cider and taffy, which they helped "pull." Games, such as pinning pasteboard hearts on a Jack O'lantern's face while blindfolded, produced prizes of an imitation tomato and

HENRY L. JOHNSON PHOTO – JACK D. CLEMENSON COLLECTION

IT WOULD NOT have been Christmas in Marble if the wee ones failed to have a tree, all decorated with strings of popcorn, shiny metal ornaments and cotton snow around the base. This little girl received more Christmas gifts than would fit into her toy chest.

[1] Letter to the author from Esther Baumli Sanchez.

[2] Crystal River Current, August 27, 1887.

EDWIN S. PORTER, director of the classic movie, "The Great Train Robbery," selected Marble for his next film, entitled "The Big Bear Hunt." Edwin is shown mounted on a handsome steed, with camera at his side. Frank Dickens, on the white horse, was accompanied by Jim Downing, considered to be one of the "most fearless" bear hunters in the Rockies. This 1909 "epic" movie ended with the poor bear being brought down with innumerable bullets — with a "grand finale" featuring hunting dogs tearing the bear's body to shreds. Needless to say, the unfortunate bear never had a chance in this Hollywood silent-movie charade.

a hand-painted dish. Dinner was provided, and "The sumptuously arrayed table showed a magician had been to work here the past half hour and had applied his magic art with a lavishing hand. Mrs. Holland was the magician." After eating, they turned out the lights and gathered around the fireplace to hear ghost stories. Mr. Philips related a weird tale from Kipling. There was dancing to tunes such as "Arkansas Traveler," "Lost Indian" and other tunes of the day, played by W.W. Wood on his violin. At the end of the party, the tallyho driver came to take everyone home.

Fourth of July was always an occasion for a variety of entertainments. In 1909, almost 400 persons visited Marble for the celebrations, many riding a special train, with reduced fares from Glenwood Springs, New Castle and Silt. The local newspaper credited this good attendance to the "special," the good roads and an opportunity to visit the marble quarries free of charge. The celebrations started off with minor sports: races for boys and girls under 12, a wheelbarrow race for men and a nail driving contest for women. Then, it was time for the trip to the quarry in two specially equipped cars. In the afternoon, there was a ball game between Carbondale and Marble, which the hosts lost. Next came a bucking mule contest and cow pony races followed with a 100-yard dash for men, automobile races, a picture show with a standing room only crowd extending out into the street, and after dark, fireworks were shot

Continued on Page 260

TO-NIGHT!

The Masons will entertain with a

Dancing Party

Masonic Hall.   Marble Orchestra.   Supper Served.   Tickets $1.50.

THE MARBLE Masonic Lodge, No. 137, was chartered on September 20, 1910, and it lasted until 1918, when it closed after the Colorado-Yule Marble Company closed the quarry. The Slate Cliffs are in view in this 1910 photograph. Notice the fire escape, leading off the dance floor on the second floor, where occasional Saturday-night dances were held until 1942. The structure was later torn down.

THIS FOURTH OF JULY "Bar-B-Que" in Marble was being prepared during 1908, over a large open pit in a forested area, down by the Crystal River. The meat was strung-out over the barbeque pit, with steel rods placed on top of rails. This delightful area is now a recreation-vehicle (RV) campground, not far from the Marble General Store, and is operated by Dave and Meredith Jones (as of 1992).

MEMBERS OF ST. PAUL'S Boys Club met at this shingle-covered building behind the St. Paul's Episcopal Church in Marble. Most of the members held a potted plant — for some unknown reason.

ST. PAUL'S BOYS CLUB room and library, behind Marble's St. Paul's Episcopal Church, appears in this photograph, taken by an unknown photographer during 1912. Some of the Colorado-Yule Marble Company's houses are in view across the street from the church. The dirt roadway beside the club building is West Second Street.

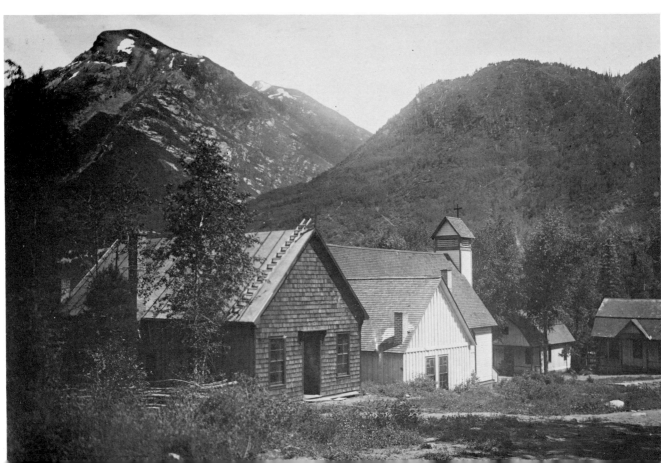

ST. PAUL'S BOYS CLUB of Marble was on one of their summer outings in 1915. This festive occasions included picnics, as well as hunting, fishing and camping excursions into the hills above the town.

ONE OF THE MANY SPORTS enjoyed by Marble residents during the "good old days" was baseball, considered to be the true all-American game and the most popular game in small towns. This sport took the Marble team off to play other teams on the Western Slope of Colorado. It was unthinkable, of course, to "play ball" without regulation uniforms for everyone.

HENRY L. JOHNSON PHOTO – JACK D. CLEMENSON COLLECTION

THE PRINCESS THEATER had been built in 1912 on West Main Street, near the Marble Band Stand. This group of performers posed to have their picture taken at the entrance on opening day. By 1913, the theater was run by a man named Faussone, and two weekly shows were performed for the pleasure of the townspeople of Marble, as well as for the residents of the nearby area.

off from the hill above Beaver Lake. Then, at 9:30 p.m., it was "On With the Dance" until 2 a.m. The day's program was planned and sponsored by the local Great Northern Scouts, and enjoyed by all.[3]

Another form of entertainment in the valley after the turn of the century was motor car touring. The second motor car ever owned in Marble came to town in August, 1913. The machine was a 22-horsepower Metz "...and it sings around these hills like a thing of life."[4] It was owned by Dr. H.G. Haxby, who was constantly with his car since its arrival, and his friends twitted him about sleeping out in the barn with it. Frank Gertig taught him how to drive and care for it and "...Curb the tendency of the thing to buck and snort and climb telephone poles until now he has it pretty well tamed." The doctor was the town's first automobile bug.

The young people never were at a loss for something novel to provide a release from the tensions of the day. As in many parts of the country, it was the usual custom to "serenade" newlyweds by their peers. In July, 1923, this opportunity presented itself when "...three gallant young men, John Parsons, Tom Kissel and W.J.

Hodgson, each with a June bride" returned to town. The three young couples were so engrossed in their own raptures, they naively assumed they had escaped the custom. By "clever tactics," the three couples were captured and placed in the People's Store under guard, while an express wagon was confiscated. "The benedicts and the brides were forced into the conveyance and drawn by a happy, noisy crowd to the camping grounds where Strickland's orchestra was camping, and given their choice to negotiate for a free dance or go to jail." After initial objections, the newlyweds quickly arranged for the music, spurred on by the town marshal's presumed backing of the threat, and all repaired to the Masonic Hall and danced until eleven o'clock to everyone's enjoyment. The occasion offered a favorable time for a general introduction to the brides, while the husbands were tied in a corner as the crowd danced with their wives.[5]

Dancing probably was one of the most popular forms of entertainment and was sponsored by various groups, or occurred spontaneously. The local volunteer firemen were often the instigators, with the help of the Marble Band, either for free, or as a money-raiser. In

[3] The Marble Column, July 11, 1923.

[4] The Marble Booster, August 16, 1913.

[5] The Marble Column, July 11, 1923.

Continued on Page 264

JACK D. CLEMENSON PHOTO

A GATHERING OF FRIENDS was being entertained by Esther Baumli Sanchez at the piano, with her sister, Rose Baumli Rassano. Elmer Kneedler and Jim Allen (students in Crystal) were sitting between the two girls. They were in the living room of the Baumli home at East Second and State streets during 1942. This house had wooden walls and no insulation, making it difficult to heat in the winter.

IT WOULD NOT be a "real party" in Marble without music during the "good old days." The accordianist was a man by the name of Sven, who was in front of an unidentified lady. Otto Schultz and Elmer Bair were to the right of Sven. Canned goods were a safeguard against bad winter storms, which could blockade the roads into town for days at a time.

HENRY L. JOHNSON PHOTO – JACK D. CLEMENSON COLLECTION

HENRY L. JOHNSON PHOTOS –
JACK D. CLEMENSON COLLECTION

EVEN THE "BIG KIDS" of Marble found pleasure from the snow of winter. This little group was known as the "Marble Snowshoe Club," about 1915. Elmer Bair (on the right) has authored a book entitled "Elmer Bair's Story." Notice the old-style skis.

JOHN, BING AND TOMMIE Brooks took advantage of perfect snow conditions in Marble during 1915. The snow depth varies to a great extent here, although there is nearly always enough on the ground for good skiing from December until March of every year — good enough to satisfy everyone looking for winter sports.

THE MARBLE BAND of 1910 performed in their specially-made uniforms at the Fourth of July celebration. It was an important thing to do in those days, to play a musical instrument — to give of yourself. Although the band was small, the musicians had a good assortment of instruments.

THE MARBLE BAND was photographed along the outside wall of the Princess Theater during about 1915. Notice the familiar instruments still in use in today's orchestras.

THE MAY DAY PROCESSION of 1912 came marching down West Main Street, past the Marble City State Bank, on their way to the band stand. The procession had formed earlier at the school grounds farther up the street.

1921, the townspeople held a party and dance to celebrate the opening of the quarry and mill after the wartime closing. A notice in the Crystal River Current as early as 1886, informed the boys of the Crystal River to "Look out for the grand ball and supper at the Elk Mountain House on New Year's Eve at Crested Butte."[6]

Indications are that a number of the husky bachelors crossed the forbidding Schofield Pass through the deep snow to enjoy an evening. The sixteen-mile trip was undertaken as casually as if they were reporting to a local silver mine for work. Those who did not wish to go to that lively town were cordially invited to a New Year's dinner in Crystal, given by Mrs. G.W. Melton. The Marble Hall on State Street in Marble was available in 1910 for "Hops, Entertainments, Social Gatherings, and Gabfests." In 1916, there was a social dance at the Crystal Club in Crystal, which "now has a piano." The O.N.O. Dancing Club offered a turkey supper and dance in 1912 for 109 members and guests. The Walsh family catered, and the dances included: waltzes, two-steps, schottisches, with "Chains" and "Tags."[7] Dancing and entertainment were offered by the Emanon Club at its party in March, 1913, and the next year, there was a Nickel Dance at the Masonic Hall on July fourth. Music for the dances often was provided by Paul Tischhouser and his orchestra of six pieces: piano, violin, clarinet, cornet, trombone and drums. Fourth of July dances had the entire Marble Band in attendance. Leo Liston sometimes played the piano, sometimes with drums and coronet joining in.

[6] Crystal River Current, December 15, 1886.

[7] The Marble Booster, December 28, 1912.

Miscellaneous entertainments included the 1912 firemen's "smokeless" smoker at the pool hall, with amateur boxing, an Italo-Greek picnic the same year, trips to Redstone (by special train for 50 cents) for dancing, horseshoe pitching, marble pitching by children, and many picnics in Lead King Basin and other popular spots. Oldtimers swapped yarns whenever they got together.

Winter sports occupied a top position from the beginning in this beautiful area of pristine powder snow. By December of each year, the wagon road over Schofield Pass was closed by snow, and the mail had to be carried from Crested Butte to Crystal on the backs of men traveling on skis. These skis, which in the 1880's were called snow shoes, were made by hand from boards nine feet long. Those used by Ambrose Williams are in the Aspen museum. They were needed in winter to reach many of the operating mines, and the men became quite daring and skillful. By 1886, the Gunnison County Snowshoe Club had been organized and consisted of members from all over the county. A small group of members from Crystal and Schofield, including Tom Boughton, Frank Williams, and Al and Fred Johnson, usually ran off with the prizes and became quite cocky. They would issue challenges to all comers, and prizes might be as much as $150, $75 and $25 for first, second and third places (substantial amounts in those days). Club winners often entered state championships. Frank Williams' skis were called the Devil's shoes.

On one occasion, the Crystal River members challenged Ouray and Silverton skiers to race any of the following ways: "Fastest speed downhill, with or without

THE MAY POLE DANCE was being celebrated on May 25, outside the elementary school, where Mrs. Herman kept an old Marble tradition alive. Notice the original Marble City Band drum (at the right).

THE TRADITIONAL MAY DAY celebration was in full swing in 1912. This observance was held each year on May 1. The holiday featured "May poles," with colorful streamers held by children.

MAY DAY FESTIVITIES were under way at the Marble Band Stand in 1912, which provided this seating arrangement for onlookers. Colonel Meek, with the aid of school and Sunday-school participation, sponsored this annual event. The Woods home, which was built of logs, sat across West Main Street. The primary subject of this picture was the youthful May Day queen, sitting on her throne under the canopy.

pole, or take another man, weight not less than 135 pounds, on their shoulders and run down, or they will run on level ground with or without a pack, from 500 yards to 50 miles, if to travel with pack take anywhere from 25 to 100 pounds. Alternatives: run downhill on one shoe, run down with two men standing on one pair of shoes, or two men on three shoes, or three men on four shoes, or run down with rider facing up hill."[8]

[8] _Crystal River Current_, February 19, 1887.

A.A. Johnson, who operated a store in Crystal, sometimes carried the mail from Crested Butte to Crystal, over Schofield Pass and down the Crystal River gorge, past the Devil's Punch Bowl. Once, someone asked how he had the nerve to ski down the canyon, with its severe avalanche danger. He replied that he pushed off hard at the top and went as fast as possible, in hopes of outrunning any avalanches. This technique always worked for him.

Much enthusiasm was whipped up over the "snow shoe" races held by the Gunnison County Club at Crested Butte, Gothic and Gunnison. Many men were not occupied during much of the winter, and were willing to spend several days traveling to these contests. The Current reported on a race at Crested Butte in 1887, with headlines: "Our Winter's Sport, Crested Butte Opens Up the Snow Show Season With A Grand Race." The race, scheduled for a Sunday, was postponed until Monday on account of a snow storm. "A large crowd came out on snow shoes and in sleighs to witness the fun, among them were all the young ladies who highly enjoyed the tramp on shoes. A splendid track was selected, north of town, on what is known as the Chicken Ranch hill, and a course laid out to run three at a time. Ten entries were made and the winner of two heats laid off for the final run to determine the winner of the prizes..." Frank Williams and Tom Boughton were the

OSCAR McCOLLUM JR. PHOTO

THERESA HERMAN, former Marble teacher and author of the "Crystal River Saga," posed at her soda-pop stand on West Park Street, where she greeted passersby. She has a copy of her book in her hand.

Our Winter Sport
(written for the Current by D. Evil)

Tis not a sport of childhood,
Nor is it called a play;
It always does our old folks good,
And makes the young folks gay.

It gives our lassies bright red cheeks,
And our laddies those of brown;
It makes the old folks pleasure seek,
And of all sports it's the crown.

For you always get plenty exercise
While climbing up the hill;
And when descending how the snow flies
When you show your acrobatic skill.

It is the sport of sports of all sports,
This one we cherish so—
It is justly called the open port
Of Heaven here below.

In wonder, no longer will I keep you,
But straight-way let you know,
That it is the Norweigan snow-shoe
We use for gliding o'er the snow.

Now just try this little episode,
Then straight-way let me know;
How many successive times you dove
Head-first in the snow.[10]

These men probably were better skiers than poets. Perhaps all the skiers were not expert, as a later story reports: "A course has been cleared through the timber on Mineral point above Crystal for snow-shoeing and boys have great sport tumbling."[11]

Bobsledding was a popular winter sport. A course was made on Main Street from the Marble high school building down through the center of town, all the way to Beaver Lake. The fire department sprinkled the street with water to form ice, and some merchants estimated that the bobsleds raced past their establishments at speeds up to 55 miles per hour. They raced even at night, and there were a number of accidents, when someone failed to get out of the way in time, or when the sleds turned over in the snow. At one point, a town councilman promised to install a street light at West Second to make the course safer.

One of the popular sports was fishing in the river and lakes for trout. Game limits were high or ignored, and newspaper reports indicated catches of 30 and 40 fish. The Marble museum displays a net fish trap used at Crystal before 1900. The large catches depleted the fish in the river, and efforts were made to get the county to build a fish hatchery. By 1913, the Sportmens' Club was working to improve fishing. Many Easterners were so impressed with the fishing in the Crystal River, they came all the way out here to spend their vacations.

All kinds of sports were enjoyed. The town had a baseball team, complete with uniforms, and played teams from nearby towns. Teams came to Marble from New Castle and Carbondale, and in August, 1913, the Marble team won a game against the Spring Gulch boys, 10 to 4. The Marble ball field had a grandstand holding 200

1st and 2nd prize winners. "After the race several young ladies climbed the hill to make the descent, showing splendid skill in the art of snow-shoeing." The club painted the town red. "Capt. Burton ate too much dinner to be present at the race."[9]

The club challenged any shoers in the United States or Canada. Their view of the sport is clearly revealed by the following poem:

[9] Crystal River Current, January 22, 1887.

[10] Crystal River Current, January 22, 1887.

[11] Crystal River Current, February 5, 1887.

people. In 1910, the Marble Association Foot-Ball Club bragged that its coach was Bob Williams, a native of Wales, who had coached at Johns Hopkins University last season (he was now a marble worker). It also had several good players from Scotland, England and Ireland.

Moving picture theaters were popular and had shows Friday and Sunday evenings, and in 1916, Joe Faussone's Marble Theatre advertized that a four piece orchestra played at each performance, and prices were 25 cents for adults and 15 cents for children. Four years earlier, he had proudly called his establishment the Marble Opera House, though no evidence can be found of any opera performances.

COLLECTION OF MR. AND MRS. CHARLES ORLOSKY –
COURTESY OF MARBLE HISTORICAL SOCIETY

CHARLES AND MARJORIE ORLOSKY were considered to be Marble's oldest residents when they lived there. This photograph was taken from inside the kitchen of their modest home during the 1970's. Their house was east of Beaver Lake. The Orloskys were some of the nicest folks you could ever hope to meet — unless you trespassed on their property! Their son, Jack, now runs the Gold Pan Shop (as of 1992), on the road to Crystal City, east of Marble.

COLLECTION OF MR. AND MRS. CHARLES ORLOSKY – COURTESY OF MARBLE HISTORICAL SOCIETY

WILD GAME ABOUNDED in the mountains surrounding Marble. Some of Charles Orlosky's trophies were photographed on his cabin wall.

Fraternal organizations were plentiful, with the Masonic Lodge No. 137 being organized in 1910. It owned its own two-story building on East State Street, with a popular dance floor upstairs. In the same year, the Brotherhood of American Yeomen, Homestead No. 2233, and the Fraternal Order of Eagles, Marble Aerie No. 1827, were organized. Both met twice monthly. Two years later, the Homesteaders' Lodge was organized and the Marble Hive No. 9, L.O.T.M., was in existence. The Woodmen of the World, Camp No. 702, was active through many years, and in 1913, ordered fifty monuments of marble to be placed around the country, as well as several "Temples of Fame" chapels. A tombstone it placed can still be seen in the Marble cemetery. The Elks were also in evidence and held a convention in Marble in the 1920's.

The churches in Marble were an important social element. In 1908, the St. John's Episcopal church building in Aspen was dismantled and moved to Marble and renamed St. Paul's. Church services of several denominations were held in this building. For a few years, an Episcopal priest was assigned to Marble, but after World War I, priests usually came for services from Aspen or Glenwood Springs. The Women's Auxiliary, the Ladies' Aid Society of the Union Church and the Lady Maccabees supported the work of the churches, with luncheons, bazaars, teas and bobsled rides.

Other clubs included the Ladies' Auction Club, a Boys Club, organized by the Rev. Oliver Kingman, which met in the library building behind the church. This library was stocked with books and periodicals donated by the stockholders of the marble company, and members of the church congregations. The high school Literary Club encouraged reading among the youth. The Frost Lending Library offered memberships at 75 cents, with book rentals at 10 cents per week, and had 600 first class fiction volumes.

A sewing club, called the Columbine Club, met regularly, and one summer, its girls presented a ladies black-face minstrel show at the Faussone Theatre, with music by the high school orchestra. In 1927, the Marble Sportsmen Club was organized and sponsored Troop No. 128, Boy Scouts of America, which functioned for several years.

As in most mining towns, Marble boasted of several saloons, where the men could relax from their labors with a drink and convivial conversation. Among the early saloons were counted the Silver Dollar Saloon, the Taaley & Heberling Saloon and Joe Faussone's Senate Saloon. At the urging of the marble company, the town citizens voted in 1909 to become dry, and all saloons disappeared. The large number of Italian and eastern European marble workers liked their liquor, so secret stills and bootlegging became a big industry, which could not be controlled by the many ordinances passed by the town council.

This thirst and the need for places to gather was partially met by the New Pastime Parlor, offering soft drinks and cigars, under Joe Gallo's management. Winn & Brownell opened the Mission Billiard Parlor, which also sold cigars and tobacco, candies and gum.

Marble and Crystal probably were not much different from many other isolated mining towns, and the

270

A BABY PORCUPINE was photographed outside the Orlosky's home in Marble.

THIS UNFORTUNATE COYOTE had his leg in a trap when the family dog tried to finish him.

ROCKY MOUNTAIN BIGHORN SHEEP are occasionally spotted in the area around Marble.

THE BETZ BARN stood in pasture land above the town of Marble. It was photographed by the renowned Marble artist, Thanos Johnson, in 1942, shortly after he arrived there to make this his home. Whitehouse Mountain, covered with a blanket of snow, and the Yule Creek drainage area (at the right) appear in this picturesque scene.

residents were left to their own devices in providing opportunities for recreation and relaxation from their labors. Their attempts to provide entertainment were varied, and in the high and beautiful mountains of the upper Crystal River Valley, they took advantage of what nature provided. Modern recreational developments have grown from the base provided by their predecessors.[12]

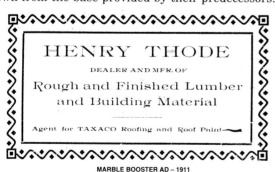

HENRY THODE

DEALER AND MFR. OF

Rough and Finished Lumber
and Building Material

Agent for TAXACO Roofing and Roof Paint

MARBLE BOOSTER AD – 1911

MR. BETZ SR. and Kenny Herman were busy shoveling snow off the roof of T. V. Herman's home after a heavy snowfall in Marble during December of 1950. This heavy accumulation of snow would sometimes cave-in a roof due to the tremendous weight of it.

[12] This chapter was originally published in _Trails Among the Columbine, A Colorado High Country Anthology,_ Sundance Publications, Denver, 1985; and is reprinted here with revisions.

Marble and the Crystal Valley are now at their Prettiest; what about that Vacation?

MARBLE BOOSTER

BY FRANK P. FROST   MARBLE, GUNNISON COUNTY, COLO., SATURDAY, JULY 14, 1917   VOLUME 7; NUMBER 19

Where are the friends of yesteryears?

Oscar Lehow, brother of Mrs. L. C. Summers, came up this week for a visit.

The river still continues to recede, creeks are at normal Summer stage again, and some trout have been caught this week on flies.

Mrs. C. C. McWilliams celebrated a birthday anniversary last Thursday and had several friends in for the afternoon in honor of the occasion.

Sheep coming in via road from Hot Springs to Placita certainly put the road in awful condition, but they promise to clean it up as soon as they get around to it.

The Lead King mine is reported to have nearly forty tons of concentrates ready to ship if the wagon road was passable to let them down to Marble with ore wagons.

Mrs. John R. Brooks and children, Jack and Dagmar, and Mrs. Terry Mullin and daughter, Kathleen, went down to Redstone to visit over Sunday with Mrs. Ernest Ericsson.

Strawberries were a fine crop here this year, all of the gardens having vines being fairly loaded with fruit. Potatoes are doing fine, too, and most of the patches have plants about ready to bloom.

Rupert Messenger, the old reliable Reuben Glue, has sold his cigar store here to Milt Campbell, and will shake the dust of Marble off his feet very shortly. He probably will join his son, Clyde, at Salt Lake.

Tom Boughton, deputy assessor here, has had his hands full this week rounding up an assessment of the sheep which have been brought in. The owners have not been particularly anxious to seek Boughton out and deliver their schedules.

Our idea of a painful memory is that pretty little bandstand on Main street that we have to pass several times a day. The nearest we come to hearing music from it now is when a stray burro climbs on the steps and brays, as happened the other day.

Sheriff Hanlon came in Monday and remained a couple of days on business. A report had reached the sheriff that one of our citizens here was off his nut but personal investigation convinced the officer that the man in question is sane and able to take care of himself.

Roadmaster Walsh certainly has had his hands full this year, with the unusual work coming up from high waters. The work has been the hardest of any for many years and yet less permanent improvement to the roads has been accomplished than ever before, due to the

NEIGHBORHOOD NEWS

Happenings of Interest Gathered for the Benefit of Our Readers.

necessity for making temporary repairs in a hurry and then removing to another scene of trouble to repeat the program. Life on the roads near Marble has been just one cussed thing after another, Dad Walsh says.

Left from our magazine agency, we have in this office a large number of splendid magazines, fiction, scientific, sporting, outdoor, etc. We will sell these magazines at a nickel apiece as long as they last. Come in and get some cheap reading matter.

Several Marble people are planning on taking in the Cattlemen's Day celebration at Gunnison, among the number being Henry Mertens, Wilford Parry, Ernest Mazza, Tom Boughton, and possibly The Boosters. The celebration starts the 19th, running to the 21st.

Jimmie Morrison, engineer, and Mike Ross, fireman, of the train crew were both on the sick list a few days this week. Both were off duty when the train hit the cloudburst below Redstone and they were not sorry to miss the long hike home which the others had to take.

Joker Walsh came in Monday from Lige Brigg's sawmill near Minturn where he had been working for a couple of weeks. He was on the train which got held up by the cloudburst on the other side of Redstone and he telephoned to John Brooks here who went down for him in an auto.

The Gallo family all left Marble this week, boarding up their store building until conditions become so they can return here. Tony and Josie Gallo have found positions at Glenwood, where their brothers and sisters are working, and Joe Gallo will work at Aspen, where the father, A. Gallo, is already located.

There was a time in the history of country newspapers when the most of the subscribers paid with potatoes, chickens, eggs, butter, apples, etc. But these days, if a subscriber brought in a bushel of potatoes, he probably would want us to advance his year's subscription and throw in the printing office to boot.

The sheriff had orders to postpone the sale of a motor truck and various mining appliances, formerly the property of the Universal Sales company, which sale was advertised to be held last Monday, and he and his deputy, Joe Faussone, went up to Crystal Monday and publicly announced the postponement of the sale until August 1. The chances are that the difficulty will be fixed up before that time so that there will be no sale.

The wagon road between Redstone and Carbondale, in Pitkin county, was again tied up for traffic the fore part of this week, making about the steenth time this road has been closed since Spring came. Cloudbursts caused several bad rock slides last Sunday and Monday. A force of men have been working all week to clear the road.

Henry Thode has at last gotten permission from John C. Osgood to build a wagon road from his lumber setting on the forest reserve down through Redstone to the railroad, and this week he started work in earnest at his setting and on the construction of the road. Gus Magnussen and his partner, and Tom Williams went down the fore part of the week to work for Henry. The consent of Osgood to build this road has been withheld for nearly a year.

While over at Aspen for the 4th, the editor of this paper was told by W. D. Beck, a brother of Tom Beck, formerly of Marble, that Tom is to go from Gunnison to Denver the 15th of this month to take a place as bookkeeper with the auto truck concern owned by Izett brothers, one of the partners being Arch Izett, a former Marble citizen. Ike Kobey has been bookkeeper but he is to go on the road as a travelling salesman for the Izetts and Tom Beck takes his place in the concern. The Izetts are building up a big business converting Ford cars into trucks.

Those of us left in Marble have been doing considerable speculating since the news came out about the proposed sale of the C. Y. M. under foreclosure beginning August 1. The most of us feel that whoever buys this property in will have to do considerable work on it this coming Winter to put it in shape and we are all of us eager to see the plant running. The expense of an idle plant

such as this, counting insurance and caretaking, amounts to $1,500 or $3,000 a month, which is a considerable item of dead expense, besides the loss of interest on money invested, taxes, etc. It seems certain that in whose ever hands the property falls will do something toward rehabilitating it.

From exchanges of The Booster it is noted that all the old mine dumps in this part of the state are being worked over very carefully, the prevailing prices of metals making it profitable. There are several mine dumps in this neighborhood that would pay to work over. And what about the old smelter dump, across the river from Marble? That is said to have splendid values in it, the dump having been made at the time the old smelter was in operation, many years ago and before present-day methods of smelting were discovered. As a result of the crude methods then in use, it is highly probable that much value still remains in that old dump. Silver is now 78 cents and lead $11.

The heavy rain of last Sunday assumed the proportions of a cloud-burst on Slate mountain north of town, and Ambrose Williams, who was walking up that way, says an enormous quantity of mud came down the creek, along with big bowlders the size of an office desk. At the division of the creeks where the mud used to come this way, and which the town spent considerable money to prevent in the future, the main lot of mud took down the other branch, but quite a lot of it leaped the barrier and came down the old route for quite a distance. Ambrose said there needs to be a little work done there right away as a precaution against possible property damage in the town of Marble. A stitch in time might save more than nine.

Sunday school children of Marble had a fine picnic and basket dinner at the big spring below Holland's ranch last Monday, starting out from town at 10:30 and returning in the middle of the afternoon. Ambrose Williams, superintendent of the Sunday school, was in general charge of the arrangements and was assisted by a number of ladies, including Mrs. Granger, Mrs. Barton, Mrs. Tays, Mrs. Williams, Mrs. Coryell, Mrs. Faussone, Mrs. Sallgren, Mrs. Howe and her sister. Joe Faussone took some of the children down in his car, Johnnie Williams drove a couple of loads down in a spring wagon, and the rest walked. About fifty children, altogether, took part in the picnic. They had a great dinner and afterward played a lot of games and held athletic sports, foot races, etc.

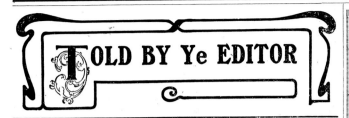

TOLD BY Ye EDITOR

A LOOK INTO THE FUTURE.

[The Booster has at various times printed items taken from the files of the Crystal River Current, published twenty-eight years ago. It has occurred to us that a few items taken from the advance files of this paper, to be published twenty-eight years hence, might also be of interest. Here are the items as we think they will appear along about 1935. —EDITOR.]

Drop into Rube Messenger's cigar store, 222 Main street, for a game of rummy and a cigar.

The new addition to Henry Mertens' store is now ready for occupancy. This immense, fine store now occupies a solid block from Center to East Third street. There are branch stores located at Crystal, Schofield, Placita, Prospect and Avalanche. Mr. Mertens travels from one store to another exercising a general supervision over his immense interests.

The latest unit of the Colorado-Yule company was opened for work this week. It is located at McClure Flats, the power plant and dam being at Prospect. The new plant is employing about 2,000 men and added to the plants at Marble, Redstone and Carbondale, it now makes about 20,000 on the payroll of the company.

W. D. Parry and George Tays left the fore part of this week for a prospecting trip. This paper predicts that one of these days these boys will find something good in the way of a mine, although they are not at all in need of such luck, both being wealthy men. Once a prospector, always a prospector.

The Crystal River & San Juan railroad is about to discard the old caboose which has seen service for so many years on its line, and will install in its place a train of solid steel Pullmans. Joe Larkin, superintendent of transportation of the system, is our authority for this report. It seems too bad in a way to retire this old caboose. It has seen faithful service.

For a novelty, at his palatial picture theater the other night Manager Faussone introduced some selections on his electric pianola, among the lot being "After the Ball" and "There'll be a Hot Time." While his 30-piece orchestra waited, the audience was regaled with these and other selections, proving to be quite interesting and novel.

The 4th of July was celebrated here with an old-fashioned picnic in the City Park, adjoining the magnificent new railway station. Tischhauser's concert band of 100 pieces was a feature of the celebration, giving concerts at the marble auditorium in the center of the park, adjoining the Catholic cathedral. The Marble Tramway company handled the crowds on its street car lines without an accident of any kind.

Cookman brothers this week completed the tearing down of the old Ko-

(Continued on third page)

A LOOK INTO THE FUTURE.

(Continued from Second Page)

bey burned building at the corner of Main and Center streets. A handsome 20-story office building is to be erected on this corner.

Aviation flights and other special features all this week at the Beaver Lake park. Come and shoot the chutes See Baptist Targhetta in his famous act of catching trout.

Three cases of violation of the state law against selling lemon extract were tried by Police Magistrate Budlong this week and heavy fines imposed. Judge Budlong is also impounding considerable live stock found running at large, it having been decided to again enforce this ordinance, after a lapse of twenty-eight years.

The bridge across Carbonate creek, adjacent to the Colorado-Yule hospital, which was made unsafe in the flood of 1917, so long ago that old residents will scarcely remember it, was fixed up this week, and is again in service for traffic.

Three taxicab drivers for the Brooks Auto Service company were fined in police court this week for speeding up high school hill faster than ninety miles an hour.

A committee representing the mine owners association of Crystal appeared before the county commissioners here this week to protest against the condition of the wagonroad between Marble and Crystal. A section of the road is unfit for travel, having been washed out by floods years ago—no one remembers just when—and the mine owners would like to have it repaired.

How'd you like to be a railroader on the Crystal River and San Joo-an?

Will the audience now join in singing that beautiful hymn, "Bringing in the Sheep."

Only a few days more now, boys, and you will know whether you are to go to the wars or not. The drafting is about to begin.

Of the four great disasters—fire, flood, famine and pestilence—we have had some experience with the first three this Summer, but, thank the Lord, we have yet to undergo the last.

In these days of uncertain mail service, it seems to this paper it would give better value received if the fire bell was rung when the mail arrives, rather than for the curfew.

Will any brother editors of the Western Slope, knowing of a nice healthy cat, please express it to "Cap" Dailey of the Aspen Times. Cats having litters of kittens preferred. "Cap" is very fond of cats, it is reported.

A visit this week of the head officials of the Crystal River railroad, which owns the line between Carbondale and Placita, gave rise to rumors here that

THESE PICTURES WERE TAKEN ALONG CRYSTAL RIVER, WHICH IS NOW RECEDING AFTER THE WORST FLOODS IN ITS HISTORY

they were contemplating abandoning the service. George B. Taylor, who was with the party, said there was nothing in the report.

The sheep men have announced that they will put the road to Redstone back in better shape than it ever was before, beginning the work the last of this week. This is the right spirit and if more sheep men had it there wouldn't be so much opposition to them coming into a neighborhood.

Following along the lines of "waste not," laid down by the tide of affairs, why doesn't some genius step forward and gather in for conservation the floating cotton that bothers housewives half to distraction? Chunks as big as your fist wait in whenever a door or window is opened. Cotton ought to be worth conserving, eh?

Great disappointment was ours the other day, due to poor eyesight after years of reading in newspaper work. We thought we saw a crowd of men down the street and fairly split ourself getting down to see what it was all about, but upon drawing near it turned out to be a bunch of burros quietly feeding on the grass along the main street through the business center.

Looking around on the hills, adjacent to Marble, just now one can hardly re-

member last Winter except as an unpleasant memory. The hills are perfectly beautiful now, with all trees in full leaf and the most attractive flowers growing everywhere. Again let us remark, there isn't a prettier place in the world in the Summer time than Marble,

Efforts have been made this week to convince the county commissioners of Gunnison county of the importance of building a new road around the place where the river washed out the old road, just the other side of the Black Queen mine on the way to Crystal. The only revenues now coming into Marble, about, are those derived from the mines in the vicinity of Crystal and now operations there are handicapped and curtailed by reason of there being no road.

There are a number of subscribers to

this paper who evidently think we mean to give it away to them, thinking, too, that we have so much money and are so philanthropic that cash is no object to us. These people have another think coming. Every week now we are lopping off some names of people of this disposition, because we absolutely cannot afford to carry subscribers who do not pay. Some time we hope to be in a position where we do not have to be so careful about expenses, but just now every nickel counts and it certainly costs money to produce and send YOU that paper which you get every week. Are you paying for it or do you think we ought to give it to you?

Morning and afternoon showers, and some heavy rains, broke the drouth here since the last Booster—the first precipitation for about six weeks. The rains were badly needed.

THE MARBLE BOOSTER

BY FRANK P. FROST, - EDITOR AND PROPRIETOR.

Entered in the postoffice at Marble, Colo., as second class
matter, under Act of Congress of March 3, 1879.

=== OFFICIAL PAPER OF THE TOWN OF MARBLE ===

MEMBER COLORADO EDITORIAL ASSOCIATION | An independent newspaper published weekly. Subscription $2 a year. Display advertisements 25 cents a single column inch. Readers 10c line.

MARBLE, COLORADO, SATURDAY, JULY 14, 1917

One trouble is no more than cleared up on the railroad between Carbondale and Marble this year than another trouble comes. Last Monday on the return trip from Carbondale, the train ran up to a series of rock and mud slides near Hot Springs, three miles below Redstone, which had been caused by a cloudburst that afternoon. The track was covered by slides in two places, half a mile apart, to a depth in each case of about ten feet. There were a number of smaller slides. Dynamite will be required to get them out. Frank Mueller said it would be a week or more before another train can get through. There was no mail Monday, but on Tuesday, the track auto went down as close as it could get from this side and the mail which was on the stalled train was carried on men's back two miles and brought into Marble. Intermittent mail service may be had in this manner for the next week yet, and then again there may not be any mail after the coal supply on the engine runs out, for there is no place to get any more except to get a car sidetracked at Carbondale and employ men to coal the engine by hand shoveling. Because of illness of the regular engine crew, Mueller, himself, ran the engine the first of the week, while Lou Reynolds was taken from the power house to do the firing, which resulted in no lights here in town on Monday and Tuesday nights. Even after these recent slides are cleared out,

which is an immense job, there remains further trouble at the Holland ranch bridge over Crystal river, a mile below Marble, which bridge is in bad shape from high water and is not safe for an engine to run over. Passengers, mail and freight have been transferred across this bridge from one train to another since the structure became unsafe, what times the train has run at all. Most of the time for the last month all the train service we have had has been the track auto, whose capacity is so limited that many disappointments among would-be passengers have resulted and, of course, freight has piled up at Carbondale which has been impossible to move.

There is more Catarrh in this section of the country than all other diseases put together, and until the last few years was supposed to be incurable. For a great many years doctors pronounced it a local disease and prescribed local remedies, and by constantly failing to cure with local treatment, pronounced it incurable. Science has proven Catarrh to be a constitutional disease, and therefore requires constitutional treatment. Hall's Catarrh Cure, manufactured by F. J. Cheney & Co., Toledo, Ohio, is the only Constitutional cure on the market. It is taken internally in doses from 10 drops to a teaspoonful. It acts directly on the blood and mucous surfaces of the system. They offer one hundred dollars for any case it fails to cure. Send for circulars and testimonials.
Address: F. J. CHENEY & CO., Toledo, Ohio.

Estate of Joseph Fisher, Deceased

All persons having claims against said estate are hereby notified to present them for adjustment to the County Court of Gunnison County, Colorado, on the 6th day of August, A. D. 1917.
PETER MATTIVI,
Administrator of the estate of Joseph Fisher, deceased.
First publication July 14, 1917.
Last publication Aug. 4, 1917.

W. R. Hood made a business trip to Carbondale on Thursday of this week.

Uriah McLean and George Clayton, both former residents of Marble, were visitors here this week at the home of Dan Barnes.

Mr Reynolds is no longer with the Sheep Mountain mine here. It is reported that on account of heart trouble he had to go to sea level.

The unwatering of the Black Queen mine is proceeding slowly, although a good job is being made of it. Just what is to be done after the unwatering is not announced.

In leavetaking of the Misses Gallo—

Tony and Josie—a steak fry was held Wednesday evening across the river from the trolly bridge, in which a dozen friends helped make a jolly occasion.

When you have an item of news tell it to The Booster.

A sheepherder with the Turner & Osborne flock was hurt in some manner unknown Wednesday, being found unconscious in the trail.

A dog belonging to A. R. Ambrosini bit the little son of Mr. and Mrs. John B. Moruzzi one day the early part of this week so badly that the child's welfare demanded an immediate examination by a doctor. The fangs of the dog struck the little boy beneath one eye and the face swelled to nearly twice the original size, both eyes being closed. John B. Moruzzi came out from Pueblo, where he is now located, to help his wife with the injured child.

LOOKING TOWARD THE WEST from the Marble City Hotel, the 1941 flood was subsiding, after severe damage had been done along the channel of Carbonate Creek — as may be seen down by the Marble Band Stand. In the next flood (which came in 1945), buildings made of marble had their first floors inundated with mud, almost to the ceilings. Before 1941, the grocery store (at the far left) had a gasoline pump out on East Main Street.

THIS WAS THE 1941 FLOOD DEBRIS at the Marble Band Stand on Main Street. The girls were taking the risk of stepping on nails as they scavenged for sovenirs. The shed visible beneath the bell tower may have housed the Marble Fire Department's fire-extinguisher cart. The other two hose carts were stored beneath the band stand.

Chapter 7

The End of A Dream?

In the summer of 1941 the future of Marble was not very bright. The marble quarry and mill were still functioning at a much reduced rate after surviving the Great Depression. But the company announced in September that all operations would cease by the end of the year as the war in Europe had seriously depressed the markets for marble. Marble extraction in the quarry was centered on an area of very good stone and the workers were trying to remove as much marble as possible before the end. Less than 200 residents of the town were trying to carry on while considering what they would do after the marble business was gone. The Williams Brothers General Store, with its marble sidewalk in front and the single gas pump, continued to open every day. Ambrose Williams in his dark suit and stiff celluloid collar seemed like a page from the past as he searched through the store for just the item a customer wanted, or worked the lever on the gas pump to fill the glass chamber at the top, so it could flow by gravity into the car tank. Everyone came there every day to pick up their mail at the post office facility in the front corner of the building. There had been no newspaper published in the town for about twenty years but there was not much local news and the residents were not too interested in outside happenings, as the news from elsewhere always seemed bad.

OSCAR McCOLLUM JR. PHOTO

THE MARBLE BAND STAND and Fire-Alarm Tower still stood firm, although engulfed in flood debris when this photograph was taken in 1958.

August 8th began as usual with a warm sun but by mid-afternoon the usual afternoon shower appeared over the basin north of town. Suddenly, Carbonate Creek contained in its little ditch through the center of town, was flowing with black mud. Soon it was a raging torrent carrying rocks and trees along with it. One could hear the hollow clunking sound of the boulders bumping against each other. The terrible black flood spread out relentlessly around and through the buildings along Main Street carrying away flimsy additions to the rear and sides. A portion of the hospital disappeared into the flow, but fortunately, no one was sick at the time. A young woman with two small children was living in the big Williams house on West First Street, heard a strange sound and looked out the window to see a wall of mud and rocks approaching. She grabbed a child under each arm and rushed out to higher ground, up Silver Street to the west. Looking back she saw the house shudder and slide about fifty feet down the gentle slope. Forty years later she still vividly recalled her terror as she described the incident to the author in the museum.

Marjorie Orlosky was alone in her home on the east side of the flooded area and rushed out of the house when the mud pushed in her front door. As she struggled to open the gate against the strong flow of mud about knee deep, rocks scraped against her legs scratching the skin and bruising her, but doing no serious harm. Marge felt fortunate to get out without suffering seri-

Continued on Page 284

MUCH OF THE 1941 FLOOD went down Center Street, as this view (above) shows, where the Kobey clothing-and-shoe store once stood on Main Street (on this corner).

FARTHER TO THE LEFT (below), the 1941 flood had nearly undermined the drugstore, next door to the site where the Kobey' clothing-and-shoe store formerly stood, at the corner of Main and Center streets.

278

THIS PHOTOGRAPH (above) shows the path taken by Carbonate Creek during the 1941 flood — as it cut through the business section of Marble, along East Main Street. The boarded-up Marble City Hotel survived, as did several homes behind it, on East Marble Street.

THIS IS ANOTHER VIEW of the 1941 flood. Here, you are looking toward the northeast at the Marble City Hotel, Elite Bakery and Carey's Ice Cream Parlour, which were not damaged during the flood.

MARBLE WAS PHOTOGRAPHED by Ron Ruhoff during September of 1958, just before the aspen leaves turned to autumn gold. The central part of Marble is visible here — where the town originated. The remains of mud and rock slides from Carbonate Creek are very much evident (at the left). This scene may be enjoyed from the old grade of the former Colorado-Yule Marble Company's tramway line to the quarry.

HERE ARE TWO VIEWS (above) of the same house on Marble Street, between East First and Center streets. This two-story house was the first home to be hit by the flood of 1941.

AS THE 1941 MUD SLIDE continued down Carbonate Creek, this was the scene on Silver Street (below) — or rather, what was left of Silver Street — as men attempted to channel the creek away from this house.

THE HORACE WILLIAMS HOUSE was caught in the path of the 1941 flood; however, it was restored on its original site in better-than-original condition. Although it had been carried 35 feet from its foundation, it was built of solid four-inch timbers and covered with siding, and was not severely damaged.

THE WOOD'S CABIN on Main Street, across from the Marble Band Stand, was badly damaged by the wall of water and mud in 1941.

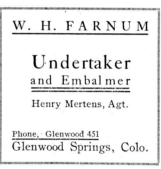

ANOTHER VIEW (at the left) of the 1941 flood damage shows the imposing mess that had to be cleaned up.

HIGH WATER and debris endangered the Treasury Mountain Railroad bridge during the 1945 flood. This span crossed the Crystal River. When this type of debris piles-up, it obstructs the flow of water like a dam. In this case, the debris had pushed-up against the bridge, which could have damaged the bridge pillars and caused extensive damage downstream. The Colorado-Yule Marble Company's electric-tramway grade is visible along the distant river bank.

THIS IS YET ANOTHER PHOTOGRAPH of the 1945 high-water and flood debris, which collected against the Treasury Mountain Railroad's pile trestle over the Crystal River. The former railroad spur that ran along the north bank at this location was the site where Crystal River & San Juan engine No. 3 was scrapped. As of this date (in 1945), the boiler had been tipped over on its side, and you are viewing the bottom, where the grate area was located. Scavengers had carted off most of this engine for scrap dollars — something that has happened to so many artifacts that relate to this area's history.

THE CRYSTAL RIVER DURING FLOOD AT MARB

Marble, Colo. After the flood in 1945

JOHN B. SCHUTTE PHOTO – MARBLE HISTORICAL SOCIETY COLLECTION

AT 7:00 P.M. ON JULY 31, 1945, the worst flood ever to hit Marble cascaded over the already-devastated area bordering the Carbonate Creek channel. No sign of the Marble City Hotel remains in this photographic spread (above and on the following page), and the two buildings made of marble are gone from sight. At the left, the Marble Fire Bell Tower and Marble Band Stand were still standing. The Slate Cliffs are in view above the gorge, where Carbonate Creek cuts through slate rock.

ous injury. Miraculously, no one in town was badly hurt. Most of the buildings in the flooded section of town were destroyed or badly damaged. The buildings with basements had them filled with the thick concrete-like flow which still entombs their contents.

In the aftermath of the flood efforts were made to open some of the streets and the damaged buildings were removed. Many families lost everything and left the dying town. The John Brooks family closed up their flooded house with many things still inside, and moved to Denver, only to have most of their possessions stolen. Those who remained continued their life in the best way they could. By the end of the war in 1945 there were still about fifty persons still hanging on in Marble, making a living through various activities.

Then, in the first week of August in 1945, ac-

cording to Marge Orlosky the week of the year when all the floods occurred, another big one hit. This flood of more mud and rocks spread out over the area so badly damaged four years before. The town truly seemed doomed this time. Most of the damaged buildings and many of the houses remaining were torn down or moved out so the owners would not have to pay taxes on them. Today there are less than thirty old structures remaining in the entire town.

RICHARD A. RONZIO COLLECTION

A BULLDOZER WAS BORROWED from New Castle to clear away the debris from the 1941 flood in Marble. It was in use at Slate Creek in this view, clearing away rocks where the main road enters Marble, at the west end of town.

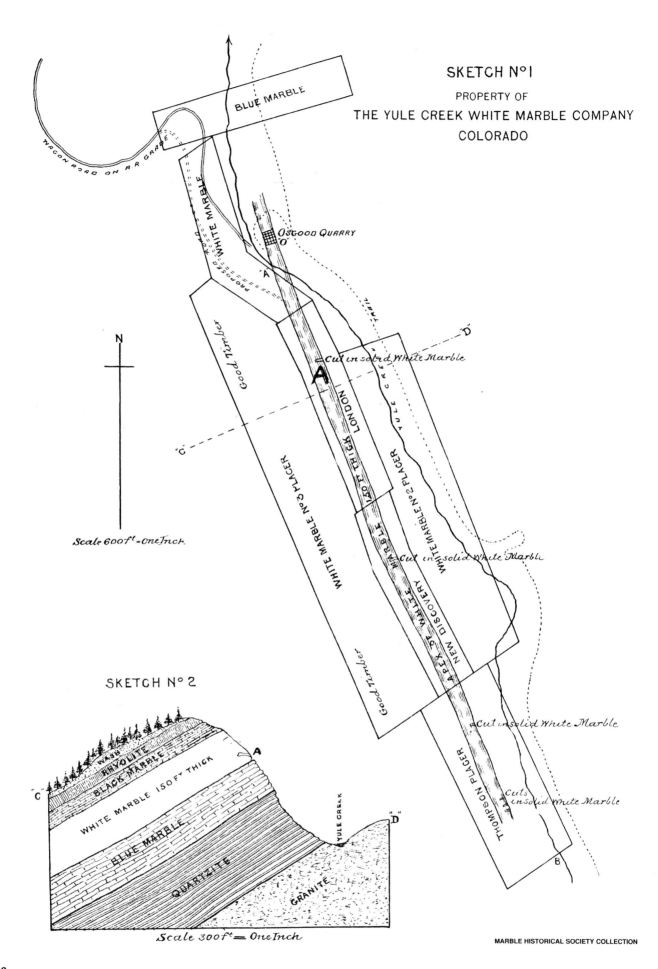

SKETCH N°1

PROPERTY OF

THE YULE CREEK WHITE MARBLE COMPANY

COLORADO

BLUE MARBLE

WAGON ROAD ON R.R GRADE

PROPOSED ROAD WHITE MARBLE

Osgood Quarry "O"

"A"

"D"

Good Timber

Cut in solid White Marble

"A"

"C"

Scale 600ft = One Inch.

WHITE MARBLE N°3 PLACER

150 FT THICK LONDON

WHITE MARBLE

Yule Creek Trail

Yule Creek

WHITE MARBLE N°2 PLACER

APEX OF WHITE N EW DISCOVERY

Cut in solid White Marble

Good Timber

Cut in solid White Marble

Thompson Placer

Cuts in solid white Marble

"B"

SKETCH N° 2

RHYOLITE
WXSB
BLACK MARBLE
WHITE MARBLE 150FT THICK
BLUE MARBLE
QUARTZITE
GRANITE

"A"

"C"

YULE CREEK

"D"

Scale 300ft = One Inch.

Chapter

QUARRYING THE WHITE STONE

Knowledge of the extensive marble deposits up Yule Creek preceeded the arrival of the white explorers and prospectors in the upper Crystal River Valley, early known as Rock Creek. The Ute Indians who had for many centuries used this valley for summer hunting grounds were aware of the "white stone." Since the Indians had no use for the marble, it was left undisturbed by them. Large sections of marble were exposed in cliffs on the west side of Yule Creek and in many places on Treasure Mountain, east of the creek. Geologists among the early explorers noted a large outcrop of marble containing deep scratches or grooves caused by the glaciers which had moved down these valleys.

Trappers and explorers had been in the Rock Creek area before 1880, but it was not until after this date that prospectors arrived in some numbers with the dream of finding gold, silver and other valuable ores. Among them, in 1873, were Sylvester Richardson, and George Yule the next year.[1] Both recognized the marble deposits and knew that they had value. Yule took more action on this knowledge and because of his efforts to publicize it the outcrops in the cliffs west of the creek later were named after him.

By 1890, John C. Osgood had been attracted to the valley by the extensive coal deposits near Redstone and elsewhere, and about this time became interested in the marble. He sent some men up Yule Creek to begin development on the claim he acquired on the east side of the creek, a short distance below the present Yule quarries. At this time, the commercial qualities of the marble were not known but Osgood committed a considerable amount of money and effort over the next ten years to trying to determine this. By 1893, he had extracted blocks for testing and shipped a large block to the Chicago World's Fair. Its superior quality attracted much attention in the stone industry, and this undoubtedly contributed to the later increased efforts in the valley.

Locally this deposit was referred to as the Osgood Marble Quarry and was the source of the large amount of marble supplied for the interior floors, wainscoting and stairways of the new state Capitol building in Denver. This marble was removed from the quarry in 1893 and 1894, and was hauled to the railroad at Carbondale over the newly-completed wagon road. Before 1893, there was only a trail down the valley. The marble was dragged on sleds in the winter and on wagons in the summer the 34 miles to the railroad.

The Marble Times & Clarence Chronicle,
October 13, 1893.
Governor Routt and Otto Mears, members of the

capitol board, inspected the Keene marble quarries last week, with the view of finishing the interior of the state capitol with our beautiful Yule creek marble.

. . . . .

In 1900, increased efforts were expended to produce marble in commercial quantities, and this required a regular wagon road from the Town of Marble up the four miles to the quarry. Items from The Marble Times and Crystal Silver Lance newspaper published in Marble chronicle the road construction, beginning in September, 1900.

The Marble Times & Crystal Silver Lance,
September 14, 1900.
J.C. Osgood, Mrs. Osgood, J.T. Kebler and Paul Blount were here Monday and visited the company's marble property up Yule creek and viewing the proposed new wagon road that is to be built.

The marble quarry is a point of interest to visitors especially the young ladies. The dining room is now supplied with table-cloths, and the menu is much improved, and we Frank-ly [sic] admit there is attraction.

. . . . .

The operation was becoming somewhat civilized, and even at this early date, the activity was of interest to tourists. It also became necessary to import some specialists in stone quarrying.

The Marble Times & Crystal Silver Lance,
September 28, 1900.
Wednesday's stage brought in Wm. Rogers from Luttrell, Tennessee, and he will join the force at the Osgood marble quarry.

The Marble Times & Crystal Silver Lance,
October 5, 1900.
Tuesday we had the pleasure of paying a visit to the Osgood marble quarry to witness the hoisting of the first block of marble. Although the block measured 8-0x3-6x2-0, the derrick is so arranged that it was comparatively an easy task to swing the big block of stone out. As the block was taken from the surface it was not expected it would be of marketable value, as the action of the weather would naturally render it too soft, but it proved conclusively to Supt. F.H. Eaton that the stone will be entirely free of seams after the surface layer is removed.

---

[1] Vandenbusche, Duane & Myers, Rex, "Marble, Colorado: City of Stone," p.7, Golden Bell Press, Denver, 1970.

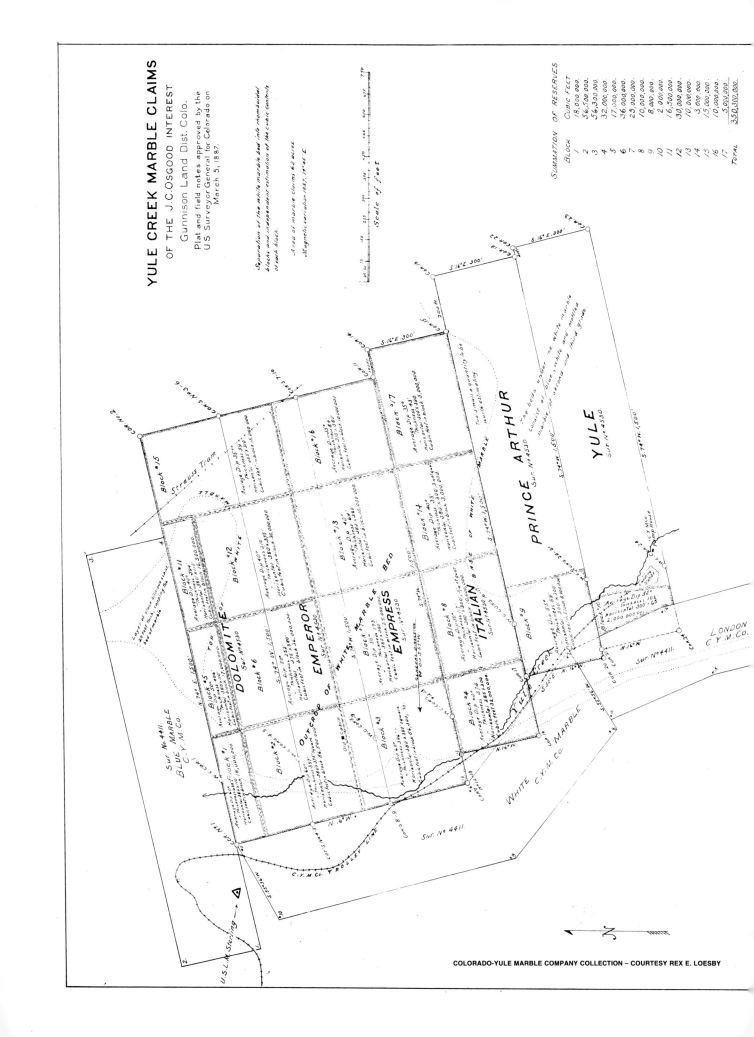

YULE CREEK MARBLE CLAIMS

OF THE J.C. OSGOOD INTEREST
Gunnison Land Dist. Colo.

Plat and field notes approved by the
U.S Surveyor General for Colorado on
March 5, 1887.

Separation of the white marble bed into rhomboidal
blocks and independent estimation of the cubic contents
of each block.

Area of marble claims 62 acres

Magnetic variation 1887, 14°45' E.

Scale of feet

SUMMATION OF RESERVES	
BLOCK	CUBIC FEET
1	18,000,000.
2	56,500,000.
3	56,300,000.
4	32,000,000.
5	17,000,000
6	36,000,000.
7	25,000,000.
8	10,000,000.
9	8,000,000.
10	2,000,000.
11	16,500,000.
12	30,000,000.
13	10,000,000
14	3,000,000
15	15,000,000.
16	10,000,000.
17	5,000,000.
Total	350,300,000.

COLORADO-YULE MARBLE COMPANY COLLECTION – COURTESY REX E. LOESBY

Another block was removed Wednesday, and it is a fine piece, measuring 8-0x5-9x2-2, or in round numbers weighing 10,000 pounds, and of a perfect white texture and good quality.

The channeler will now be put to work cutting out another surface layer farther into the hill, which will possibly take a month's time, then the cutting out of the second layer will be commenced.

The quarry is operated by a practical and competent force of men, namely, F.H. Eaton, superintendent; Pat O'Keefe, foreman; Wm. Rogers, Bob Robinson and J.E. Wiliford, all from the marble quarries at Luttrell, Tenn.

The channeler, drill and other machinery were furnished by the Sullivan Machinery Co. of Chicago, who build the best quarry machinery in this country, and the channeler and drill are running smoothly and doing excellent work.

This increasing production required with some urgency a better road.

The Marble Times & Crystal Silver Lance,
October 12, 1900.

Monday, James Legget brought up Surveyors Utley and Scott who will run another line for a wagon road to the Osgood marble quarry in order to get an estimate of the cost of building such a road. Paul Blount came up with them.

The Marble Times & Crystal Silver Lance,
October 19, 1900.

At the Osgood marble quarry the boys are getting along nicely cutting out the second layer of stone and in a short time will have several blocks out ready for shipment east for testing purposes. But before this can be done a mile and a half of wagon road must be built.

IN 1886, JOHN C. OSGOOD of the White Brest Fuel Company — along with the Colorado Midland Railroad — purchased bonds covering many of the marble claims along Yule Creek, above the town of Marble. In 1891, John C. Osgood acquired a quit-claim deed on some of the marble holdings, which included both the London and the White Marble claims. One of these claims produced the block of marble Osgood took to the Columbia Exposition in 1893. During 1905, Osgood organized the Redstone Marble Company, but the company was dissolved in 1918, after producing very little finished stone. However, marble for the floors and stairs of the Colorado capitol came from the Osgood quarry in 1893–1894. It should be noted that Otto Mears, of Rio Grande Southern and Silverton Railroad fame, was a member of the Colorado Capitol Board that chose this marble for the construction of the state capitol.

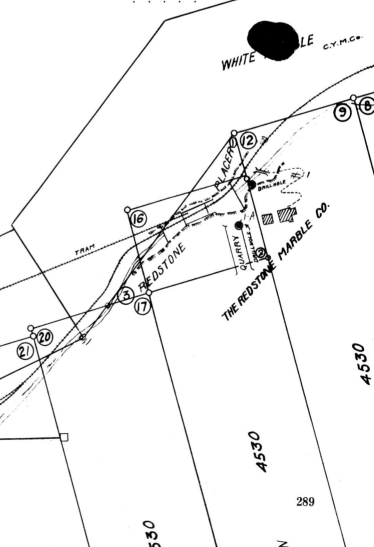

© ROBERT AND SALLY OSGOOD LAWRENCE

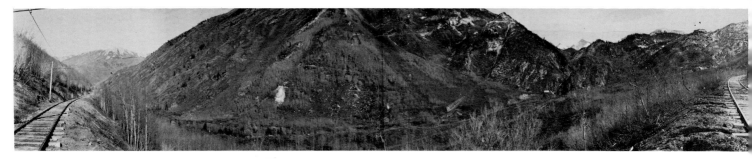

HENRY L. JOHNSON PHOTO – JACK D. CLEMENSON COLLECTION

THIS PRINT (above) is a miniaturized version of the same one printed on this and the following three pages. The original photograph was exposed on a continuous roll of film with a "circuit" camera, which operated on a gear track that rotated 360 degrees. The illustration below and on the following three pages is printed at 110 percent of the original-print size. Henry Johnson's camera is on display at the Marble Historical Society Museum.

THE FIRST PAGE (below) illustrates the grade of the Colorado-Yule Marble Company's standard-gauge electric-tramway line as it came up the hill from the town of Marble. Mount Daly is visible in this scene, which is located in the Maroon Bells–Snowmass Wilderness. This magnificent wilderness area is between Crystal City and the Maroon Bells, near Aspen.

Success breeds competition, so other marble deposits in the vicinity were beginning to be developed. Kline Falls is the large water fall on the Crystal River, a short distance upstream from the town of Marble.

The Marble Times & Crystal Silver Lance,
November 2, 1900.

Messrs. Anderson and Parry have completed work on the black marble claims, near the Kline Falls, the property of Griffith and Hoagland.

The Marble Times & Crystal Silver Lance,
November 9, 1900.

Paul Blount was up the last of the week looking after the construction of the wagon road to the quarry.

The Marble Times & Crystal Silver Lance,
November 16, 1900.

Work on the wagon road to the Osgood marble quarry is now progressing very satisfactorily, as workmen are becoming more plentiful, and in a few days it is expected all the men desired will be on the ground. The contractors, Flaharity & Farrell, are both now on the ground pushing the work. They have sublet portions of the work to some of our home people.

The Marble Times & Crystal Silver Lance,
November 23, 1900.

S.C. Hodgson has accepted a position as engineer at the marble quarry and will move his wife up there as soon as accommodations are provided.
. . . . . .

THE SECOND PAGE of this panorama (below) illustrates the Colorado White Marble Company's exploratory opening on the side of Treasure Mountain. An electric-wire support tower is in view at the bottom of this photograph. The two other openings are on the pack trail climbing up beside Yule Creek, beyond the lower pine trees.

HENRY L. JOHNSON PHOTO – JACK D. CLEMENSON COLLECTION

The "accommodations" consisted of quarters in a log cabin. Of course, this did not include amenities such as running water and electric lights. Women of those days did not expect much in the way of comfort or convenience and were willing to join their husbands when there was barely a roof over their heads. Remains of an old log cabin can still be seen at the Osgood quarry site.

The Marble Times & Crystal Silver Lance,
November 23, 1900.
Owing to the snow storm, Pat O'Keefe and Wm. Rogers suspended work on the marble quarry and spent a couple of days down here. This is the first lay-off the boys have taken since they started work.

. . . . . .

The heavy snows at the altitude of the quarry, about 9000 feet, continued to hamper work at the quarries and particularly the transportation of the marble down the steep road to town.

The Marble Times & Crystal Silver Lance,
November 23, 1900.
Edwin Eaton, a brother of F.H., was in from Tennessee this week looking over the marble quarry, and we understand that he was highly pleased with the blocks already out. He says there is plenty of demand for Colorado marble in the east.

THE THIRD PAGE of this spectacular panorama (below) illustrates the end-of-track at the Treasury Mountain Railroad's power plant and the adjacent boarding houses. It appears that the property was idle around the loading area (at the left), where a mast stood, minus the boom that transferred marble from the funicular cable car to regular railroad cars on the Treasury Mountain Railroad. The old Strauss Quarry is located at the upper ridge.

The Marble Times & Crystal Silver Lance,
November 30, 1900.

Melton's jack train is packing another carload of coal up to the marble quarry for use during the winter.

The Marble Times & Crystal Silver Lance,
January 4, 1901.

The force of men on the marble road is being constantly increased, and this fine weather is a God-send for the contractors.

The Marble Times & Crystal Silver Lance,
January 11, 1901.

Last Saturday about a dozen new men arrived in camp to work on the quarry road. The contractors now have quite a force of men employed.

The Marble Times & Crystal Silver Lance,
January 18, 1901.

The road up Yule creek was again opened for travel last Friday, and on Saturday Phil Moore's jack train took a load of supplies up to the marble quarry.

The standard method of getting supplies up into the high country was by means of mules and burros. It is amazing the amount and kind of materials that could be strapped to the backs of these patient and sure-footed beasts. Also, there seemed to be a labor shortage, as not everyone wanted to work on the heights in the winter.

Continued on Page 297

THE FOURTH PAGE of this panorama (below) illustrates the Redstone Marble Company's building, to the left of "Windy Point," below Purple Mountain, the taller snowcapped peak. The Colorado-Yule Marble Company's quarry opening is farther back and higher in this canyon. "Lumber Siding," or "Sawmill Curve," as it was variously known, was near the right — on the grade of the electric-tramway line. Unfortunately, the date for this this view is unknown.

HENRY L. JOHNSON PHOTO – JACK D. CLEMENSON COLLECTION

Property of The Colorado WHITE Marble Co

THE DATE IS UNKNOWN for the time this photograph was taken of the property named "The Colorado White Marble Company." This prospect is located on the west side of Whitehouse Mountain, not far north of the end-of-track of the Treasury Mountain Railroad. Apparently, the company could not find investors to con-

tinue developing this property, and it decayed in later views. Three prospect openings are on the hillside — the largest one visible at the cabins, above and to the right of them on the second switchback road. The third opening is on the upper right-hand section of the photograph, a bit below the snow.

PRECEDING PAGE: After taking the curve around "Windy Point," this view opens up, as you look toward the south, toward Mount Baldy (on the right) and Purple Mountain (on the left). J. C. Osgood had his marble quarry located where the mill building appears, beneath the peaks. The marble dump appears to the north (left) of this. Beyond (to the right) is the marble dump of the Colorado-Yule Marble Company, with a glimpse of Quarry Town (at the far right). Yule Creek tumbles down through this chasm.

PART OF THIS OLD CABIN (above) was still standing at J. C. Osgood's Redstone Marble Company quarry when photographed ca. 1990.

The Marble Times & Crystal Silver Lance,
January 25, 1901.

Frank Smith, employed on the new marble road, was down in the valley the fore part of the week trying to get rock men, but had poor success.

The Marble Times & Crystal Silver Lance,
February 1, 1901.

While up here last week, Superintendent Cornell advanced the price of Flaharity & Farrel's contract on the marble road and gave them until the first of April to complete the work.

The fine weather we have enjoyed so far this winter has very materially aided in all out-door work. Supt. F.L. Eaton says that work at the marble quarry is going along nicely and could not proceed any faster in any mountainous country, and by the time the wagon road is completed he hopes to have ready for shipment many blocks of fine stone.

. . . . . .

Only the relatively mild winter of 1900-01 enabled work on the road to continue throughout the winter months. In the meantime work was continuing at the quarry.

The Marble Times & Crystal Silver Lance,
February 22, 1901.

Supt. Eaton informs us that they are working in fine marble at the present time, and that he is more encouraged than ever with the stone. He expects the wagon road to reach the quarry in about six weeks, if we have good weather, and then he will ship out a few blocks for testing purposes.

The Marble Times & Crystal Silver Lance,
April 26, 1901.

The contractors on the quarry road are in their heaviest work—just across the creek from the quarry; it is

Continued on Page 301

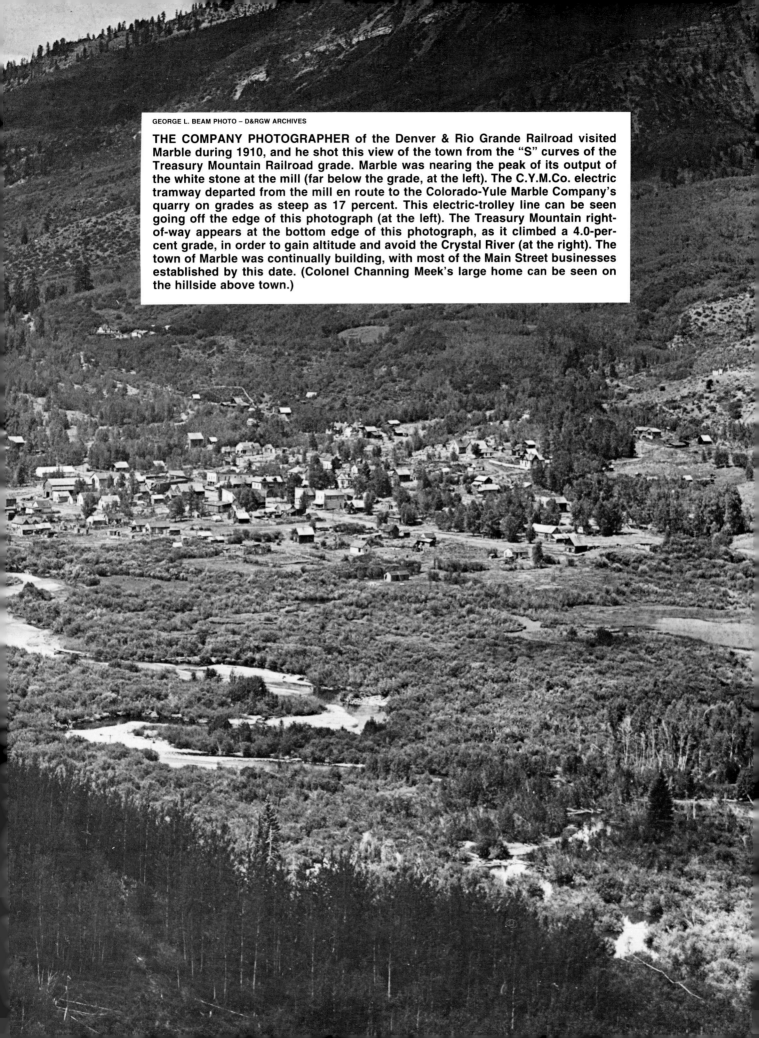

GEORGE L. BEAM PHOTO – D&RGW ARCHIVES

THE COMPANY PHOTOGRAPHER of the Denver & Rio Grande Railroad visited Marble during 1910, and he shot this view of the town from the "S" curves of the Treasury Mountain Railroad grade. Marble was nearing the peak of its output of the white stone at the mill (far below the grade, at the left). The C.Y.M.Co. electric tramway departed from the mill en route to the Colorado-Yule Marble Company's quarry on grades as steep as 17 percent. This electric-trolley line can be seen going off the edge of this photograph (at the left). The Treasury Mountain right-of-way appears at the bottom edge of this photograph, as it climbed a 4.0-percent grade, in order to gain altitude and avoid the Crystal River (at the right). The town of Marble was continually building, with most of the Main Street businesses established by this date. (Colonel Channing Meek's large home can be seen on the hillside above town.)

THE FORMER GRADE of the Treasury Mountain Railroad appears in the lower part of this color view, which was taken from the old grade of the Colorado-Yule Marble Company's tramway line to the quarry. Beaver Lake is visible at the far left, and the man-made pond (center) covers the area where the Colorado-Yule Marble Company's power plant had been located. Mount Daly is covered with golden aspen (at the left), with a glimpse of Snowmass Peak beyond (in the distance). Hat Mountain is at the right, next to the base of Whitehouse Mountain.

IN THIS LATE AUTUMN SCENE, shot in 1966, the support poles that had carried electric-power lines to the Colorado-Yule Marble Company's quarry were still standing. One was in view (at the lower left). Looking back, in the direction of Marble (lower center), is a glimpse of the old grade of what was originally the Treasury Mountain Railroad. Mount Daly is the snowcapped peak in the distance.

all solid rock work for quite a distance and in some places the side cut is 70 - 80 feet high. It will be many weeks yet before the road is finished. It will be a fine piece of road when done.

. . . . .

1911

THE TREASURY MOUNTAIN

RAILROAD ✦ **COMPANY**

Pass **H W Conard,**

Colorado Midland R R

UNTIL DECEMBER 31ST 1911 UNLESS OTHERWISE ORDERED

E. T. Guymon
PRESIDENT

No. **70**

PERHAPS THE ONLY known pass to exist from the Treasury Mountain Railroad, this one was printed on gold-colored paper stock.

Cutting a road through solid rock along a vertical cliff was difficult and dangerous work.

The Marble Times & Crystal Silver Lance,
June 14, 1901.
A piece of rock was hurled over the gulch last Saturday while blasting on the wagon road and landed on the boiler at the quarry, damaging it considerable, causing delay in channeling until the new pieces arrive from the foundry at Enterprise, Kans.

. . . . .

The man who platted the portion of the town of Marble west of Carbonate Creek also was investigating the marble outcrop in the Crystal River, as many of the early developers diversified their holdings.

The Marble Times & Crystal Silver Lance,
July 5, 1901.
W.W. Wood is doing some work on his marble holdings between here [Marble] and Crystal.

. . . . .

With summer weather of 1901, the pace of work at the Osgood quarry was stepped up. At this time Osgood was president of the Colorado Fuel & Iron Company (C.F.&I.), which he had organized several years before, and was conducting his social experiment at Redstone. This theory was based on the idea that coal miners could benefit from decent living conditions and some cultural amenities, and thus produce more.

Continued on Page 305

THE TREASURY MOUNTAIN RAILROAD right-of-way crossed the Crystal River flood plain on the south side of the river, before making the climb to the Strauss quarry. Two boxcars and the Crystal River & San Juan's long combination coach-caboose, No. 2, had been spotted ("parked") on the mainline shortly after the collapse of the Crystal River Marble Company in 1912. To the right of the com-

bine is a short passing track. The residential and business sections of Marble (shown at the right) was called "Clarence" until July 4, 1892, when the two towns merged into one. Carbonate Creek flows through the gulch just above town. Beaver Lake is to the far right, on the road to Crystal City. (Some people say that this body of water was called "Marble Lake" during the early days.)

THE TREASURY MOUNTAIN Railroad had only one locomotive, No. 1, which was a Lima-built Shay geared engine, designed for work on steep, rough track. She was a standard-gauge locomotive, with small 28-inch driving wheels. No. 1 was capable of hauling two empty cars up the 4.0-percent grade to the end-of-track, which took approximately 45 minutes over the distance of nearly 2-1/2 miles. Ties, rail joiners and tie plates were stacked in Marble for tracklayers — in this view taken during September of 1909.

SNOWBOUND IN MARBLE, the Treasury Mountain Railroad's Shay geared locomotive was blanketed with snow. The little Shay was at the end-of-track at the lower end of the line. Pistons and gears are located on the right side of this type of engine, below and ahead of the crew's cab.

OSCAR McCOLLUM JR. PHOTO

LOIS ANN McCOLLUM, the wife of the photographer/author, was walking down the 4.0-percent grade on the Treasury Mountain Railroad in the direction of Marble when this picture was shot. Mount Daly, located in the Maroon Bells–Snowmass Wilderness is in the high country, to the right (northeast of Marble).

LOCOMOTIVE No. 1 of the Treasury Mountain Railroad was taking-on water at the CR&SJ standpipe in Marble during 1910. This standpipe was located near the Colorado-Yule Marble Company's office. At this time, the Treasury Mountain engine made trips to the upper end-of-track every other day.

MARBLE HISTORICAL SOCIETY COLLECTION

Marble
Colo.
13.

SNOWCAPPED MOUNT DALY is the high point of this 1980 autumn view. You are looking out toward the old abandoned grade of the Treasury Mountain Railroad, across Yule Creek Canyon. The road leading up along Daniels Hill from Marble to Crystal, is plainly in view below the trail leading up to the Bair Ranch. The photographer was standing on the Colorado-Yule Marble Company's tramway grade.

The Marble Times & Crystal Silver Lance,
August 2, 1901.

The C.F. & I. Co. has established a new department in connection with its vast undertakings. It is called the Sociological department, and will be under the immediate charge of Dr. Corwin. The object is to look after the education of the children and the sanitary conditions of all families in every camp belonging to the company. It is a laudable object and the officers of the company are worthy of praise for inaugurating the movement.

. . . . . .

Though C.F.&I. was doing the development work at the Osgood quarry, there is no evidence that these social theories were being applied there.

Continued on Page 322

U.S. GEOLOGICAL SURVEY MAP
ROUTE MAP of the TREASURY MOUNTAIN RAILROAD

23

9409
24

8681

Marble
BM 7953

8103

Hat Mtn
9172

26

COLORADO-YULE MARBLE COMPANY

8250

8500

SWITCHBACK

8750

9000

9500

10000

10500

11000

11500

TREASURY MOUNTAIN RAILROAD

ELECTRIC TRAMWAY

Whitehouse
Mtn

(COLORADO WHITE MARBLE COMPANY)

8710

LOADING AREA

END-OF-TRACK

FUNICULAR CABLE TRAMWAY

STRAUSS QUARRY (lower)

STRAUSS QUARRY (upper)

CRYSTAL RIVER
MARBLE COMPANY

COLORADO-YULE MARBLE COMPANY QUARRY

YULE-COLORADO
QUARRY

10500

A WOODEN DAM had burst somewhere upstream on the Crystal River, which in turn, slammed debris up against the Treasury Mountain Railroad's bridge in Marble. It is interesting to notice the large inventory of cut marble in storage alongside the Crystal River Marble Company's grounds — beside the track, along the east end of the wooden barn used by the Crystal River & San Juan Railway.

COLORADO RAILROAD builders usually followed the contours of the mountains when they constructed their grades. In this photograph (to the right) of the Treasury Mountain Railroad grade, a short, straight section had been cut through rock. The town of Marble is out sight, below the ridge known as Gallo Hill.

SHOOTING TOWARD THE EAST — almost into the sun — the yellow-and-orange leaves on the aspen trees appear nearly translucent. The abandoned grade of the Treasury Mountain Railroad is above the cabin rooftop. This colorful Indian-summer view was shot in 1980.

THANOS A. JOHNSON PHOTOS

THE MARBLE ARTIST, Thanos A. Johnson, re-discovered the Treasury Mountain Railroad's Shay locomotive parked at the end-of-track on July 30, 1945. This was a few-hundred feet beyond the funicular cable-railroad connection with the TMR. The Lima-built Shay geared engine (with builder's number 2052) had been lettered as No. 1 for the TMR and was purchased in 1909. She was a standard-gauge engine, with 28-inch drivers, and she was used extensively during 1912, on the run from Marble to Redstone, when the CR&SJ was short of motive power (because No. 6 was being refueled). TMR No. 1 had been stored inside the enginehouse, which had disintegrated due to the severe climatic conditions at this altitude. In 1948, a man appeared on the scene with cutting torch in hand and reduced the locomotive into pieces — to be hauled out for scrap metal. This was another rape of the area's historic artifacts, all for the "quick buck." The lower view is the northern exposure of this engine, with the power house in the background.

HENRY L. JOHNSON PHOTO – JACK D. CLEMENSON COLLECTION

THE TREASURY MOUNTAIN Railroad grade gained altitude with this switchback en route from Marble to the Strauss Quarry. This rail line climbed on a steep 4.0-percent grade. The curved track is that of the leg between switches on the switchback, and you are looking downgrade. The track from Marble was to the right.

THE END-OF-TRACK of the Treasury Mountain Railroad is in this view, near the center of the scene. It is believed the picture was taken in 1910, as the photographer looked at the property of the Crystal River Marble Company. At the far left, the funicular cable tramway began its climb toward the quarry opening, which was located on the side of Whitehouse Mountain. White tents dotted the landscape near the boarding house, above the Treasury Mountain Railroad's right-of-way. The railroad ended at the powerhouse (near the right of center). Although not in view, the Colorado-Yule Marble Company's electric tramway turned the corner to approach its end-of-track, below the quarry that is located in the basin where Purple Mountain tops out.

DAVID S. DIGERNESS COLLECTION

THE POWERHOUSE and engine shed of the Crystal River Marble Company's Strauss Quarry occupied the buildings in this photograph. This was located beside Yule Creek, at the end-of-track on the Treasury Mountain Railroad. TMR locomotive No. 1 was housed inside the building, reached by crossing over a short timber bridge. Yule Creek is behind these buildings. Track had been removed by the time this photograph was taken.

THE NORTH AND WEST WALLS of the Crystal River Marble Company's Treasury Mountain Railroad engine shed were photographed at an unknown date. Large, high doors allowed the Treasury Mountain's Shay locomotive access through the building.

TWO MORE COLOR VIEWS are presented on the preceding page, taken on July 30, 1945, before the scrapper arrived to cut up and haul off the TMR engine. Brass fittings, such as the bell, whistle, gauges and headlight were already gone. Notice that the gold-leaf lettering still looked nearly new, even though it was some 35 years old as of this date.

THIS IS THE ENGINEER'S SIDE of the Treasury Mountain Shay locomotive, taken during the 1940's, showing the pistons and gears that drove the engine. The metal shed, now gone, protected this machine for many years — however, after the shed collapsed, hikers were provided a rare sight, a Shay in the wilderness! The extremely good condition of this Shay is surprising.

THE CRYSTAL RIVER Marble Company's power-house, located at the end-of-track, appears in this scene (at the left), with the Treasury Mountain Railroad grade leading to it. The Strauss Quarry boarding house is at the center, while the bunkhouse is higher up (at the right).

FAIRY MAE (MATTINGLY) McKEE PHOTO –
MARBLE HISTORICAL SOCIETY COLLECTION

THE WORKERS at the Crystal River Marble Company's quarry were quartered in this boarding house, near the end-of-track (above). The old building was still intact when photographed in 1951. It had been operated by a relative of the photographer, Esther Mattingly.

THE CRYSTAL RIVER MARBLE Company's powerhouse and locomotive shed appear in this view (at the far right), beside Yule Creek. The boarding house and bunkhouse are higher up the hillside (at the left). Notice the funicular tramway that was built up the side of Treasure Mountain. This cable-car line had grades reaching 26 percent, equaling 26 feet of vertical rise for every 100 feet of horizontal roadway. It ended at the Treasury Mountain Railroad's siding (at the far left), where a derrick lifted loads from the funicular car to railroad cars. The old Strauss Quarry is at the end of the funicular tramway.

HENRY L. JOHNSON PHOTO – JACK D. CLEMENSON COLLECTION

GEORGE L. BEAM PHOTO – D&RGW ARCHIVES

GEORGE L. BEAM PHOTO – D&RGW ARCHIVES

THE CRYSTAL RIVER MARBLE Company's funicular tramway operated with two incline cable cars (in the view at the left). Workers loaded one cable car at the upper end (where the quarry was located), while the other one was being unloaded at the bottom. A passing track was located mid-way on the line and made the operation possible. The tramway had a maximum grade of 26 percent as it went up the mountainside. This operation is commonly known as the Strauss Quarry. As of 1992, the cable drums and machinery for this funicular line were still in place, while rails and gear are strewn about (to the rear of this scene).

LOOKING DOWN the funicular track from the Crystal River Marble Company's Strauss Quarry in 1912 provides you with a splendid view, where Yule Creek meanders through the valley. The Treasury Mountain Railroad grade is visible at this location. On the opposite slope are wagon roads, working their way down from the halfway house of Colorado-Yule Marble Company's electric tramway. The halfway house contained an electric sub-station and is at the far right.

317

THE LOADING AREA of the Crystal River Marble Company was at the lower end of the funicular incline-cable line, and it appears in this greatly-enlarged view of the picture on Page 317. A railroad gondola had been spotted on the siding to be picked up by the standard-gauge Shay locomotive to be hauled off to Marble, after stone was loaded by the derrick. Yule Creek meanders beyond the tracks. Funicular-tramway workers are in view, near the bottom of the photograph. Notice the wagon road that had been built to reach this quarry, on the west bank of Yule Creek. Positioned at the end of the funicular line is a mast-and-boom derrick, with a block-and-tackle, used to unload the cable-incline cars onto standard-gauge railroad cars.

IT IS QUITE POSSIBLE that this was the first "official" photograph of the upper workings of the opening of the Strauss Quarry, ca. 1906. This was located on the side of Whitehouse Mountain. A wooden derrick, consisting of a mast and boom, had been installed to hoist blocks from the opening. The log cabin provided shelter and contained a blacksmith shop for the quarry workings.

THIS COMPARRISON PHOTOGRAPH was taken in 1990, and it reveals the ruins of the revolving derrick lying on the rock. This derrick had been installed by the Crystal River Marble Company at the workings of the old Strauss Quarry. This was the upper workings, which were abandoned in favor of a tunnel quarry lower down the slope. John Petrocco, Jack Clemenson and his son, Tony, are in this scene.

LOOKING DOWN at the end-of-track of the Treasury Mountain Railroad, this summer photograph shows the scar left by the funicular tramway. This line brought marble blocks down from the Strauss Quarry, high up on the hillside, to the standard-gauge railroad (at the lower left). The lower workings of the Strauss Quarry are visible about three-quarters of the way to the top of the ridge, where the larger waste dump appears. The distant peaks (at the far right) are Mount Baldy (left) and Purple Mountain (right), where waste rock can be seen from the Colorado-Yule Marble Company's quarry (just below the two peaks).

321

GEORGE L. BEAM PHOTO – D&RGW ARCHIVES

IMPROVEMENTS HAD TAKEN PLACE on the side of Whitehouse Mountain, at the end of the funicular line. The surface works of the former Strauss Quarry were photographed in 1912. Equipment consisted of a revolving steel derrick and a horizontal drilling machine, fed by compressed-air lines. The Crystal River Marble Company (incorporated on March 30, 1909) had taken over the property of the Strauss Quarry; however, it subsequently became completely idle by 1915. This photograph was taken at the original quarry.

The Marble Times & Crystal Silver Lance,
July 12, 1901.

Tuesday we paid a visit to the Osgood marble quarry and found everything moving along nicely. The channeler is cutting away in some fine looking stone; the outside block was taken out on Monday; the next couple of blocks are expected to be of a shipping quality. It must be re- membered that the work now carried on is of a prospecting nature and as the plant is small it is necessarily slow work; but once the quality of the stone is assured the company will undoubtedly erect a large plant and go at it in a busi- ness-like manner, as the fuel company has never been known to do anything in a hap-hazard way.

OSCAR McCOLLUM JR. PHOTO

TURNING TOWARD THE RIGHT with his camera, the photographer picked up more of the ruins left behind at the upper-quarry opening of the Crystal River Marble Company's operation on Whitehouse Mountain.

The following item mentions a different marble deposit then being investigated, which was about four miles up Yule Creek from the Osgood, and the present Yule quarries.

The Marble Times & Crystal Silver Lance,
July 19, 1901.

F.G. Zugelder of Gunnison, in company with a gentleman from New York, were at the head of Yule creek Saturday and Sunday examining what is locally known as the Keene marble.

The Marble Times & Crystal Silver Lance,
August 9, 1901.

Supt. Eaton is making preparations to ship out several blocks of marble from the Osgood quarry to be sawed up into slabs. We understand the blocks will be sent to Chicago.

The Marble Times & Crystal Silver Lance,
August 23, 1901.

The new wagon to haul the marble blocks to the railroad reached here on Tuesday and it surely has the appearance of being strong enough to haul any block horses can pull.

The same day a hoister was brought in for use at the quarry. The first two blocks of marble from the Osgood quarry were taken down to Placita yesterday from whence they will be shipped to Chicago to the mill of Sherman & Flavin to be sawed up into slabs. The blocks look solid and free from any seams, hard and pure white. We will now soon learn the verdict of those who will examine this stone.

• • • • • • •

Osgood soon was involved in the problems of corporate take-over of his C.F.&I. by John D. Rockefeller, and likely did not have the time or inclination to pursue his development of the marble deposit. It also is possible that the quality of that deposit of marble was not adequate for continued production.

THE LOWER WORKINGS of the Crystal River Marble Company's Strauss Quarry were photographed by Ron Ruhoff in July of 1971. This is an exploratory hole, 100 feet northeast of the main tunnel, shown on the next page. A cable-winding hoist drum is in the foreground.

THIS PHOTOGRAPH (above) shows the main opening in Whitehouse Mountain on the lower level. Notice the cable-winding hoist drum, also seen in the picture on Page 324. The funicular tramway passed through the notch to the left of this opening, and the company's exploratory opening is out of sight, to the left of where the boy in shorts is standing.

A HOIST DRUM was resting in its original position at the lower Strauss Quarry when this photograph was taken during 1971.

325

STEPPING INSIDE the opening on the lower level, you can see these two four-wheel drilling-machine bases, blocked-up on short sections of rail. (These bases were used to support channeling machines to cut marble blocks.) The mast still stands at the rear wall in this photograph, but the boom is missing.

OSCAR McCOLLUM JR. PHOTO

THE BACK WALL inside the main tunnel of the Strauss Quarry appears in this view (at the left). A derrick with a wooden mast still stood in one corner, minus the boom, blocked into position against the tunnel roof. Cable was still in position at the time this picture was taken (in 1990). A branch tunnel leaves this section of the main tunnel — shown in the series of photographs below.

OSCAR McCOLLUM JR. PHOTO

THE MAIN STRAUSS TUNNEL, on the lower level, goes into the mountain about 100 feet, where two branch tunnels are located (at the left). The boom lays on the tunnel floor (at the right) in this photograph, which reveals one of the openings (to the left) that penetrates into the mountain for an additional 50 feet.

OSCAR McCOLLUM JR. PHOTO

CONTINUING DEEPER into the quarry on the lower level, this 50-foot-long branch tunnel was photographed in 1990, showing the end of the workings. Notice the opening at the right, which goes in for about 10 feet. The tunnel ceiling is approximately six feet tall.

NOTICE THE STRAUSS QUARRY branch tunnel, off to the right of the longer 50-foot tunnel at this location. This is not far from the outside entrance (or portal).

OSCAR McCOLLUM JR. PHOTO

SYLVIA T. SMITH
PUBLISHER OF *THE MARBLE CITY TIMES*
Died during March of 1932 in Denver

IT IS SOMEWHAT OF AN ENIGMA that the only-known photograph of Sylvia T. Smith made its appearance in Elmore Frederick's carriage house in Denver (at the rear of 221 Sherman Street), the second business home of Sundance Publications, Limited, during 1972. It had probably arrived in Denver via an old steamer trunk from one of the relatives of Mr. Frederick, who had lived in Crested Butte, Colorado.

SYLVIA SMITH vs. THE MARBLE COMMUNITY

This story had a profound effect on Marble; its community spirit, social tolerance and even its economic health, during the period of its greatest growth. At the time, the citizens of Marble reacted to what they perceived as a threat to their dream of a prosperous life and secure future. They did not consider the legal consequences of their actions or the civil rights of one of their members. This was a one-industry town, and whatever was good for the Colorado-Yule Marble Company was good for the community.

Sylvia Taylor Smith came to Marble in the fall of 1908, as an experienced country newspaper editor. For eight years she had published a paper in Crested Butte and later the implication was made that she had not been overly welcome in that town, though her paper was initially well received.

The Marble Times & Crystal Silver Lance,
September 7, 1900.

The initial number of the Crested Butte Weekly Citizen has reached our table, and it is indeed a very newsy and creditable issue. Miss Smith is to be congratulated upon the appearance of the initial number and we wish her success in the journalistic field.

· · · · ·

It appears that Sylvia had a deep-seated hatred of big business and immediately focused on the marble company as an evil entity. On arriving in Marble she began publishing a weekly newspaper, the Marble City Times, with the printing equipment she brought with her. It was a reasonably good paper, and within a year and a half was competing with the later-founded paper, The Marble Booster, published by Frank Frost. Her paper printed about 200 copies each week and was supported by local advertising and the usual national advertising. About 40 copies were sold locally and about 50 copies were sent east to stockholders of the Colorado-Yule Marble Company, selected in rotation from her list of 400 marble company owners. Occasionally, she employed Miss Mary Quinn to help with getting out the paper.[1] But there were not many persons in Marble favorably inclined toward Miss Smith.

She published the usual local news and liked to include articles on women's sufferage.

The Marble City Times,
April 29, 1910.

ON EQUAL SUFFERAGE. In Colorado It Is A Successful Fact. Some difference of opinion exists as to whether or no the world is growing better, but there is little room for question that it is growing more liberal in sentiment. The increase of toleration and respect for the views of others in religious matters is apparent, and so it is in economical and governmental theories. Mankind may not have reached the point of hopeing that there is "good in everything" but it is close to recognition of the fact that there is some good in any system or custom that is adopted by any considerable portion of mankind, and retained by them.

· · · · ·

It is ironic that this more liberal attitude she was praising later proved not to exist in her own town. Almost every issue of her paper included something derogatory to her greatest hate, the marble company.

The Marble City Times,
April 29, 1910.

SIXTY CUTTERS WALK OUT.

Another strike has been inaugurated at the Yule Marble's mill by sixty cutters laying down their tools and walking out into the unhoused world because the company refused to pay the wages agreed upon. Labor Commissioner Brake states that there is a constant stream of complaints flowing to his office from marble workers who are not receiving the wages the Yule company promises to pay when they bring the workers into Marble.

Later—Just as the paper is on the press a compromise has been made.

The Marble City Times,
November 2, 1911. Quoting from the New York Sun.

GOVERNMENT SEEMS TO ENCOURAGE THE USE OF MAILS IN PROMOTING YULE MARBLE. What is the conjuration used on government officials?...

"From the office of the Fidelity Bond and Mortgage Company at 2 West Thirty-third street, opposite the Waldorf-

[1] Bennett, John F., "Sylvia T. Smith: Her Day In Court," The 1970 Denver Westerners Brand Book, Jackson C. Thode, Editor, pp. 365-391, 1971.

Astoria, Charles Austin Bates is sending out some letters to sound sentiment on the attractiveness of a proposition which looks like 50 to 100 per cent a year in the near future."

　　　. . . . .

On March 20, 1912, a huge avalanche of snow roared down the mountain side above the marble mill and destroyed a portion of it. Sylvia Smith could not contain her glee.

The Marble City Times,
March 22, 1912.

DESTINY KEPT HER APPOINTMENT AND RE-DRESSES MANY WRONGS.

Colorado-Yule Marble Mill Crushed Like an Egg Shell by Avalanche, Warnings Unheeded. Company Never Will Pay Dividends. Organized by Strenuous Promoters Its Stock-Selling Scheme has Carried Desolation into Many Homes and Written "Dispair" Over Many Lives that Cannot Give Worthless Paper Back for Hard-earned Lifetime Savings.

Certain, unhesitating, with the awful noise peculiar to such destruction, like the crash of doom came the snowslide that wrecked the Colorado-Yule Marble Company's mill Wednesday morning about 6:40.

For days and days snow has hung threateningly over the mill on the mountain to the south; winter after winter old-timers have warned and shaken their heads over what they were certain was inevitable as taxes. When the whistles of distress from the new power house, situate about one hundred fifty yards east of the mill out of the path of the slide, pierced the snow-ledened air, there was no questioning and but little excitement. The long-expected had happened.

...That there was no loss of life or injury to any one was because of supernatural design, the night workmen having left the shop but a short time previous.

...According to "Marble in 1912," a pamphlet issued by Meek in January, begging stockholders to buy corporation notes just issued, so he could hasten back from New York and continue work at Marble, the company is badly in need of funds, so it cannot yet be stated what will be done about rebuilding the destroyed section of the mill. Stock selling, which has been the great source of revenue to this gigantic swindle has been stopped by magazines and papers sounding a note of warning, but, as Nat Nasby relates, "There is a new crop of fools coming on every year."

　　　. . . . .

This was the last issue of Sylvia Smith's newspaper. The Marble Booster presented a factual and less emotional picture of the disaster.

Continued on Page 335

SYLVIA T. SMITH NOTED in her newspaper, *The Marble City Times,* on March 15, 1912, that the accumulation of snow from a storm looked dangerous above the Marble mill. On March 20, a massive avalanche of snow came down off Mill Mountain and crushed part of the mill. Luckily, the snowslide was at 6:40 a.m. and hit between work shifts, and no deaths occurred. In this photograph, linemen were already restoring electric power, while workers on the ground probed the wreckage to make sure no bodies were beneath the hard-packed snow and timbers. The mill office was sagging heavily at the roof, and Shop No. 1 had vanished.

THE MARBLE CITY TIMES
Newspaper sheet size: 22 x 30 inches

One of Marble's needs is a Hospital. Thousands have been taken from working men for such an institution. Where is this money?

MARBLE CITY TIMES

VOL. III — Marble, Colorado, Friday, March 22, 1912 — No. 48

THE MARBLE-CITY TIMES
S. T. SMITH, Editor and Proprietor
MEMBER COLORADO EDITORIAL ASSOCIATION

SUBSCRIPION PRICE

ONE YEAR	$2 00
SIY MONTHS	$1 00
SINGLE COPY	5 ct

Entered at Marble postoffice for transmission through the mail as second-class matter.

OPPORTUNITY FOR CAPITAL

Many people possess the mistaken idea that the Crystal-river slope of Gunnison county has been well prospected. The early-day prospector of this section searched the exposed veins and dikes for [illegible] lead or zinc ores were found the high cost of transportation via burros and wagons to the nearest available railroad prohibited the shipping of the ores.

Gold values were thought not to exist in this vicinity, therefore few assays were run for this "metal of metals." Now all is different. We not only have a railroad of standard gauge, but have mountains of low grade smelting ores as well as large bodies of shipping grade of copper, lead, silver, zinc and other metals.

From the head of Yule creek comes reports of bodies of molybdenite and vanadium ores and it is up to you, Mr. Miningman, and prospectors, to act in a body and put the existing conditions before the smelting and milling world.

We have the ore; we have the natural resources of water power and immence bodies of fine timbers, which are always available for mining purposes. All that is needed is the combined efforts of those interested in the future developement and prosperity of this part of the county.

Other mining districts are mining and milling at a profit lower grades of ore, on a general average, than we have here. They are, also, prospering and improving their towns and cities. Many of them not possessing one-half the natural resources found in this section.

Another point worth considering is, that when our latter-day prospectors pay more attention to the sulphide ores and cease looking entirely for metalic gold and silver in the oxidized zones and areas then will gold and silver finds be made which will startle the mining world. The old adage, "Gold is where you find it," has proven true in every sence. Some of our largest gold finds have been made in mining districts covered time and again by prospectors, and thought to be barren of gold values. We have here the economic geological conditions favorable to the existance of gold ores. The writer's opinion is that "it is here" and remains for you, Mr. Prospector, to get busy. We venture to make the prophecy, that within the next five years gold and silver finds will be made here which will prove a second Cripple Creek or Klondike.—Howard Batt.

The last issue of the Financial World shows in a statement concerning the Sears, Roebuck Co., Chicago, the fast passing of the small merchants. The article is as quoted:

"The common stock, of which there is $40,000,000, continues to go up, but with some profit-taking as the advance proceeds. This advance is just the means of taking profit. What helps the move is the enormous business at present. February sales amounted to over $7,000-000, agains $5,5000,000 in February 1911. But the first three months of the year are always the best mail order months."

The foregoing is explanitory of why great catalogue houses save you from thirty-five to forty per cent on every article of household goods as well as every stich of clothing you buy from them. Many of the great houses manufacture almost every thing they sell and they retail at almost wholesale prices. That is the reason they can give you a better article for less money than you can get elsewhere, and no power on earth can sustain the middle man against such pressure.

Thirty-five per cent saved on a cheap suit of clothes means a nice pair shoes for Mary and John. Ten dollars saved on a kitchen range means a nice floor covering for that room. "You have gloves just like mine. Let's see the brand," said one lady to another. "How much?" "Ninty-six cents with four for postage. Got them at Sears, Roebuck's,' came the answer. "What," said the first speaker, "I paid one twenty-five for mine in Denver.'

If one believes he owes it to a locality to stand and be fleeced, he should read the Colorado Court-of-Appeal's decision upon the middlemen of Denver, who have been fleecing an unsuspicious public to the tune of 500 per cent profits.

The chances are the next mayor will not be convinced of the truth of the French saying that "there is no indespensable man." Mr. Tischhauser is leaving the council with an open mind on the subject.

LOCALS

There was not a second to the motion to drop the sleighbells for the balance of the season.

Harry Pratt is to have the position of timekeeper when the Yule quarry again begins work.

The only discord in the Easter celebration will be the old jokes about Eastern millinery. Mrs. Bantock should try to induce paragraphers to devise something new on the subject.

Leon Campbell wrote Marble friends a few days ago from Ogden, stating he was journing to Seattle.

Mrs. M. [illegible] Fowker, representing Napier & Co., Glenwood, came last week to carry on a week's special sale of children and ladies new spring garments. She started on her return to the Springs Wednesday and had the pleasure of walking the railroad three miles back to town, from where the train was stuck in the snow.

Mrs. Emmitt Wilkins and children accompanied by Mrs. Cowels will return to her home to Spokan, Washington, next week. Mrs. Cowels will spend a month on the coast.

Lydia Clarkson, employe of the TIMES, went to Denver to meet her brother today who has been in the McLean sanitarium, St. Louis, since December. He returns home cured of his lameness. They will spend two weeks with friends in Denver before returning.

Joe Chance, who has been afflicted with rheumatism, is improving. A Rhode Island man has been cured of this complaint by a stroke of lightning. Nevertheless Joe is not hankering for that kind of treatment.

John Harper and Pat O'Kief journeyed to Denver Tuesday. Mr. Harper will spend two weeks with his family before returning. O'Kief will return as soon as work has resumed its normal condition.

Registration time is approaching.

Buletin No. Two, issued by Strauss, Parson & Co. (incorporated) mine operators, with office rooms in the Central [illegible] building, Denver has just been received at the TIMES office. The bulletin is to keep stockholders informed about the work going on at the mines and dumps the company is handeling.

If, after viewing the condition of the main thoroughfair as it has existed the past five months, that sidewalk ordinance is again taken up by the council, evidently the commandment "Love thy neighbor as thyself" will never be taken as seriously as it should.

Don't let the dance prevent you seeing the excellent pictures in the Opera house tonight and tomorrow night. Remember Sunday evening always has extry attractions.

Bishop Brewster was to have come from Glenwood to day to hold seavices this evening, and morning and evening services Sunday, in St. Paul's mission but owing to slides blocking the railroad he will not be able to fill his appointment. The Congregation Sunday school is preparing Easter services, to be held in the Mission. The little ones are showing great interest in the work.

GAVE ONE OF HIS STOCK-SELLING STUNTS

Kunnel Meek went through one of his Waldorf-Astoria, stock-selling stunts Wednesday evening when he was chairman of the caucus called to select deligates to the Republican convention to be held in Gunnison Tuesday. The women showed their interest by being absent.

MARBLE'S ATHLETIC CLUB

Basketball Game Tomorrow Eve at 8 p. m. Sharp

The Athletic club is to have a Basketball game in Adrian's hall tomorrow eve to which an admission fee of twenty-five cents will be asked of adults and one of fifteen cents will be demanded of children. Seventy-five cents will be the admission for the dance which begins at the close of the game, 9 o'clock. Good music is promised.

The Marble Basketball team challanges any other team on the Western slope for $100 to winner. It has players from Denver, Glenwood, Aspen, West Rutland Vt., University of Chicago, Middlebury, Vt., and other places. The list of membership follows: "Bob" Hart, general manager, "Jack" Shaud, "Buck" Yirak, "Fat Robl, "Ike" Fabian, "Baldy" Fabian, "Budd" Woodman, "Frenchy" Vondette, "Davy" Davidson, "Sambo Richards, "Shorty" Halnon, "Bnnny" Greer, "Curley" Cowles, "Doc" Luris, "Hans," Heisse, Frank Brooks, "Wahos Sam" Crawford, and others.

There were interested spectators at Sunday's practice game.

DESTINY KEPT HER APPOINTMENT AND REDRESSES MANY WRONGS

Colorado-Yule-Marble Mill Crushed Like an Egg Shell by Avalanche Warnings Unheeded

COMPANY NEVER Will PAY DIVIDENDS

Organized by Strenuous Promoters Its Stock-Selling Scheme has Carried Desolation Into Many Homes and Written "Despair" Over Many Lives that Cannot Give Worthless Paper Back for Hard-earned, Life-time Savings

Certain, unhesitating, with the awful noise peculiar to such destruction, like the crash of doom came the snowslid that wrecked the Colorado-Yule-Marble company's mill Wednesday morning about 6:10

For days and days snow has hung threateningly over the mill, on the mountains to the south; winter after winter old-timers have warned and shaken their heads knowingly over what they were certain was inevitable as taxes. When the whistles of distress, from the new power house, situate about one hundred fifty yards east of the mill out of the path of the slide, pierced the snow-ladened air, there was no questioning and but little excitement. The long-expected had happened.

The slide crossed the river as if there was no river, just as previous slides have done in the same place. It swept away the machine shop, electrial-store house, "Shop No. One," and damaging "Shop No. Three, spent its force on the slope to the north. Windows and doors in the houses facing the mill were blown in by the concussion and the rooms filled with snow. Some of the dwellers were preparing breakfast while others had not yet risen. The Bu[illegible]marks' rooms received an ample supply of snow before they were awakened. Their neighbor, Mrs. Cooper, whose husband is engineer on the five-o'clock-morning train to Carbondale, was frightened almost to death by her bed being covered with about two feet of snow. That there was no loss of life or injury to any one was because of supernatural design, the night workmen having left the shop but a short time previous.

The company will, no doubt, report the disaster as, "causing but little damage;" "loss lighter than at first suppoesd," and so on, but to one viewing the scene the reck is complete. Misjudgement, ruin, desolation speak in heaps of broken timbers, twisted and misshapened machinery, shattered monuments,—"No. One" having been the Monumental shop—and the recked office building, the north side and east end of which were torn away. The cupola, on the top of the office, had an occupant, Miss Salters, the night telephone girl, who was blown out upon the main roof without injury, although unconscious when taken from the dangerous position.

Trolley Line Blocked Three Weeks

The quarry has been shut off from the outside world, so far as geting supplies up to the place is concerned, for three weeks. Tuesday shovelers had opened the way to the rotary house where a team took supplies which men were to have carried on to the quarry. A number of men made their way down from the quarry yesterday. Some have not gone back but are awaiting a train to take them out.

Company Hard Pressed for Money

According to "Marble in 1912," a pamphlet issued by Meek in January, begging stockholders to buy corporation notes just issued, so he could hasten back from New York and continue work at Marble, the campany is badly in need of funds, so, it cannot yet be stated what will be done about rebuilding the destroyed section of the mill. Stock selling, which has been the great source of revenue to this gigantic swindle, has been stoped by magaziens and papers sounding a note of warning, but, as Nat Nasby relates, "There is a new crop of fools cuming on every year."

ST. PATRIC'S DAY SATURDAY

The band celebrated the anniversary of the birth of the illustrious St. Patric with a dance in Masonic hall in the evening. The bright green was not conspicious on coat lapells as pedestrians skimble scambled through the deep snow and breathed the white crystal-ladened air. The heavens were blotted out; everywhere silence and snow; everywhere bonds and fetters and desolation; hard, glittering, inexorable Death supreme in earth and air.

So it looked to one who braced to meet the force of the gale, and in the partial shelter of the Opera house, gazed out at the wind-driven snow. So it would have been, in reality, to one who knew not of the wisdom of Nature. The partially-sheltered one smiled, and, if Nature had been less intent on her work far away she too would have smiled; for we always smile when some one recognizes us behind our mask. This person knew the mask so well that, perfect as was its counterfit of death, they were not for a moment in doubt. They knew that behind the mask, life was pulsing, coursing, throbbing, beating, gathering volume for a tide that should presently break like a fountain out of the depths of the earth and strew the world with flowers from sky to sky. Behind that mask, secure from prying eyes, from profane curiosity, from the cold searching of the fact-gatherer, the ancient mysteries were being enacted, the primeval miracle was being wrought again; in darkness and silence all things were moving to birth, behind the face of death. Life was passonately brooding over the radiant loveliness in her heart.

The school's literary society will not be held this afternoon,

The train is expected to get through the snowslide today, Tuesday's mail is the last that has been received.

Papers and magaziens have pictures of London's suffragettes, and they are generally allright if their pictures tell the truth.

A Denver girl has applied to the Circut court to have her name changed. Girls in Marble could tell her a quicker and more satisfactory way of securing the same results.

Forfeiture Notice

Marble, Colo., February 9, 1912

To Gus Johnson:

You are hereby notified that I expended for the years 1911, 1912 Two Hundred Dollars in labor and improvements upon the Humboldt mining claim, situate in Rock Creek Mining District, County of Gunnison, State of Colorado, the location certificate of which is found of record in the office of the Recorder of said Gunnison county, in order to hold said claim under the provisions of SECTION 2324 of the Revised Statutes of the United States and the amendment thereto concerning annual labor upon mining claims, being the amount required to hold said claim for the period ending December 31 A. D. 1911

And, if within ninety days from the personal service of this notice or within ninety days after the publication thereof, you fail or refuse to contribute your proportion of such expenditure as co-owner, your interest in the said claim will become the property of the subscriber, your co-owner, who has made the required expenditure as required by the terms of said section.

GUS LARSON.

First pub. Feb. 9; last May 3, 1912.

MARBLE CITY TIMES

MARBLE, - - COLORADO

WANT TO KEEP WESTERN POSTS

COLORADO AND WYOMING SENATORS WORKING FOR APPROPRIATION FOR THEM.

BORAH BILL FAVORED

FAVORABLE REPORT HAS BEEN RECEIVED ON MEASURE EXTENDING TIME OF ENTRY.

Western Newspaper Union News Service.

Washington. — Senators Warren, Guggenheim and Chamberlain, who are members of the sub-committee which is now considering the army appropriation bill, are endeavoring to have dropped from the bill the provision inserted by the House proposing to prohibit the expenditure at military posts recommended for abandonment of any portion of the funds appropriated by the bill for the construction, maintenance and repair of barracks and quarters.

Among the posts affected are Fort Logan, Colo.; D. A. Russell, Mackenzie and Yellowstone, Wyo.; Douglas, Utah; Boise Barracks, Ida.; Missoula and Harrison, Mont.

It is believed the Senate military affairs committee, upon the recommendation of the sub-committee, will eliminate the provision from the bill, so that the posts named for abandonment may be maintained.

The United States Supreme Court set October 15th next as the date for hearing arguments upon the demurrer filed by the state of Colorado to the bill of complaint of the state of Wyoming in the suit involving the right of citizens of Colorado to divert the waters of the Laramie river from their natural watershed for use in Colorado.

Attorney General Preston, who is here representing the state of Wyoming, and Clyde Dawson, who is representing the state of Colorado and the other defendants in the case, agreed upon the date set for the argument and it was set by the court in accordance with this agreement.

A favorable report has been received from the Interior Department on the bill extending for three years the time of all desert land entrymen who through no fault of their own cannot make final proof at the end of the regular period, on account of the non-delivery of water.

A similar bill applying only to two counties in Colorado, was recently passed by the House.

The House public lands sub-committee which has been considering the Borah three-year homestead bill, has agreed upon the bill, amending it to require the entrymen to build a habitable house upon the land and furnish proof of continuous residence for seven months during each year of the three required to complete the entry.

An amendment also is proposed making the act apply to all existing homestead entries requiring residence.

The secretary of the interior has temporarily withdrawn until March 5, 1913, the lands on the Pike's peak watershed applied for by the cities of Colorado Springs and Manitou for the protection of their water supply. Hearings on this application will be had before the House committee on public lands and the secretary of the interior the latter part of the present week.

Senator Guggenheim introduced a bill to authorize the Interior Department to sell these cities the lands desired.

The Postoffice Department has accepted the proposal of Timothy D. Foster to lease new quarters for the Victor postoffice for ten years from May 1, including postoffice and postal savings equipment.

Strikers May Return to Work.

Lawrence, Mass.—A general return to work by employes within a short time is predicted by textile mill managers, following the anouncement that 3,000 operatives who have been on strike already have resumed work. The ranks of the strikers have also received additions.

No Special Rates Granted.

Chicago.—Passenger traffic officials say there will be no special railroad rates this year to either the Republican or Democratic national convention.

Ships Lodged in Ice.

Racine, Wis.—Five ships are lodged in the ice in Lake Michigan near Racine. Some are said to carry passengers.

Kilbane to Meet White.

Cleveland, Ohio.—Champion Johnny Kilbane has agreed to box Charlie White of Chicago here March 25. It is reported that Kilbane consented to meet White here so his Cleveland friends may see him in action, although he had intended to remain out of the ring for three months.

AN EPITOME OF LATE LIVE NEWS

CONDENSED RECORD OF THE PROGRESS OF EVENTS AT HOME AND ABROAD.

FROM ALL SOURCES

SAYINGS, DOINGS, ACHIEVEMENTS, SUFFERINGS, HOPES AND FEARS OF MANKIND.

Western Newspaper Union News Service.

WESTERN.

Bert Franklin of Los Angeles, the former McNamara detective, entered a plea of guilty to the charge of jury bribery.

John Chambers, a Healdsburg, Cal., wood chopper, has confessed to the operation of an elaborate mint for making counterfeit coins.

Gov. Edwin L. Norris of Montana, has issued a proclamation establishing state quarantine against Wyoming sheep on account of scabies.

The bodies of Samuel J. Fisher and his wife and two grown daughters were found in the family home in San Francisco, each with a bullet hole in the head.

Farmers of Weld county, Colo., will invest $25,000 in Eastern dairy cattle this spring, and Paul Maris, dairy expert at the State Agricultural college, has offered his services free to select and purchase the stock. It is impossible to secure the best dairy stock in Weld county.

The two-year-old daughter of Joseph Bona, a miner living at Stumptown, Colo., died as a result of falling into a tub of scalding water. During the temporary absence of the mother, who was washing, the child fell into the tub and was severely burned before she was rescued.

Claude Huff, a Denver youth, was riding a bicycle in Salt Lake when his hat blew off and the boy seemed to turn on his wheel to follow it and ran directly in front of a street car. The car struck the back of his head, almost severing it from the body. Both legs were broken and mangled.

His left foot torn off by the accidental discharge of his shotgun, Henry Schwartz, thirteen years old of Marysville, Kan., picked up the severed member, took the lace out of his shoe and used it to bind up his leg to check the flow of blood. He crawled a quarter of a mile and got help, but died.

WASHINGTON.

Wireless messages will hereafter be known as radiograms in the Navy Department.

Many fine warships have gone into the reserve fleets by orders from the Navy Department recently issued.

The House passed a bill granting citizenship to the people of Porto Rico. The measure will now go to the Senate.

The Postoffice Department designated Walsenburg, Colo., and Deming, N. M., to be postal savings depositories after April 1.

Increased activity in commerce, due to the approach of spring, has reduced the deficit of the federal government to $20,570,000.

The gravity of the situation in Mexico caused President Taft to issue a proclamation virtually warning American citizens to refrain from entering that country and those now resident there to leave.

The ways and means committee agreed to report favorably the free sugar bill, together with the excise bill providing for a tax on the incomes of individuals and corporations in excess of $5,000 net a year.

President Taft's recommendations for the establishment of a commission on industrial relations are embodied in a bill introduced in the House by Representative Hughes of New Jersey. The bill is significant in view of the labor troubles at Lawrence, Mass., and elsewhere.

Representative Knowland of California told the House commerce committee that officials of the Pacific Mail Steamship Company had been told by members of the New York clearing house that no money would be advanced for shipbuilding if Cogress legislated against the transcontinental railroads in connection with the Panama canal.

Insisting that any act of corruption that contributes to nomination in a senatorial primary is just as culpable as if it occurred in election by a Legislature, Senator Bristow, of Kansas, urged the Senate to reject the majority report of the committee on privileges and elections exonerating Senator Stephenson, of Wisconsin, of the charges that corrupt practices were employed in his election.

The United States government has manifested its purpose of standing without abridgement, alteration or amendment upon the original petition filed in its suit for the dissolution of the United States Steel Corporation and its subsidiary concerns.

By a vote of two to one the board of cabinet officers charged with the enforcement of the pure food law entered a final decision against the use of saccharine in prepared foods. Secretaries Wilson and Nagel confirmed the decision that food containing saccharine was adulterated.

FOREIGN.

A Shanghai cablegram to Chicago says General Huang, Chinese minister of war, has ordered shot all soldiers found smoking opium.

Eighteen children died of meningitis aboard the steamship Avon, between Lisbon and Rio Janeiro, and three between Rio Janeiro and Saltos.

The brewery belonging to Andwandter Brothers of Valdivia, Chile, the largest in South America, was destroyed by fire. The loss is estimated at $5,000,000.

The paralyzing effect on other industries on account of the coal miners' strike in Great Britain is being keenly felt. It is computed that 150,000 workers outside of the coal miners are idle. More than 1,000,000 miners in England, Scotland and Wales are out.

Because the coal miners had been able to gain government recognition of their grievances by threatening the business of the country, the suffragettes entered upon a policy of menace to trade in London. They carried it out suddenly and with an ardor that resulted in heavy financial losses, brought consternation to merchants of the most prosperous shopping district of the city, and paralyzed business. Before the police could muster their forces and restrain the women, streets were covered with shattered plate glass from the show windows of stores.

In a desperate battle at Chihuahua, Mexico between the forces of Gen. Pascual Orozco and Col. Francisco Villa, thirty-five men were killed. Villa reached the city from Bustillo with 700 men and sent envoys to Orozco with a demand that he turn command of the city over to him. Orozco, urged by the citizens of the capital not to allow the bandit leader to enter, sent back a curt refusal. Within an hour Villa attacked the city. The fight lasted three hours and while details were not obtainable, the fact that thirty-five were killed was telegraphed to Juarez by a government operator whose dispatch was shown to a correspondent. The dispatch also contained the information that Villa drew off after the battle, leaving Orozco in command of the city.

SPORT.

"Billy" Uvick, the Omaha welterweight, has been matched with Walter Coffey of Los Angeles for a twenty-round match in that city March 15.

Knockout Brown had one of the softest picnics of his strenuous young career in trimimng Young Bob Fitzsimmons in the ten-round windup before the Longacre Athletic Club in New York.

GENERAL.

Mrs. Abigail Morrill, 103 years old, celebrated her birthday recently at Newburyport, Mass. She is in good health and retains all her faculties.

The universal chiropractors' association has adopted resolutions urging legislatures to pass laws to allow the practice of healing without drugs.

Indiana leads all other states in good roads. Its total mileage of improved highways is 24,955. Ohio comes next with 24,106. New York is third with 12,787.

For the first time in the history of heavier-than-air flying, a man leaped from an aeroplane at Jefferson Barracks, St. Louis, and descended 1,500 feet to the earth in a parachute.

The last scrap of the old battleship Maine which could be used as a relic has been disposed of. All the pieces allotted to patriotic societies and other organizations have arrived at the Washington navy yard. The fortunate ones can have them by paying the costs of transportation and packing.

Mrs. Isabella Goodwin, a police matron of New York, to whose credit is placed the capture of the taxicab robbers who recently held up two bank messengers and procured $25,000, was advanced to the rank of first grade detective at a salary of $2,250 by Police Commissioner Waldo in recognition of her services.

Chicago is to be the headquarters of a national war to the finish on the white slave traffic in every city and town of the United States. The secret formation within the last few weeks of a national organization having behind it almost unlimited capital and a large number of the most influential citizens of the country became known in Chicago through negotiations to secure a federal charter in Washington.

Because 800,000 British coal miners have gone on a strike the demand for American coal for shipment to England has increased to the limit of transportation facilities. Meantime coal operators in various parts of the United States predict a strike involving several hundred thousand men April 1. New York coal dealers have notified their customers that they fear a strike and have advised them to prepare for it.

The Missouri Supreme Court denied the writ of ouster asked by the state against the Missouri Pacific, Iron Mountain and Wabash railroads, the Pacific Express Company and the American Refrigerator Transit Company.

The papal legation at Washington has been advised from Rome that the diocese at Omaha, Neb., had been divided and a new diocese created with the episcopal residence at Kearney, Neb. A new bishop will be appointed later.

COLORADO NEWS

GATHERED FROM

All Parts of the State

Western Newspaper Union News Service.

COMING EVENTS IN COLORADO.

March 11-16.—Denver Automobile Show, Denver.
April 29.—Democratic State Convention, Colorado Springs.
May 6-11.—State Y. M. C. A. Convention, Pueblo.
June 18-20.—State Sunday School Convention, Colorado Springs.
June 11-July 19.—Summer Term, State Teachers' College, Greeley.

Minister Gets $2,000 Damages.

Pueblo.—After deliberating for five hours, the jury in District Court awarded Rev. Albert Buxton $2,000 for a fall he received when he stumbledover a portion of defective sidewalk a year ago. Buxton sued the city for $10,000.

Idaho Springs' New Hotel.

Idaho Springs.—Work on the $100,000 hotel building of the Hot Springs Hotel Company at Idaho Springs will be commenced April 1, and by Aug. 1 the structure is expected to be complete. In many respects the establishment seems destined to be one of the most unique in Colorado.

High-Grading Is Charge.

Denver.—Charges that high-grading on a wholesale scale is being carried on by a gang of Greeks, with headquarters in Denver and with the Smuggler-Union and Tom Boy mines of Telluride as its sources of supply, were made during the hearing of the case against Detectives George Saunders and John Kenney of the police department before the fire and police board.

Greeley-Poudre Nearing Completion.

Greeley.—"We expect to have the Greeley-Poudre irrigation system completed by the middle of April, and the waters of the Laramie river flowing through the Laramie-Poudre tunnel by May 1," was the statement of D. A. Camfield, president of the construction company. Mr. Camfield said also that it is hoped to have all the ditches and reservoirs in the district completed so that all the moisture from the recent snows may be conserved in the reservoirs. The main ditch is completed east of McGrew reservoir a distance of twenty-one miles and only gaps in the long line of main ditch westward need connecting up to complete the chain of 165 miles of ditches, laterals and sub-laterals. McGrew reservoir will hold 900,000,000 cubic feet of water and there are also Dover reservoir, Douglas, Cobb and Mitchell lakes. The district is now cementing the big tunnel. Never in recent years has there been such a fall of snow at the headwaters of the Laramie river as this winter. This means all kinds of water for the tunnel reservoir and the Laramie river. Land holders in the district are optimistic over the future of their holdings.

"The New Frontier."

Dolores.—"The New Frontier," the Western slope of Colorado, bids fair to surpass in 1912 its $29,000,000 production of last year. Its prosperous stock farmers and fruit growers expect the largest profits they have ever known. Abundant snows insure plenty of water and the reservoirs are almost certain to contain water to last two seasons.

The territory includes an area of 37,000 square miles or an empire as large as Massachusetts, Delaware, New Hampshire, Rhode Island, New Jersey and Vermont combined. It contains nineteen counties: Delta, Dolores, Gunnison, Montezuma, Eagle, Garfield, Grand, Hinsdale, La Plata, Mesa, Montrose, Ouray, Pitkin, Rio Blanco, Routt, Moffat, San Juan, San Miguel and Summit. Their population is but 112,132 at present. They have room for several million people.

There are 10,000,000 acres of government land open to entry on the Western slope, and 441,167 acres of unsold state land. The irrigated lands assessed are 459,000 acres. Attractive improved land close to bustling towns may be bought by those who seek the advantages of civilization. Beautiful sites for farms and homes in more remote valleys may be bought at low prices or homesteaded. It is a question of pocketbook or fancy.

As examples of production it may be said that Palisade shipped 196 cars of peaches worth $151,900; 177 cars of apples which sold for $88,500, and potatoes worth $254,000. Grand Junction shipped 194 cars of pears worth $97,000; 826 of apples worth $413,000, and other products, making a total value of $516,000. Clifton shipped 320 cars of apples worth $165,000.

Fruita produced 182 cars of apples worth $91,000. Mesa county shipped four carloads of honey and 297 cars of cantaloupes. Delta town shipped twenty-one cars of cantaloupes and one car of honey. Grand Valley shipped one car of honey and eight cars of mixed produce.

Farmers Organize.

Sterling.—The ways and means committee of the Logan County Agricultural Association met at the court house recently. The plan adopted was to organize a corporation, not for profit, and secure subscriptions for stock in the association from citizens of the county, which subscriptions will be due April 1, 1912, at which time a meeting of all persons subscribing for stock will be called and officers elected to manage the affairs of the company.

DOCTORS FAILED RESTORED BY PERUNA.

Catarrh of the Lungs Threatened Her Life

Miss Ninette Porter, Braintree, Vermont, writes: "I have been cured by Peruna.

"I had several hemorrhages of the lungs. The doctors did not help me much and would never have cured me.

"I saw a testimonial in a Peruna almanac of a case similar to mine, and I commenced using it.

"I was not able to wait on myself when I began using it. I gained very slowly at first, but I could see that it was helping me.

"After I had taken it a while I commenced to raise up a stringy, sticky substance from my lungs. This grew less and less in quantity as I continued the treatment.

"I grew more fleshy than I had been for a long time, and now I call myself well."

FOR SALE—10 ACRE BEARING ORCHARD IN Mesa Co., Colo.; Palisade irrigation dist.; near town; all conveniences. Barby, Box 319, Chicago.

FOR GOOD MEASURE.

Tommy—Say, Pop, does a person ever get something for nothing?

Papa—Sometimes, and a prison sentence usually goes with it.

A Beautiful Decline.

Ollie James, the gigantic and genial congressman and senator-elect from Kentucky, was in conversation the other day with a Washingtonian when the latter made certain inquiries with reference to a mutual friend from he had not seen for a number of years.

"And how does Colonel Prescott spend his declining years?" he asked.

"Beautifully, sir; beautifully!" answered James. "He has a fine farm, sir. A string of trotters, sir. And a barrel of whisky 16 years old—and a wife of the same age, sir!"

Work Begets Work.

George W. Perkins, the New York financier, was talking about the scarcity of the $10,000 a year man—the man actually worth a $10,000 salary.

"The advantage of the $10,000 a year man," he said, "is not alone that he works splendidly—it is also that under him everybody else works splendidly. There's a Chinese proverb," he said, "that expresses exactly what I mean:

"'If a farmer is diligent the soil will not be lazy.'"

A Poor Guesser.

Wedmore—Before I married, I learned to live on half my income.

Singleton—And found that it was a wise step, eh?

Wedmore—Yes, only a half was the wrong proportion—I should have made it an eighth.

Elegant Language.

"A poet speaks of himself as a 'blind voyager across the bitter seas.'"

"Perhaps an overindulgence in fancy food has given him an acute sensation of mal de mer."

A WOMAN DOCTOR
Was Quick to See That Coffee Poison Was Doing the Mischief.

A lady tells of a bad case of coffee poisoning, and tells it in a way so simple and straightforward that literary skill could not improve it.

"I had neuralgic headaches for 12 years," she says, "and have suffered untold agony. When I first began to have them I weighed 140 pounds, but they brought me down to 110.

"I went to many doctors and they gave me only temporary relief. So I suffered on, till one day, a woman doctor advised me to drink Postum. She said I looked like I was coffee poisoned.

"So I began to drink Postum, and gained 15 pounds in the first few weeks and am still gaining, but not so fast as at first. My headaches began to leave me after I had used Postum about two weeks—long enough, I expect, to get the coffee poison out of my system.

"Now that a few months have passed since I began to use Postum, I can gladly say that I never know what a neuralgic headache is like any more, and it was nothing but Postum that relieved me.

"Before I used Postum I never went out alone; I would get bewildered and would not know which way to turn. Now I go alone and my head is as clear as a bell. My brain and nerves are stronger than they have been for years." Name given by Postum Co., Battle Creek, Mich.

"There's a reason," and it is explained in the little book, "The Road to Wellville," in pkgs.

Ever read the above letter? A new one appears from time to time. They are genuine, true, and full of human interest.

Attendant Was Wise

Jones had just run over to see if Mr. and Mrs. Blank would go to the theater with them. Mrs. Blank was sorry, but unfortunately, Blank was out. Probably he was at the club. She would telephone. The following conversation ensued:

"Halloa! Is this the——club? Is my husband there? Halloa! Not there? Sure? Well, all right, then; but, hold on, how do you know? I haven't even told you my name."

"There ain't anybody's husband here—never." was the wise attendant's reply.

How She Landed Him.

Maisie—I hate sofa pillows, cozy corners and tidies. If I ever keeep house I'll arrange everything solely for comfort, for——

Morton—Sweetheart, name the day.

His Friendship.

He—I know how this catastrophe has crippled you, and as one of your oldest friends I should like to help you. I will buy your furniture for 300 francs.

She—You're very kind, but I have just sold it for 325 francs.

He—What? You allowed yourself to be robbed like that?

Pointed Paragraphs.

Fate seems to have picked out some men to be punching bags and some to be door mats.

When it comes to getting something for nothing, his Satanic majesty is at the top of the heap.

An old bachelor says it is time for a man to think of marrying when he hasn't anything else to worry him.

Breathes there a man with soul so dead who never to himself has said, "How much easier I could bear my neighbor's burden than my own!"

At the Aviation Meeting.

Mme. Vanite—Well, it certainly was not worth putting on my nice new pair of boots!

The Careful Valentine.

There is a young man in this town who likes the ladies, but who doesn't wish to be captured. Consequently his attentions are rather timorous. He went to a poetical friend recently, and spoke thusly:

"Say, old man, you are something of a poet."

"What of it?"

"I want you to help me get up a valentine for a young lady."

"What do you want to say?"

"Well, I want to say something sort of tender, don't you know, but at the same time I don't want to commit myself, understand."

"But you don't want a poet to draw up your valentine. What you want is a lawyer."

Excusable Mistake.

The irascible old gentleman had ordered a chicken, but when he got it he wasn't satisfied—some people never are.

"Waiter," he yelled, "bring a charge of dynamite and a hatchet and an extra double steam power coke hammer. This chicken's got to be carved, even if it is made of dreadnought steel."

The waiter was desolate. "Very sorry, sir," he said, "but that always was a peculiar bird. It even objected to be killed, though we do everything with the greatest of kindness. But this bird, sir, actually flew away, and we had to shoot it, sir—yes, shoot it—it flew on to the top of a house and—"

"Say no more," said the old gentleman. "I see it all now. You shot at it and brought down the weathercock by mistake. John, it is all forgiven."

Rules for Business Men

Don't worry; don't overbuy; don't go security.

Keep a high vitality; keep insured; keep sober; keep cool.

Stick to chosen pursuits, but not to chosen methods.

Be content with small beginnings and develop them.

Be wary of dealings with unsuccessful men.

Be cautious, but when a bargain is made stick to it.

Keep down expenses, but don't be stingy.

Make friends, but not favorites.

Don't take new risks to retrive old losses.

Stop a bad account at once.

Make plans ahead, but don't make them in cast iron.

Don't tell what you are going to do until you have done it.

HIDES-PELTS-FURS

The L. A. Watkins Mdse. Co. Dealers in Hides, Wool, Pelts, Tallow, Furs. 925 Wazee St., Denver, Colo. Write for our Price Lists and Shipping Tags

SEEDS

40 packages $1.00. Write for catalogue.
THE WESTERN SEED CO., 15 & Blake, Denver, Col.

BEE SUPPLIES

of best quality at right prices. Send for free Illustrated Catalog, with instructions to beginners.

HONEY of absolute purity, just as it comes from the yards of our members. Sample by mail, 10c.

The Colorado Honey Producers' Assn.
1442 Market Street, Denver, Colorado

$25.00 $25.00 $25.00 $25.00 $25.00 $25.00 $25.00

COLONIST FARES
from
ALL MAIN LINE POINTS and ALL POINTS ON MARSHALL PASS LINE, SALIDA to GRAND JUNCTION,
on the
DENVER & RIO GRANDE RAILROAD
in COLORADO, to
CALIFORNIA AND THE PACIFIC NORTHWEST,
Via The Denver & Rio Grande Railroad and the Western Pacific Railway.
The Royal Gorge-Feather River Cañon Route.

Tickets on Sale March 1 to Apr. 15, 1912. By depositing tickets with Agent, stop-overs of five days will be allowed at and west of Cañon City on the Denver & Rio Grande Railroad in Colorado and Utah, and at Elko, Hazen, Reno, Las Vegas, Lovelock, Shafter, Winnemucca, Nevada, and all points in California; at all points on the Great Northern at and west of Billings, Montana; at all points on O. S. L. and O. W. R. & N. Co., and all points on Southern Pacific between Portland, Ore., and Weed, Calif.

Colonist Tickets will be honored over the Rio Grande via Glenwood Springs or via Gunnison and Montrose.

For detailed information, inquire of nearest Agent.

FRANK A. WADLEIGH,
General Passenger Agent, Denver, Colo.

His Mother's Valentine

* * *

By E. L. HENDERSON

(Copyright, 1911, by Associated Literary Press.)

V. J. was a valentine. There could be no doubt about this. He was born on the 14th of February; his mother had named him Valentine, and he bore the outward semblance of one—one, moreover, of that offensive type popularly known as comic.

No one knew what V. J. Vincent, as he invariably signed himself, had suffered from this combination of circumstances. Hair of unmitigated red, a nose of unconventional length, inquiring ears and a dimpled chin were, he told himself, heavy enough burdens to bear, without the necessity of smiling cheerfully at the endless jokes to which he submitted on each recurring 14th of February. He had learned to accept the hair and ears and nose with resignation, but the dimples, perpetually laughing at the rest of his face, were still a sensitive point; and in a beardless era when fashion demanded glaring honesty in chins, a conspicuous one. He could only fall back on an unfailing sense of humor for support.

V. J.'s name was appropriate in more than one respect. In the lace-trimmed, Cupid-adorned creations displayed in February, there is usually found, hidden under a heart-shaped leaf, a little apartment warm with sentiment. In V. J.'s being, there was a similar recess, but so cunningly concealed that few suspected its existence.

Its sentiment was, however, bubbling up on this particular morning of the 14th of February as he passed the Merrill home, bound officeward. He had hoped to see Marcia Dillon at the window. Instead, he caught a smile from her young cousin, Dana Merrill. Fortunately, he did not catch the remark that followed it: "Doesn't Val Vincent look like a comic valentine?"

"His face is rather an intelligent one for a comic valentine," responded Marcia. "He has good eyes."

"Oh, yes, but eye-glasses are not becoming. I wonder if anything would be very becoming to Val?" laughed Dana.

"He has a fine forehead." Marcia spoke in the manner of one determined to see justice done to an unpromising subject.

"It's a high one, certainly, and improving right along. Actually, Maria,

"It's a freak of a face," he declared.

I believe Val Vincent is getting bald, and he isn't so awfully old either—not near thirty yet."

Marcia looked up with the amused and tolerant glance of twenty-five directed toward sixteen.

Dana ran on lightly. "Of course, no one could help liking Val. He's bright and witty, and as good as he is funny looking. He was devoted to his mother, and I'd be willing to have a comic valentine for a brother myself, if he'd treat me as Val does that harum-scarum Gwen. She has two girls visiting her now, and the whole bunch depend on him to entertain them, as if he were of high school age too. The girls all like him, even if they do regard him as sort of a joke. I'm glad you're such a good friend to him, Marcia."

"He's by far the cleverest man I've met here," asserted Marcia.

"Oh, he has brains, all right," agreed Dana.

Could V. J. have heard Marcia's defense, it might have sugar-coated the annual dose of witticisms he was called upon to swallow. As it was, a growing conviction that he had been indulging in some very foolish dreams of late, was emphasized by the light jests.

He sat in his office in the afternoon, smiling rather wanly at a feeble joke from the office boy that hinged on his unfortunate cognomen. "He isn't exactly an Apollo himself," he thought as he watched the lank, grinning boy withdraw from the room. Then, "Confound the name, anyway!" he exclaimed.

If V. J. ever wavered in a deep sentiment of reverence for his mother it was when he thought of the name she had given him. At home there was a series of valentines, pictures taken on his successive birthdays, by which she had emphasized the name's absurdity. They ran up to thirteen, when the subject had rebelled. Then, after an interval, there was one more, sent from a distant college—a poorly finished, staring caricature of a youth in his teens, of which a fastidious regard for dress and a sentimental pose were conspicuous features. How delighted his mother had been with this particular valentine! Could any other woman, he asked himself, ever overlook his defects as she had done?

He arose and walked to a mirror. "It's a freak of a face," he declared, surveying his reflection sternly and critically. "It looks," he said, "as if it had repented at the last and tried to do something in the beauty line. Could anything be more harrowing and inharmonious! No sane girl could ever bring herself to the point of accepting the wearer of such a face." He would never make a fool of himself by asking it. No! The matter was settled definitely, finally and forever, he declared.

The role he was to play henceforth seemed, however, a tame and colorless one as he sat that evening in the Merrill library talking to Marcia. He delayed taking up the book they were reading together.

It had been a dangerous experiment, the reading of that book. An interest in it had led to regular meetings, during which Propinquity had been busy after the manner of that efficient ally of Cupid.

In V. J.'s case the mischief had been done before he reached chapter three. This was inevitable. Marcia was pretty. She had a merry face, with all sorts of charming little curves playing over it; and his heart leaped out toward the sense of humor it indicated. Then no one could look at her mouth and chin and not gain a hint as to her character. Sane, sweet and sensible were the adjectives those features spelled. But V. J. understood. For him there could be only frank friendship. He resolutely picked up the book for the closing chapters.

And just then Dana opened the door and tossed into Marcia's lap a large envelope. "It came this afternoon while you were out," she explained. "I thought you had it."

"Who in the world is sending me a valentine of this sort?" exclaimed Marcia, picking up the flimsy, fancy envelope. "Oh, I know. It's Dickey, Mrs. Ashton's little boy. I was over there yesterday, and he was valentine crazy. Don't you want to see it?"

V. J. leaned over as Marcia drew out the valentine; and then there fell a thick and sudden silence. From a setting of lace paper, rose-hued hearts and plump cupids, there looked up at him his own face, the familiar college caricature, beneath which in letters which seemed clamoring to be read, were the words:

"I am your valentine.
Will you, sweet maiden, not be mine?"

Marcia's face was flushed and angry. "Those silly girls!" she exclaimed. "I do not think girls of that age—"

Her voice broke as she began to replace the valentine in its envelope.

V. J. put out a restraining hand and took the picture. "It looks to me," he observed, "as if St. Valentine has had some odds and ends left when he finished his yearly assortment and had thrown them together to save the scraps. An old fellow of his experience ought to know that an incongruous mixture of the comic and the sentimental is never successful."

But Marcia did not laugh. "I know all about that picture," she said indignantly. "Mrs. Ashton told me yesterday how happy it made your mother one Valentine's day. Gwen should be thoroughly ashamed of herself!"

To V. J. there was something wonderfully sweet and intimate in this mention of his mother by Marcia. Certain resolutions melted in its warmth. There was a moment's silence. Then, "I am waiting," he reminded.

Marcia looked up inquiringly.

"There is a question, you know. I couldn't ask it myself, but this young fellow has had the audacity to ask it for me. You haven't answered it yet."

And the answer must have been satisfactory, for V. J. never, as he had sworn to do, destroyed his mother's valentine. Something in a nature full of sentiment forbade his doing so.

Supply of Sable Cut Off.

The true Russian sable being in danger of complete extermination, the duma has passed a bill prohibiting the trapping of sable from February 14, 1913, till October 29, 1916. Hitherto there has not been even a closed season, and sable have been caught when moulting and with young in such a reckless fashion, especially in the Yakootsk, Lena and Amoor districts, that their numbers have been steadily decreasing for years. The sable is the true marten, a variety of the pine marten, and the size of the skin rarely exceeds eight inches by twenty inches. The bluish tint of the overhair and the softness of the pelt distinguish the real from the imitation sable.

Only a few hundred pelts of the choicest kind are trapped in the year, but no less than 20,000 so-called sable skins are sold annually at the Irbitsk fair. The majority of these are the skins of squirrels from Tartary and Siberia, dyed to imitate the genuine sable.

IS THE PAIN THERE?

"Every Picture Tells a Story"

Then Your Kidneys May Be Weak and in Need of Quick Attention

Backache is enough cause to suspect the kidneys. The kidneys are in the small of the back. Congested kidneys swell and throb. The back naturally aches. It hurts to bend or stoop or to sit down.

Kidney trouble may come on all unnoticed. A cold, a chill, a fever, a strain or irregular habits may start it. While sick kidneys can be cured in the beginning, it is a serious matter when dropsy, gravel or Bright's disease sets in.

Doan's Kidney Pills have made a reputation in the cure of backache, and kidney and bladder ills. The best proof is the testimony of the users. Here are two typical testimonials. Thirty thousand others are being published in the newspapers. A postage stamp will bring you reports of cases nearer home.

If you suspect your kidneys, get the best-recommended kidney remedy.

MRS. MARY I. REMINGTON.

A Resident of Gilroy, Cal.

Cured of Serious Case at a Critical Period.

"I suffered so severely from pain and soreness over my kidneys," says Mrs. Remington, "that it was a task for me to turn in bed. My kidneys acted very freely but secretions were retarded and scalded in passage. I was weak and much run down.

"After taking other remedies without benefit, I began using Doan's Kidney Pills and was completely cured. I was going through the critical period of a woman's life at the time, and after using Doan's Kidney Pills there was a miraculous change for the better in my health."

SHELDON SMITH.

Prop. Arlington House, Woodland, Cal.

Cured of Serious Case and Feels Like a Boy, Despite His 76 Years.

"Three years ago I was almost helpless," said Mr. Smith, "Kidney secretions scalded terribly and obliged me to arise ten to twelve times a night. My left limb became so stiff and sore I could hardly walk—just hobbled around with a cane.

"I had almost every complaint that diseased kidneys produce and Doan's Kidney Pills cured them all. At the age of 76 I feel like a boy, and enjoy health and comfort. Can anyone wonder at my gratitude?"

DOAN'S KIDNEY PILLS

SOLD AT ALL STORES. 50 CENTS A BOX. FOSTER-MILBURN COMPANY, BUFFALO, N. Y.

THEN ALL WILL PRAISE.

Scribbler—What's the best way to become a great poet?

Ruyter—Write a bunch of junk that no one can understand.

HANDS WOULD CRACK OPEN

"About two months ago my hands started to crack open and bleed, the skin would scale off, and the good flesh would burn and itch dreadfully. When my hands first started to get sore, there were small blisters like water blisters which formed. They itched dreadfully, it just seemed as though I could tear the skin all off. I would scratch them and the skin would peel off, and the flesh would be all red and crack open and bleed. It worried me very much, as I had never had anything the matter with my skin. I was so afraid I would have to give up my employment.

"My doctor said he didn't think it would amount to anything. But it kept getting worse. One day I saw a piece in one of the papers about a lady who had the same trouble with her hands. She had used Cuticura Soap and Ointment and was cured. I decided to try them, and my hands were all healed before I had used one cake of Cuticura Ointment. I am truly thankful for the good results from the Cuticura Soap and Ointment, for thanks to them I was cured, and did not have to lose a day from work. I have had no return of the skin trouble." (Signed) Mrs. Mary E. Breig, 2522 Brown Street, Philadelphia, Pa., Jan. 12, 1911.

Although Cuticura Soap and Ointment are sold everywhere, a sample of each, with 32-page book, will be mailed free on application to "Cuticura." Dept. L, Boston.

Blissful Ignorance.

"Have you seen Joe lately?"

"Why, yes; I saw the old chap yesterday. And what do you think?—he's going to be married?"

"Can it be possible? To whom?"

"He's going to marry Mary Merrie."

"What! Why, I didn't know they knew each other."

"They don't. That's why they're going to be married."

Out of Date.

"Every time he opens his mouth he puts his foot in it."

"That's a great pity. Contortionists are no longer in demand as vaudeville attractions."

HIS THOUGHT.

Henson—He said he could never forget his alma mater. I wonder what he meant?

Henpeck — His mother-in-law, I guess.

Fortissimo.

When a certain Baltimore matron returned home one afternoon not so long ago the first sight her eyes beheld was a badly damaged youngster of hers. Little Bobby's forehead bore a bump almost the size of a doorknob.

"Heavens!" exclaimed the mother. "What has happened to Bobby?"

"Nuthin' much, mum," explained the new nurse. "You told me, mum, he might play on the pianner if he wanted to. Well, mum, wanst while he was sliding on the top, he slid a bit too far, mum; an' that accounts for the bump ye see, mum."

The Keynote.

Knicker—I thought simplicity was to be the keynote of your gowns.

Mrs. Knicker—It is; I have simply got to have them.

ONLY ONE "BROMO QUININE."
That is LAXATIVE BROMO QUININE. Look for the signature of E. W. GROVE. Used the World over to Cure a Cold in One Day. 25c.

Fairy Story.

"They married and lived happily ever after."

"You forget that you are talking about two people on the stage."

Ten smiles for a nickel. Always buy Red Cross Bag Blue; have beautiful clear white clothes.

The Reason.

"This purse is real alligator skin."

"I suppose that is why it has such snap."

Mrs. Winslow's Soothing Syrup for Children teething, softens the gums, reduces inflammation, allays pain, cures wind colic, 25c a bottle.

Occasionally we meet a man whose train of thought reminds us of a row of flat cars.

Garfield Tea will keep the whole system in perfect condition.

An oculist can do nothing for a man who is blind to his own interests.

A Bad Beginning.

"Whenever Jiggers starts to tell anything he prefaces his remarks by saying, 'Believe me.'"

"That's why I never do."

Important to Mothers

Examine carefully every bottle of CASTORIA, a safe and sure remedy for infants and children, and see that it

Bears the Signature of *Chas. H. Fletcher*

In Use For Over 30 Years.

Children Cry for Fletcher's Castoria

It isn't difficult for a man to see his affinity in a woman with an obese bank account.

Use Allen's Foot-Ease

The antiseptic powder to be shaken into the shoes for tired, tender, smarting, aching, swollen feet. It makes your feet feel easy and makes walking a Delight. Sold everywhere, 25c. For free trial package, address Allen S. Olmsted, Le Roy, N. Y.

Many a girl repents at leisure because she didn't marry in haste.

For liver and kidney troubles, nothing is quite so mild, pleasant and effective as Garfield Tea.

Some men don't know very much, but they don't know it.

DEFIANCE Cold Water Starch
makes laundry work a pleasure. 16 oz. pkg. 10c.

Brown's Bronchial Troches
Unexcelled for relieving Throat Troubles. No opiates Sample free. JOHN I. BROWN & SON Boston Mass.

Make 25 to 50 Weekly

selling the Automatic Combination Tool in your home county. A Fence Builder's Tool, Post Puller, Lifting Jack, Vice, Wrench, etc. Used by Farmers, Teamsters, in Factories, Mills, Mines, etc. Weight 24 lbs. Capacity 3 tons. No experience necessary. Free instruction. Write for special offer to live agents. Send no money. Name county where you live.
AUTOMATIC JACK COMPANY
Box 257 Bloomfield, Ind.

FERRY'S SEEDS

Good gardeners are those who raise good flowers and vegetables. Good flowers and vegetables come from good seeds. We produce good seeds—the inference is obvious. For sale everywhere.

1912 SEED ANNUAL
Free on Request
D. M. FERRY & CO.
Detroit, Mich.

W. N. U., DENVER, NO. 10–1912.

Do You Feel This Way?

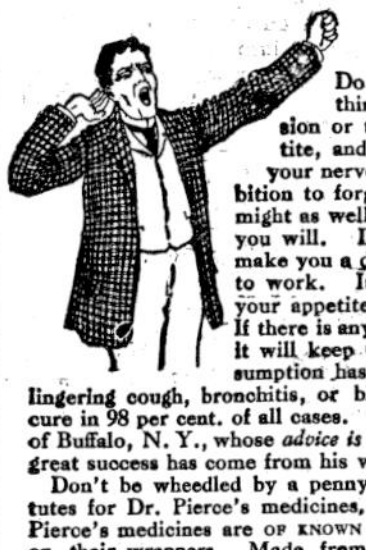

Do you feel all tired out? Do you sometimes think you just can't work away at your profession or trade any longer? Do you have a poor apetite, and lay awake at nights unable to sleep? Are your nerves all gone, and your stomach too? Has ambition to forge ahead in the world left you? If so, you might as well put a stop to your misery. You can do it if you will. Dr. Pierce's Golden Medical Discovery will make you a different individual, It will set your lazy liver to work. It will set things right in your stomach, and your appetite will come back. It will purify your blood. If there is any tendency in your family toward consumption, it will keep that dread destroyer away. Even after consumption has almost gained a foothold in the form of a lingering cough, bronchitis, or bleeding at the lungs, it will bring about a cure in 98 per cent. of all cases. It is a remedy prepared by Dr. R. V. Pierce, of Buffalo, N. Y., whose *advice is given free* to all who wish to write him. His great success has come from his wide experience and varied practice.

Don't be wheedled by a penny-grabbing dealer into taking inferior substitutes for Dr. Pierce's medicines, recommended to be "just as good." Dr. Pierce's medicines are OF KNOWN COMPOSITION. Their every ingredient printed on their wrappers. Made from roots without alcohol. Contain no habit-forming drugs. World's Dispensary Medical Association, Buffalo, N. Y.

W. L. DOUGLAS SHOES

$2.25 $2.50 $3.00 $3.50 $4.00 & $5.00

For MEN, WOMEN and BOYS

THE STANDARD OF QUALITY FOR OVER 30 YEARS

THE NEXT TIME YOU NEED SHOES give W. L. Douglas shoes a trial. W. L. Douglas name stamped on a shoe guarantees superior quality and more value for the money than other makes. His name and price stamped on the bottom protects the wearer against high prices and inferior shoes. Insist upon having the genuine W. L. Douglas shoes. Take no substitute. If your dealer cannot supply W. L. Douglas shoes, write W. L. Douglas, Brockton, Mass., for catalog. Shoes sent everywhere delivery charges prepaid. *Fast Color Eyelets used.*

PUTNAM FADELESS DYES

Color more goods brighter and faster colors than any other dye. One 10c package colors all fibers. They dye in cold water better than any other dye. You can dye any garment without ripping apart. Write for free booklet—How to Dye, Bleach and Mix Colors. MONROE DRUG COMPANY, Quincy, Ill.

SUCH A POOR INHERITANCE

Tears of a Rival Attorney Were Explained, Not in Too Friendly a Fashion.

At the trial of Horne Tooke, Lord Eldon, speaking of his own reputation, said:

"It is the little inheritance I have to leave my children, and by God's help, I will leave it unimpaired."

Here he shed tears, and to the astonishment of those present, Mitford, the attorney general began to weep.

"Just look at Mitford," said a bystander to Horne Tooke, "what on earth is he crying for?"

Tooke replied:

"He is crying to think what a small inheritance Eldon's children are like to get."

COMMON FORM OF CRUELTY.

Bessie—Yes, he claimed his wife pinched him severely whenever she asked him for money.

Bert—Well, he needn't flatter himself that he is the only man who has been pinched for money.

Puzzle of Living.

Religionists chided about their inability to agree on points of faith might point out that they differ only in fundamentals and not essentials, whereas the scientists differ on everything. Take the science of living. A week ago you would have "died if you drank water with your meals." Now they say it doesn't do any harm at all. One variety says: "Eat meat, lots of it, to build good, rich blood." Another says meat is poison; that vegetables are the only food. A third declares meat and vegetables both increase debility, and that you will live twice as long on raw fruits and nuts. Some say "Talk with your meals, laugh; it makes the food digest." Others insist silence is never so golden as at the table.

Wheat Goes Down.

De Broker—Hear about De Curbb?

De Ledger—No. What's happened to him?

De Broker—Knocked flat.

De Ledger—You don't say? Was he caught by the drop in wheat?

De Broker—Well, yes; something like that. A barrel of flour fell on him.

Be happy. Use Red Cross Bag Blue; much better than liquid blue. Delights the laundress. All grocers.

Good Advice.

"I will have my pound of flesh."

"Be a vegetarian instead, and take a peck of potatoes."

Dr. Pierce's Pellets, small, sugar-coated, easy to take as candy, regulate and invigorate stomach, liver and bowels. Do not gripe.

Every man has a future before him, but too often his past behind him acts as a handicap.

Garfield Tea, taken regularly, will correct both liver and kidney disorders.

We can do more good by being good than in any other way.—Burton.

Coat and Costume

DARK green cloth with reverse side in blue and green plaid is used for this very useful coat. The large collar, which is pointed on sleeves and center back, has the plaid outside, so have the turn-up cuffs. Horn buttons form fastening below collar. Hat of dark green straw, trimmed with spotted ribbon. Materials required for the coat: 5 yards 50 inches wide, 4 buttons, 4½ yards satin 22 inches wide for lining to hips.

Cloth Costume.—Almond-colored cloth makes as well in this style. The skirt is quite plain and short. The coat is one of the newest designs, cut like a man's morning coat, the collar and turn-up cuffs being faced with black satin. The double-breasted waistcoat is also of the black satin; a black satin button with simulated buttonhole trim each side front of coat. The toque has a crown of fold-ed almond-colored silk with brim of black satin. A bow of black ribbon trims the side. Materials required for the costume: 5 yards 46 inches wide, 1 yard black satin 22 inches wide, 4½ yards satin 22 inches wide for lining coat.

CHEAP TONIC FOR THE HAIR

Preparation That Will Increase the Growth and Impart Beautiful Sheen to Tresses.

Eagerly the eyes of a woman will scan the pages of papers and magazines for the thousand and one little helps, especially those that are for beautifying the completion or hair, or to remedy some physical defect. It sounds very good, and so it is, but when one mentally calculates the price of the much desired, it is with a sigh that the article is cast aside.

There is nothing more beautiful than a woman's hair. It fulfills a mission when ugly features are beyond repair, for angularity and sharpness is softened with a delicate frame of beautiful hair around one's face.

It is not possible to change the color without injurious results, and nature provides the shade of hair which best suits your complexion. But when it is dead looking, dusty appearing, broken, not properly arranged it destroys the best appearance in the world.

Let the hair be ever so tawdry, broken or dull of appearance this preparation will increase its growth, impart a beautiful sheen and change its dull, dead appearance. Boil a double handful of sage with one-half teaspoonful of salt and sulphur in one quart of water. Use leaf sage. Strain it into a large bottle, add as much quinine as you can hold on the end of a knife blade and put into the mixture 5 cents' worth of bay rum and 5 cents' worth of witchhazel. Apply it to the scalp with a medicine dropper. If the scalp is dry use a very little vaseline on the hair. The liquid will "cut" the grease. This is good.

RIBBONS ON LACE CANVAS

Lovely Work Possible When Care is Taken to Secure Properly Suitable Colors.

Very lovely work can be done with ribbon, wide and narrow, self-colored or shaded, on some of the very pretty lace canvases so easily procurable in most fancy shops. The sort of articles best suited for this work are sachets, cushion covers, table centers, nightdress cases, etc.

The lace canvas on which many examples has been worked is ecru in color and somewhat stiff.

Care should be taken never to let your ribbon, be it wide or narrow, get twisted.

Especially if the whole of the canvas is not threaded with cross lines of ribbon, it is necessary to line your work with a suitable color to show under it.

China Silk for Petticoats.

Women in increasing numbers are turning to china silk as the solution to the present petticoat problem. It outwears the usual petticoat silks and sateens by far, and if of an ordinarily good quality, will launder without the damaging effect. Not the smaller of its advantages is its light, supple nature, which does not permit the tiniest suggestion of clumsiness, and moreover, it can be had in any suit of dress shade.

ENGAGED GIRL'S PRETTY IDEA

Will Announce Coming Marriage to Her Friends at a Typical Cupid's Luncheon.

A charming maiden who has yielded to Cupid's earnest pleading is to announce the fact to her friends in this pretty way: Eight of her nearest and dearest girl chums are to be bidden to a luncheon. The table is to be done in pure white, the centerpiece of bride roses, the candles white with white silken shades. At each plate a pink bridesmaid rose, except that of the hostess, where a pure bride rose will tell you the story. The place cards are to represent brides, the face being a photograph of the real bride. The favors are to be white suede card cases containing the cards of the happy girl and the lucky man. Can you imagine anything sweeter?

In the evening the girl's mother is to issue cards for a dance to which all the gay circle of young people will be asked, and the cotillion figures are to be symbolic of the good patron saint who presides untiringly over "affaires de coeur." There will be necklaces and fobs of tiny silver and gilt hearts. Hearts will be represented in fans, cups, aprons and cushions. One figure will be especially attractive: Red fencing hearts for the girls, bows and arrows for the men. The ices and cakes will all be hearts, with a plentiful supply of gilt Cupids with arrows.

ONE OF THE NEWEST BLOUSES

New Doilies Are Thin.

Dollies as thin as gossamer are now being used with crystal glasses and dainty china. The latest importations of these are fine as cobwebs. Each disk is embroidered with the finest linen floss, and while the pattern seems to cover the bit of tissue it by no means gives it a thick look. The finger bowl set which expresses the newest style in the perfectly appointed table is of sheer bolting cloth finished on the edge with a tiny embroidered scallop and garland of microscopic flowers worked in a trellis design.

LITTLE COLORADO ITEMS

Small Happenings Occurring Over the State Worth While.

Western Newspaper Union News Service.

Akron reports a heavy fall of snow.

Palisade will hold its spring election April 2.

Georgetown has secured a perpetual water right.

The Swedish Baptist church in Greeley has been nearly completed.

During the month of February there were 291 deaths in Denver.

The twenty-seventh storm of the winter has visited Trinidad.

James Conners, a resident of Georgetown for thirty years, is dead.

A new grandstand at the Longmont baseball grounds is being constructed.

Construction work has been started on a new Catholic church at Meeker.

Col. A. W. Jones, a resident of Greeley for twenty-eight years, is dead.

The Silverton branch of the Denver & Rio Grande is tied up by snowslides.

On the ranch of Joe Kunzman, near Kersey, there is a six-legged yearling lamb.

A railroad will be built from Meeker ten miles south to tap the coal fields.

Forty-two miles of the Old Santa Fe trail from Denver will be a twenty-foot pike.

Boulder has secured an addition of three elk for the Chautauqua park in that city.

At the Wilson park saw mill, 20 miles from Meeker, snow eight feet deep is reported.

Mrs. Marian C. Gilbert, who was accused of killing her husband in Pueblo, was acquitted.

For the first time pea acreage will be contracted for in the Fort Lupton district this season.

Claude Streppy, a miner of Victor, fell sixty-three feet from a hoist and was fatally injured.

A special grand jury has convened in Grand Junction to investigate the bootlegging situation.

A movement has been started in Trinidad to do away with the nickel-in-the-slot telephones.

In a wreck on the Rio Grande four miles east of Salida one trainman was killed and three injured.

In June Grand Junction will celebrate the thirtieth anniversary of the incorporation of the town.

The Windsor creamery has been opened for business. Cream will be furnished from 250 cows.

El Paso, Boulder, Weld and Pueblo counties have decided to hold presidential preference elections.

In a slashing battle at Longmont Karl Puryear of Denver won a decision over Al Tobin of Longmont.

Members of the Kersey Commercial Club are going out among the farmers and soliciting membership.

Many people who attended a church supper in Greeley were taken violently ill with symptoms of poisoning.

The Routt county extension of the Laramie, Hahn's Peak & Pacific railway will be commenced April 1.

Adjutant General Chase has requested the State Land Board to loan $150,000 for the erection of an armory at Denver.

The Greeley Hydro-Electric Company will ask that city for a franchise to furnish a current for heat, light and power purposes.

Several of the Farmers' Union Trading Compay stores on the Western slope, recently closed, have been reopened.

The Colorado Grain Dealers' Association has decided to establish a state bureau of inspection in Denver, with deputies in the principal towns of the state.

Burglars broke into the hardware store of Ellis at Hood at Florence and stole $500 worth of goods. Three men were arrested and put in jail at Cañon City pending investigation.

Stockmen of Moffat county have organized a wolf bounty association and $20 each will be paid for grown wolves and $10 for pups, this amount being in addition to the bounty paid by the county.

The Aurora State bank was entered by a lone robber recently who secured between $500 and $600 in cash. While the bandit was attempting to make his escape he was shot and mortally wounded.

Grand Junction has raised the $2,500 bonus asked by the Ziegler Brothers, of Muscatine, Ia., and the latter will invest $100,000 in a cannery in that city. The plant will be completed in the spring.

By an agreement entered into recently the coal strike in Southern Colorado, which has existed for nearly two years, has been practically ended. The agreement has been ratified by the union miners of Lafayette and Louisville. As a result of this arrangement 1,000 miners will return to work.

Trinidad merchants and shippers have taken steps to reduce the rates charged by railroads and express companies hauling out of that city.

Glenwood Springs is trying to secure the annual midsummer meeting of the Colorado Stockmen's Association, which will be held some time in July.

The Republican state convention will be held in Colorado Springs March 27th, at which time delegates will be named for the national convention.

COLD COMFORT FOR MOTHER

Comment of Boston Belle on Young Man's Conduct Was Icy in the Extreme.

General F. D. Grant, at a Washington's birthday dinner in New York some years ago, told a story about a young Boston Tory.

"This Tory," he said, "fought during the Revolution neither on one side nor on the other. He took a pleasure trip on the continent, and he didn't come back home again until the war was over.

"He was treated very coldly by society on his return, and this grieved his good old mother to the heart.

"The dear old lady tried to explain the matter one afternoon to a Boston belle.

"'Naturally, as the head of the family,' she said, 'my son could not take part in the war. To him fell the duty, perhaps the more arduous duty, of protecting his mother and sisters and looking after the interests of the estate.'

"'Oh, madam,' said the belle, with an icy smile, 'you need not explain. I assure you, I'd have done exactly as your son did—I'm such a coward!'"

Natural Avoidance.

Mayor Gaynor of New York was defending his anti-suffrage views: "Woman has her place and man has his," he said, "and when I think of the confusion that would come from intermingling their places, I am reminded of an anecdote about Lady Holland. Lady Holland once said to Lord John Russell: 'Why hasn't Lord Holland got a post in the cabinet?' 'Well, if you must know,' Lord John answered, 'it is because nobody would work in a cabinet with a man whose wife opens all his letters.'"

Hard to Find.

"Here are some verses entitled 'The Road to Arcady.'"

"Pshaw! Almost any poet can tell the way to Arcady, but none of them ever gets there."

A Hint From Shakespeare.

"Why do you call your dog Hamlet?"

"Can't you see why? He's a Great Dane."

The Paxton Toilet Co., of Boston, Mass., will send a large trial box of Paxtine Antiseptic, a delightful cleansing and germicidal toilet preparation, to any woman, free, upon request.

He who reigns within himself and rules passions, desires and fears is more than a king.—Milton.

When a man does things he hasn't much time to talk about them.

The Remedy that revolutionizes and regenerates the victim of constipation is Garfield Tea, a herb combination.

Two heads are better than one—in a cabbage patch.

The Marble Booster,
March 23, 1912.

COMBINED SNOWSLIDE AND CYCLONE HITS MARBLE MILL. Damage Will Reach $15,000. Monumental Shop Destroyed and Other Damage Done. None Killed or Hurt. Miss Evaline Salter, Night Telephone Operator, Had A Miraculous Escape and There Were Several Other Very Close Calls.

A few minutes before 6 o'clock Wednesday morning the people of Marble were awakened by the prolonged screeching of the siren whistle at the new power plant of the Colorado-Yule Marble company. The whistle kept repeating the signal, 32, and that meant the Colorado-Yule office. The whole town was quickly alarmed everyone believing the mill was on fire. Soon the streets were filled with men struggling through three feet of new and heavy snow which had fallen during the night atop an equal amount of old snow. Breaking a trail was very difficult.

. . . . .

There was a "Second Edition of The Marble Booster, Saturday Night, March 23, EXTRA," with a further report on subsequent activities at the mill.

The Marble Booster,
Extra, March 23, 1912.

WORK NOW RESUMED IN ALL DEPARTMENTS.

It takes more than a combined snowslide and cyclone to put the Colorado-Yule Marble company out of business— or even to give the company a serious setback.

What on Wednesday morning appeared to be a complete disaster, is this Saturday night hardly more than a temporary inconvenience. Indomitable spirit and loyalty has brought quick results, and, too, the damage proved not nearly so great as was at first supposed.

This Saturday night marks a resumption of work in all departments in the big mill. In fact, work started yesterday, Friday, in most of the mill, but today all departments are working as usual.

. . . . .

The editor, in a separate article, explains the reasons for the slide and that "Conditions Bringing on this Slide were Unprecedented." There was not an unusual amount of snow on the mountainside, but when the heavy wet snow began to fall, Col. Meek, anticipating the danger at 9:30 Tuesday night ordered Mr. Frazier to check that all fires were extinguished in Shop No. 3, which was in an old slide path. Then the paper focused on the report in the Marble City Times.

The Marble Booster,
Extra, March 23, 1912.

STRONG INDIGNATION OVER A NEWSPAPER ATTACK ON COMPANY.

Tonight the outlook is very cheerful. The workmen employed by the company have rallied to its support in splendid fashion and the town people are lending their services wherever needed. Only one thing occurred today to mar the general cheerfulness and that was the appearance of a so-called newspaper on the streets containing an article which in every line expressed the greatest satisfaction that the disaster had occurred. This pseudo newspaper has upon many other occasions attacked the Colorado-Yule company, but it was thought that the present situation would call for a square deal from even the bitterest enemy of the company. As a matter of fact the party who prints this sheet has no reason to attack the company at any time, except for the money there is in it, but to print a spiteful, goody-goody article when misfortune came like it did Wednesday morning is just about the last straw and

The Booster would not be surprised to hear of summary action being taken, such is the general feeling of indignation.

. . . . .

Frank Frost continued this theme in his next issue.

The Marble Booster,
March 30, 1912.

"DESTINY" ON THE JOB AGAIN. The Marble City Times is Suppressed. Acting Under Orders from Mayor, Marshal Mahoney Takes Possession. MISS SMITH GOES. Marshal Escorted Her to the Depot Thursday Morning—The People Held Mass Meeting At the Masonic Hall Last Monday Night.

Indignation at the continuous publication of articles in the Marble City Times, which they believed to be hurtful to the town and its interests, and brought to the climax by an article in the last issue which was accepted to mean that the paper was glad the recent slowslide damaged the Colorado-Yule mill, therby throwing many persons temporarily out of employment, caused 300 persons to meet at the Masonic hall last Monday night to give expressions to their feelings in the matter and to adopt a set of resolutions calling upon Miss Sylvia Smith, editor of the paper, to leave Marble and never return. This action was taken after many vain efforts had been made to get the paper to quit "knocking" the town's interests. The article in the last issue was the last straw and the people acted.

W.B. Frazier called the meeting to order as the temporary chairman. John F. Parrish acted as temporary secretary and upon motion of the Rev. J. A. Walton, seconded by Henry Thode, the temporary officers were made permanent. Mr. Frazier then explained the object of the meeting, speaking in part as follows:

"In presenting this vital matter," he said, "I wish first to impress upon you that my position is simply that of an individual. I am not representing the Colorado-Yule Marble company here, but simply myself, and I have only the interest that every other person here tonight should have— that of persons, men and women, whose bread and butter depend in large measure upon the industries of Marble. Therefore, let us start right with a clear understanding that this is not a company meeting.

"I am in a position to state to you here tonight that no one thing has so hurt the company as these reports that have been given wide publicity as coming from the Marble City Times that the Colorado-Yule company is a stock-selling swindle. It is true that the company has sold stock; all such companies have to do it in order to develop...

"It is hard to believe that the editor of such a sheet is a woman. I am now coming to the point of what I have to say and that is that the time is here when the town of Marble must be rid of this woman."

At this point Mr. Frazier was interrupted by prolonged applause, practically every person in the vast audience joining in.

...Mr. Frazier then read a set of resolutions, printed elsewhere in this paper with the signatures, and when he came to the words, "and never to return," there was prolonged applause again. At the conclusion of the reading of the resolutions, the Rev. James A. Walton, pastor of Union church here, took the floor.

Continued on Page 338

THE MARBLE BOOSTER
Newspaper sheet size: 22 x 30 inches

Extra Copies of this issue of The Booster may be obtained at Blackstock's Drug Store or at this office at 5 cents per copy

The Booster will always fight for the things which make a prosperous town

THE MARBLE BOOSTER

The Booster is an independent newspaper devoted to the interests of Marble

Five Cents a Copy. MARBLE, GUNNISON COUNTY, COLORADO, SATURDAY, MARCH 30, 1912. VOL. 2. NO. 3

"DESTINY" ON THE JOB AGAIN

THE MARBLE CITY TIMES IS SUPPRESSED

Acting Under Orders From Mayor, Marshal Mahoney Takes Possession.

MISS SMITH GOES

Marshal Escorted her to the Depot Thursday Morning—The People Held Mass Meeting at the Masonic Hall Last Monday Night.

Indignation at the continuous publication of articles in the Marble City Times, which they believed to be hurtful to the town and its interests, and brought to the climax by an article in the last issue which was accepted to mean that the paper was glad the recent snowslide damaged the Colorado-Yule mill, thereby throwing many persons temporarily out of employment, caused 300 persons to meet at the Masonic hall last Monday night to give expressions to their feelings in the matter and to adopt a set of resolutions calling upon Miss Sylvia Smith, editor of the paper, to leave Marble and never return. This action was taken after many vain efforts had been made to get the paper to quit "knocking" the town's interests. The article in the last issue was the last straw and the people acted.

W. R. Frazier called the meeting to order as temporary chairman. John F. Parrish acted as temporary secretary and upon motion of the Rev. J. A. Walton, seconded by Henry Thode, the temporary officers were made permanent. Mr. Frazier then explained the object of the meeting, speaking in part as follows:

"In presenting this vital matter," he said, "I wish first to impress upon you that my position is simply that of an individual. I am not representing the Colorado-Yule Marble company here, but simply myself, and I have only the interest that every other person here tonight should have—that of persons, men and women, whose bread and butter depend in large measure upon the industries of Marble. Therefore, let us start right with a clear understanding that this is not a company meeting.

"I am in a position to state to you here tonight that no one thing has so hurt the company as these reports that have been given wide publicity as coming from the Marble City Times that the Colorado-Yule company is a stock-selling swindle. It is true that the company has sold stock; all such companies have to do so in order to develop. This applies to mining companies, stone companies and every other kind of company that attacks and develops these rugged mountains. The articles that have been published in the Marble City Times have, as I say, been widely disseminated and in places where we expected the company to gain financial encouragement copies of that miserable sheet have been pulled on us and timidity encountered. The interests also affects each of us; it is a matter of self protection with us and it is no excuse to say that you are not connected with the company, for your business and your livelihood here depends entirely upon the success of this company. Let me say, too, that no enterprise ever was started upon a more firm foundation. There is no marble deposit in the world that compares with ours. We always win out in competition with any other marble in the world and you people here tonight know that our mill is simply swamped with orders, that we can't produce the finished marble fast enough.

"The position of Miss Sylvia Smith, as expressed in her paper—The Marble City Times—in the last issue, published March 22, 1912, is such that it hardly can be believed. She openly exulted in the disaster to the company plant and in reading the article one cannot fail to draw the inference that she is sorry no one was killed, so that the disaster might be more complete. She does not say that openly, but the inference is there, and you will all bear me out in this statement. She does not say, you may have noticed, that she is glad that no one was killed. This article is headed 'Destiny Keeps her Appointment and Redressed many Wrongs.' Would it have been destiny, or justice, if Miss Salter had lost her life? Would it have been destiny, or justice, if the slide had occurred an hour and a half later when the shops would have been crowded with workmen? The inference is that the loss of lives would have more completely 'redressed the wrongs.'

"It is hard to believe that the editor of such a sheet is a woman. I am now coming to the point of what I have to say and that is that the time is here when the town of Marble must be rid of this woman."

At this point Mr. Frazier was interrupted by prolonged applause, practically every person in the vast audience joining in.

"Every man here tonight hates to tackle this proposition because she is a woman," Mr. Frazier resumed, "but a duty like this must be met. We have put up with this long enough. She has openly boasted that her skirts have saved her many a licking. We have the right as citizens of this town to say who are objectionable characters and this privilege is to be extended here tonight. Everyone here who feels that he or she can speak for the success of the town, with all of its businesses and industries, is invited to take this opportunity for expression."

Mr. Frazier then read a set of resolutions, printed elsewhere in this paper with the signatures, and when he came to the words "and never to return," there was prolonged applause again. At the conclusion of the reading of the resolutions, the Rev. James A. Walton, pastor of Union church here, took the floor.

"It is not an easy matter for me, situated as I am, to stand here and refrain from expressing the thoughts that boil up within me," said Mr. Walton, in opening. "There is always a certain amount of respect and courtesy due a woman. However, I have read this woman's paper for a year and a half and I have long since reached the conclusion that she is not engaged in publishing that paper for the purpose of disseminating news. She is not publishing it to tell of our local affairs; she is publishing it to hurt, to injure Marble. Not a single feature of the town—educational, religious, commercial or social—has escaped her scathing pen. She has harpooned them all. What seems to me most remarkable is that the people here have endured it this long—three years I believe. Here are your homes, your interests, your living. She scarcely prints an issue of her paper but what derogatory articles hurt your interests. How much will your interests here be worth if the machinations of this woman should be successful? They are your interests and she is aiming at them; they are your homes and she is trying to destroy them.

"Sylvia Smith is a menace to all of us. We all know right well that the minute the Colorado-Yule company quits Marble, so do all the rest of us that have the price of a ticket out. There will be no more groceries, no more clothing, no more paregoric sold here. Why? No money.

"I say to you all, protect your interests. Had the publisher of this paper been a man, as Mr Frazier has pointed out, there would have been no necessity for this meeting tonight. In conclusion, I want to say that if you have one iota of interest in Marble, you will join here tonight in asking that woman to go out and quit our homes, our streets and our community life."

When Mr. Walton sat down the applause was deafening. He had warmed to his subject as he went along and by the time he reached the closing sentences he had the big audience "going," as one man expressed it. In contrast to the natural oratory of Mr. Walton was the talk of Judge C. E. Budlong, who followed with an appeal, none the less eloquent but more in the language of one man speaking to another.

"I came here three years ago," said the Judge. "Nearly as soon as I got off the train I began to hear some 'knocks' against the Colorado-Yule company. I listened patiently but I could not discover that they were based upon any reason. There are a few of those 'knockers' still with us, but the number has dwindled very considerably—in fact, I could count them upon the fingers of one hand today. Today the great Colorado-Yule enterprise is three times the size that it was when I came. Now, mark my prediction: In three years from this time, it will have grown to be three times larger still. (Applause.)

"We meet here tonight for a very serious purpose. I say to you, Brother Kobey, that if the Colorado-Yule company was to shut down its mill here, within sixty days you would not sell enough socks to buy a ticket to Redstone.

"Now, in regard to that article this Miss Silvia Smith has published. When a woman takes a man's place she must expect to receive what a man would receive in the same position. This Marble City Hatchet is chopping the blood out of our town. These resolutions say that she must pack her suitcase and get out of this town. Shall we sit idly and let this thing go on? I say no. Too many people read those articles of hers and do not take the pains to find out whether they are true or not. If she'll pack her suitcase and get out it will be well for her. If she stays, Lord have mercy on her. We expect the committee to tell her that if she does not obey the mandate of that resolution she will often wish she had."

A great wave of applause again broke over the house as Judge Budlong resumed his seat. Dr. H. G. Haxby followed.

"My position, briefly," said Dr. Haxby, "is that this woman is hurting everyone of us. Every dollar that her articles divert from the support of this great industry here means a loss of part of that dollar to me, and to every other person within the sound of my voice. Her publications are undoubtedly inimical to the interests of this town."

Other speakers followed in rapid succession. The Booster here presents the remarks, in brief, of each:

Dan Barnes—"The other speakers have voiced exactly my sentiments in much better language than I can express myself."

George L. Swigart—"I am too much of a gentleman to say what I think of this woman in the presence of so many ladies as are here tonight. I'll stay here until midnight, if necessary, to sign that resolution."

Prof. A. M. Willson—"It seems so queer that this woman would stay here year after year in a town which she so evidently hates. This is a large country. Why not move on?"

Homer Harrington—"I can't help but feel that the continuance of this sheet is an outrage upon us all. I stand ready to sign that resolution with a hearty endorsement of all it contains. There are many others who feel as I do and who are as sincere as I am."

E. O. Pratt—"I have been here almost since the start of the Colorado-Yule company and I always have been paid a regular salary at a regular time. So far as the people of this town are concerned I cannot see how it would adversely affect them if the company sold a gold brick every other day back east. The company has made the town and it is the only thing which makes it possible for a town to be here. We all know what a lie it is to speak of this gigantic industry as a stock selling scheme."

Dr. H. H. Swift—"I have served on several boards of health where my duty was to abate nuisances such as had a bad smell, dead horses, dead dogs, etc.—things that made people sick. I say to you, though, that never in all my experience have I met with anything so offensive and so badly needing abatement as this newspaper, so-called. Those who have given the matter thought know right well that the editor is the paid agent of people who are trying, for gain, to hurt the company. If this editor had been a man she would have been ridden out of town on a rail a long time ago."

M. E. Granger—"We have met here to discuss a common enemy in Sylvia Smith. The snow slide has not damaged us. Colonel Meek will take care of the slide. But its up to us to take care of Sylvia Smith. (Applause.) This is an indignation meeting and I believe we are all indignant. My name will be on that resolution."

Mr. Frazier—"There is no half way point tonight. Let's see where everyone stands. What we do here will have effect. Let us stand up for Marble."

Tim Salter—"I have been in Marble three and one-half years and one month after I came and read Miss Smith's paper I was forced to the conclusion that she was an undesirable citizen. At that time she had some friends; now I don't believe she has more than two or three at the most. I'll guarantee five or six names on that resolution."

H. L. Sweet—"Money is the most timid thing and the quickest to take to cover. That's why the articles Miss Smith publishes are harmful, because money is frightened without reason, and the owners of it do not take the time or trouble to investigate. I am at a loss to understand the motives which prompted this woman to gloat over the recent misfortune, which, only by a miracle, happened with no loss of life. As Professor Willson aptly says, there is plenty of room in this country. She can move south, north, east, west or straight up."

At this point Rev. Walton took the floor to make a motion that a committee of fifteen men and ten women be appointed to deliver a copy of the resolution to Miss Smith. Henry Thode seconded the motion and it was carried. The chair being asked to appoint the committee, Mr. Frazier named the following men:

Dan Barnes, Dr. H. G. Haxby, Ambrose Williams, Charles McWilliams, John F. Parrish, I. M. Kobey, W. R. Frazier, Judge C. E. Budlong, Rev. J. A. Walton, W. R. Hood, Henry Mertens, Homer Harrington, Frank P. Frost, W. D. Parry, Henry Thode.

Mr. Frazier then announced the appointment of a nominating committee of ladies to name the committee of ten. The nominating committee presented the following list of ladies for membership on the general committee;

Mrs. Homer Harrington, Mrs. Jack Clayton, Mrs. A. M. Willson, Mrs. W. R. Hood, Mrs. Thomas Walsh, Mrs. J. F. Parrish, Mrs. Dan Barnes, Mrs. Ida B. Carey, Miss Elva Ward, Mrs. H. G. Haxby.

The talks were then resumed, after Mr. Frazier had asked the general committee of twenty-five to remain after the meeting and make plans for presenting the resolution to Miss Smith. Dan Barnes said he would like to hear from Williams brothers. John Williams said:

"I am tired of this thing and I am glad to sign that resolution to have this person to take up her abode elsewhere."

Ambrose Williams said:

"I would have been glad to have had Miss Smith here tonight so she could have been heard. If there are any extenuating circumstances we should hear them. The first impression I had after reading her article was that it was rather glorifying in a calamity and I felt that it injured her more than it did the company. I am in hopes this matter may be handled in such a way by the committee that a just settlement may be reached."

Mrs. Dan Barnes said:

"I am heartily in favor of this resolution and may say that I have always believed this woman to be a nuisance and a detriment to the town. I am willing to do what I can to rid the town of her."

Mrs. Montgomery said: "Mr. Chairman, the ladies present deeply deplore the necessity of such a meeting."

Mr. Frazier replied that the men, doubtless, were the most embarassed. He then called for an expression from all the women present, asking all those in favor of the resolution to please stand. Fifty or more women stood; two or three did not.

The meeting then was adjourned, after the audience had been told where the resolution might be signed. The people lined up and passed in front of the secretary's table, affixing their signatures. It required more than an hour to do this, while the crowd patiently stood in line.

At the committee meeting, held immediately afterward, it was agreed to present the resolutions to Miss Smith the next afternoon at 3 o'clock. Mr. Frazier was elected chairman of the committee and the members were asked to be at Kobey's store the next afternoon at 2:45 o'clock.

The next morning the resolutions were placed at the postoffice for further signatures of all who cared to sign. By noon there was an additional list of names on the paper. Then a copy was made, showing that the resolutions had been signed by just 232 persons in all. Of this number 197 signed at the meeting held in Masonic hall.

(Continued on last page.)

MARBLE TIMES IS SUPPRESSED

(Continued from first page.)

The committee met, as per schedule, at 3 o'clock and it was soon discovered that Miss Smith had sent notes to two members of the committee warning not only them but all the other members of the committee not to set foot upon her property. It was quickly ascertained that a newspaper is public property and as such is open to the public. In the face of the concealed threat of the notes, however, the committee first made sure of its right to call upon Miss Smith, then the roll was called. It showed only one absentee—one of the ladies. The committee then set out for the office of Miss Smith, Mr. Frazier bearing the resolution in his hand.

At the entrance to Miss Smith's office, the leaders of the committee met Miss Smith, who brandished a stove shovel in their faces and warned them not to come upon her property. Mr. Frazier offered to read her the resolutions. She would not listen, but kept repeating her demand that the visitors take themselves off her property. In this demand, she was backed up by Tom Boughton, who stood back of her. Ugly words flashed back and forth from Boughton to those members of the committee who stood in the front. Boughton observed the Rev. Mr. Walton and shouted to him that he was a hyprocrite, whereupon the dominie offered to lay aside the ministerial cloth long enough to prove that he was a man as well as a minister. Other hot words were spoken, when it was seen that Boughton was taking the part of the woman who was asked to leave Marble. Several members of the committee advised Boughton in certain tones to shut up. A leader said there might have been serious trouble where the intention before was merely to leave the resolution and depart.

Miss Smith, meanwhile, was circling the buildings in the immediate vicinity, brandishing her stove shovel and iterating and reiterating her demand for the visitors to leave. Mr. Frazier read the resolutions while he followed her around, and when he had finished he left the paper she could get it. She refused to take it from him. The committee then returned to Main street. As soon as they had gone, Miss Smith recovered the resolutions from the ground where Mr. Frazier had dropped the paper, and took them with her, laughing heartily as she read aloud to Boughton and others. Some one asked her if she wasn't afraid.

"Why, no, why should I be," she replied. "I have to grin and bear it and protect my property."

An officer had gone to Miss Smith before the committee approached her office and told her that the committee was coming upon a peaceful mission and that neither she nor her property should come to any harm. She refused to give her permission for the committee to visit her, however, and sent back word warning them to stay away. The committee went anyhow.

The last words Mr. Frazier spoke to her were: "Miss Smith, you have just seventy-two hours in which to leave Marble, never to return." She made no reply.

MAYOR ORDERS THE CITY MARSHAL TO ACT

Wednesday afternoon the situation became acute. Marshal Mahoney heard a great deal of talk about violence and he was preparing to protect Miss

---

Smith and her property when he received an order from Mayor Tischhauser commanding him to "do that very thing."

Acting under this order, the marshal took charge of Miss Smith and Thursday morning sent her out of Marble. He also took charge of the plant of the Marble City Times and stored it in the basement of Kobey's store. The marshal told a reporter for The Booster that he had excellent reason to believe Miss Smith was in danger of violence here and that her property was in danger, so he was acting for her interests as well as obeying the order of the mayor when he threw about her the protection of the law.

The mayor's order to the marshal commanded him to remove Miss Smith from the town in order to protect her from violence and to prevent disturbance which was certain to ensue from the enraged state of the public mind.

When Marshal Mahoney was taking possession of the Times office, he and the men he had employed to store the plant discovered the type all set for another issue of the paper, which was to re-print the article of last week which gave so much offense.

Miss Smith left Marble with the expressed intention of going straight to Governor Shafroth.

Miss Smith advanced no objection to leaving Marble—in fact, according to Marshal Mahoney, she appeared rather anxious to leave.

Since her departure the town has been quiet and there has been little talk of a riotous nature. The people, however, are determined that the "knockers" shall and must go and they are also determined to rule their own affairs according to what they believe is for the best interests of the town of Marble.

THE RESOLUTIONS AND THOSE WHO SIGNED

Whereas, The editor of the Marble City Times, Miss Sylvia Smith, has at all times endeavored to injure the chief industry of Marble, The Colorado-Yule Marble Company, by publishing in its columns scurrilous and untruthful statements, and that she is antagonistic to all the interests of the community, business, educational, religious and social, and

Whereas, The wrecking of the mill by the recent snow slide was a disaster to the community as a whole; that the article in the Marble City Times under date of March 22, 1912, was untrue, vicious and filled throughout with a fiendish satisfaction over the loss to the company and the community, and seeming to regret that there was no loss of life, and

Whereas, Such an attitude is in direct opposition to all community interests and the continued publication of this scurrilous sheet a menace to the people of Marble as a whole, be it

Resolved, That we hereby request Miss Sylvia Smith to take her departure from the town of Marble at once, never to return. Be it

Resolved, That a copy of these resolutions be presented to Miss Smith.

W R Frazier	F B Kendrick
W A Brown	Mrs Harvey
C R Duff	T L Harvey
J R Nunn	H B Day
P Ceacco	Joe Chance
Arthur West	John J Walsh
Chas Gerken	Frank J Clovel
Ernest Mazza	A A Lockwood
E R Walsh	N Westergard
W C Robnet	L Brown
F M Chinaworth	C J Fisher
W Cowles	Eugene Fabian
Ted Long	P J Sallgren
C C Judd	E O Pratt
J H Larkin	Frank Smith
H Harrington	P E Tully
R J Woodward	W G Campbell
Emanuel Constant	C P McHugh
Wm Tobin	Stephen Weber

A Ambrosini	S M Murphy
C C McWilliams	A Agnew
M Ceshini	J B Hanley
A H Cowles	Mrs Perdue
Jay Green	Helen M Tardy
Walter Parks	May Phillips
J A Williams	T F Mullin
J H Garrison	Mrs T F Mullen
Robert O Stanley	Bessie Parks
Q A Harrison	Mrs Jas B Hanley
E E Elliott	Mrs L P Montgomery
H E Robinson	ery
G Gober	Lillian M Granger
Wm Jaynes	Nellie D Perdue
Fred P Dehilde	Katherine Frazier
Frank K Chinn	Mary A Salter
Chas G Green	M E Granger
George Healy	John Walsh
Henry King	T R Salter
P J Tischhauser	Evaline Salter
W F Mason	W A Lenihan
G C Faltz	Thos Evans
M W Davidson	Mrs Frank Gertig
Robert B Hart	Mrs Thos Walsh
Henry King	Mrs John Fisher
H H Wlliams	I M Kobey
M F Magnus	Mrs Ida B Carey
H F Lee	Mr D Parry
Helen Tays	J Widdicombe
John Johnson	C E Budlong
Geo H Tays	D H Barnes
H M James	C A Williams
C G Gokey	H G Haxby, M D
Geo E Backus	J P Parrish
Mr and Mrs Berg-mark	Miss Maggie Larkin
Mr and Mrs Cooper	Miss Mary Larkin
H H Swift	Phil Larkin
Jos Seaforth	Mrs W T Barr
Mrs Thos Cooper	Mrs Lucy Hill
Mr and Mrs Froebei Jones	Mrs Irena Lambert
Mrs N W Ward	Mrs Minnie Sweet
John Fisher	Mrs A L Izett
Emil Constant	A L Izett
J Tweed	Mrs D H Barnes
H L Sweet	Mrs A W Reinecke
W G McManus	A W Reinecke
Mrs W G McManus	George S Swigart
E T Hack	Mrs Swigart
E L Osborne	Mrs Tessie Brown
Mrs E L Osborne	Philip S Arnold
W C Goodwin	M S Ives
Mrs Anna Goodwin	Thomas A Beck
Lou Allen	X Greer
G N Kinney	J M Richards
E D Barton	A Johnson and wife
A H Lyon	Mrs E Erickson
Mrs Mable Lee	Geo E Brown
Mrs Maud Harrison	Ernest Erickson
Mrs Perry Sallgren	Jennie Clayton
June Carey	E C Chaumbers
Mrs G E Brown	J B Blackstock
Mrs E D Barton	Mrs Metta Meads
Mrs T J Beesley	- Walton
Mrs R J Woodward	Frank Gertig
Mrs P J Tischhauser	Ada L Haxby
Mrs I M Kobey	A T Teeter
Mrs G E Backus	M E Parry
Mrs Ed Lewis	Mrs H Harrington
Ed Lewis	Elva M Ward
N Ward	Geo E Brown
J T Beesley	Henry Thode
R G Taylor	Mrs E F Adrian
V L Clift	E F Adrian
Mrs A M Willson	J A Walton
H C Budlong	Frank P Frost
Mrs W R Floyd	Henry Mertens
W R Hood	Rich Thomson
A W Willson	P R Lipson
H Bozung	Susie Healy
Mrs D A Williams	F E Heisse
H H Jorgensen	Mrs F E Heisse
J F Breeden	W H Baker
H D Pratt	D R Snider
V T Brown	Mrs D R Snider
Mrs V T Brown	William Rollman
Mrs Frank Morse	Tony Nerone
Frank Morse	Mrs C S Ronald
Mrs H V Knouse	C S Ronald
Annie M Long	H O Anderson
Homer V Knouse	H W Kirk
Mrs Frank Frost	Al Wood
Ed Sorrell	Mae Sallgren
H W Batt	Helen C Beck

New Spring toggery of all kinds at Kobey's.

See the new styles of Sorosis underskirts for sale at Mrs. Carey's; are now on exhibition.

Spectators will be charged 25c at the Yeomen masquerade ball next Monday night at Masonic hall.

FOUND—Pair of gold-rimmed spectacles. Owner call at this office and pay for this notice.

FOR SALE—Stove Wood at $2.50 a cord; also firewood in any length out of seasoned slabs at low prices.—Thode's Lumber Yard.

Carbondale Item:—I. M. Kobey, one of Marble's most popular business men, was in Carbondale last Thursday. He was on his way home after spending several days in Glenwood resting up.

Extra copies of The Booster may always be had at the office of the paper on State street for 5c each.

FROM THE RAILROAD YARD at the mill, the photographer aimed his camera toward the east. The office still stood, with coal smoke coming from the boiler-room heating plant. Shop No. 1 was gone, and wreckage covered the CR&SJ tracks. Smoke was also coming out of the stack on the steam power plant (at the right). A boxcar remained upright on the house track beside Shop No. 2. The company's two white sheds (next to the tracks) had been smashed, and this was the debris that covered the tracks.

"It is not an easy matter for me, situated as I am, to stand here and refrain from expressing the thoughts that boil up within me." Said Mr. Walton in opening. "There is always a certain amount of respect and courtesy due a woman. However, I have read this woman's paper for a year and a half and I have long since reached the conclusion that she is not engaged in publishing that paper for the purpose of disseminating news. She is not publishing it to tell of our local affairs; she is publishing it to hurt, to injure Marble... What seems to me most remarkable is that the people here have endured it this long—three years I believe... How much will your interests here be worth if the machinations of this woman should be successful? They are your interests and she is aiming at them; they are your homes and she is trying to destroy them.

"Sylvia Smith is a menace to all of us...

"I say to you all, protect your interests..."

When Mr. Walton sat down the applause was deafening...

· · · · ·

In spite of Mr. Frazier's assertions, everyone knew that the marble company was instigator of the meeting, and that all employees, as well as those only indirectly dependant upon the marble business, must support the proposed action or suffer the consequences. The next speaker was Judge C.E. Budlong.

The Marble Booster,
March 30, 1912.

"I came here three years ago," said the judge. "Nearly as soon as I got off the train I began to hear some 'knocks' against the Colorado-Yule company. I listened patiently but I could not discover that they were based upon any reason...

"Now in regard to that article this Miss Sylvia Smith has published. When a woman takes a man's place she must expect to receive what a man would receive in the same position. This Marble City Hatchet is chopping the blood out of our town..."

· · · · ·

These speakers were followed by Dr. H.G. Haxby, Dan Barnes, George L. Swigart, Prof. A.M. Willson, Homer Harrington, E.O. Pratt, Dr. H.H. Swift, M.E. Granger, Tim Salter and H.L. Sweet. All spoke in much the same vein. Then Mr. Frazier spoke again and said,

The Marble Booster,
March 30, 1912.

"There is no half way point tonight. Let's see where everyone stands. What we do here will have effect. Let us stand up for Marble."

The Marble Booster,
March 30, 1912.

At this point Rev. Walton took the floor to make a motion that a committee of fifteen men and ten women be appointed to deliver a copy of the resolution to Miss Smith. Henry Thode seconded the motion and it was carried. The chair being asked to appoint the committee, Mr. Frazier named the following men:

Dan Barnes, Dr. H.G. Haxby, Ambrose Williams, Charles McWilliams, John F. Parrish, I.M. Kobey, W.R. Frazier, Judge C.E. Budlong, Rev. J.A. Walton, W.R. Hood, Henry Mertens, Homer Harrington, Frank P. Frost, W.D. Parry, Henry Thode.

Mr. Frazier then announced the appointment of a nominating committee of ladies to name the committee of ten. The nominating committee presented the following list of ladies for membership on the general committee:

Mrs. Homer Harrington, Mrs. Jack Clayton, Mrs. A.M. Willson, Mrs. W.R. Hood, Mrs. Thomas Walsh, Mrs. J.F. Parrish, Mrs. Dan Barnes, Mrs. Ida B. Carey, Miss Elva Ward, Mrs. H.G. Haxby.

...Dan Barnes said he would like to hear from the Williams brothers. John Williams said:

"I am tired of this thing and I am glad to sign that resolution to have this person to take up her abode elsewhere."

Ambrose Williams said:

"I would have been glad to have had Miss Smith here tonight so she could have been heard. If there are any extenuating circumstances we should hear them. The first impression I had after reading her article was that it was rather glorifying in a calamity and I felt that it injured her more than it did the company. I am in hopes this matter may be handled in such a way by the committee that a just settlement may be reached."

· · · · ·

This last voice of moderation was largely ignored, except that Mrs. Montgomery said, "Mr. Chairman, the ladies present deeply deplore the necessity of such a meeting."

The Marble Booster,
March 30, 1912.

Mr. Frazier replied that the men, doubtless, were the most embarassed. He then called for an expression from all the women present, asking all those in favor of the resolution to please stand. Fifty or more women stood; two or three did not.

The meeting then was adjourned, after the audience had been told where the resolution might be signed. The people lined up and passed in front of the secretary's table, affixing their signatures. It required more than an hour to do this, while the crowd patiently stood in line.

At the committee meeting, held immediately afterward it was agreed to present the resolutions to Miss Smith the next afternoon at 3 o'clock. Mr. Frazier was elected chairman of the committee and the members were asked to be at Kobey's store the next afternoon at 2:45 o'clock.

The next morning the resolutions were placed at the postoffice for further signatures of all who cared to sign. By noon there was an additional list of names on the paper. Then a copy was made, showing that the resolutions had been signed by just 232 persons in all. Of this number 197 signed at the meeting held in Masonic hall.

The committee met, as per schedule, at 3 o'clock and it was soon discovered that Miss Smith had sent notes to two members of the committee warning not only them but all other members of the committee not to set foot upon her property. It was quickly ascertained that a newspaper is public property and as such is open to the public. In the face of the concealed threat of the notes, however, the committee first made sure of its right to call upon Miss Smith, then the roll was called. It showed only one absentee—one of the ladies. The committee then set out for the office of Miss Smith, Mr. Frazier bearing the resolution in his hand.

At the entrance to Miss Smith's office, the leaders of the committee met Miss Smith, who brandished a stove shovel in their faces and warned them not to come upon her property. Mr. Frazier offered to read her the resolutions. She would not listen, but kept repeating her demand that the visitors take themselves off her property. In this demand, she was backed up by Tom Boughton, who stood back of her. Ugly words flashed back and forth from Boughton to those members of the committee who stood in the front. Boughton observed the Rev. Mr. Walton and shouted to him that he was a hypocrite, whereupon the dominie offered to lay aside the ministerial cloth long enough to prove he was a man as well as a minister. Other hot words were spoken, when it was seen that Boughton was taking the part of the woman who was asked to leave Marble. Several members of the committee advised Boughton in certain tones to shut up...

Miss Smith, meanwhile, was circling the buildings in the immediate vicinity, brandishing her stove shovel and iterating and reiterating her demand for the visitors to leave. Mr. Frazier read the resolutions while he followed her around, and when he had finished he left the paper where she could get it. She refused to take it from him. The committee then returned to Main street. As soon as they had gone, Miss Smith recovered the resolutions from the ground where Mr. Frazier had dropped the paper, and took them with her, laughing heartily as she read aloud to Boughton and others. Someone asked her if she wasn't afraid.

"Why, no, why should I be," she replied. "I have to grin and bear it and protect my property."

The last words Mr. Frazier spoke to her were: "Miss Smith, you have just seventy-two hours in which to leave Marble, never to return." She made no reply.

The Marble Booster,
March 30, 1912.

The Resolutions:

Whereas, the editor of the Marble City Times, Miss Sylvia Smith, has at all times endeavored to injure the chief industry of Marble, the Colorado-Yule Marble Company, by publishing in its columns scurrilous and untruthful statements, and that she is antagonistic to all the interests of the community, business, educational, religious and social, and

Whereas, The wrecking of the mill by the recent snow slide was a disaster to the community as a whole: that the article in the Marble City Times under date of March 22, 1912, was untrue, vicious and filled throughout with a fiendish satisfaction over the loss to the company and the community, and seeming to regret that there was no loss of life, and

Whereas, Such an attitude is in direct opposition to all community interests and the continued publication of this scurrilous sheet a menace to the people of Marble as a whole, be it

Resolved, That we hereby request Miss Sylvia Smith to take her departure from the town of Marble at once, never to return. Be it

Resolved, That a copy of these resolutions be presented to Miss Smith.

[Signed by all the members of the committee.]

The Marble Booster,
March 30, 1912.

MAYOR ORDERS THE CITY MARSHAL TO ACT.

Wednesday afternoon the situation became acute. Marshal Mahoney heard a great deal of talk about violence and he was preparing to protect Miss Smith and her property when he received an order from Mayor Tischhauser commanding him to do that very thing.

Acting under that order, the marshal took charge of Miss Smith and Thursday morning sent her out of Marble. He also took charge of the plant of the Marble City Times and stored it in the basement of Kobey's store. The marshal told a reporter for The Booster that he had excellent reason to believe Miss Smith was in danger of violence here and that her property was in danger, so he was acting in her interests as well as obeying the orders of the mayor when he threw about her the protection of the law.

Miss Smith left Marble with the expressed intention of going straight to Governor Shafroth.

Miss Smith advanced no objection to leaving Marble—in fact, according to Marshal Mahoney, she appeared rather anxious to leave.

. . . . . .

It appears that the marshal's action to "protect" Miss Smith involved putting her in the town jail for the night. Her testimony at the trial gave her view of the events.

Sylvia Smith vs. C.F. Meek et al,
Case No. 1515, Gunnison County District Court,
Gunnison, Colorado.

I stayed in the jail from 4:00 o'clock in the afternoon of Wednesday until between 4:00 and half past four the next morning, Thursday morning. The jail is a log cabin, hewed logs, healthy as to ventilation since the logs don't fit and between the logs were open places. But they put their coal right in this room, too, and there was quite a big pile of coal there and, of course, it couldn't be very clean under those circumstances. The coal had been taken in there and was in bad condition. There was a space of perhaps two and one-half or three feet between the two cells and the logs in the jail and there was thrown in the space what may have been a doubled up mattress or part of a mattress and I got weary and begged the man that had been left in charge, Mr. Fisher, not to lock me in a cell and I asked him if he was going to put me in a cell and he didn't answer me and I begged him not to lock me in a cell and there was a woman in the jail and she said, "Miss Smith, you can't go in there, there was a drunk man, a drunken dago, in there."

I ignored her and I said to Fisher, "Are you going to lock me up there?" and I says, "I don't want to be locked up, I don't want to sleep. I can stay here." and he says, "I guess I won't lock you up." And after awhile I became weary and I realized I hadn't had any dinner that day. In the excitement I had forgotten it and Mrs. Curley, the woman who was in the jail divided up something they had brought her from the house and cooked it on a little stove she had there to cook on. And I said to her, I looked at this mattress when I became so very weary, and I said, "What is that bundle of stuff down there?" The mattress being covered with loose newspapers I couldn't tell if it was a mattress with a lot of old stuff piled over it. She told me the bundle was clean clothes and I spread the newspapers over this and laid down and she gave me part of her quilt. She told me her bedding was clean and I laid down between the logs of the jail and the cell in that narrow place, but I did not sleep much. I caught cold and was pretty nearly two months getting over the cold.

. . . . .

The Marble Booster printed articles from other area newspapers commenting on this drastic action of the townspeople to remove a notorious "knocker." This included comments from the Glenwood Post, Granite Mining Journal, Pitkin Miner, Glenwood Avalanche, Paonia Booster, and they were careful to not express approval of the action, though it seemed to be implied. The Denver Rocky Mountain Herald, however, implied definite approval, but the Gunnison News Champion was non-committal, and merely reported:

The Marble Booster,
April 13, 1912. Quoting from the Gunnison News-Champion.
Sheriff Pat Hanlon went to Marble Tuesday in response to a report that a condition of lawlessness prevailed over there consequent upon the displeasure created by the writings of Sylvia Smith, editor of the Marble Times. Miss Smith was deported, and it was rumored that other "undesirables" were to follow. Sheriff Hanlon expected to be gone several days.

. . . . .

The Booster printed two letters under the heading:

The Marble Booster,
April 20, 1912.
It's All in the Point of View.
New York, April 10, 1912.
Dear Mr. Frost:—The way The Booster has covered the news of Marble for the last three weeks, should make other Colorado papers sit up and take notice. It couldn't have been better done by the New York Sun.

I congratulate you, also, on your determination to increase to eight pages and on your straightforward, virile announcement of it in the April 6 issue. When Marble is as big as Rutland, Vt., (24,000) or Carrara, Italy, (34,000) The Booster will be a model and prosperous daily and a piece of property whose value will repay you for all the money and brains you now put into it.

Yours truly,
CHARLES AUSTIN BATES

Marble, Colorado, April 13, 1912.
F.P. Frost, City:—As my subscription to The Marble Booster expires April 10, 1912, you can please stop my paper.

Respectfully,
T.A. BOUGHTON.

. . . . .

First indication of troubles in the aftermath of the eviction of Sylvia Smith was printed in The Marble Booster, quoting from the Glenwood Post.

The Marble Booster,
April 27, 1912. Quoted from the Glenwood Post.
Glenwood Post:—Miss Sylvia Smith, the erstwhile editress of the Marble City Times, who says she was recently deported from the Marble camp as a result of some of her anarchistic utterances, has begun suit against the Colorado-Yule Marble company, the San Juan and Crystal River Railroad company, Col. C.F. Meek, Rev. J.A. Walton and others for damages in the sum of ONE MILLION DOLLARS. My goodness, Sylvia, how your advertising rates have gone up the last few weeks.

. . . . .

The suit named thirty-seven townspeople, the Colorado-Yule Marble Company, the Crystal River & San Juan Railroad and the town of Marble as defendants. The claims were reduced from one million dollars to $52,500; $22,500 being for actual damages, and $30,000 in punitive or exemplary damages.[2]

When the case came to trial in Gunnison in April, 1913, many Marble people were on hand. This did not include W.R. Frazier, who happened to be in Omaha at the time. He claimed he had not been notified, but this excuse did not sit well with the Marble people. They felt they had been let down by the marble company.

The Marble Booster,
May 3, 1913.
WHY HE WAS NOT AT TRIAL. W.R. Frazier Tells Why He was not at Gunnison. NO NOTIFICATION SENT. Says he was to Have Been Notified Through the Chicago Office of Colorado-Yule Company but no Word Came until Mrs. Frazier Wrote.

. . . . .

The attorney for the defendants, Dexter T. Sapp, sent The Booster copies of his correspondence with Frazier, notifying him of the trial date. His transmittal letter stated that, "I regret exceedingly that Mr. Frazier was not here and also regret that he misunderstood his own understanding."

The Marble Booster,
May 17, 1913.
Gunnison, Colo., Mar. 24, 1913.
Mr. W.R. Frazier
c/o C-Y M. Co.,
Western Union Bldg.,
Chicago, Ill.
Dear Mr. Frazier:—The Smith case has been notified for trial and I expect to reach it on the 15th or 16th of April, and most certainly want you here.

If anything occurs so the case will probably not be tried I will either write or wire you at your Chicago address.

Yours very truly,
D.T. SAPP.

[2] Smith vs. Meek.

THE DAY AFTER the big snowslide, cleanup operations had begun in earnest, and tent canvas had been fastened over the exposed office wall. Only the tele-phone-switchboard operator had been in the office on top of the building at the time of the avalanche. She fled from her station upon the impact — with utmost haste!

Youngstown, Ohio,
March 29th, 1913.

Dexter T. Sapp, Esq.,
Gunnison, Colo.
Dear Mr. Sapp:—Your letter of the 24th instant has just reached me in Chicago. I will be on hand in April for the Smith case, though I wish it could be put off until another term of court.
Very truly yours,
W.R. FRAZIER.

. . . . .

In August, 1912, Col. Meek had died as a result of a trolley runaway, so Frazier was the highest remaining company official who had orchestrated the removal of Sylvia Smith, and certainly should have been at the trial. In a letter to Frank Frost, editor of The Marble Booster, dated April 24, 1913, he claimed he had not been notified of the trial date, and added

The Marble Booster,
May 3, 1913.

In any way that I can ever help, I will, and I certainly expected to have been at Gunnison to do all I could to help the company and the people of Marble to help in their fight against Sylvia Smith.

. . . . . .

Frank Frost printed "The Real Facts in Sylvia Smith Case," since the defendants believed Judge Black at the trial had unfairly not permitted the jury to hear the background to the action taken by the citizens of Marble to protect their interests. He reviewed the arrival of Miss Smith in Marble and the history of her paper there.

The Marble Booster,
April 26, 1913.

The paper [Marble City Times] dwindled until it consisted of only a single sheet, printed on one side by herself and on the other by the "patent insides" company. The advertising it contained, she admitted on the stand at Gunnison, brought her in not to exceed $11 a month...

Miss Smith lived during this time at one of the Marble hotels, dressed well, bought property here, paid her help and her bills promptly and appeared to be well supplied with money. The people of Marble believed she was being paid for the articles that she printed that were designed to hurt the Colorado-Yule Marble company—and they still believe it after having heard her testimony in the trial. It would not have been possible for her to live on the proceeds of her newspaper business alone.

Notwithstanding loss of patronage and friends, she continued to attack somebody or something in every issue of the sheet she published. She threw slime on the public schools, the church, the chamber of commerce, the band, the Masonic hall, the merchants, private citizens and the company that made it possible to have a town here The situation became almost unendurable but the people of Marble did not know what to do about it. Of what use to bring a suit? She had nothing or claimed to have nothing. Of what use to protest? She laughed at people who tried to remonstrate with her. She told them that she was going to fight the Colorado-Yule Marble company until she died...

...the defendants were unable to get any evidence in justification of their acts past the judge, and the jury brought in a verdict for Miss Smith in the sum of $10,000.

The case will be taken to the supreme court, of course, and if a new trial is secured...there will be a change of venue asked for.

The Marble Booster,
June 28, 1913.
Supersedeas in Smith Case.

Word was received here last week too late for publication in The Booster that the state supreme court had granted a supersedeas in the Sylvia Smith case, which, reduced to common English, means that a hearing is allowed before the higher tribunal and meantime the lower court cannot make any move in the case. The attorneys for the defendants have ninety days from next September to prepare an abstract of record and file it with the court and the court, itself, has anywhere from one to fifty years to take up the case for review, according to how far the judges are behind the docket. It is believed here that it will be several years before the case will be reviewed by the court. Meantime a bond of $16,000 has been supplied and there the case rests.

· · · · ·

In June 1915 the supreme court acted in the Smith case.

The Marble Booster,
June 12, 1915. Reprinted from the Denver Post, June 7, 1915.

A judgement of $10,000 obtained by Miss Sylvia Smith against the Colorado Yule Marble Company and the Crystal River & San Juan Railway company was affirmed by the supreme court this morning...

· · · · ·

Action to collect on the judgement was taken promptly.

The Marble Booster,
June 26, 1915.
ATTACHMENTS ARE MADE TO SATISFY A JUDGEMENT.

Sheriff Pat Hanlon came over Monday with papers to serve on defendants in the Sylvia Smith case, and Tuesday attachments and levies were made on several of the business houses and on some residences with the result that some of the business houses were closed for from one to two days, but, by now, all except one store are doing business just as though nothing had occurred.

The judgement will be fully settled in the next few days.

The Marble Booster,
July 3, 1915.
The story wasn't ended, however.
Sheriff Attaches The Booster.

A Plain Statement by the Editor Concerning the Refusal of the Colorado-Yule Marble Company to Make Good its Obligations in the Sylvia Smith Case and what then Happened to Individuals.

As editor of this paper, I want to make a statement which will be concerned with the inside story of the Sylvia Smith case, as relating to the settlement of the damages, now pending. I hope this statement will not be construed as unfriendly to the Colorado-Yule Marble company, for it is not so intended to be. It is simply intended to be a plain, unbiased statement of facts, susceptible of proof, to the end that many of the readers of this paper, who are stockholders of the Colorado-Yule company, may understand the real, inside facts and form their judgement accordingly. These readers are entitled to know what methods were used to close up The Booster office, if it is closed, and why it was done.

...The office is at this time in the custody of the sheriff—taken in charge while I was away—although, through the insistance of Sheriff Hanlon and Deputy Sheriff Faussone, it was not closed, as were other places that were levied upon.

Failure on my part to pay the sum demanded of me probably will put The Booster up to sheriff's sale, and this I cannot stop, if, as has been suggested to me, the sum demanded is of exorbant size.

To begin at the beginning, then, in a statement of the facts—the inside facts, that did not come out at the trial, for reasons that will be stated hereinafter—the individual defendants in this case who have had to pay this judgement, or the most of it, had no more to do with driving Sylvia Smith out of Marble than they had to do with driving Adam and Eve out of the Garden of Eden. The most they did was to attend the meeting held in Masonic hall to protest against her and her paper and to sign a petition calling upon her to leave Marble. The actual act of arresting her and placing her in jail, followed the next morning by her deportation, they knew absolutely nothing about. They were not consulted in those actions and positively did not know anything about it until she was gone. Colonel C.F. Meek was the man who dictated that action, absolutely, and the statement is easy to prove. There are at least three persons who heard him dictate to his stenographer, now living in Marble, the order which he caused Paul J. Tischhauser, as mayor, to sign, which order gave the marshal authority to go and take the woman and send her out of town; the order also authorized the marshal to take Miss Smith's plant, type, presses, etc., and store them, which he did and the entire plant is today in the basement under the Kobey store, and was not destroyed, as has been so frequently stated on the outside. Mr. Tischhauser, mayor, was at that time an employee of the Colorado-Yule Marble company and did not dare disregard the Colonel's orders, even had he been so inclined.

Even those who signed the petitions asking Miss Smith to leave Marble were coerced into doing so. Mr. Frazier, assistant to Colonel Meek, circulated the petition and practically every person he solicited to sign the paper was approached with words something like these:

"This town has got to get rid of Sylvia Smith and we want you to sign this paper if you are a friend of the Colorado-Yule Marble company. If you are not we want to know it."

What would you have done in a case like that?

Some there were who did refuse to sign [and lost their jobs].

...immediately after the suit was filed and service of the papers was made Colonel Meek called all the defendants together at Masonic hall and there stated to them openly that they should none of them have any worry about the case; that the Colorado-Yule company would take care of everything, including the attorneys to defend the suit and any judgement or compromise that might be reached.

· · · · ·

Editor Frost then went into a long explanation of events which followed; that the new president of the company, Mortimer Matthews, refused an offer to settle the case for $3,200, choosing instead to go to trial. The individual defendants first began to have doubts about the good faith of the company after the trial, when Matthews insisted the marble company and the railroad company would only pay their proportional share, six-tenths, of the cost of a new trial or an appeal to the supreme court. Total cost was $906, of which amount the companies paid $142, plus attorney costs. Since thirteen of the defendants had left Marble, it fell on the remaining ones to pay the entire costs. The paper listed the amount each person paid toward the judgement. Frost then emphasized that the next company president, J. Forrest Manning, recognized the company's obligation, but that the board of directors would not let him put out the money. This caused great hardship for some of the defendants.

The Marble Booster,
July 17, 1915.

According to a sheriff's sale notice, published in the last week's issue of the Gunnison News-Champion, the home of Mrs. Ida B. Carey, one of the unfortunate defendants in the Sylvia Smith case, is to be sold at public auction at the courthouse steps on the morning of the 31st day of July to satisfy an execution in behalf of the unpaid balance due on Miss Smith's judgement.

. . . . .

The Booster attempted to end the discussion of the case and give "The Final Word."

The Marble Booster,
July 24, 1915.

We have said our say about this case...

From this time on, then, The Booster will be just the same as it always has been—the strongest kind of a "booster" for Marble, the Colorado-Yule Marble company, and all other industries of the town and vicinity. Every bit of news we can get of interest to our readers will be published, the same as always, and, as far as we are concerned, the dead past is dead.

IT IS BELIEVED that Sylvia Smith made the Marble City Hotel her home while operating her newspaper in the town of Marble. This arrangement allowed her to have an office to work from at the hotel, and it also provided an advantage for her by allowing her to eat her meals in the restaurant on the main floor.

LOCOMOTIVE NO. **2052** ORDER NO. **2993** SPECIFICATION NO.   PLAN NO. *1976*   INDEX NO. *97*

BUILT FOR *Crystal River Marble Co.*

ROAD NUMBER _____ NAME *Treasury Mountain*   DUPLICATE OF NO.

SHIPPED TO *Pueblo, Colo.*   DATE SHIPPED *Aug. 3, 1909*

Gauge of Track *56½"*   Gauge of Locomotive *55¾"* Kind of Rail *steel*

Style of Locomotive *32 Ton Shay 2 truck*   Cylinders *3-8 X 12*

Empty weight on Trucks—Front ___ No. 2 ___ No. 3 ___ Rear ___   Total empty weight *55,000*

REPAIR BOOK NO.	BOILER	DRAWING NO.	PATTERN NO.	STOCK NO.	REPAIR BOOK NO.	MACHINERY	DRAWING NO.	PATTERN NO.	STOCK NO.
	Built From Card No.	5347				Bottom Bracket	155-11	5974	
	Size and Style	39⅜ Straight				Bottom Bracket Cap	8717	6038	
	Working Pressure *160#* Fuel *Coal*					Bracket Box Bearing—Lower	8716	6040	
	Cinder Pot Base	12913	01828			Bracket Box Bearing—Upper	"	6039	
	Cinder Pot Gate	12913	01829			Cylinders	15922	6163	
	Exhaust Extension	5244	4207			Cylinder Barrel	—	—	
	Exhaust Pipe	12827	1378			Cylinder Frame	—	—	
	Exhaust Nozzle *2¼"*		1246			Cylinder Head	7201	01239	
	Exhaust Tip	—				Cylinder Head Casing			
	Fire Door	12702	C-32			Cylinder Crank Box Bearing—Lower	—	—	
	Fire Door Frame		C-34			Cylinder Crank Box Bearing—Upper	—	—	
	Fire Door Liner		C-33			Cylinder Crank Box Cap.	—	—	
	Fire Box Length *54¼* Width *33⅝* Height *52½*					Connecting Rod	8934		
	Flues, No. *85* Size *2"* Length *108"* Gauge *12*					Connecting Rod Strap	8934		
	Grates—Rocker or Stationary Finger or Plain		01920			Crank Pin Brass (in pairs)	8929	02232	
	Grates—Dump	11851	G-186			Crank Shaft	15734	73	
	Grates—Dead or Cover Plate (Front)		D-4			Crank Counter Balances	—	—	
	Grates—Dead or Cover Plate (Rear)					Crosshead	7808	6042	
	Grates—Dead or Cover Plate (Sides)					Crosshead Pin	8934		
	Grate Frame—Right	302	D-1083			Crosshead Shoe			
	Grate Frame—Center					Crosshead Guide R. Front and L. Back	7901	6370	
	Grate Frame—Left	302	D-1082			Crosshead Guide L. Front and R. Back	7901	6370	
	Jacket	Planished iron				Crosshead Pin Brass (in pairs)	8927	6048·6049	
	Lagging	magnesia block				Eccentric No. 1 Cylinder	8412	5997	
	Petticoat Pipe	12935				Eccentric No. 3 Cylinder	"	5996	
	Stack *Taper*	12626	6324			Eccentric (Split) No. 2 Cylinder Top	"	5994	
	Stack Cone					Eccentric (Split) No. 2 Cylinder Bottom	"	5995	
	Stack Saddle	4221	3333			Eccentric Strap Top Half	8414	6102	
	Stack Ring					Eccentric Strap Bottom Half	"	6103	
	Stack Netting Mesh — Gauge	—				Eccentric Blade R. Front and L. Back	8411	#4	
	Smoke Box Front	12954	02108			Eccentric Blade L. Front and R. Back	8411	#4	
	Smoke Box Door	12954	02112			Link Radius *35"*			
	Smoke Box Netting Mesh *3½* Gauge *12*					Links *Solid*	8107	6099	
	Smoke Box Cleaning Hole Flange and Lid	12911	01836-01883			Link Bushings	"		
	Steam Pipe Elbow	12151	6202			Link Block			
	Steam Bracket	15633	5999			Link Block Pin	8505		
	Steam Bracket Supplement	15655				Link Hanger	8105	#2	
	Soft Plugs *662A 5000 66-113*	H449	6883			Link Hanger Bushings			
	Throttle Valve	152	2541			Link or Eccentric Rod Bolts	8505		
	Throttle Valve Case	5394	4677			Piston Head	7504	01162	
	Washout Plugs	11417	1½-2"			Piston Packing Rings	4488	6274	
	(steel dome cap)				19/16	Piston Rod No. 1 *std* No. 2 *std* No. 3 *std*	7507	#3	
						Piston Rod Key			
						Piston Rod Stuffing Box	7711	5360	
						Piston Rod Stuffing Box Gland	7711	5361	
						Piston Rod Vibrating Cup			
						Piston Rod Packing *Garlock*			
						Piston Rod Packing Rings (Babbitt)			
						Steam Chest Cover	7410	6037	
						Steam Chest Cover Casing			
						Slide Valve	7405	6011	
						Slide Valve Balance Plate	7405	6012	
						Slide Valve Balance Rings or Strips	4488	6298	
						Slide Valve Balance Springs	#5		
						Tumbling Shaft Box	5308	01634	
						Tumbling Shaft Cap	5308	01635	
						Universal Coupling Ball	8316	02166	
						Universal Coupling Centers	15½"		
						Valve Yoke	7602	#6	
						Valve Stem Stuffing Box	7703	5417	
						Valve Stem Stuffing Box Nut or Gland	7703	5418	
						Valve Stem Packing		ch	
						Valve Stem Packing Rings Babbitt			
						Valve Stem Vibrating Cup			
						Valve Stem Crosshead	3	01633	
						Valve Stem Crosshead Guide	3	01562	
						Valve Travel *2½* *¼"* Angular Advance			

THESE ARE THE SPECIFICATION sheets showing names of all the parts, drawings and patterns used to construct the Treasury Mountain Railroad's standard-gauge Shay locomotive. This Shay had the Lima Locomotive Works builder's number of 2052, and it was shipped to Marble in 1909.

TANK			
Built From Card No.	15762	L-1	
Style *Leg*			
Cap. *1000* Gals. Water Tons Coal Cords Wood			
Size, Length *100"* Width *40"* Depth *34"*			
Valves *1¼"*			
Valve Seats *1¼"*			
Coal Bunk Cap.	—		

FUEL OIL TANK	
Built From Card No.	—
Cap. Gallons	—
Size, Length Width Depth	—

For this loco use repair plates Nos. 1-4-5-7-10-12-14-18

205[illegible]

REPAIR BOOK NO.	TRUCKS	DRAWING NO.	PATTERN NO.	STOCK NO.
	Axles	10230	#62	
	Bolster Channel—Top 9"-13¼#	9547		
	Bolster Channel—Bottom 9"-13¼#	9547		
	Bolster End Casting—Right	—	—	
	Bolster End Casting—Left	—	—	
	Bolster Springs	¾"×3½"×6"		
	Brake Beams	7" 15#		
	Brake Beam Fulcrums	9855	6717	
	Brake Heads	9842	6715	
	Brake Shoes	3060	2972	
	Center Plate—Top	14	H15	
	Center Plate—Bottom	5066	4784	
	Coupling Ring Whole F	4835	4264	
	Coupling Ring Half F	4835	4265	
	Coupling Ring Whole 2nd Truck	—	—	
	Coupling Ring Half 2nd Truck	—	—	
	Coupling Ring Whole 3rd Truck	—	—	
	Coupling Ring Half 3rd Truck	—	—	
	Coupling Ring Whole Rear Truck	4835	4264	
	Coupling Ring Half Rear Truck	4835	4265	
	Coupling Ring Bushings	4835	02601	
	Crank Coupling—Front End	9016	6200	
	Crank Coupling—Rear End	9016	6200	
	End Separators	9411	5083	
	Gear Rims—~~Plain—Lugged~~—Keyed		16	
	Gear Bolts	8818	#5	
	Journal Bearings—Right	291	J-74	
	Journal Bearings—Left	291	J-74	
	Line Shaft—Front 3⅛"-7" collar 50"⌀	9161 ~~[illegible]~~		
	Line Shaft—2nd	—	—	
	Line Shaft—3rd	—	—	
	Line Shaft—Rear 3⅛"-7" " 50"⌀	9161 ~~[illegible]~~		
	L. S. Couplings—Front Shaft	9016	6200	
	L. S. Couplings—2nd Shaft Forward End	—	—	
	L. S. Couplings—2nd Shaft Rear End	—	—	
	L. S. Couplings—3rd Shaft Forward End	—	—	
	L. S. Couplings—3rd Shaft Rear End	—	—	
	L. S. Couplings—Rear Shaft	9016	6200	
	L. S. Bearings—Inner F. Truck	9223	6095	
	L. S. Bearings—Outer F. Truck	9223	6094	
	L. S. Bearings—Inner 2nd Truck	—		
	L. S. Bearings—Outer 2nd Truck	—		
	L. S. Bearings—Inner 3rd Truck	—		
	L. S. Bearings—Outer 3rd Truck	—		
	L. S. Bearings—Inner Rear Truck	9223	6095	
	L. S. Bearings—Outer Rear Truck	"	6094	
	Line Shaft Washers	9118	K215	
	Pinions		16	
	Pedestal Springs	1½"×6"×6"		
	Sleeve Couplings—F	5493	4936	
	Sleeve Couplings—No. 2	—		
	Sleeve Couplings—No. 3	—		
	Sleeve Couplings—Rear	5493	4936	
	Square Shaft—Front 3½"×36"	3328		
	Square Shaft—2nd	—		
	Square Shaft—3rd	—		
	Square Shaft—Rear 3½"×39"	3328		
	Side Bearing Base	5509	3044	
	Side Bearing Block	3164	3043	
	Spring Plate—Center	—		
	Spring Plate—Ends	—		
	Truck Box, F. Truck	9226	6086	
	Truck Box Cap., F. Truck	9221	6088	
	Truck Box, 2nd Truck	—	—	
	Truck Box Cap., 2nd Truck	—	—	
	Truck Box, 3rd Truck	—		
	Truck Box Cap., 3rd Truck			
	Truck Box, Rear Truck	9226	6086	
	Truck Box Cap., Rear Truck	9221	6088	
	Truck Pedestal	111	2a46	
	Truck Pedestal Cap.	111	2871	
	Truck Pedestal, Inside Box	3041	3090	
	Thrust Plate	3041	3092	
	Truck Column—Right	94.2	5830	
	Truck Column—Left	"	5831	
	Truck Arch Bars	4927		
	Truck Bottom Bars	"		
	Truck Top Bars	"		
	Tires Number 7 Section No. 3			
	Wheels 28 Diam. 7'-6¼" Circum.	9965	0735	
	Face 4½ Flange 1⅛" Bore 4⅜			

REPAIR BOOK NO.	ACCESSORIES	DRAWING NO.	PATTERN NO.	STOCK NO.
	Air Sanders	Ours		
	Brake Lubricator Mich 106 Type 15936	~~1¼" Plain Powell~~		
	Brake—Air and Steam ~~Hand~~			
	Air Brake Material Ord. No. 106			
	Air Pump No. 107929 - 9½" W.A.B.			
	Steam Brake Cylinder	13517	6502	
	Steam Brake Piston	13513	3528	
	Steam Brake Piston Rings	3176 / 4488	6785 / 6273	
	Steam Brake Valve	#5		
	Bell 50#			
	Bell Ringer			
	Blow-off Valve	1"		
	Cab	11181	Closed	
	Cab Lamp	Dayton		
	Check Valve	1" Strong		
	Connecting Rod, ~~Oil~~—Grease Cups	#23		
	Crosshead Guide, Oil—~~Grease~~ Cups	1½" Powell		
	Crosshead Pin Oil Cups	#4 spring top		
	Crank No. Forg. No.			
	Crank Test T. S. Elong. Red. Area			
	Cylinder Cocks	6-⅜" union bible		
	Cylinder Lubricator	Mich B.L. 21278		
	Draft Gear	—	—	
	Drawhead—Front	10419	5666	
	Drawhead—Rear	10419	5666	
	Drawhead—Automatic	Lima		
	Drawhead Knuckles	"		
	Fire Extinguisher	—	—	
	Gauge Cocks	3 -		
	Hand Rail	1" Pipe		
	Headlight	1-14" Rd case		
	Headlight Chimneys	#90 Macbeth		
	Hose on Feed Pipe			
	Injectors	2-#5 Metropolitan		R-178951 L-178950
	Injector Lubricator	1¼" Plain Powell		
	Link Pin Collars, No. 1 ¼" No. 2 ⅜" No. 3 ¼"			
	Log Buffer	—	—	
	Oil Pipe to Cylinders No. 1 ½"×4' No. 2 ½"×5⅝' No. 3 ½"×79"	10518		
	~~Pilot or~~ Pilot + Foot Board	10399		
	Piston Rod Packing Oil Cups	—		
	Pop Valves	One-2" Kunkle		
	Sand Box—Front	Hand Sander		
	Sand Box—Rear	" "		
	Sand Pipe Hose	1¼"×8'-front 7' rear		
	Siphon	2½		
	Siphon Hose	2½"×16 feet.		
	SnowPlow	—		
	Snow Flanger	—	—	
	Steam Gauge	Irm Ashcroft 564767		
	Steam Chest Relief Valve	154	2641	
	Steam Heat Hose and Coupling	—		
	Steam Heat Gauge	—		
	Steam Heat Reducing Valve	—		
	Steam Pipe to Injectors	~~3/4"×30½~~ 1¼" inn		
	Steam Pipe to Lubricator	¾"×30½" copper.		
	Steam Pipe to Steam Gauge	⅜"×28"		
	Steam Pipe to Water Gauge	⅜"×10" "		
	Steam Brake Drip Valve	201		
	Steam Turrett	27	0457	
	Track Water Sprinkler	—		
	Valve Stem Packing Oil Cup			
	Water Gauge	½" single		
	Water Gauge Lamp	Dayton		
	Water Gauge Glass	⅝"×14"		
	Whistle	4"		

FRAMES

Engine Frame 9	Inch Beams—W. T. 30#
Tender Frame —	Inch Beams—W. T. —

Gunnison County School District-4
School Teachers

This list is not complete, but was compiled from Teacher's record books, District-4 pay records, old newspapers and information from former Marble students and teachers.

.YEAR	TEACHER	SALARY	GRADES TAUGHT

MARBLE

YEAR	TEACHER	SALARY	GRADES TAUGHT
1893-94	Hattie M. Evans		
1899	Hattie M. Evans		
1900	Miss A.M. Malony		
1901	Emily R. Johns		
1901-02	Jennie Copeland		
1906	Dolly Duncan Webb		
1907	Teresa Mahoney		
1910-11	Prof. F.A. Walker - Principal		
"	Mary Sharp		Primary
"	Nellie Perdue		
"	Helen M. Tandy		3
"	Mrs. L.P. Montgomery		
1911-12	A.M. Wilson - Principal		6-12
"	Nellie Perdue - Asst. Prin.		6,7
"	Mrs. L.P. Montgomery		4,5
"	Helen M. Tandy		2,3
"	Elizabeth "Bessie" A. Parks		1
"	May Phillips		
1912-13	Prof. Montello Gray - Prin.	125./mo	8-12
"	Mrs. L.P. Montgomery-Asst.Prin.	80./mo	5,6,7
"	May Phillips	75./mo	8-12
"	Esther L. Dame	75./mo	4,5
"	Mabel Parker		2,3
"	Pansy Woodward		2,3
"	Bessie A. Parks	75./mo	1
"	Prof. A.R. Ambrosini		Man. Training
1913-14	Prof. Montello Gray - Supt.		
"	Mary V. Whiteman		9-12
"	Prof. A.M. Willson		6,7
"	Esther L. Dame	75./mo	4,5
"	Pansy Woodward		2,3
"	Bessie A. Parks	75./mo	1,2
1914-15	Prof. Vivian Sadler - Supt.		
"	A.M. Willson - Principal		6
"	Mary Truxall		8-12
"	Mary V. Whiteman		8-12
"	Esther L. Dame		4,5
"	Bessie A. Parks		1
"	Helen Williams		2,3
"	Miss Locke		6
1915-16	Prof. T.H. Pease - Supt.		9-12
"	Bessie A. Parks		1
"	Helen Williams		2,3
"	Mrs. L.P. Montgomery		4,5
"	Miss Locke		6,7
"	Mary Bowman		9-12
"	Mary Truxall		9-12
1916-17	Prof. T.H. Pease - Supt.		
"	Mary Elizabeth Skinner	75./mo	3,4
"	Miss Derry		
1917-18	Anna G. Ross	100./mo	1,4,6-9,12
1919-20	Ruth A. Howland	100./mo	1,2,4,5,7-9
1922-23	D.M. Elder		5-8
"	Katherine Miller		3
1923-24	Helen Williams	1125./yr	4-6
1924-25	M. Pancoast - Principal	2000./yr	9-12
"	Nina Riddle	125./mo	3,4
"	Margaret E. Watt	125./mo	5,6
1925-26	Nina Riddle	125./mo	3,4
"	Mary L. Beesley	125./mo	1,2
1926-27	C.H. Coyle - Supt.	1700./yr	9,10,12
"	Mary L. Beesley	125./mo	1,2
"	Helen Williams	1125./yr	7,8
"	Margaret E. Watt	125./mo	5,6
"	Nina Riddle	125./mo	3,4
1927-28	E.M. Andres - Principal		
"	Mary McHugh	1035./yr	1,2
"	Mildred Evans	1035./yr	3,4
"	Myrtle R. Rogers	1125./yr	3-6
"	Amy Yorke		7,8
1928-29	Cecil Morgan - Principal	1800./yr	9-12
"	Helen Williams	1125./yr	5,6
"	Mildred Evans	1135./yr	3,4
"	Mary McHugh	1035./yr	1,2
"	Myrtle R. Rogers	1035./yr	5,6
"	Amy Yorke	1170./yr	7,8
1929-30	Harry U. Foster - Supt.		
"	Dorothy V. Chapman	1125./yr	7,8
"	Ernestine Johnston	1125./yr	3,4
"	Myrtle R. Rogers	1125./yr	2
"	Mary E. McHugh		
1930-31	Harry U. Foster - Supt.		
"	Helen L. DeVany	1125./yr	5,6
1931-32	Harry U. Foster - Supt.	1900./yr	9-12
"	Mary E. McHugh	1170./yr	1,2
"	Esther Foster	1170./yr	9-12
"	Lucille M. Jewell	1170./yr	4-6
"	S.B. Talton		
1932-33	Harry U. Foster - Supt.		
"	S.B. Talton		
1933-34	Harry U. Foster - Supt.		
"	Dwight A. Williams		
"	Lucille M. Jewell		
"	Iva Faletti		10,11

YEAR	TEACHER	SALARY	GRADES TAUGHT
1934-35	Elvin W. Sloan - Supt.		
"	Lucille M. Jewell	990./yr	1-4
"	Florence D. Potts		5-8
1935-36	Elvin W. Sloan - Supt.		
"	Ellenrose Attane Mirabella	100./mo	4-6
1936-37	Kenneth Lucy - Supt.	125./mo	9-12
"	Prudence Barrett		9-12
"	Ellenrose Attane Mirabella		
1937-38	Owen Kenneth O'Fallon - Supt.	1125./yr	1-12
"	Prudence Barrett	900./yr	9-12
1938-39	Owen Kenneth O'Fallon - Supt.	1260./yr	9-13
"	Prudence Barrett	990./yr	9-11,13
1939-40	Owen Kenneth O'Fallon - Supt.	1500./yr	7-12
"	Mary Leda Lewellen	990./yr	9-12
"	Mary McHugh	110./mo	
"	Miriam Bunce	110./mo	
"	Alice S. Greene	110./mo	
1940-41	Owen Kenneth O'Fallon - Supt.	1600./yr	
"	Mary Leda Lewellen	990./yr	9-12
"	Mary McHugh	110./mo	
"	LaVee Beck Lamb	110./mo	
1941	Malcom Drake	110./mo	
1941-42	Mary Leda Lewellan	110./mo	
"	Margaret Mahoney	120./mo	
1942-43	Theresa V. Herman	110./mo	
1943-44	Theresa V. Herman	1200./yr	
1944-45	Theresa V. Herman	1600./yr	
1945-46	Theresa V. Herman	1600./yr	
1946-47	Theresa V. Herman	1950./yr	
1947-48	Theresa V. Herman	2500./yr	
1948-49	Theresa V. Herman	2500./yr	
1949-50	Theresa V. Herman	50./mo	

CAMP GENTER

YEAR	TEACHER	SALARY	GRADES TAUGHT
1928-29	Marguerite Deti	115./mo	

CRYSTAL

YEAR	TEACHER	SALARY	GRADES TAUGHT
1887	Mrs. J.C. Johnson		
1891	Miss Enwall		
1893	Dora Cochran		
1894	Bertie Smelcer		
1900-01	Hattie Evans		
1901-02	Agnes Carlbert		
1904-05	Miss Cross		
?	Edna Richards		

PLACITA

YEAR	TEACHER	SALARY	GRADES TAUGHT
1900-01	Maud Cole		

RAGGED MOUNTAIN

YEAR	TEACHER	SALARY	GRADES TAUGHT
1929-30	Ruth A. Gardner	990./yr	1-7
1930-31	Demis O. Gardner	990./yr	2-6,8
1936-37	Alta Thomas		
1937-38	Alta Thomas		
1938-39	Alta Thomas		
1939-40	Alta M. Beuten	110./mo	
1940-41	Alta M. Beuten	110./mo	
1941-42	George J. Bale	176./mo	9,11,12
1949	Margaret Lee	173./mo	
"	Mrs. LeRoy Smith	200./mo	
1950	Jean Marie Sperry	131./mo	

SPRING CREEK

YEAR	TEACHER	SALARY	GRADES TAUGHT
1926-27	Elsa Berg	110./mo	1,2
1927-28	Marguerite Deti	990./yr	1,2,4-7
1928-29	Ernestine Johnston	1125./yr	3,4
1930-31	W.D. Coleman	110./mo	1-5
1931-32	W.D. Coleman	120./mo	1-4,6
1935	Viola Howison	810./yr	2-4,6,8
1938-39	Bruce Bon Durant		
1939-40	Bruce Bon Durant		
1942-43	Fern Schafer	107./mo	
1943	Mary Childress	117./mo	
1943-44	Leta A. Shaeffer	117./mo	
1944-45	Leta A. Shaeffer	118./mo	
1945-46	Leta A. Shaeffer	120./mo	
1946-47	Leta A. Shaeffer	150./mo	
1949-50	Leta A. Shaeffer	200./mo	
1950	Margaret S. Lee	185./mo	

YULE CREEK

YEAR	TEACHER	SALARY	GRADES TAUGHT
1894	Daisy Baker		

1900 Federal Census
Gunnison County, Colorado

T623, Roll 124, Enumeration District 140, Sheet 17, p.135, Precinct 24, 19 June 1900,
T.T. Higby, enumerator.

MARBLE VILLAGE

	Sex	Relation	Born		Place	Occupation
Repfl (?), Charles F.	M	head	May	1858	Iowa	miner, quartz
— Paul M.	M	brother	—	"	—	
Sandburg, R.G.	M	head	Jun	1831	Sweden	miner, quartz
Thomas, O.F.	M	head	Jan	1859	Indiana	freighter
— E.V.	F	wife	Apr	1867	Canada	
— Olive	F	daughter	Jun	1890	Colorado	at school
— Estella	F	"	Sep	1896	"	
Penny, Jeanie	F	sis in law	Nov	1876	"	
— Alice	F	niece	May	1898	"	
Johnson, Cora	F	boarder	May	1876	"	
— Helen	F	"	Aug	1898	"	
Sahw, A.B.	M	servant	Sep	1872	Indiana	teamster
McNeil, Ronald	M	boarder	Oct	1858	Canada En	miner, quartz
Mason, W.F.	M	head	Aug	1858	N.Car.	" "
Bardine, Joseph	M	head	Jun	1832	Penn.	" "
— Anna	F	wife	Nov	1839	"	
Myers, Mary	F	gr. dau	Jun	1888	Colorado	at school
— Cleveland	M	gr. son	May	1891	"	" "
Brown, Ia	F	gr.gr.dau	May	1896	"	
Edgerton, A.J.	M	head	Aug	1857	Ohio	miner, quartz
— Hattie	F	wife	Sep	1875	Iowa	
— Stella	F	daughter	Jan	1894	Colorado	at school
Evans, William	M	head	Apr	1832	Illinois	shoemaker
— Mery Ann	F	wife	Jul	1841	"	
— Joseph M.	M	son	Aug	1865	"	mine carpenter
— Cora	F	dau in law	May	1866	"	
— Ina L.	F	gr. dau	Oct	1887	"	at school
— Merrick W.	M	gr. son	Oct	1889	"	" "
— Hattie M.	F	daughter	Nov	1870	Missouri	school teacher
Barnes, D.G.	M	head	Jun	1862	Iowa	miner, quartz
— Mamie	F	wife	Nov	1868	"	
— George D.	M	son	Sep	1889	Colorado	
Rummell, F.	-	head	Aug	1859	Iowa	
— Anna	F	daughter	Aug	1884	Colorado	at school
— William	M	son	Oct	1887	"	" "
— Maude	F	daughter	Mar	1893	"	" "
— Eunice	F	"	May	1900	"	
Pace, Ida	F	head	Feb	1869	Iowa	
— Emma	F	daughter	Oct	1892	N. Dak.	at school
— Lulu	F	"	Sep	1895	Colorado	
Stevens, Stella	F	lodger	May	1882	"	
Melton, William	M	"	Jan	1872	Wisconsin	farmer
Clayton, J.F.	M	head	May	1859	New York	burro packer
— Jennie	F	wife	May	1874	Wyoming	
— Lydia	F	daughter	Nov	1894	Colorado	at school
— George	M	son	Oct	1896	"	
— Frank	M	"	Feb	1900	"	
Goodman, F.S.	M	head	Jan	1872	Austria	miner, quartz
— Emile	F	wife	Jan	1879	Iowa	
Rohrer, Leonard S.	M	boarder	Aug	1872	Kansas	bookkeeper
Tischhauser, P.J.	M	head	Feb	1867	Kansas	day laborer
— Lena	F	wife	Sep	1867	Switzerland	
— Paulina R.	F	daughter	Oct	1888	Kansas	at school
— John L.	M	son	Jun	1893	"	" "
— Oscar B.	M	"	Mar	1898	Colorado	
Hoffman, J.H.	M	head	Dec	1864	Switzerland	mech.& miner
— Lizzie	F	wife	Sep	1870	"	
— Henrietta	F	daughter	Mar	1890	Kansas	at school
— Daisy	F	"	Jan	1898	Colorado	

	Sex	Relation	Born		Place	Occupation
Hoffman, Leonard	M	head	Jan	1857	Switzerland	Merch & miner
— Leona	F	daughter	Jan	1892	Kansas	at school
— Viola	F	"	Jan	1894	"	" "
— Emmet	M	son	Nov	1899	Colorado	
Lambert, J.H.	M	head	May	1844	New Jersey	real est agen
Wood, W.W.	M	head	Oct	1840	Ohio	" " "
— Martia A.	F	wife	Sep	1863	Illinois	
— Paul M.	M	son	Nov	1895	Colorado	
Fuller, E.W.	M	head	Feb	1828	Mass.	physician
Flagg, Rosina	F	sister	Nov	1824	"	
Parry, William	M	head	May	1855	England	miner, quartz
— Mary	F	wife	Feb	1864	"	
— Wilfred	M	son	Sep	1888	Colorado	at school
Downing, James	M	head	Oct	1854	Iowa	day loborer
— Addie	F	wife	Dec	1855	"	
— Nellie	F	daughter	Feb	1887	"	
— Elsie`	F	"	Nov	1889	"	at school
— Clarence	M	son	Aug	1899	Colorado	
Mellhollin, Orin	M	head	Nov	1869	Iowa	burro packer
— Eva	F	wife	Jun	1873	"	
— Lorran	M	son	Sep	1894	"	
Downing, Madison	M	bro in law	Dec	1877	"	burro packer
Lottale, Peter	M	head	Mar	1859	Italy	saloon keeper
Briggs, D.M.	M	head	Mar	1855	Illinois	" "
Bush, J.M.	M	head	Dec	1843	Michigan	engin, stat.
Brown, Daniel	M	head	Apr	1840	New York	farmer
— Elizabeth A.	F	wife	May	1840	Illinois	
— Robert	M	son	Aug	1869	"	miner, quartz
— William H.	M	"	Sep	1878	Iowa	" "
Tatum, A.M.	M	boarder	Feb	1865	Missouri	sawmiller
Reyland, Frederick	M	head	Aug	1870	Illinois	notions store
— Jessee L.	F	wife	Sep	1874	"	
— Evalyn	F	daughter	Mar	1900	Colorado	
Reyland, Eugen	M	head	Mar	1834	Germany	retired
— M.E.	F	wife	May	1839	Illinois	
Bowman, A.	M	head	Jan	1860	Sweden	miner, quartz
— Blonda	F	wife	Apr	1860	"	
— Fritz	M	son	Jan	1892	Colorado	
— Louisea	F	daughter	May	1894	"	
— Battina	F	"	Sep	1897	"	
Williams, Evan	M	head	Jun	1862	Wales	printer
Thompson, R.	M	partner	Jun	1840	Scotland	miner, quartz
Melton, George W.	M	head	Sep	1840	Illinois	" "
— Martha	F	wife	Mar	1844	Ohio	
— Gladys	F	daughter	Sep	1883	Colorado	
Melton, Charles	M	head	Sep	1871	Wisconsin	miner, quartz
— Aldean	F	wife	Nov	1877	Colorado	
Melton, William	M	head	Dec	1832	Illinois	farm laborer
Moller, Charles	M	head	Aug	1845	Germany	farmer
Anderson, H.W.	M	head	Sep	1848	Penn.	farmer
Fisher, Joseph	M	head	Apr	1850	Portugal	farmer

BIBLIOGRAPHY

Bennett, John F., "Sylvia T. Smith, Her Day In Court," The Denver Westerners Monthly Roundup, vol. XXVI, July-August 1970, pp. 1-14.——, "Sylvia T. Smith: Her Day In Court," The 1970 Denver Westerners Brand Book, Jackson C. Thode, Editor, Denver, pp. 365-391, 1971; This is a slightly different version of Bennett's article in the Westerners Roundup.
Campbell, Rosemae Wells, "Crystal River Valley-Jewel or Jinx?," Sage Books, Denver, 1966.
Colorado State Business Directory.
Colorado State Census, Gunnison County, 1885
Edgerton, Frank W. & Rose, "Journal of Events Jerome Park and Crystal," 1886 - 1895; deposited at Colorado State Historical Society, Denver.
Federal Census: Gunnison County, Colorado, 1880, 1900, 1910, National Archives & Record Service.
Foote, Alvin, "The Fabulous Valley," A. & T. Company, Inc., 1950.
Francis, Theresa V., "Crystal River Saga," Betts Printing Co., Tucson, 1959.
Gunnison School District No.4; "Permanent High School Record, Marble, Colorado;" book deposited at Colorado State Archives, Denver.
Isler, Ruby, "Date History of Marble Colorado," Reminder Pub. Co., Glenwood Springs, n.d.
Marble, Colorado, "Petition for Incorporation," filed in County Court of Gunnison County, Colorado, May 15, 1899.
McCoy, Dell, & Collman, Russ, "The Crystal River Pictorial," Sundance Publications Ltd., Denver, 1972.
Town of Marble, "Board of Trustees Minute Book," July 1899 to December 1921; book deposited at Colorado State Archives, Denver. ——; "Police Docket, Marble, Colorado;" book deposited at Colorado State Archives, Denver.
Vandenbusche, Duane, & Myers, Rex, "Marble, Colorado: City of Stone," Golden Bell Press, Denver, 1970.
Vanderwilt, John W., "Geology and Mineral Deposits of the Snowmass Mountain Area Gunnison County, Colorado," Bulletin 884, U.S. Geological Survey, Government Printing Office, Washington, 1937.

NEWSPAPERS;

The Aspen Daily Times, November 8, 1886 - January 1, 1887.
The Aspen Democrat, September 12, 1908.
The Crystal River Current, (Crystal & Marble), October 9, 1886 - August 4, 1905.
The Crystal Silver Lance, April 20 1893.
The Marble Booster, March 18, 1911 - September 15, 1917.
The Marble City Times & Clarence Chronicle, September 22, 1893 - July 20, 1894.
The Marble Column, July 11, 1923.
The Marble Times, April 7, 1899.
Marble City Times, July 27, 1894 - March 22, 1912.
The Marble Times & Crystal Silver Lance, June 29, 1900 - September 6, 1901.

OSCAR McCOLLUM JR. PHOTO

THIS SNOW CORNICE on the ridge of Mill Mountain forms each winter, as the prevailing wind blows snow into deep drifts. It is believed that this formation broke loose during March of 1912 to devastate the Colorado-Yule Marble Company's mill on the edge of town.

INDEX